CSR and Competitiveness in China

中国快速成长的民营企业：企业社会责任和可持续性发展

A report prepared for IFC PEP-China

沈艳　姚洋　著

外文出版社
FOREIGN LANGUAGES PRESS

图书在版编目（CIP）数据

中国快速成长的民营企业：企业社会责任和可持续性发展：英文 / 沈艳 姚洋 著.
－北京：外文出版社，2009
ISBN 978-7-119-05599-2

I. 中… II.①沈…②姚… III. 私营企业－调查报告－中国－英文 IV. F279.245

中国版本图书馆CIP数据核字（2008）第210447号

责任编辑 　王　蕊
封面设计 　吴　涛
印刷监制 　冯　浩

中国快速成长的民营企业：企业社会责任和可持续性发展

作　　者 　沈　艳　姚　洋

©2008外文出版社

出版发行 　外文出版社
地　　址 　中国北京西城区百万庄大街24号　　　邮政编码　100037
网　　址 　http://www.flp.com.cn
电　　话 　(010) 68995875（编辑部）
　　　　　　　(010) 68995844（发行部）
　　　　　　　(010) 68995852 / 68996188（邮购部）
　　　　　　　(010) 68320579 / 68996067（总编室）
印　　制 　外文印刷厂
经　　销 　新华书店 / 外文书店
开　　本 　1/16
印　　张 　14.75
装　　别 　平
版　　次 　2008年12月第1版第1次印刷
书　　号 　ISBN 978-7-119-05599-2
定　　价 　50.00元

ACKNOWLEDGEMENTS

This report is produced with the assistance of the IFC Private Enterprise Partnership for China (PEP-China). In the course of the study, we have benefited from the supports of many organizations and individuals.

IFC PEP-China played a valuable role in organizing and administrating the study. Mr. Jingchang Lai and Ms. Ling Huang of IFC PEP-China provided tireless inputs and advices throughout all phases of the study. The Danish government provided financial supports to the project. The Bureau of Small and Medium Enterprises, the National Development and Reform Commission and the National Bureau of Statistics, the People s Republic of China provided great assistance in the survey period of the project. In particular, we are indebted to Madam Di Na, Mr. Zhang Haiying, and Mr. Zhou Xuewen for their superb leadership in organizing case studies and the firm survey. Local government agencies in the 12 survey cities provided competent assistance in organizing and participating in focus group interviews and the survey.

The project also benefited from inputs provided by various institutions and people in China. The Institute of International Labor and Information, the ministry of Human Resources and Social Security (the former ministry of Labor and Social Security), under the leadership of Mr. Zhang Junfeng, conducted a supplementary individual survey and provided a background report based on the survey. Mr. Guo Jun provided a background paper on labor protection in China; Professor Tong Xin provided a background paper on environmental standards and their impacts on Chinese exports. Mr. Guo Jun, Professor Li Lulu, and Mr. Gu Qiang, Mr. Dai Jianzhong, Mr. Zheng Yisheng, Mr. Xu Zhong, Professor Wang Shiweng, Miss Cheng Rong, Professor Tong Xin participated in preparatory and draft review workshops of the project and provided helpful comments.

Graham Bannock read and edited the manuscript. We are grateful for his help. The flow of the text has been improved by his editing.

Jian Lian, Hu Weiwei, Yang Xi, and Zhong Ninghua provided competent research assistance. The China Center for Economic Research at Peking University sponsored the project and provided administrative supports.

The opinions expressed in this report do not represent those of either the China Center for Economic Research, or IFC. The authors take full resporsibility for the opinions and possible errors in this report.

ACRONYMS

ACFOE:	All-China Federation of Enterprises
BSR:	Business for Social Responsibility
CPDF:	China Project Development Facility
CSR:	Cooperate Social Responsibility
DID:	Difference In Difference
EP:	Environmental Protection
ERM:	Enterprise Risk Management
FDI:	Foreign direct investment
FIAS:	Foreign Investment Advisory Service
GRI:	Global Reporting Initiative
HMT:	Hong Kong-Macao-Taiwan
IFC:	International Finance Corporation
IILI:	Institute of International Labor and Information
ILRF:	International Labor Rights Fund
ISO:	International Standard Organization
MLSS:	Ministry of Labor and Social Security (the present Ministry of Human Resources and Social Security)
MNCs:	Multi-National Companies
MoA:	Ministry of Agriculture
MOL:	Ministry of Labor (the former body of MLSS)
NGOs:	Non-government Organizations
NLU:	National Labor Union
NPC:	National People s Congress
NBS:	National Bureau of Statistics
QM:	Quality Management
SETC:	State Economic and Trade Commission
SMEs:	Small and medium enterprises
SOEs:	State-owned Enterprises
TCS:	Three-party Coordination Scheme
UNIDO:	United Nations Industrial Development Organization
WBCSD:	World Business Council for Sustainable Development
WRC:	Workers' Representative Conference

CONTENTS

EXECUTIVE SUMMARY

In 1999, the International Finance Corporation (IFC) carried out a major study of the private sector in China and published a report, *China's Emerging Private Enterprises: Prospects for the New Century* (IFC, 2000). That report has become a standard reference for researchers on the Chinese private sector both inside and outside China. The private sector has grown rapidly since 1999 and now accounts for more than two thirds of China's industrial GDP. However, the quality of the growth has not been uniform across the board. As China gains share in international commodity trade and becomes the world factory, this issue has increasingly gained international attention. Recent international exposure of the low quality and hazardous products that China exports is but one example. The international community as well as serious scholars and policy makers within China are becoming increasingly concerned with the implications of the private sector development for the sustainability of the Chinese economy. The concept of corporate social responsibility (CSR), has been gaining ground in both public debate and within the business arena. It is against this background that the IFC, under the assistance of the China Project Development Facility (CPDF), helped to initiate this study. The China Center for Economic Research at Peking University was the organization that conducted the study.

This new study covered 12 cities and surveyed more than 1,200 firms, most of which were private. The aim of the study is several-fold. First, it is intended to establish the status quo of CSR performance of private firms as compared with state owned enterprises (SOEs), foreign firms, and domestic-foreign joint ventures. Second, it tries to find the link between CSR performance and the financial performance of enterprises, that is, it tries to find a business case for firms to engage in CSR activities. Third, it aims, based on the findings of the study, to provide concrete suggestions to the Chinese government and enterprises to strengthen the private sector contribution to the sustainability of the Chinese economy. Lastly, it is intended to provide a case study of sustainable development strategies for other emerging economies.

The results of this study have strong implications for government policies and business operations. This executive summary will first summarize the main findings and then put forward a set of recommendations for government and enterprises, respectively. We would like to emphasize that our findings are based on the analysis of a relatively large sample of 1,268 firms from twelve cities with different geographic, social, political, and economic characteristics. Although this does not mean that our sample is representative of the whole country, the size of the sample allows us to test our results by sophisticated statistical methods and thus gives us confidence in our findings. At the very minimum, this study provides the first set of systematic empirical results for CSR and its relationship with firm performance in China. In particular, it builds up a clear business case for CSR in China.

1. Summary of findings

Chapters 3 10 provide rich sets of results. Two sets of findings are especially consistent through all these chapters and bear important policy implications. One is that market competition and supply chain pressures have an unambiguous effect in promoting CSR among firms, and the other is that there is a real business case for CSR because it improves firm profitability by helping firms to retain a more stable workforce, gain a larger market share, and obtain more external finance. More specifically, the main findings of the chapters are:

CSR Awareness

- A firm is more aware of CSR than other firms if it is an SOE, an exporting firm, a large firm, a firm operating in a competitive market, or a firm with better educated management.

- CSR activities are mainly confined to the first generation type, i.e., providing donations and meeting the expectations of the law.

- Joining business associations helps firms to increase their CSR awareness.

Labor Standards

- Only half of the correspondents in the individual survey had a written contract with their employers in their last job. The majority of the contracts were short term. Worker age (middle-age workers are favored) and education, firm ownership, size, and sector are factors affecting whether a worker can get a written contract. Firms offering written contracts tend to have shorter working hours, pay their workers higher wages and provide larger coverages for pension and medical insurance.

- Labor unions play a positive role in worker protection. Firms with a labor union tend to have shorter working hours and offer a larger coverage for pension and medical insurance. However, they do not offer significantly different wage rates from those offered by firms without unions.

- Collective bargaining does not provide tangible benefits to employees. It still takes time for collective bargaining to have an impact.

- SOEs and foreign-invested firms and Hong Kong, Macao, and Taiwan-invested firms are much better than domestic private firms at treating their employees.

- Local employees enjoy much better treatment than migrant employees.

Environmental Standards

- Firms facing more intense competition put more effort into complying with national environmental standards and spend more on environment-related investment.

- Firms that are more aware of CSR perform better in protecting the environment in all aspects than firms with low awareness.

- Domestic private firms have the smallest proportion of firms with ISO14000, and are the least aware of cleaner production.

- There are large regional and industry variations in environmental protection, suggesting that government efforts and industrial policies are an important driver for better environmental protection.

Quality Control

- Over 80% of the sample firms have a quality management department and the majority of them chose to establish the department when they established the enterprise.

- In addition to establishing the quality management department, firms enhance their product quality by obtaining product quality certificates, such as ISO9001, establishing product brand names, and inspecting the product quality of their suppliers.

- Joint ventures are more confident about the quality of their products.

- Firms that are more aware of CSR are likely to spend on establishing brand names and inspecting their suppliers.

- Firms in more competitive markets often outperform those operating in markets with moderate or low degrees of competition. These firms spend much more on establishing brand names. They are also much more careful in inspecting the quality of their suppliers.

Corporate Governance

- Firms operating in more competitive markets are more likely to have a better governance structure, hire professional managers, and have better information disclosure and risk control.

- Firms that are more aware of CSR perform equally well in these respects.

- Privatized (gaizhi) firms are more eager to establish modern governance structures and provide contracts for their managers than traditional SOEs. They also do better in information disclosure and risk control.

The supply Chain and CSR

- The majority of the sample firms are subject to labor and environmental requirements imposed by their customers. By the frequency of requirements, the order is: customers in developed countries, large FDI firms in China, customers in developing countries, small and medium FDI firms in China, SOEs, and domestic private firms.

- However, only one fourth of the sample firms place labor standards and half of them place environmental standards on their suppliers. Firms own records of labor standard compliance are not a significant factor affecting their decision to impose labor standards on their suppliers, but their better environmental compliance does increase their tendency to impose environmental standards on their suppliers.

- Large firms are far more likely than SMEs to impose CSR requirements, especially environmental standards, on their suppliers. Foreign and HMT-invested firms are doing better than domestic firms, and exporting firms are doing better than non-exporting firms. In both cases, environmental standards are more emphasized than labor standards.

- In general, firms impose CSR requirements on their suppliers not because they value CSR themselves, but because they face outside pressures to do so.

- Firms favor court settlements over private settlements in commercial disputes. There is weak evidence showing that firms in cities with a better legal environment tend to trust the court more than firms in cities with a slacker legal environment.

CSR and Financial Performance

- Better compliance with labor and environmental standards is associated with higher rates of profitability and labor productivity, but better quality control does not have a significant impact on either profitability or labor productivity.

- In the case of environmental standards, a causal relationship between better compliance and better financial performance can be established.

- There is also a causal relationship between supply chain requirements of labor and environmental standards and better financial performance.

- The positive effects of CSR on financial performance come through the following channels: lower turnover rates, larger market shares, and better access to external finance.

2. Recommendations for the government

The results of this report have important policy implications. They provide insights for several important areas in the current CSR debate in China.

- The race to the bottom story does not hold; instead, there is a story of race to the top. That is, market competition has not forced firms to lower their CSR standards, but instead has encouraged them to enhance their CSR performance. This has a lot to do with the business environment in China. One critical factor is the transmission of international standards and practices through the international supply chain. Another factor is the demonstration effect of better performing firms, including SOEs and FDI firms. In such a business environment, trying to save on cutting CSR expenditures will not fulfill the goal of long-term profitability; instead, better CSR performance can help firms get ahead of others in retaining a better workforce, getting a larger market share, and obtaining more external finance.

- Multinational companies have played a positive role in promoting CSR in China while not having hurt the profitability of Chinese firms in serious ways. This positive role is played through supply chain transmission of international standards and the local demonstration effects of FDI firms.

- SOEs are doing better than other types of firms in most areas of CSR. However, they do not play an active role in transmitting their code of conduct to a larger part of the business world.

- Firms adopt CSR more because of the external pressures they face than because of their own willingness.

Based on these clarifications and the relevant results summarized in the last section, we propose the following recommendations for the Chinese government. They may also be useful for governments in other developing countries.

- Leveling the playing field and providing equal opportunity to all firms are not only pivotal for fair competition, but also helpful in promoting CSR.

- Setting up their own CSR standards is needed by government and society so as to take a proactive role in promoting CSR and gain ground in multinational endeavors. However, those standards should not be used to discourage international companies from pressing their suppliers to implement higher standards. International companies can serve as catalysts for better CSR.

- Implementation of existing laws and government regulations provide incentives for firms to build CSR into their business strategies.

- Policy and media coverage should direct attention away from the first generation type of CSR activities in which philanthropy is the most significant part; instead, they should induce more efforts on the part of the companies to build CSR into their business strategies.

3. Recommendations for companies

The most important result that this study offers to companies is that CSR can be an important source of competitiveness in China. In particular, we have the following recommendations for companies.

- Companies should seriously consider making CSR an integral part of their business strategies.
- The kind of CSR activities that may bring immediate payoffs are improving the treatment of workers, increasing compliance with environmental standards, and strengthening corporate governance.

- SOEs should think hard about how to cash-in on their superior CSR performance in the market. They can play this card in getting more orders and better deals in the international market. They should also transmit their own code of conduct through their own supply chains, for doing so not only brings significant social gains, but also helps leveling the playing field in which they operate.

- Multinational companies should continue to use CSR as leverage in the marketplace. Companies producing in China should continue to be the role models for better CSR performance. Companies having suppliers in China should continue to impose relevant code of conduct on their suppliers, but in the meantime realize that standards applied in the developed world may not be immediately applicable in the developing world. It is thus important for them to manage a delicate public relations campaign in their home countries.

- Small domestic firms may be under smaller pressures to strengthen their CSR. However, they would better be prepared if they wanted to expand to medium and even large scale. They should realize that CSR can be one of the bottlenecks in this transformation. Getting acquainted with CSR is the first step towards putting them on the right track.

- Overall, firms need to scale up their efforts to comply with the national laws and regulations regarding labor, environment, and product quality. Opportunism will bring short-term benefits, but honesty will deliver payoffs that last longer.

Chapter 1
Introduction

In 1999, the International Finance Corporation (IFC) carried out a major study of the private sector in China and published a report, *The Emerging Private Sector in China* (IFC, 1999). That report has become a standard reference for researchers on the Chinese private sector both inside and outside China. The private sector has grown rapidly since 1999 and now accounts for more than two thirds of China s industrial GDP. However, the quality of the growth has not been uniform across the board. As China gains share in international commodity trade and becomes the world factory, this issue has increasingly gained international attention. Recent international exposure of the low quality and hazardous products that China exports is but one example. The international community as well as serious scholars and policy makers within China are becoming increasingly concerned with the implications of the private sector development for the sustainability of the Chinese economy. The concept of corporate social responsibility (CSR), has been gaining ground in both public debate and within the business arena. It is against this background that the IFC, under the assistance of the China Project Development Facility (CPDF), helped to initiate this study.

This new study covered 12 cities and surveyed more than 1,200 firms, most of which were private. The aim of the study is severalfold. First, it is intended to establish the status quo of CSR performance of private firms as compared with state owned enterprises (SOEs), foreign firms, and domestic-foreign joint ventures. Second, it tries to find the link between CSR performance and the financial performance of enterprises, that is, it tries to find a business case for firms to engage in CSR activities. Third, it aims, based on the findings of the study, to provide concrete suggestions to the Chinese government and enterprises to strengthen the private sector contribution to the sustainability of the Chinese economy. Lastly, it is intended to provide a case study of sustainable development strategies for other emerging economies.

This introduction will discuss the notion of CSR, the business case for CSR, debates around CSR, the drivers behind its emergence, and its introduction and controversies in China. At the end of the chapter, we lay out the plan of the report.

1.1   The Concept of CSR

CSR is a notion which originated in the developed economies. This section reviews its definitions, relationship to sustainability, its content, international standards, and the debates around it in the developed economies. China is at a different stage of development from the developed economies, and the notion of CSR could be different in China than in the developed economies. We defer that discussion until Section 1.5.

Definitions of CSR

Although the notion of corporate social responsibility can be traced back to 1924 when Oliver Sheldon first proposed the concept, it is in the last twenty years that CSR has become an important part of the international business environment. It mainly stemmed from consumer and civil society pressures for companies to act in a socially responsible way while pursuing profit. In developed countries, this amounts to asking companies to act beyond what the law requires them to do. The following are several examples of the definition of CSR. By these definitions, CSR is:

"Being socially responsible means not only fulfilling legal expectations, but also going beyond compliance and investing more into human capital, the environment and relations with stakeholders." (European Union, 2001).

The continuing commitment by business to behave ethically and contribute to economic development while improving the quality of life of the workforce and their families as well as of the local community and society at large." (World Business Council for Sustainable Development, see WBCSD, 2001)

"Operating a business in a manner that meets or exceeds the ethical, legal, commercial and public expectations that society has of business." (Business for Social Responsibility, see BSR, 2006)

Essential to these definitions is the broad notion of contingent stakeholders that not only include shareholders, but also workers, the local community, and society as a whole. While the shareholders are only concerned with company profits, other stakeholders are concerned with humane treatment of the workforce, the environment, the coherence of society, as well as product quality. In many circumstances, these two strands of interests conflict with each other.

While a company s abiding by the law will give workers a fair employment contract, it is not guaranteed that workers are being treated in a humane manner. For example, in economies with a flexible labor market, large layoffs are expected when economic downturns come. This is within the realm of action allocated by the legal system to the company, but for many workers, especially those in their late age of employment, it is humiliating and in many cases devastating.

Because of the classical problem of externality, companies may well ignore the negative impacts of their production and products on the sustainability of the environment and the ecosystem. Much has been dealt with by government regulation, but the problem remains because of lack of knowledge, the lack of sufficient action on the part of the government, and evasive action by companies. For instance, until cleaner production is required by government regulation, companies seldom start thinking about the environment in their product design phase. Another example is global warming. Although some scientists began to give warnings twenty years ago, it was not until the evidence became undeniably strong that world leadership as well as individual countries began to take concrete action to abate emissions. It is also noteworthy that government regulation varies with the stage of development. The southern countries have laxer government regulation, and companies in the north can move their production to the south to avoid stringent regulation in their home countries.

Companies are an intrinsic part of society. However, unattended business conduct, even if it appears lawful, may well destroy the fabric that the coherence of the society hinges on. The spread of pornography of 'quality' systems for product (ISO9000) and environmental (ISO14000) management.

The OECD Guidelines for Multinational Enterprises: These guidelines provide voluntary principles and standards for responsible business conduct consistent with applicable laws. They aim to ensure that the operations of multinational enterprises are in harmony with government policies, to strengthen relations between enterprises and society, to help improve the foreign investment climate and to enhance their contribution to sustainable development.

1.2   The Business Case for CSR

Since most companies are still in transition from the first to the second generation of CSR, it is important to make it clear that it is attractive for companies to embark on the transition. The key to this is to make a business case for the transition. In other words, it is imperative to align CSR activities with company goals for profit making. The UNIDO report identifies six areas where the business case for CSR can be established:

Cost savings. Investment in environmental efficiency measures such as waste reduction and energy efficiency often yield rates of return through cost savings that compare favorably with most commercial investments. This is especially true for companies engaged in cleaner production.

Enhanced reputation. Good company performance in relation to sustainability issues can both build reputation, while poor performance when exposed, can damage brand value. This is particularly important to companies with high-value retail brands, which are often the focus for media, activist and consumer pressure.

Increased ability to recruit, develop and retain staff. These can be direct effects of introducing family friendly policies, using volunteering programs to develop skills or may be an indirect effect such as improved morale and loyalty towards a company that employees feel proud to be a part of.

Better relations with government. The formal and informal license to operate is a key issue for many companies looking to extend their business or operating in politically unstable conditions. Diligence in meeting social and environmental concerns can result in a reduction in red tape and a more cooperative relationship with government departments.

Sharper anticipation and management of risk. Managing risk in an increasingly complex market environment, with greater oversight and stakeholder scrutiny of corporate activities, is key to the success of companies. Listening to the concerns and perceptions of stakeholders, as well as those of scientific experts, is of crucial importance.

Learning and innovation. Learning and innovation is key to the success and survival of all companies, not just those in knowledge-intensive and rapidly developing industry sectors. Addressing sustainability necessitates interaction with a wide range of individuals and organizations outside of the traditional business relationships of a company.

Complementarily, a recent report by Developing Value, a joint effort by SustainAbility, IFC, and the Ethos Institute, also identifies six factors contributing to the business case for CSR, i.e., save costs, increase revenues, reduce risk, build reputation, develop human capital, and improve access to capital (Developing Value, 2005). Clearly, some of these factors overlap with the areas proposed by the UNIDO report, but increasing revenues and improving access to capital are two added factors.

What is not covered by either of the reports is the now so-called Porter hypothesis. Michael Porter and van der Linde (1995) proposed that higher environmental standards imposed by the government will stimulate innovations that will not only cover the costs of meeting the standards, but also bring new profits to firms. This is so because inertia, management errors, and uncertainty prevent firms from innovating. For most economists, however, the Porter hypothesis is doubtful because in theory rational firms will not miss any profitable innovations. Yet, like most major social, economic, and political changes, a sense of crisis can be a key for a firm to change its behavior. Imposing higher environmental standards raises the bar for survival and acts as a catalyst for firms to search for better technologies. From the corporate point of view, meeting more stringent environmental standards can lead to higher profits through more innovation. Another potential benefit is that meeting higher environmental standards could appeal to a considerable number of consumers who have a clear taste for environmentally friendly production and products. For example, a survey by the UK-based Business in the Community finds that 86% of consumers say that they have a more positive image of a company if they see that it is doing something to make the world a better place" (UNIDO, 2002). As a result, meeting higher environmental standards has the potential to increase corporate sales volumes.

1. 3   Debates around CSR

Like other progressive concepts, CSR is not free from criticism. Milton Friedman s classic claim often rings in our ears: "there is one and only one responsibility of business – to use its resources and engage in activities designed to increase its profits so long as it stays within the rules of the game." (Friedman, 1962) For neo-classical economists, CSR by nature cannot be part of a company's business goals because it implies costs to the company. This is vividly illustrated in the debate that Porter and van der Linde had with mainstream economists regarding the Porter hypothesis. In the same issue in which Porter and van der Linde s paper was published, the *Journal of Economic Perspectives* also published papers by mainstream environmental economists who vehemently rejected the idea that more stringent environmental regulation could lead to innovations with benefits that more than compensate the costs incurred in compliance. The reason in the neo-classical mode is that if there existed opportunities to make a net profit, firms would have already explored them; the fact that companies have not voluntarily adopted stringent environmental standards shows that the cost of compliance must be higher than the potential benefits. That is, there cannot be a business case for CSR. However, this line of reasoning, besides assuming super rationality on the part of the managers, which Porter and van der Linde rightly reject, misses the dynamic nature of decision making inside the firm (Bromley, 2006). Business opportunities are not something already in the market, because otherwise there could not be any innovation at all. Business opportunities emerge as a result of the active searching activities of enterprises. Firm actions change the environment in which their business operates. As such, the classical economic maximization process loses its foundation because there are no pre-set parameters.

The above arguments may sound too academic and technical. In a broader context, two things are in favor of making CSR an integral part of corporate business strategy. One is that it is a fact that society requires companies to take more responsibility for ensuring that our world becomes a better one. These responsibilities may not be coded into law either because it is too difficult to do that, or because the legislative body has not realized their value to society. Civil movements can exert real threats to corporate business through protests, boycotts, and media coverage. In economic jargon, the parameters for the corporate profit maximization problem have been changed. As a result, caring about CSR can make a real business case for companies. In addition to changing societal preferences, there is another factor favoring a business case for CSR. It is evident that environmental and labor protection is unevenly enforced across national borders, and production activities in different countries are subjected to different environmental and labor standards. However, the commodity market is quite uniform across the national borders. As a result, firms meeting higher environmental and labor standards may have an advantage in gaining larger shares in the international market.

In an even broader context, it is legitimate to ask the question why society cannot ask companies to act in a more socially responsible way, even if that implies higher costs on their part. After all, companies are an integral and important part of society. It is noteworthy that asking companies to take up more social responsibilities is similar but in many cases more than asking them to pay taxes. Many of the issues CSR concerns cannot be solved simply by spending money. For example, for workers who suffer from toxic substances in a hazardous workplace, monetary compensation may not restore their health to their original levels. The economist's aggregate cost-benefit analysis fails on this account because the harmed party, the silent mass, will not rema in silent.

That having been said, the above argument by no means implies pushing companies to the verge of bankruptcy. The voluntary nature of CSR prevents this. For the proponents of CSR, it should always be kept in mind that a negotiated partnership between companies and the society is the best way to achieve their goal of a better and sustainable world.

1. 4 Drivers of CSR

Although the notion of CSR can be traced back as far as the 1920s, it is the new wave of globalization and the associated changes in global political and civil movements in the last twenty some years that have brought it to the front stage of the business world. There is a rich tradition of philanthropic giving in the business world in many countries. The first generation of CSR thus has a long root in history. However, the second generation of CSR has been a relatively new phenomenon, mainly as a response to changes in society and the business world.

The first driver that forces companies to treat CSR seriously has been the increasing consciousness of civil society over the environment. This has not only happened in the developed world, but also in the developing world. It is actually even more urgent in the developing world as fast industrialization has posed a serious challenge to the local environment and the global ecosystem. This time, the world is brought together by the common concern for the future of our planet. Global warming is at the center of concern. Before it became an international topic, environmental degradation had been by and large thought of as a local event having limited impact on the global environment (Lomborg, 2001). The hard evidence revealed by recent studies (such as the recent UN report) has decisively changed the course of thinking. No country can be thought of and treated as an isolated territory immune from responsibility for curbing global warming. Cross-border claims for more responsible governments and companies have been gaining legitimacy.

The second driver has to do with multinational companies. These companies have their business operations in different countries and can often evade harsh labor and environmental regulations by shifting their production to countries with loose regulations. This raises concerns of the civil society in both their home countries and their recipient countries, but especially in their developed home countries partly because civil awareness is stronger there. The recent litigation brought by the International Labor Rights Fund (ILRF) against Wal-Mart is a case for consideration. The basis for the ILRF suit was that Wal-Mart had not enforced its own code of conduct for labor treatment among its suppliers in developing countries. As the ILRF lawyer representing the case, Terry Collingsworth says, the suit seeks to require the company to implement the provisions of its code of conduct. Additionally, if successful, the suit will require Wal-Mart to more deeply operationalize the assertions it makes to its customers and others that it monitors its suppliers compliance with the code and takes effective action against those suppliers that violate the code." (Collingsworth, 2006). This opinion is challenged by Phillip Rudolph of the Ethical Leadership Group who, commenting on the case, believes that it is unfair and unrealistic to lay responsibility wholly at the feet of the companies.… Wal-Mart's incorporation of its code into its supplier contracts does not create a duty in Wal-Mart. It creates a duty in Wal-Mart's suppliers." (Rudolph, 2006) However, the intention of ILRF is precisely to break Wal-Mart's chain of duty shifting. The difference between Mr. Rudolph and Ms. Collingsworth is that the former believes that Wal-Mart has nothing to do with the enforcement of its code of conduct that it requires its suppliers to follow, but the latter believes that Wal-Mart must be part of the mechanism for enforcing the code of conduct that it promises to its customers. Although the merits of the ILRF s claim can still be debated and the court decision is still pending decisions, the interesting development brought up by the case is that civil society groups in the developed world are beginning to insist that multinational companies cannot simply wash their hands by shifting their social duties to companies in the developing world.

The third driver lies in the perceived risks in the society and environment. On the one hand, globalization has the amplifying effect that it makes the world market more fluid and volatile; on the other hand, it also transmits environmental risks across national borders and places the world as a whole in greater uncertainty. This amplifying effect of globalization is clearly evident in the international financial markets. Even the Wall Street mastermind, George Soros, has warned that large amounts of unregulated cross-border flows of capital would bring great risks to the world, although he himself had been a big winner in capital market speculation (Soros, 2005). On the environmental side, international communities are beginning to realize that small events even in the remotest corner of the world can cumulatively have a large impact. There is a sense of environmental crisis across every national border. All these factors contribute to civil society s demand for companies, especially multinational companies, to act in a more responsible way to spare the world from major social and environmental disasters.

The fourth driver comes from a paradigmatic shift in the business models of companies. Globalization opens up new fronts for competition. In response to increasing global civil society activism, companies can build a business case around CSR and use it as a competitive tool in competition for market share, better public relations, and a better handling of risks. In addition, globalization also brings competition for top talent onto the international level. Providing better treatments for the workforce serves as a competitive tool for attracting the best employees.

1.5   Phases of CSR in China

CSR is a relatively new concept in China. Its introduction has been clearly linked to the pace at which China is melting into this new wave of globalization. As a large developing country heavily relying on exports, China is an interesting case to study for its resistance to, engagement in, and debates on the introduction of CSR.

Weizhong Zhou, the director of BSR's China office, summarizes the introduction of CSR in China into three phases (Zhou, 2006). The first phase spans from 1996 to 2000. China began to introduce the concept of CSR in this phase mainly through the auditing of Chinese suppliers by multinational companies. The 1993 fire disaster in Shenzhen Zhili Toy Factory, a foreign invested firm, raised serious concerns in international business circles. ILRF, Global Exchange and 19 other international labor, consumer and human rights organizations enacted a charter, *China Business Principles,* to which many multinational companies signed up (Guo, 2006). These were then only confined to a limited business circle that had frequent contacts with the outside world. Governments, scholars, and the media were largely unaware of the concept. The second phase, between 2000 and 2004, was what Mr. Zhou calls "the wait-and-see years". In this period, Chinese suppliers were under frequent and in many cases duplicative auditing efforts and demands from customers in developed countries. This caught the attention of several key government ministries including the Ministry of Labor and Social Security and the Ministry of Commerce. Their overriding concern, however, was that CSR was being used as a non-tariff barrier against Chinese exports. As a result, Chinese officials and scholars took a wait-and-see attitude toward CSR.

The third phase, beginning in 2004, has seen engagement of businesses, governments, media, and scholars in the introduction and implementation of CSR in China. The most notable development has been active initiatives from all walks of the society. Governments and the business community have joined hands to enhance CSR and made it an integral part of business strategies. Besides the establishment of several government-business organizations devoted to promoting and enhancing CSR performance in Chinese companies, the Ministry of Commerce is enacting China s own CSR standard and in 2005 the textile industry started to implement a standard specifically for the industry, China Social Compliance for Textile & Apparel Industry, or CSC9000T, (see Box 1.1 for an introduction to the standard). The textile industry was the first to feel serious pressures from abroad as it is China s largest exporting sector, so it makes sense that it became the first to act. A handful of large Chinese companies, including the three petroleum companies and Baosteel, the largest Chinese steel company, have regularly issued their CSR or sustainability reports for several years.

In addition to government and business initiatives, the media has been playing an increasingly important role. Although they may not use the term CSR, many media reports help reveal serious violations of labor rights, environmental regulations and product quality accidents. One sign of CSR's getting increasingly popularity among Chinese media is that a search on www.google.com by the keyword corporate social responsibility" yielded 14,600,000 results on Chinese websites by the end of August 2007.

The *China News Weekly* is a news organization that explicitly promotes CSR through various activities. One of them is the annual international forum for social responsibility that gathers renowned scholars, government officials and people from the business world. It has been held bi-annually since 2006. Many multinational companies such as Intel, HP, Samsung, and Shell as well as large domestic companies such as Baosteel, The State Grid Corporation, and Lenova have participated in the forum. One of the forum events is to issue the Most Socially Responsible Company Award. This award started in 2005 and became one of the major events of the forum. Most of the award winners have been multinational companies operating in China, but domestic companies such as Lenova and the State Grid Corporation have also won the award.

Box 1.1

CSC9000T: A UNIQUE CHINESE SOCIAL COMPLIANCE MANAGEMENT SYSTEM

CSC9000T, China Social Compliance for the Textile & Apparel Industry, was introduced by the Responsible Supply Chain Association (RSCA) of the China National Textile and Apparel Council (CNTAC) in May 2005. The RSCA is an industry specific, self-disciplinary and voluntary association for the Chinese textile and clothing industry with a particular focus on putting the CSR ideas and concept into practice primarily to protect workers rights and enhance capacity building of businesses for sustainable development. CSC9000T is the first CSR management system developed and maintained by a Chinese industrial sector. China's textile exports accounted for 17% of the world total in 2003 and were expected to reach 50% by 2008. There have been many controversies regarding the labor and environmental standards in this largest export sector in China, which have drawn tremendous international attention. Companies in major importing countries have increased their auditing efforts when they buy textile products in China. CSC9000T is a response by the industry to this increasing international demand for higher labor standards.

It has ten key components providing guidance for management systems, employment contracts, child labor, forced labor, working hours, wages and welfare, discrimination, trade union & collective bargaining, harassment and abuse, and health & safety, respectively. While the majority of the standards are within the limits of the Chinese laws, some of them go beyond the Chinese laws and incorporate codes of conduct in developed countries.

Unlike SA8000, the prime mandate of CSC9000T is not on auditing and accreditation, but on the establishment and improvement of CSR management systems within factories." (Sun, 1996) In other words, it is mainly a guide for self-discipline and self-appraisal.

RSCA is the primary driver pushing for the adoption of CSC9000T in the Chinese textile industry. Companies adopting the system have reported tangible benefits. For example, after being in the first batch of experimenting companies, Gaiqi Garment, Co. Limited in Fujian province immediately obtained a one million US dollar order from a Canadian customer and was exempted from on-site auditing. This example is not unique; other CSC9000T companies have had the same experience. In addition to helping companies get orders, CSC9000T also helps companies to retain workers. There has been a shortage of workers in recent years and low return rates of workers after major national holidays have become a major issue for many companies. One achievement of CSC9000T is that it has significantly increased the worker return rate. For example, after the 2007 Spring Festival, companies adopting CSC9000T had a worker return rate of 90%, but the average return rate of the whole textile industry was only 60%.[*]

CSC9000T has to face the competition from international standards, especially SA8000 and ISO14000. These standards, although they are expensive to certify, are more familiar to both international customers and domestic textile companies. Hopefully, with its voluntary characteristic and low costs, CSC9000T will gain more support from Chinese textile companies.

[*] China Garment Network (Zhongguo Fuzhuang Wang),
http://www.efu.com.cn/data/2007/2007-08-23/208452.shtml, August 23, 2007.

Multinational companies are under greater pressure to take on more social responsibilities in China. They had enjoyed preferential tax treatment before the National People s Congress passed a law in the spring of 2007 to get rid of these tax benefits. The law was a result of a long-lasting debate about leveling the playing field for both domestic and foreign companies. There had been a strong call for subjecting both kinds of firms under the same national treatment . The resistance put forward by multinational companies has tarnished their image in China. In addition, people suspect that multinational companies are merely passing the burden of social responsibility to their suppliers, most of which are small and medium Chinese firms, while they do not provide proper treatment for employees in their own factories. Under this situation, multinational companies have begun to engage with the Chinese public. Their active participation in the competition for the Most Socially Responsible Company Award is one example. Their engagement culminated on August 27, 2007 when Min Yida, CEO of Dell (China), representing 1,400 foreign and joint venture companies, read a statement at a Beijing conference on CSR of foreign and joint venture companies, to call for all foreign companies operating in China to take more social responsibilities in product safety, labor welfare, environmental protection, and philanthropic activities. (Wang, 2007).

Overall, CSR in China remains mostly at the stage of early transition from the first generation to the second generation. It is thus pivotal to find a business case for CSR for it to thrive in China. These issues have been what the debates surrounding CSR have been all about.

1. 6   Debates on CSR in China

The introduction of CSR in China has been accompanied by fierce debate. This subsection reviews the debate from three perspectives, the definition of CSR, its business case, and international competition.

A Chinese Definition of CSR?

CSR has been recognized in the developed world as embracing social responsibilities beyond legal expectations. Most Chinese officials, scholars, and practitioners believe that this notion of CSR is beyond the reach of Chinese reality. Zhang Junfeng, a leading scholar on China's CSR issue, identifies three layers of CSR. The first is abiding by the law; the second is to contribute to the local community, especially in the area of environmental protection; and the third layer is to participate in philanthropic activities. Zhang believes that the first layer is the most fundamental for Chinese firms (Zhang, 2006). This view is shared by many people.

China is known for its weak legal system, especially at the enforcement stage. It is an open secret that most firms, especially SMEs, are operating in a "grey area", namely, in a semi-legal manner. While the causes are very complicated, over-regulation and high legal burdens are often cited as two of the major reasons (e.g., CPDF, 2005). However, this does not exempt Chinese firms from their legal duties. The problem is often complicated by local governments interference with legal enforcement efforts. For most local officials, economic growth is the most important goal for their jobs. It is not only because it has a lot to do with their promotion, but also because many of them sincerely believe that it is morally acceptable to sacrifice the environment and workers welfare for the rise of a strong China. The consequence is that many firms can ignore laws and openly defy law enforcement efforts by the concerned government agencies (see Box 4.1 for an example). Most of China's environmental disasters in recent years were linked with local governments intentional avoidance of implementing the existing national environmental protection laws and regulations. One of the worst cases is Shanxi, China's largest coal mining province, where the environmental problems are so bad that a scholar uses environmental wars to describe the tension between businesses and the local communities (Song, 2007).

Neglect by government officials is not without in academic circles. Some mainstream economists argue that the fact that mining workers are still willing to go down the mines and migrants still work in hazardous workplaces shows that the current situation is welfare enhancing. Others simply avoid talking about the environment altogether. To them, the Kuznets curve applies and will ultimately bring China onto the right track; that is, China will have to follow the western model of "pollution first and abatement next . The problem, however, is that there will be millions of lives deformed and even lost before the Kuznets curve takes a down turn. Thanks to the long-lasting debates and the thrust of the government policy, income inequality is a real issue of justice for most economists. What they have not realized, or have not been ready to accept, is that environmental degradation is a no less severe issue of justice than income inequality. Economic growth sacrificing the environment is unjust because it hurts a large portion of the population for the benefits of a small group of people. The Shanxi case is the most obvious in illuminating this point. The mine owners have made a large amount of money in recent years thanks to the rise of energy prices. Most of them, however, have ignored the serious problem of land collapses and their consequences for local people, many of whom have chosen to leave their villages and towns. In the meantime, the owners have no long-term plans for the mining areas and are prepared to emigrate to large cities and even abroad (Song, 2007). This is a more serious issue of injustice than income inequality.

Amidst this unfavorable atmosphere, it is even hard to ask companies to fulfill their basic responsibility to society, i.e., obeying the law. Mr. Zhang's emphasis on the first layer of CSR is well justified in the Chinese context. However, obeying the law is a passive process. Because the implementation of the law is often distorted by local governments, it is easy for companies to find an excuse for not following the national law. It is imperative to make abiding by the law a voluntary action by the corporate sector.

Therefore, a proper notion of CSR could be:

Fulfilling the needs of shareholders without compromising the needs of other stakeholders in the local community and the society at large.

Without compromising the needs of other stakeholders in the local community and the society at large is a prerequisite for "fulfilling the needs of shareholders". Obeying the law is the first step to fulfilling that prerequisite. When it is listed as a component of CSR, this first step should be an automatic impulse, not a passive response by the company. But CSR should not stop at the level of law actually implemented because the law may be quite below the standard that CSR requires. Beyond that, firms need to take into account the needs of the local community and society that may not even be written into law. This is a demanding requirement for firms in China as it is today. The key is to make a business case for CSR.

A Chinese Business Case for CSR?

Is there a business case for CSR even in an irregular legal and market environment as bad as that in China? Some, like CSR's opponents in the developed world, believes that CSR is a redundant concept – what it asks for are either stated by the law or would be fulfilled by fuller development of the market. Anything beyond market discipline would hurt not only the enterprise but also the people it is intended to protect. To quote one scholar:

"No matter by what names – including by the name of 'social responsibilities', to force enterprises to deviate from market signals and to sacrifice profits for the improvement of labor conditions will not fulfill the objective; instead, it will only lead to the decline of enterprises competitiveness and in the end hurt the real interests of labor – especially the interests of the marginalized groups of people whom 'social responsibilities' claim to help." (Li, 2006)

Less extreme comments can be found doubting whether Chinese enterprises are ready to take up the social responsibilities that go beyond their profit making activities. As one business professor puts it, "it is clear from the quality of listed companies that some Chinese enterprises have not even established an effective concept of being responsible to their shareholders, not to mention taking up corporate social responsibility." (Shutao Cai, quoted from Guo 2006)

However, like it or not, CSR is knocking on the door of many Chinese enterprises. International pressures are building up on China. As the second largest greenhouse gas emitter, China is under great pressures from the world community to raise energy efficiency. The Chinese government has taken up the challenge. In as early as 1992, the central government began to promote cleaner production; in 2005, a cleaner production standard was issued. In its 11th Five Year Plan that runs from 2006 to 2010, the central government pledged to raise energy efficiency by 15% in 2010 over the level of 2005. This has been proven to be no easy task; the target set for 2006 was missed. There is currently a national campaign to speed up progress so the final target will not be missed by 2010. Large SOEs are especially urged to take more active measures to lower their energy consumption (Huang, 2007). The recent environmental accidents in Song-hua-jiang and Tai-hu have also added momentum to the call for more responsible and prudent behavior on the part of enterprises. The domestic and international pressures for the improvement of labor conditions faced by enterprises are no less challenging. In a word, CSR is increasingly becoming an unavoidable part of the business environment in China.

It is against this background that a Chinese business case can be argued for CSR. While the six factors presented in Section 1.2 may all make a contribution, it is the competitiveness created by meeting the expectations of domestic and international pressures that contributes the most to the Chinese business case for CSR. The competitiveness arises as a result of a firm moving ahead of others in a business environment where compliance with labor and environmental laws is universally unsatisfactory. When most firms do not provide enough protection to their workers, it becomes easier for a firm to retain its workforce if it improves worker treatment (see Box 1.1 for some examples); when most firms do not meet environmental standards, it becomes easier for a firm to get new orders from environmentally conscious buyers – there are many of them in the world – if it starts a cleaner production program; when most firms hide their true financial information, it becomes easier for a firm to get bank loans if it publishes third-party audited financial reports under a well-defined and transparent corporate governing structure. This is one good thing about living in a latecomer country like China: it does not demand great efforts devoted to innovation for firms to get ahead of others.

The role played by international pressures needs more discussion. Many Chinese scholars and government officials worry that CSR is used by developed countries as a non-tariff barrier against Chinese exports. Some of them call for a balanced duty-sharing between Chinese suppliers and international buyers. As Jun Guo, an official from the National Labor Union points out:

"Our standpoint is that corporate social responsibility has to be shared in a fair manner. That is why the ISO especially emphasizes a balance between the south and the north and a joint effort between developing and developed countries to promote CSR when it enacts its CSR standards. Firms in developed countries claim that they are responsible firms and require firms in developing countries to take up social responsibilities, but in the same time suppress again and again the prices paid to their suppliers, and shorten again and again the product delivery period. How can firms in developing countries take up social responsibilities?

"… CSR standards are not rules of international trade. China should clearly define its own interests and claims and not allow the CSR issue to become a soft spot open to attacks. (Guo, 2005)

The worry that Chinese firms would be suppressed from both the CSR side and the price side is well founded; the UNIDO (2002) report also expresses the worry that SMEs would become particularly vulnerable when CSR obligations are transmitted down to them from large companies through the supply chain. There is room for multinationals to play on two grounds; one is shifting their duty of CSR to suppliers in developing countries, and the other is using the international market to suppress prices. The message that Mr. Guo wants to convey is that China should clearly define the goal that the country would achieve in terms of CSR and use it as the basis to negotiate with multinationals for better deals in business transactions. CSR is a commitment of businesses and governments to their own communities and the country as a whole and should not be negotiable with multinational companies. However, the CSR standard in China may well be lower than the one implemented in the developed world (for example, it is unrealistic to pay Chinese workers the minimum wage set in the United States or Germany). In this case, what Chinese firms can do is to negotiate a linked contract with multinational companies that ask for higher prices in exchange for a higher CSR standard. To make this strategy successful, of course, needs coordination among developing countries. Otherwise prices will be suppressed by the effect of "racing to the bottom .

On the hand, it needs to be kept in mind that 60% of China's exports are made by foreign companies or domestic-foreign joint-ventures operating in China. These companies are directly subjected to pressures from their home countries and thus may perform better than domestic companies in CSR (an assessment that this report will try to verify). Therefore, it is not a good idea to lump all multinational companies together. Those having moved their production into China can serve as an important and positive player for better CSR in China.

It is also worth noting that a higher CSR standard can serve as a policy tool for China to restructure its exports from low value-added products to higher value-added products. One way to make this restructuring happen is to follow the American pressure to revaluate China s currency. However, this approach has the drawback of hurting the people at the bottom, i.e., migrant workers in the export sector because some of them will lose their jobs and those remaining in their jobs will not get any improvements. Improving labor and environmental standards provides another way. It will accomplish what a revaluation can do for the structural change because it drives out labor-intensive products. Moreover, it brings two additional benefits that a revaluation does not provide, i.e., it improves the conditions for workers remaining in their jobs (although in the same way as revaluation, it will reduce the number of jobs) and cleans up the environment. Since the bottom portion of the population is inevitably the most vulnerable group in any structural adjustment program, any improvement made to at least a fraction of them would be better than an approach keeping their interests out of consideration.

In summary, we can argue for a Chinese business case for CSR from both the firm level and the national level. At the firm level, better CSR performance helps a firm to lead the market in attracting and retaining a better workforce and taking a larger share of market. At the national level, a higher CSR standard serves as a better policy tool to restructure China's exports. One of the objectives of this report is to verify that the Chinese business case exists at the firm level. The last chapter of the report will provide further discussion of the case at the national level when policy recommendations are put forward.

1. 7   The Arrangement of the Report

The report has eleven chapters including this one. Chapter 2 will introduce the survey and provide descriptive statistics of the sample cities and sample firms. Chapter 3 to Chapter 10 are the main content of the report and deal with CSR awareness among firms, the trend of labor protection in China, labor protection in the sample, environmental protection, quality control, corporate governance, the role of the supply chain, and CSR's role in firm performance. Chapter 11 summarizes the main findings of the report and puts forward policy recommendations for government and companies.

Chapter 2
Sampling and Descriptive Statistics

This chapter introduces the surveys and provides descriptive statistics based on them. The main survey was conducted in the spring of 2006 among 1,268 firms in 12 cities (from north to south): Changchun, Dandong, Jining, Beijing, Shijiazhuang, Xi'an, Zibo, Chongqing, Shiyan, Wujiang, Hangzhou, and Shunde. The survey questionnaire was administered to firm management and its aim was to ask the management to report information on the firm s CSR performance. This survey was supplemented by interviews conducted with government agencies and enterprises in three of the sample cities, Changchun, Chongqing, and Shunde, and an additional city close to Hangzhou, which is Taizhou. The reason that Taizhou instead of Hangzhou was chosen for the interviews was that the research team had personal ties in Taizhou and it was easier to conduct the interviews. In addition, a supplementary individual survey which was commissioned from the Institute of International Labor and Information (IILI), a research institute in the Ministry of Labor and Social Security, interviewed 345 individuals in five cities: Beijing, Zhengzhou, Chengdu, Hangzhou, and Wulumuqi. The main survey administered to the firm management might not capture the real scene of CSR performance in the sample firms. This might be particularly true for labor protection. The supplementary individual survey aimed at getting information from the employee perspective and providing a check on the results obtained from the main survey.

This chapter will first describe the organization of both surveys and the interviews, and then provide key descriptive statistics for the economic indicators of the 12 cities covered by the main survey. After that, we will provide information on the distribution of the sample firms in terms of their location, size, legal registration, and industries. The performance and growth of the sample firms will also be discussed. Finally, basic statistics will be provided for the supplementary survey.

2. 1   Organization of the Surveys and Interviews

The Main Survey

The main survey was designed by the research team and carried out by the NBS. The training of the numerators was carried out at two levels. At the first level, survey organizers from the statistical bureaus of the 12 cities were trained by the research team; at the second level, those responsible for completing the questionnaires in the sample firms in each city were gathered together and trained by the respective survey organizer in that city. These respondents filled out the questionnaire in their own firms. The city organizer was responsible for the quality of the questionnaires in their city. Because the questions asked in the questionnaire are relatively simple and straightforward, the quality of the answers was not likely to be compromised by this two-layer training scheme.

The choice of the 12 cities was based on the principle of representation rather than on a random basis. A detailed description of these cities will be provided in the next section. The original plan was to survey 100 firms in each city, but it turned out that there were a slightly larger number of firms that were actually surveyed. The survey only covered firms with an annual sales volume larger than 5 million yuan. The project did this for two reasons. One was that firms with a sales volume below 5 million yuan are very small and their behavior would not show much variation in terms of CSR. The second reason was more practical, that is, NBS only maintains a database for firms with a sales volume larger than 5 million yuan.

The NBS dataset only includes firms in industry, and does not include construction and transportation companies. So the main survey only surveyed industrial firms. This is regretful as labor protection in the construction sector is a serious issue. However, excluding the construction and transportation sectors will not affect our analysis of the other aspects of CSR because those two sectors do not have serious problems in aspects such as environmental protection and product quality. In addition, although wage arrears are more severe in the construction sector, issues of labor protection are similar in both the industrial sector and in the construction and transportation sectors.

Comparing domestic private firms with SOEs and FDI firms is the major purpose of this study. To ensure that the sample fully represented the distribution of firms, a stratified sampling strategy was adopted. The first stratum was firm ownership. Firms were divided into three categories: state-owned enterprises (SOEs), domestic private firms, and joint ventures. SOEs were firms where the state controlled the shares. Domestic private firms included companies with mixed ownership but where the majority of shares were in private hands as well as pure privately owned firms. Joint ventures were firms that had foreign shareholders including shares held by Hong Kong, Macao, and Taiwanese businesses. The shares of each of these three categories of firms in a city in the total number of enterprises were used in the sampling. The second stratum was firm size, which also included three categories: large, medium, and small. The definitions of these three size categories were the same as those used by NBS in its routine statistics, which were defined by SETC (2003). The shares of firms of these three size categories in a city were used in the sampling.

The above sampling strategy does not give exporting firms a separate treatment. To the extent that exporting is an important factor determining a firm's CSR performance, this could be a deficiency. The research team did not do so however for two reasons. One was that the sample size in each city was fairly large and a sufficient number of exporting firms should be picked up. The other was that it would have been necessary to identify all the exporting firms to treat them separately, which could be a very time-consuming task. Since the sampling was done by individual sample cities, delegating the task to the city organizers might resulted in low quality of work.

Interviews

The four cities chosen for interviews were not selected at random either. Changchun and Chongqing are large and inland cities, and Taizhou and Shunde are medium-size coastal cities. In each city, focus group interviews were conducted on government agencies and a group of enterprises. Government agencies included the department of labor, bureau of environmental protection, department of social security and health insurance, department of SMEs, bureau of industrial and commercial administration, bureau of quality inspection and enforcement, and bureau of work safety. After the focus group interviews, separate visits were paid to several important government agencies such as the department of labor, department of social security and health insurance, and the bureau of environmental protection. Several visits to the interviewed enterprises were made to obtain more detailed information. With these interviews, the research team obtained first-hand information on government regulations, firms' awareness of CSR, and how CSR affected their performance.

The City Survey

In addition to the firm survey, a simple questionnaire was administered in each sample city to extract basic city-level information such as population, economic growth, unemployment, and pension and healthcare insurance coverage. This questionnaire was filled out by the local statistical bureau staff in each city.

The Supplementary Individual Survey

It is a challenge to do an individual survey on labor protection. It is impractical to do it inside enterprises for obvious reasons. The IILI used the alternative method of distributing questionnaires in the government-sponsored employment center of each of the five cities. Employment centers were set up by cities in the late 1990s to provide employment information for laid-off workers and people in transitory unemployment. In recent years, rural migrant workers also go there to find information about job vacancies. The questionnaire asked questions on employment contracts, wage, working hours, social security, workplace safety, labor disputes, labor unions, and collective bargaining. Researchers from IILI gave questionnaires randomly to people who went to the center and asked them to fill out the questionnaires on the spot. As a result, the response rate was very high: It took only 400 questionnaires to get back the 345 valid ones. Since subsequent analysis of this chapter will focus on the information drawn from the main survey, here we provide a concise description of the profile of sample individuals in this supplementary survey.

Among the 345 correspondents, 61.6% were male, and 48.4% were female. About half of them were rural migrant workers (47.3%) and the rest were urban workers. Their educational levels were reasonably high: only 2.03% did not go beyond elementary school, 31.40% had junior high school diplomas, 45.35% had senior high diplomas (including professional schools), 15.41% had 3-year university diplomas, and the rest, 5.81%, had a 4-year university or graduate diploma. Close to two thirds of them were under 35 years old. For the sectoral distribution of their last jobs, 7.60% were in construction, 26.61% in manufacturing, 32.47% in commerce, 13.74% in hotel and catering, 3.15% in transportation, and 5.26% in other sectors.

2. 2　Profiles of the Sample Cities

Geographic Locations

The 12 sample cities constitute a reasonable representation of China in terms of geographic locations and economic, social, and legal indicators. Figure 2.1 shows the geographic distribution of these cities. Beijing and Chongqing are two provincial-level cities. Changchun, Shijiazhuang, Xi'an, and Hangzhou are provincial capitals of Jilin, Hebei, Shaanxi, and Zhejiang, respectively. Wujiang and Shunde are county-level cities.[1] The other cities are medium-sized prefecture-level cities. Beijing, Wujiang, Hangzhou, and

---

[1] Shunde is actually a district in Foshan city, but was until three years ago an independent city.

Shunde belong to the coastal region; Jining, Xi'an, Shiyan, and Chongqing belong to the western region; and the rest belong to the central region. Changchun, Xi'an and Chongqing used to be among China's industrial powerhouses, but had to go through a painful transformation in the last decade because of the shifting of the economic gravity from the inland to the booming coastal regions in the east and south. Beijing, Hangzhou, Wujiang, and Shunde are booming cities with fast growing industries and services. Zibo is catching up in industrial development, but its service sector is lagging behind in relative terms. Table 2.1 summarizes the 12 cities geographic locations and size distribution.

Figure 2.1

LOCATIONS OF THE SAMPLE CITIES

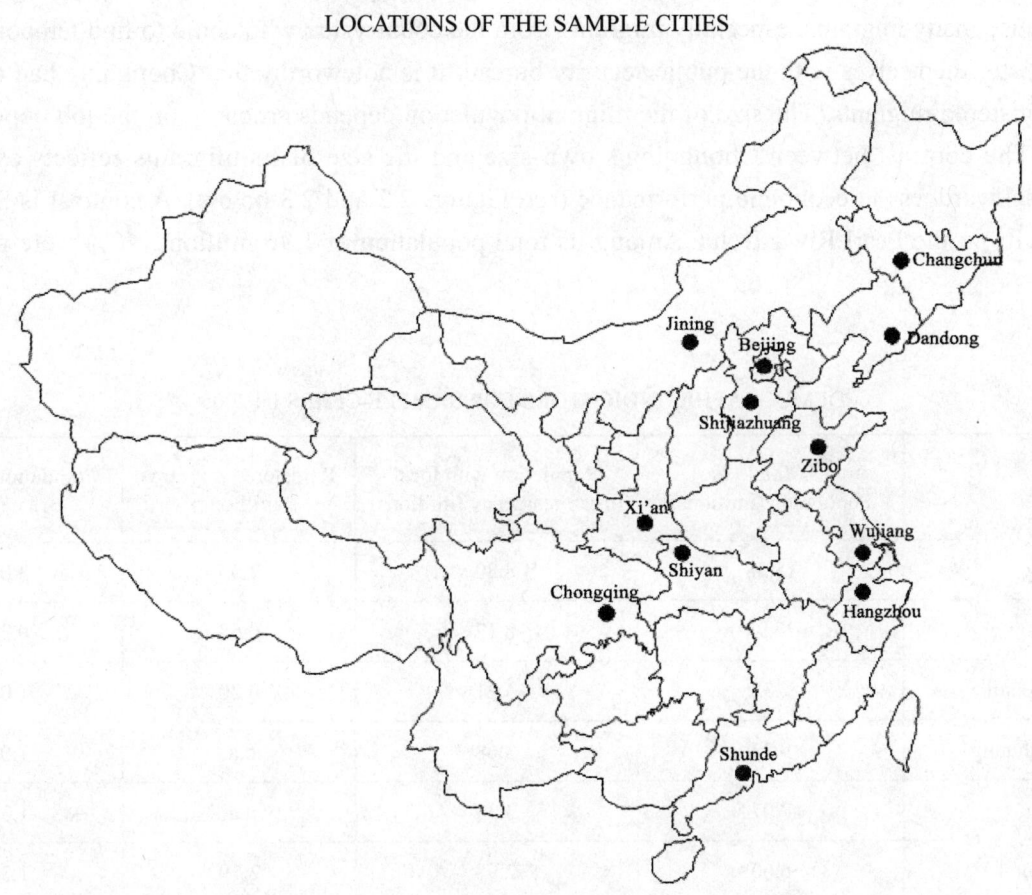

Table 2.1

SAMPLE CITIES GROUPED BY REGION AND SIZE

Region \ Size	Provincial-level cities	Provincial capitals	Prefecture-level cities	County-level cities
Coastal	Beijing	Hangzhou		Wujiang Shunde
Central		Changchun Shijiazhuang	Zibo Dandong	
Western	Chongqing	Xi'an	Shiyan Jining	

Demographics. Table 2.2 presents some key demographic data on the 12 sample cities for 2005. The total population reported in the table refers to people who live in a city for more than 6 months in a year. It thus includes both people with local residency and migrants from other cities and the countryside. By this measure, Chongqing was the largest city. It is in fact a province with a large rural area. It is a more sensible way to gauge the size of a city by looking at its population with local urban residency. In this regard, Beijing was the largest city, Chongqing became the second. The four provincial capitals occupied the next four places having close to or more than 3 million local urban residents. Among the smaller cities, Zibo was very large by having 2.11 million local urban residents. Beijing had 3.55 million registered migrants, and Hangzhou had 2.19 million. The real size of the migrant population was undoubtedly larger in both cities because many migrants, especially migrants from the countryside who come to find temporary jobs, do not register themselves with the public security bureau. It is noteworthy that Chongqing had only 0.58 million registered migrants. The size of the migrant population depends crucially on the job opportunities in a city. The contrast between Chongqing s own size and the size of its migrants reflects exactly its relative backwardness in economic performance (see Figures 2.2 and 2.3 below). A contrast is Shunde, a booming city in the Pearl River Delta. Among its total population of 1.96 millions, 40% were registered migrants.

Table 2.2

DEMOGRAPHIC INDICATORS FOR SAMPLE CITIES IN 2005

City	Total Population (millions)	Population with local urban residency (millions)	Registered migrants (millions)	Population growth rate (%)
Beijing	15.38	8.80	3.55	3.00
Chongqing	27.98	8.17	0.58	0.20
Changchun	7.32	3.21	0.20	1.00
Shijiazhuang	9.27	3.68	n.a.	1.06
Xi'an	8.07	3.33	n.a.	1.30
Hangzhou	6.60	2.98	2.19	1.35
Dandong	2.42	0.60	0.05	0.60
Jining	2.15	0.64	n.a.	-1.78
Zibo	4.42	2.11	0.17	1.19
Shiyan	3.45	0.90	0.06	0.16
Wujiang	0.91	0.24	0.12	2.80
Shunde	1.96	n.a.	0.78	0.90

Notes: Total population includes people who reside in a city for more than 6 months in a particular year. Registered migrants are people without permanent local residency but who have obtained temporary residency. Population growth rate is the rate of growth of the total population.
Source: City survey.

While the size of a city reflects its economic achievements, its population growth rate shows its growth potential because the birth rate is declining in all major Chinese cities and population growth is mainly coming from migration. In this regard, Beijing, Wujiang, Hangzhou, and Xi'an were the top four cities. Beijing's population growth rate was 3% in 2005. In fact, its population growth has been accelerating in recent years. In 2001, its population growth rate was only 1.6%. This can be contrasted with Changchun and Shunde. In 2001, their population growth rates were 8.7% and 6.1%, respectively; but in 2005, their rates declined to only 1% and 0.9%, respectively. It seems that economic expansion has decelerated in recent years. The city that really needs to worry about this, though, is Jining, which was losing population at a rate of 1.78% in 2005. However, the above trend matches the broad picture in China: population is moving from the inland regions (perhaps Xi'an is an exception) to the coastal regions, but the first movers in industrialization (such as Shunde) have begun to see deceleration in their ability to absorb labor.

Figure 2.2

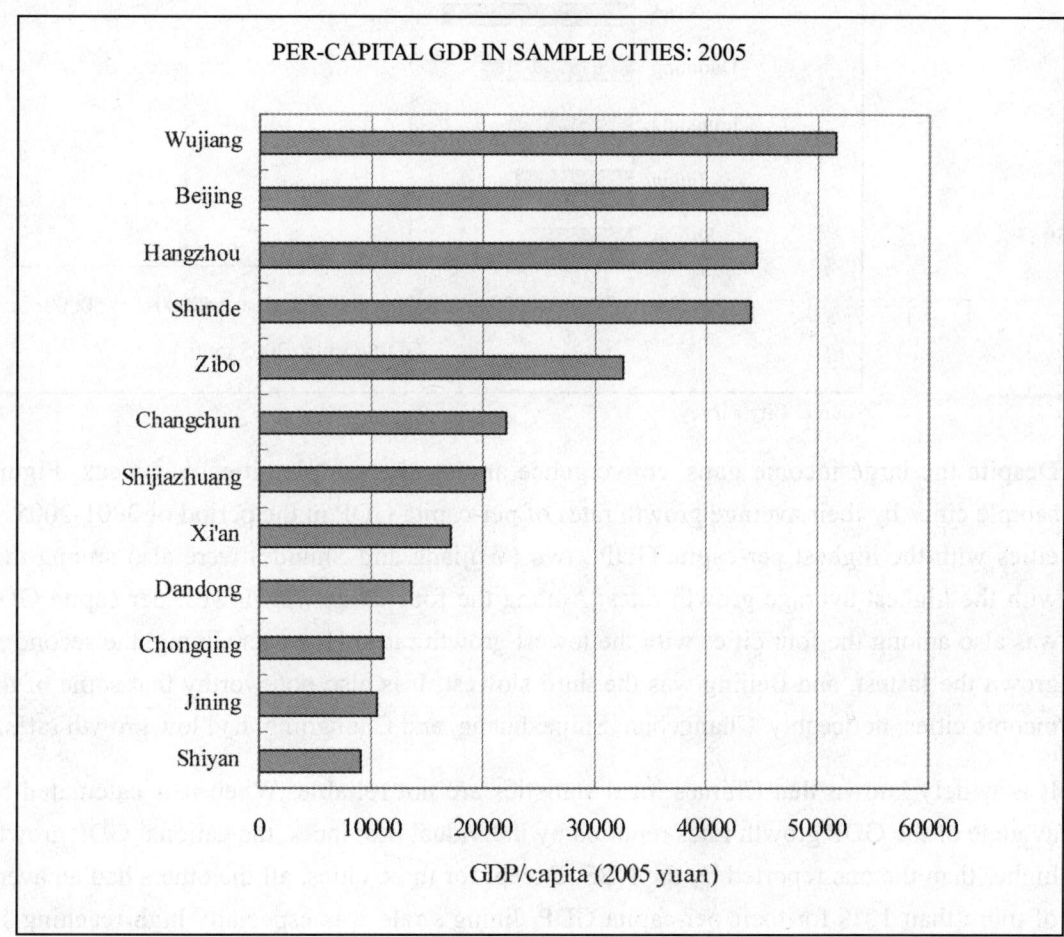

Source: City survey.

Economic Indicators

Figure 2.2 ranks the 12 sample cities by their 2005 per-capita GDP (at current prices). There was a clear downward slope running down from cities in the coastal region to cities in the central region, and then to those in the western region. The city with the highest per-capita GDP was not Beijing, but Wujiang. Standing at 51,700 yuan, Wujiang's per-capita GDP was 5.7 times that of Shiyan, the poorest among the sample cities.

Figure 2.3

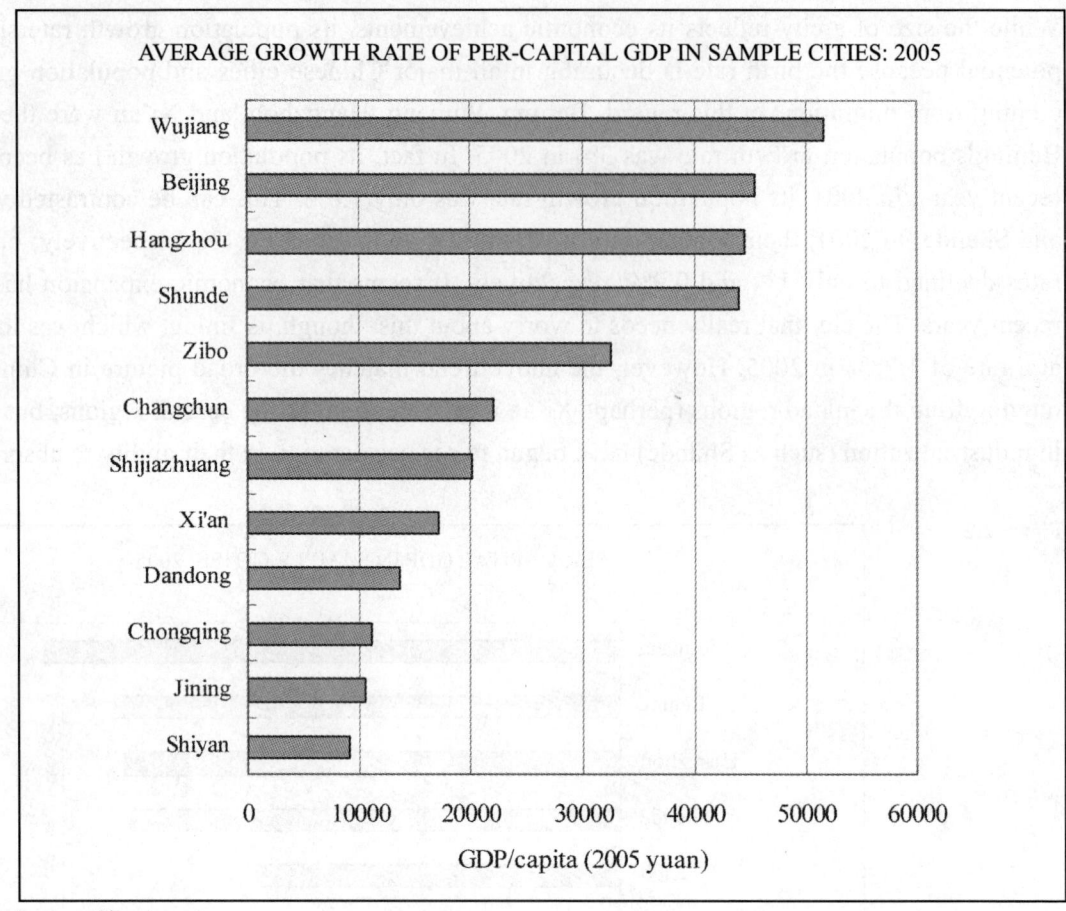

AVERAGE GROWTH RATE OF PER-CAPITAL GDP IN SAMPLE CITIES: 2005

Source: City survey.

Despite the large income gaps, convergence among the sample cities was weak. Figure 2.3 ranks the sample cities by their average growth rates of per-capita GDP in the period of 2001-2005. Among the four cities with the highest per-capita GDP[2], two (Wujiang and Shunde) were also among the top four cities with the highest average growth rates. Among the four cities with lowest per-capita GDP, one (Shiyan) was also among the four cities with the lowest growth rates. However, Jining, the second poorest city, had grown the fastest, and Beijing was the third slowest. It is also noteworthy that some of the medium-low-income cities, noticeably, Changchun, Shijiazhuang, and Chongqing, had low growth rates.

It is widely known that China s local statistics are not reliable. When it is calculated by the weighted average of the GDP growth rates reported by individual provinces, the national GDP growth rate is usually higher than the one reported by the NBS. Except for three cities, all the others had an average growth rate of more than 10% for their per-capita GDP. Jining's rate was especially high reaching 17% per annum. Therefore, caution is needed when interpreting growth rates and their associated GDP figures. However, the ranking of the cities is still indicative and meaningful assuming that the reporting bias in each city was consistent over time.

The coverage of social protection in a city is affected by the number of people with jobs. Figure 2.4 then ranks the sample cities by their registered urban unemployment rates in 2005. Since registered

---

[2] It is a conventional practice to use the ranking of the per-capita GDP of the initial year to study convergence. In our case, the ranking in 2001 was exactly the same as ranking in 2005 except Wujiang took over from Beijing as the richest city.

Figure 2.4

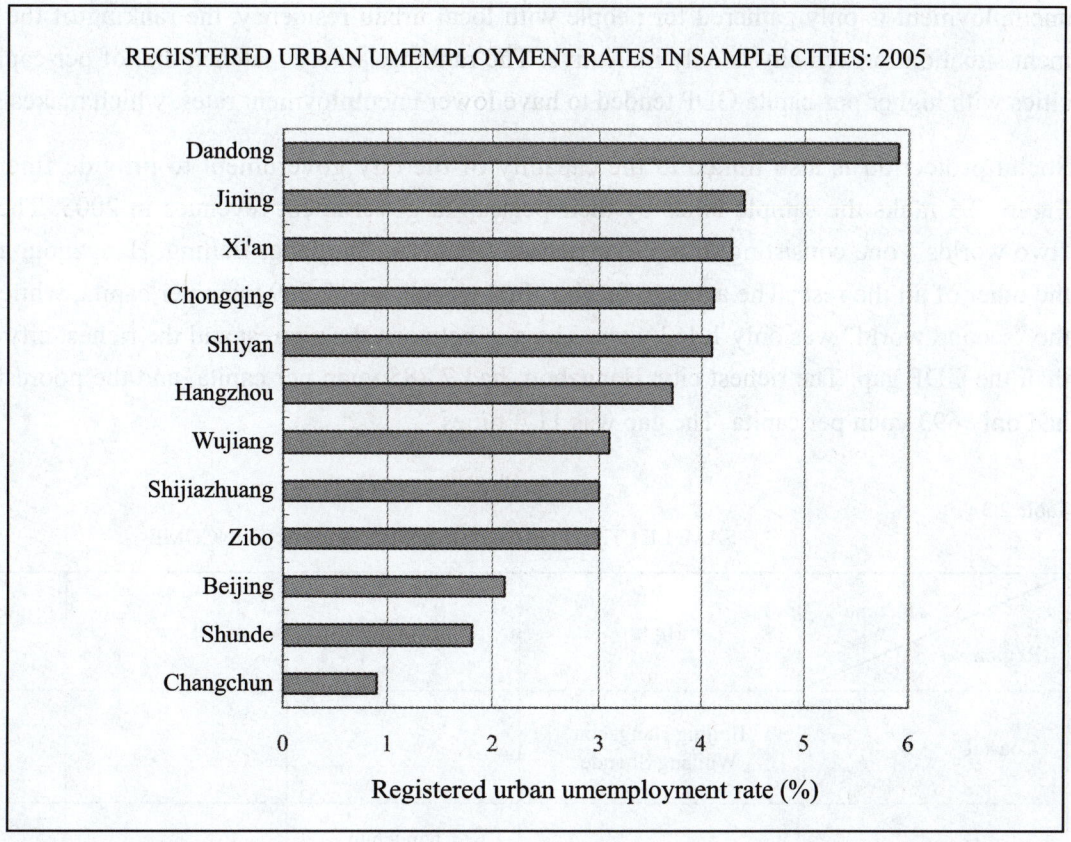

Source: City survey.

Figure 2.5

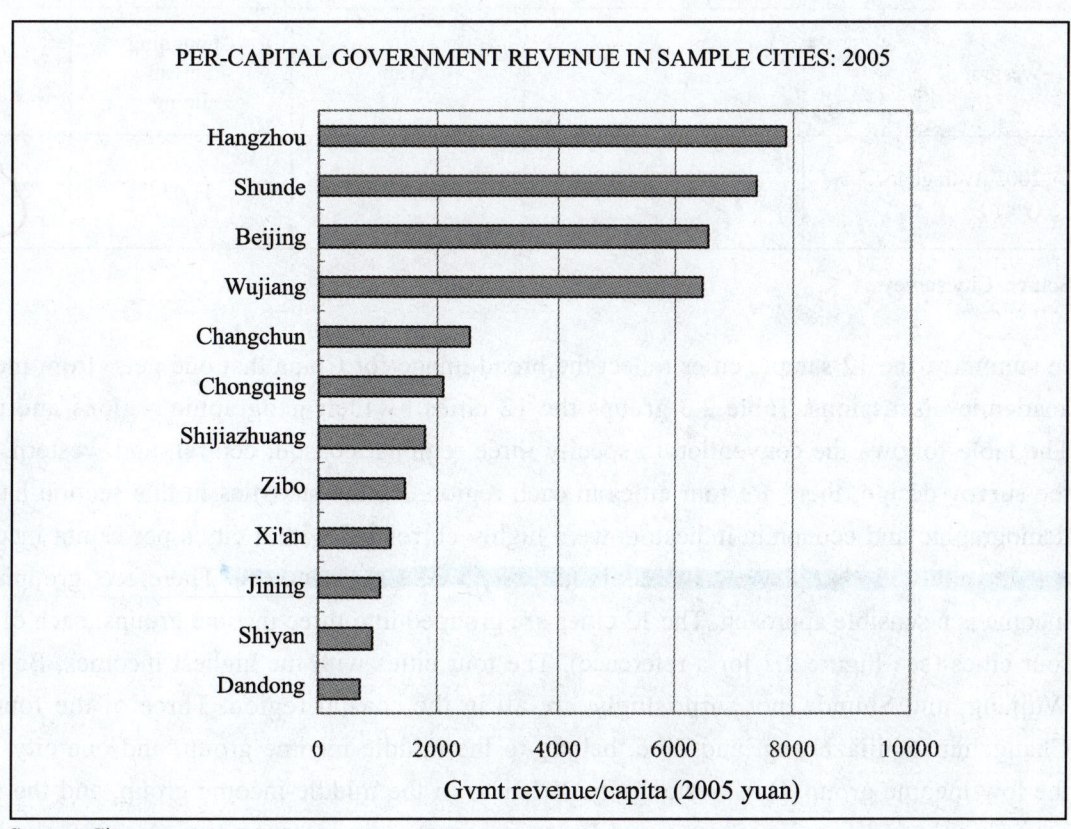

Source: City survey.

unemployment is only gathered for people with local urban residency, the ranking of the real unemployment situation in each city is only indicative. The ranking largely matched that of per-capita GDP, that is, cities with higher per-capita GDP tended to have lower unemployment rates, which makes sense.

Social protection is also linked to the capacity of the city government to provide financial resources. Figure 2.5 ranks the sample cities by their per-capita government revenues in 2005. There were clearly "two worlds", one consisting of the four richest cities, i.e., Wujiang, Beijing, Hangzhou, and Shunde, and the other of all the rest . The average for the "first world" was 7,069 yuan per capita, while the average for the "second world" was only 1,463 yuan. The gap between the poorest and the richest city was even larger than the GDP gap. The richest city, Hangzhou, had 7,885 yuan per capita, and the poorest city, Dandong, had only 693 yuan per capita. The gap was 11.4 times.

Table 2.3

SAMPLE CITIES GROUPED BY REGION AND INCOME

Income / Region	High	Middle	Low	2005 average income (yuan)
Coastal	Beijing Hangzhou Wujiang Shunde			46,401
Central		Changchun Shijiazhuang Zibo	Dandong	22,056
Western		Xi'an	Chongqing Shiyan Jining	11,939
2005 Average income (yuan)	46,401	22,961	11,034	26,799 ?

Source: City survey.

In summary, the 12 sample cities reflect the broad image for China that one gets from media reports and academic discussions. Table 2.3 groups the 12 cities by their geographic regions and income groups. The table follows the convention to specify three regions: coastal, central, and western. As intended in the survey design, there are four cities in each region. As the statistics in this section have shown, both demographic and economic indicators were highly correlated with a city's per-capita income. We expect that income will also play a critical role in a city s CSR performance. Therefore, grouping the cities by income is a sensible approach. The 12 cities are grouped into three income groups, each of which includes four cities (see Figure 2.2 for a reference). The four cities with the highest incomes, Beijing, Hangzhou, Wujiang, and Shunde, not surprisingly, are all in the coastal region. Three of the four central cities, Changchun, Shijiazhuang, and Zibo, belong to the middle-income group, and one city, Dandong, is in the low-income group. One western city, Xi'an, is in the middle-income group, and the remaining three western cities, Chongqing, Shiyan, and Jining, are in the low-income group. In 2005, the income gap was roughly 2 times between any two neighboring income groups. This gap was almost replicated between two neighboring regions, with the coastal and central regions having a slightly larger gap and the central and western regions having a slightly smaller gap. It is worth keeping this pattern in mind when one thinks about the CSR performance of the sample firms in different cities.

2.3   Profiles of the Sample Firms

A total of 1,268 firms were surveyed in the main survey. This section provides a description of their basic profiles including their geographic distribution, size, industrial distribution, ownership types, and financial performance.

Geographic Distribution

The design of the survey was to survey 100 firms in each city. In the implementation, small variations existed. While all the cities surveyed at least 100 firms, some cities surveyed more. In particular, Zibo and Shiyan surveyed 140 firms and 115 firms, respectively. Table 2.4 summarizes the distribution of the sample firms by region and income group.

Table 2.4

GEOGRAPHIC DISTRIBUTION OF THE SAMPLE FIRMS

Region \ Income	High	Medium	Low	Total
Coastal	Beijing, 100 Hangzhou, 100 Wujiang, 100 Shunde, 115			415
Central		Changchun, 100 Shijiazhuang, 100 Zibo, 140	Dandong, 109	449
Western		Xi'an, 101	Chongqing, 100 Shiyan, 115 Jining, 100	404
Total	415	441	412	1268

Source: Main survey.

Size

The average size of the sample firms was 743 workers in 2005. But the variation was large. The smallest only had two people (it might be a firm that was not in operation), and the largest had 86,991 people. By the national standard issued by the then SETC in 2003 (SETC, 2003), firms with an employment of less than 2000 people, or a fixed capital stock of less than 400 million yuan, or a sales volume of less than 300 million yuan are classified as SMEs. Most of the sample firms were SMEs. In this study, we define firms with less than 500 employees as small firms, firms with 501 to 2000 employees as medium firms, and firms with more than 2000 employees as large firms. Figure 2.6 shows the distribution of these three types of firms. Seventy-eight percent of the sample firms were small firms. In fact, 38% of these small firms had less than 100 workers.

Figure 2.6

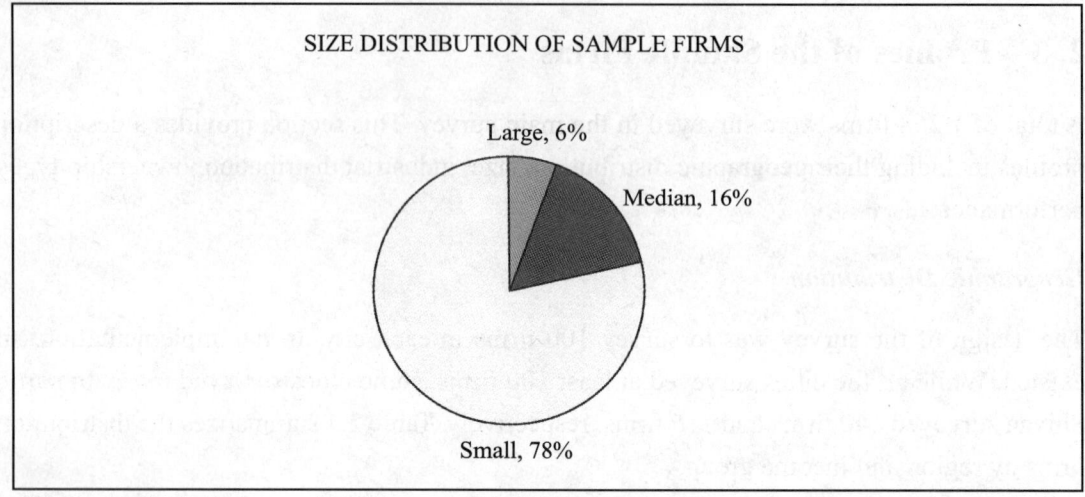

Source: Main survey.

The average amount of fixed capital at book value was 16.9 million yuan. More than 80% of the sample firms had a stock of fixed capital less than 100 million yuan (Figure 2.7). The average size of the net fixed capital was much smaller, being 9.6 million yuan. Even by SME standards, these figures are low.

Figure 2.7

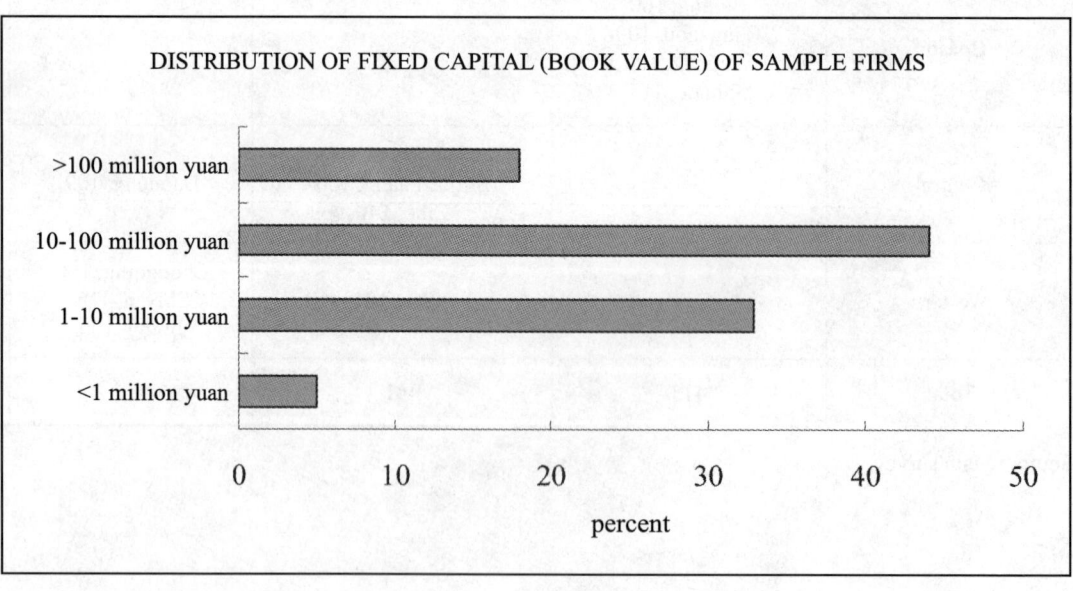

Source: Main survey.

The average sales volume of the sample firms in 2005 was fairly large, reaching 364 million yuan. However, this was so only because of the existence of some very large firms. The largest firm sold 58.9 billion yuan worth of products. Half of the firms sold less than 50 million yuan of products, and two thirds of them sold less than 100 million yuan (Figure 2.8).

Figure 2.8

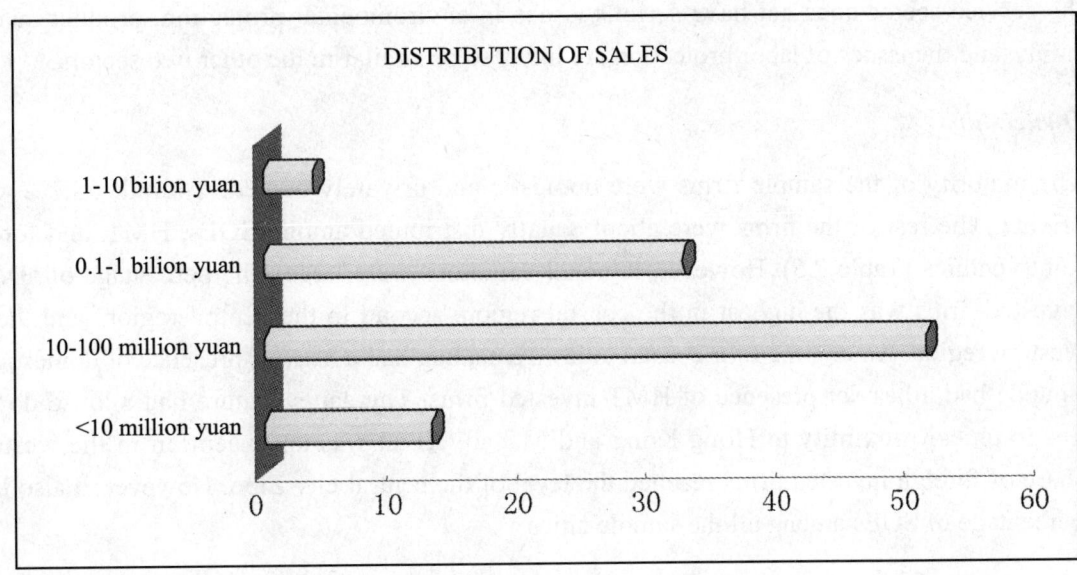

Source: Main survey.

Industrial Distribution

Figure 2.9 presents the industrial distribution of the sample firms in terms of the standard classifications of the National Bureau of Statistics. As the figure shows, the primary sector (agriculture, forestry, pasturing, fishing, mining, geological exploration, and water management) was over-sampled as 42.9% of the sample firms were in this sector. Firms in the secondary sector, i.e., the manufacturing sector, consisted of 47.7% of the sample. Accordingly, the tertiary sector was under-sampled consisting of less than 10% of the sample firms. This bias is related to the threshold of 5 million yuan of sales volume that the NBS database maintains. Many firms in the service sector cannot meet this threshold and are excluded from the NBS database. However, in terms of the focus of this study, this bias is not likely to affect our results because

Figure 2.9

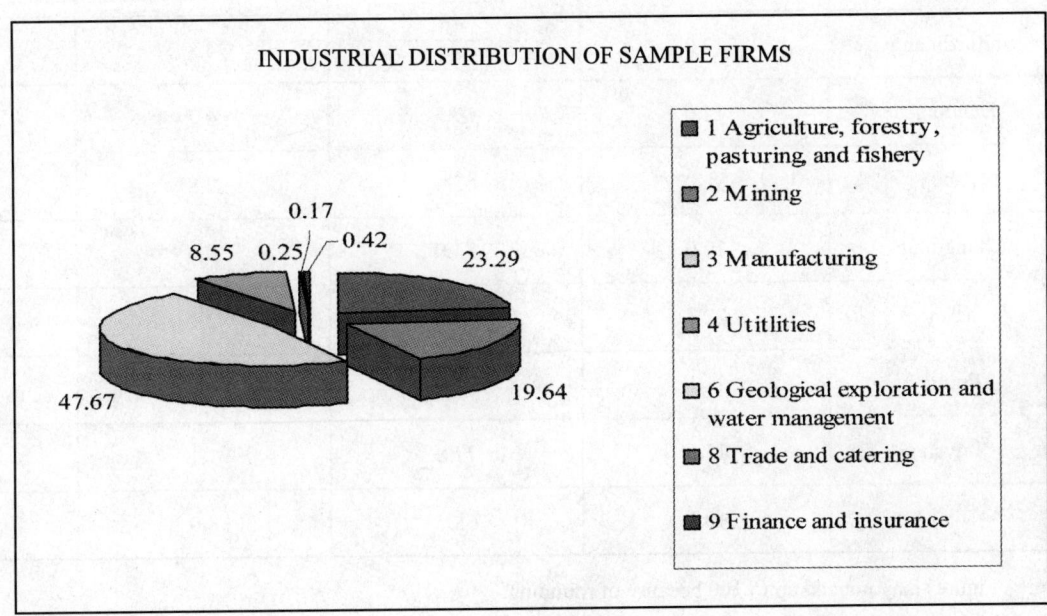

Source: Main survey.

the service sector does not have serious issues in environmental protection, product quality, and work safety, and the issues of labor protection are likely to be similar in the other two sectors.

Ownership

The majority of the sample firms were domestic and privately owned. Overall, 68.7% were domestic-private. The rest of the firms were about equally distributed among SOEs, HMT, and foreign owned or joint-ventures (Table 2.5). However, regional variations were large. The percentage of HMT and foreign invested firms was the highest in the coastal region, second in the central region, and the lowest in the western region. Among the four coastal cities, Hangzhou had a heavier presence of domestic private firms, Shunde had a heavier presence of HMT invested firms. This latter feature had a lot to do with Shunde's geographical proximity to Hong Kong and Macao. Xi'an was an exception in the western region; its share of foreign invested firms reached the level of the central city Zibo. However, it also had the highest percentage of SOEs among all the sample cities.

Table 2.5

DISTRIBUTION OF FIRM OWNERSHIP IN SAMPLE CITIES (%)

City	SOEs	Domestic private	HMT owned & joint-ventures	Foreign owned & joint-ventures
Beijing	17.2	43.4	17.2	22.2
Hangzhou	1.1	73.7	14.7	10.5
Wujiang	2.6	52.6	16.7	28.2
Shunde	0.9	57.8	33.9	7.3
Changchun	10.3	81.6	0.0	8.0
Shijiazhuang	12.0	77.2	4.3	6.5
Dandong	14.0	67.3	4.7	14.0
Zibo	8.8	65.4	8.8	16.9
Chongqing	10.0	84.0	0.0	6.0
Xi'an	22.7	58.8	2.1	16.5
Jining	11.1	88.9	0.0	0.0
Shiyan	15.6	77.8	1.1	5.6
Total	10.5	68.7	8.9	11.9

Note: Figures may not add up to 100 because of rounding.
Source: Main survey.

Exports

China's export value was 34% of total GDP in 2005 (NBS, 2006). The figure was comparable for our sample firms. The number of firms engaged in exporting was 37.2% of the total and the average share of exports in total sales was 16.1%.

There were large regional variations, however. Figure 2.10 ranks the sample cities by the share of exporting firms. It also shows the average percentage of exports in total sales volume. With a few exceptions, the downward trend from the coastal region to the inland regions was clear. Among the four coastal cities, Wujiang, Shunde, and Hangzhou were the three leading exporting cities having more than 60% of their firms engaged in exporting. Beijing's place was replaced by Dandong, a city at the border with North Korea. In Beijing, only 23.7% of its firms exported in 2005, and the average share of exports in sales was 9.1%. Clearly, the size and structure of its economy played a role here. Beijing is a service-based city. In 2005, the service sector contributed to 67.7% of its gross regional product (NBS, 2006). Dandong had an impressive performance. Although it had a smaller share of exporting firms than Hangzhou it had a higher average share of exports in total sales than Hangzhou achieved, which means that its exporting firms were more dependent on export than their counterparts in Hangzhou. In the western region, Xi'an was an exception. It surpassed Changchun in the central region and also ranked #7 in terms of the share of exporting firms. However, the exporting volume of its firms was much smaller than that of the exporting firms in Beijing because while 38% of its firms were exporting, much more than in Beijing, their average share of exports in sales was only 8.4%, smaller than the figure in Beijing.

Figure 2.10

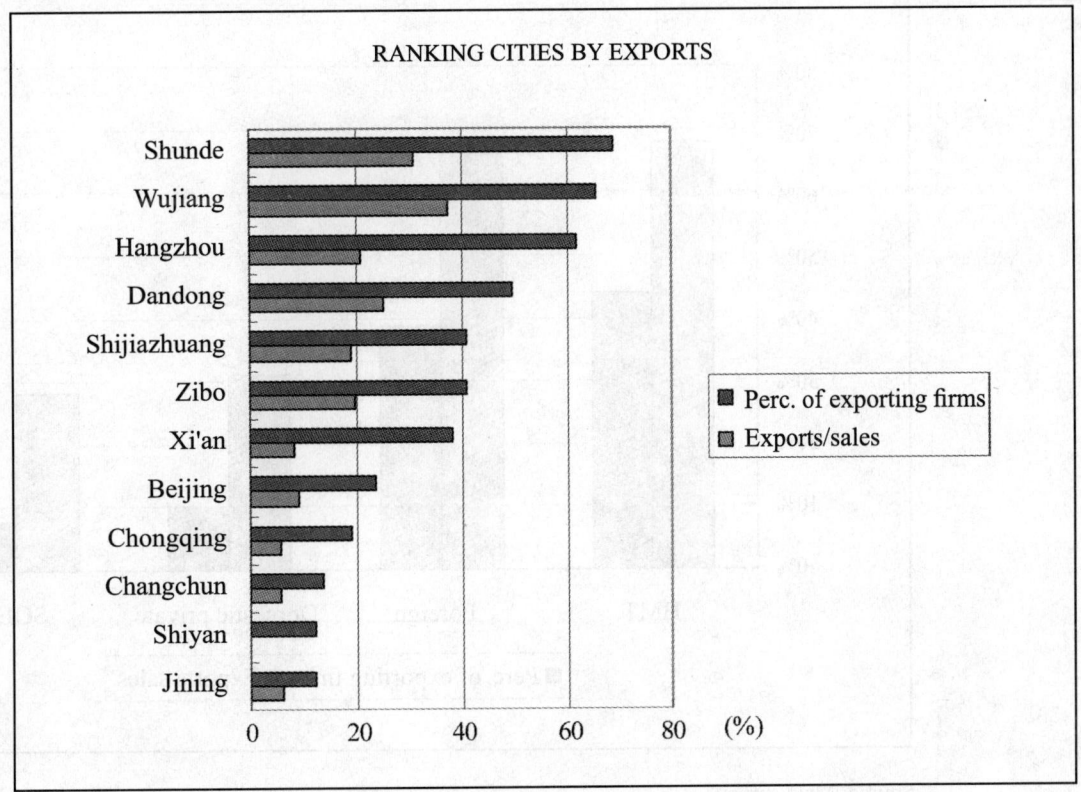

Source: Main survey.

Another interesting observation is that the exporting firms in Wujiang exported more intensively than their counterparts in Shunde. The average share of exports in total sales among the exporting firms in Wujiang was 56.8%, whereas the corresponding figure was 44.9% in Shunde. The Pearl River Delta is China's pioneer of export-oriented development strategy, but significant structural changes have begun there since the late 1990s. One of these changes is the decline of the significance of labor-intensive industries and the increase of the significance of high-tech industries in its exports. The second observation is that firms are becoming more conscious of the opportunities in the domestic market (Yao and Zhang, 2007). The third is that the Guangdong government has begun to implement an industrial policy that discourages labor-intensive and polluting industries to stay in the Pearl River Delta. Together with increasing land and labor costs, this policy is leading to a diversion of FDI from the Pearl River Delta to the Yangtze River Delta. Wujiang's emergence as a new exporting base has benefited from this shift. To a large extent, the Yangtze River Delta is replicating the experience of the Pearl River Delta.

FDI firms contribute to 60% of China's total exports (Yao and Zhang, 2007). So it is not surprising to find that among the sample firms FDI firms were much more export-oriented than domestic firms (Figure 2.11). More than two thirds of HMT and foreign-invested firms were exporting and their shares of exports in total sales were around 40%. In contrast, only 31% of domestic private firms and 28% of SOEs were exporting, and their shares of exports in total sales were 10% and 7%, respectively.

Figure 2.11

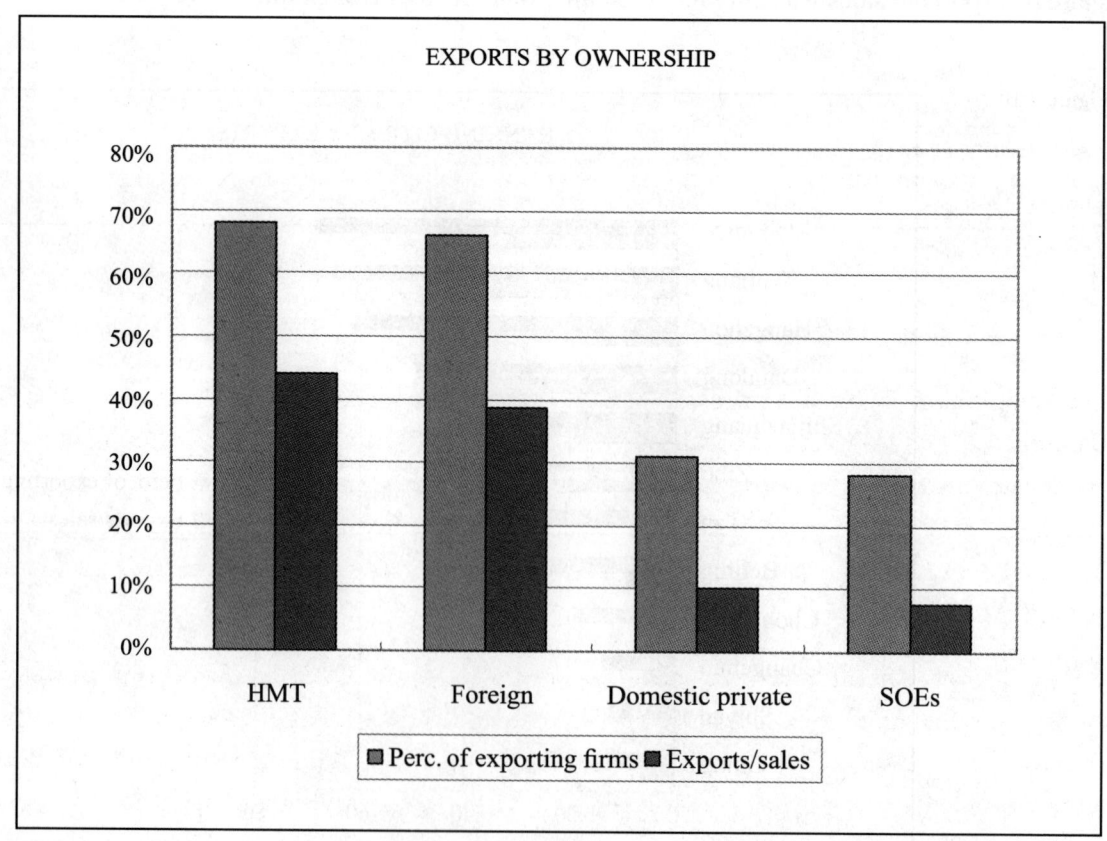

Source: Main survey.

Financial Performance

Recently, Mr. Weijian Shan questioned the World Bank's high estimates of the profitability of Chinese firms as "delusions" (Shan, 2006a) and believed that the Chinese economy was following a "low-profit growth model" (Shan, 2006b). His criticism has ignited a hot debate on China's rate of return on capital. However, two recent studies have found that the profitability of Chinese firms has been significantly improved in the last decade. Bai, Xie, and Qian (2007) using aggregate data found that the return on capital measured by pre-tax profit divided by the stock of fixed capital declined in the first half of the 1990s, but increased subsequently, at least to 2004. The range of variation was between 15% and 25%. CCER (2007) using data for firms with an annual sales volume of 5 million yuan or more produced similar results although the pre-tax profit rate was smaller.

Figure 2.12

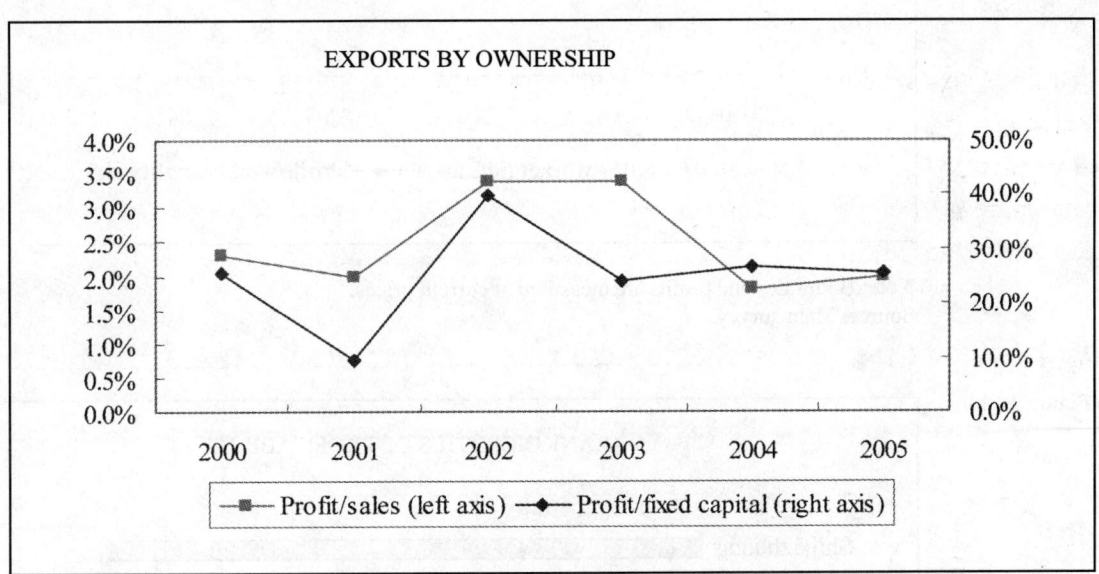

Note: Fixed capital is measured in terms of its book value because some firms had very small stocks of net fixed
     capital.
Source: Main survey.

Our sample firms had profit rates comparable to those provided by Bai et al. (2007). Figure 2.12 presents the trends of two measures of profitability of the sample firms in the period of 2000-2005. One is pre-tax profit/sales, and the other is pre-tax profit/fixed capital. Except in the year 2001,[3] the return on fixed capital was high. The average of the six years was 25.2%. The other measure, i.e., pre-tax profit/sales was low. The average of the six years was 2.5%. However, this figure was consistent with the findings of others (CCER, 2007).

Figure 2.13 provides the trends of two measures of labor productivity in the same period. One is sales/ worker, and the other is pre-tax profit/worker, both at current prices. Since the inflation rate was negligible in those years, using current prices will not distort the trend. While pre-tax profit/worker did not show a clear trend and was quite stable around 2,000 yuan, sales/worker increased steadily from 24,600 yuan in 2000 to 46,200 yuan in 2005. The average growth rate was 13.4%. This figure is comparable with the

---

[3] The low rate was caused by one firm's large loss in that year.

estimate provided by Lu and Liu (2007) who show that the average growth rate of labor productivity of the Chinese manufacturing sector was 12.6% between 1990 and 2005.

Figure 2.13

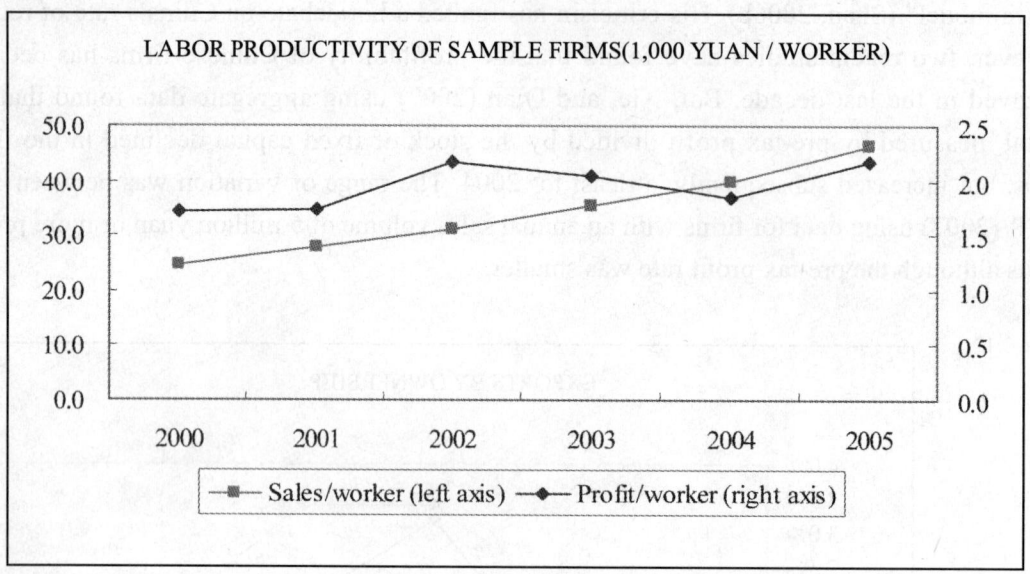

Note: Both sales and profits are measured at current prices.
Source: Main survey.

Figure 2.14

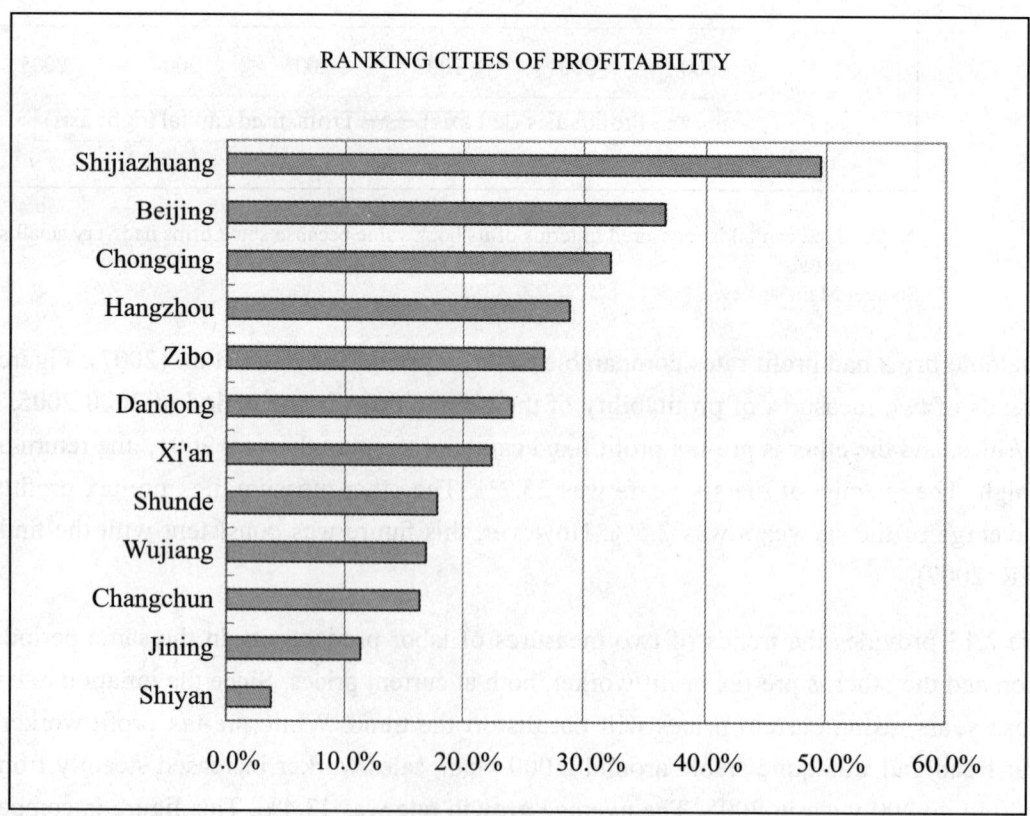

Note: Profitability is the average pre-tax return on capital in the period of 2000-2005.
Source: Main survey.

Regional variations were large, however. Figure 2.14 ranks the sample cities by the average return on capital in the period 2000-2005. There was no clear regional pattern. Shijiazhuang was ranked No.1 in terms of profitability, and Jining and Shiyan were ranked the last. The gap between Shijiazhuang and Shiyan was 45.6 percentage points. Among the coastal cities, Beijing and Hangzhou had high rates of return, but Wujiang and Shunde had relatively low rates. This might have something to do with the importance of exports in those four cities. Exports in Wujiang and Shunde are mostly processing imported components so their profit rates are low. Beijing and Hangzhou do not rely on exports as much as the other two cities do, so their profit rates are higher.

Figure 2.15

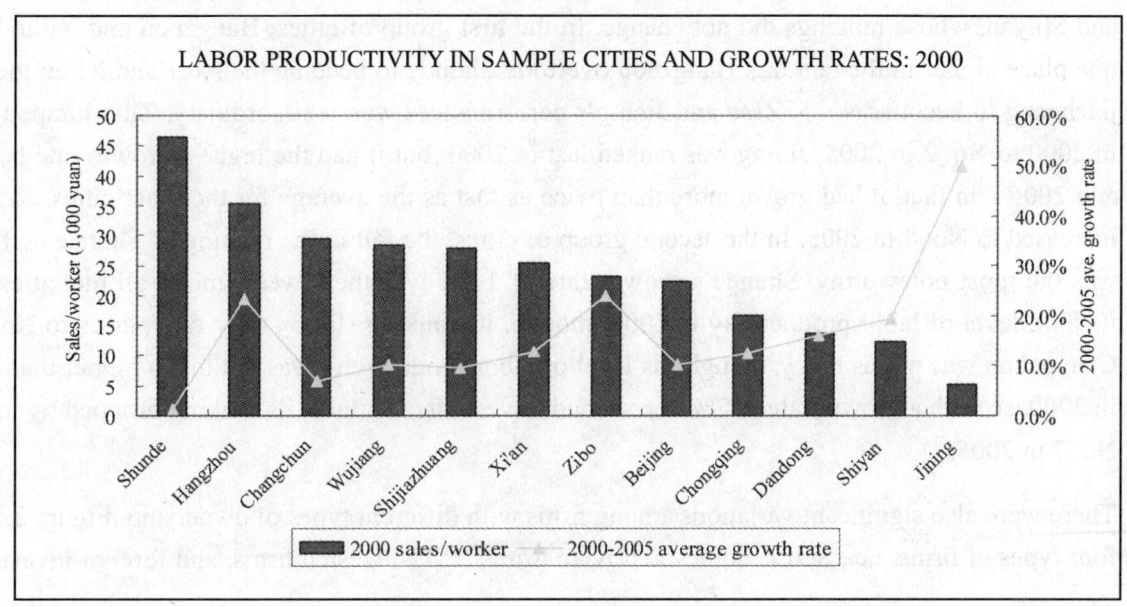

Source: Main survey.

Figure 2.16

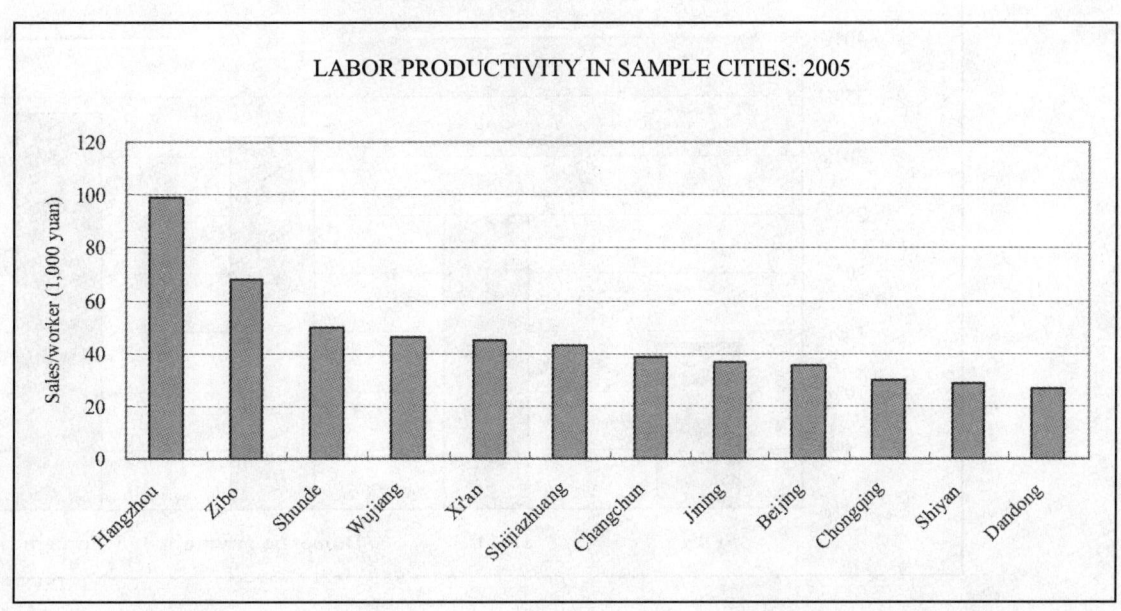

Source: Main survey.

Figures 2.15 and 2.16 further compare the sample cities in terms of their growth rates of labor productivity in the period of 2000-2005. Figure 2.15 presents two series of data. One is labor productivity in 2000, and the other is the growth rate between 2000 and 2005. The sample cities are ranked by labor productivity in 2000. Figure 2.16 then ranks the sample cities by their labor productivity in 2005. The two figures show that the 12 sample cities can be grouped into three groups in terms of their growth between 2000 and 2005. The first group comprised Hangzhou, Zibo, Xi'an, and Jining that had above average growth rates and whose rankings increased during the period of 2000-2005. The second group is comprised of those cities whose growth rates were lower than average and whose rankings fell in the same period. They are Shunde, Changchun, Shijiazhuang, Chongqing, Beijing, and Dandong. The third group has only two cities, Wujiang and Shiyan, whose rankings did not change. In the first group of cities, Hangzhou and Xi'an both moved one place higher in the ranking. Hangzhou overtook Shunde to become the No.1 and Xi'an took over Shijiazhuang to become No. 5. Zibo and Jining's performances were extraordinary. Zibo jumped from No. 7 in 2000 to No. 2 in 2005. Jining was ranked last in 2000, but it had the highest growth rate between 2000 and 2005   in fact, it had grown more than twice as fast as the average for the other cities, so its ranking increased to No. 8 in 2005. In the second group of cities, the fall in the ranking of Shunde and Changchun was the most noteworthy. Shunde's growth rate of 1.4% was the lowest among all the cities. Thanks to its high level of labor productivity in 2000, though, its ranking slid by only two places to No. 3 in 2005. Changchun was not as lucky, though. Its level of labor productivity was not much higher than the average in 2000, so with a growth rate of 7%, the second lowest after Shunde, its ranking dropped by four places to No. 7 in 2005.

There were also significant variations among firms with different types of ownership. Figure 2.17 ranks the four types of firms, i.e., SOEs, domestic private firms, HMT-invested firms, and foreign-invested firms, by

Figure 2.17

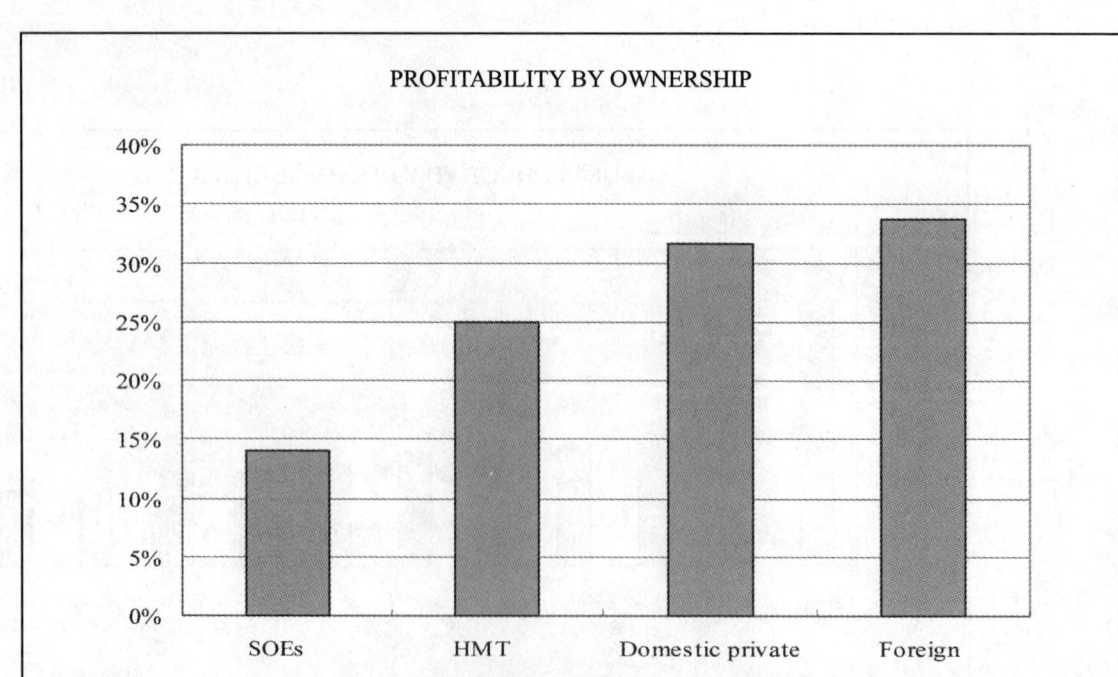

Note: Profitability is the average pre-tax return on capital in the period 2000-2005.
Source: Main survey.

their average return on capital in the period of 2000-2005. Foreign-invested and domestic private firms had very high rates of return — more than 30% indeed, but SOEs and HMT-invested firms had low returns. The high rates of return of foreign-invested and domestic private firms are consistent with the findings of CCER (2007). The low rate of return for SOEs was largely a result of their inappropriate incentive structures. A recent study by Garnaut, Song, Tenev, and Yao (2005) found that privatization significantly improved SOEs performance. However, it is a bit puzzling that HMT-invested firms had a lower return rate than domestic private firms. One explanation is that HMT-invested firms are heavily export-oriented and the competition that they face is fiercer than that found in the domestic market. Indeed, the average rate of return for exporting firms was 20% in 2005, but the rate of return for non-exporting firms was 29% in the same year.

Figure 2.18

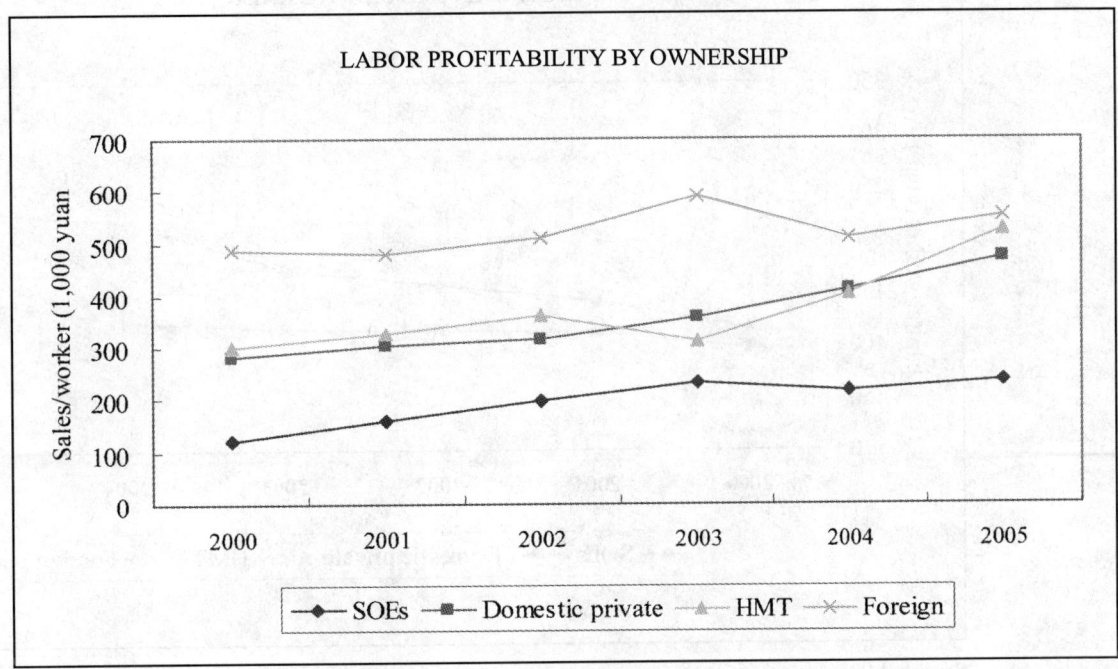

Source: Main survey.

This last explanation is supported by the comparison of labor productivity presented in Figure 2.18. This figure shows that HMT-invested firms performed as well as domestic private firms in the period of 2000-2005 while SOEs performed the worst and foreign-invested firms performed the best in the same period. There was growth for all four types of firms, but domestic private and HMT-invested firms grew the fastest. While inappropriate incentives were a reason, the low performance of SOEs was also related to their over-employment, a legacy that they inherited from the past. However, they had achieved a higher growth rate than foreign-invested firms and had narrowed the gap from 4 times in 2000 to 2.3 times in 2005.

The amount of capital per worker is an important factor determining labor productivity. It is possible therefore that the low labor productivity of SOEs was caused by their lower capital intensity. This possibility certainly conflicts with some of the recent claims that SOEs' capital intensity is high as a result of the legacy of the capital-intensive development strategy implemented in the planning period (Lin, Cai, and Li, 1996). However, Figure 2.19 provides a mixed picture. In the whole period 2000-2005, SOEs had higher capital/worker ratios than domestic private firms and these ratios had surpassed those of the HMT-invested firms in 2003 to become the second most capital intensive category of firms just behind foreign-invested firms. The gap between SOEs and foreign-invested firms was substantially narrowed in 2004 and 2005. This shows that low capital intensity cannot explain the low labor productivity of SOEs. On the other hand, their low rates of return to capital cannot be explained by their high capital intensities either. Over-employment and low quality management are more likely to be the explanation for the low levels of performance of SOEs.

Figure 2.19

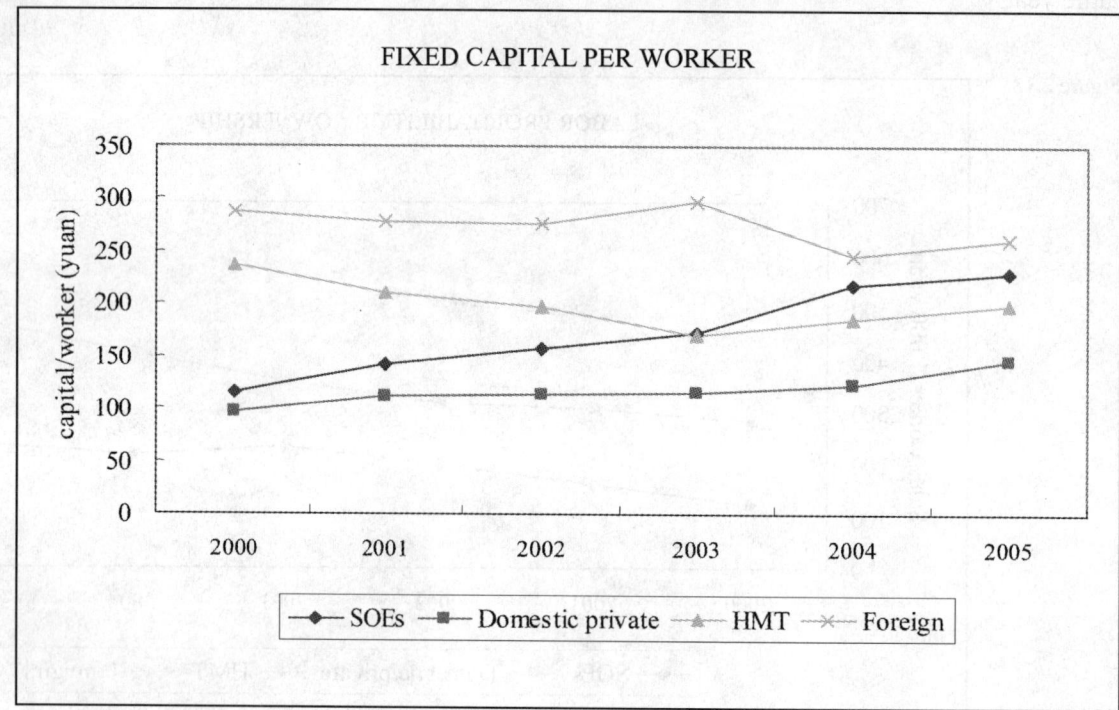

Source: Main survey.

2. 4   Summary

The 12 sample cities offer a good representation of the economic geography of China today. There are four cities in each of the three geographic regions, coastal, central, and western. If the 12 cities are further divided into three equal income groups, these groups coincide with the geographic regions except Xi'an that belongs to the western region geographically, but belongs to the middle group in terms of income. The four coastal cities are leading the other cities in terms of both economic growth and exports, but there are also signs of catch-up in some central and western cities. The performance of Zibo and Xi'an is particularly impressive.

The sample firms are also a relatively good representation of the national average. In particular, their records of exports and financial performance are comparable with the national statistics. Their distributions in size, industry, ownership, and status of exports offer rich opportunities for in-depth analyses. The mixed nature of these distributions helps one to apprehend the complex relationship between firm characteristics and CSR performance. One example is the relationship between profitability and CSR performance. While foreign-invested firms have the highest return on capital and may also maintain the highest standards of CSR, the relative performance of SOEs and domestic private firms show that higher profitability does not necessarily lead to higher standards of CSR. On the one hand, SOEs have low profitability, but it is widely believed that they have maintained relatively good records of labor protection. On the other hand, domestic private firms have high return on capital, but their CSR performance may not be as good as other types of firms. Another example is the relationship between exports and CSR performance. While the comparison of foreign-invested firms and domestic private firms supports the conclusion that more exports lead to better CSR records, the comparison of HMT-invested firms and SOEs leads to the opposite conclusion. The ensuing chapters will examine these complexities more closely.

Chapter 3
CSR Awareness and Social Participation in Sample Firms

Corporate Social Responsibility (CSR) is now an indispensable element for doing business in and outside of China. The World Business Council for Sustainable Development defines CSR as "The continuing commitment by business to behave ethically and contribute to economic development while improving the quality of life of the workforce and their families as well as of the local community and society at large. In essence, CSR reflects the belief that it is no longer enough for firms to make profits for share holders while ignoring their impacts on society and on the environment.

UNIDO (2002) documents two trends related to the development of CSR. One is that attitudes of enterprises toward CSR have changed over the last twenty years. As globalization, deregulation and *gaizhi* have deepened the interactions between the private sector and the society, increasing numbers of enterprises recognize that addressing wider social and environmental problems are not their sole obligations, but can be crucial for their long-term success[1]. In accordance with this change, more companies are reporting their social and environmental impacts. For example, 50 percent of the world s one hundred largest firms ('the G100') produced Global Environmental Reports in year 2000, and 54 percent of the G100 also report on their corporate social responsibility or corporate citizenship programs. CSR has also received increasing attention from the public. For example, the United Kingdom has established a ministry for Cooperate Social Responsibility, and the year of 2005 is designated as the year of Cooperate Social Responsibility in the Europe Union.

The second trend is although CSR has hitherto primarily been the concern of multinational companies (MNCs), CSR imposes new demands on small and medium enterprises (SMEs) in developing countries directly and indirectly. CSR will directly affect the behavior of those SMEs who wish to do business with MNCs, as they need to meet the social and environmental standards required by their business partners. The indirect impact can come from CSR's influence on local competition, the shift of consumer's demand, etc. While emphasizing that firm compliance with social and environmental standards could be beneficial to the society, the net impact of CSR on firm performance is unclear. The UNIDO report also warns against the danger that CSR can act as a protection mechanism for retaining jobs, trade and investment in developed countries so that CSR standards may undermine SMEs in developing countries.

---

[1] *Gaizhi* is a term encapsulating the transfers from the state to private firms and collectives in the non-public sector and the associated changes.

In view of these issues, CSR and its implementation has received increasing attention from the Chinese government, enterprises and service providers, non-governmental organizations (NGOs), the media, academic institutions, and online resource providers. Peng, Long and Pamlin (2005) provide an overview of CSR activities in China. A CSR database has been established as a platform for the dissemination of information on organizations with CSR activities in China[2]. However, there is no comprehensive report about the overall CSR awareness of Chinese firms. An overall evaluation of the impacts of CSR on firm performance is also absent so one cannot address the issue of whether CSR standards undermine or promote the development of SMEs in China.

This chapter describes the perceptions of CSR in the sampled firms and their participations in CSR-related social activities. In Section 1 we describe firm awareness of CSR and their understandings of the meaning of CSR. Section 2 provides information about their implementation of CSR. Section 3 considers firms' participations in CSR-related activities in a broader sense. We will focus on several key factors that are most relevant to CSR initiatives by firms.

3.1   CSR Awareness

Knowledge of CSR

Firms' CSR awareness is studied from several perspectives. We first examine firms' general knowledge about CSR through asking whether they know CSR. For those who reported they know CSR, firms understanding of CSR activities is then investigated. To better understand the characteristics of firms who are more aware of CSR, we then study CSR awareness from the perspectives of firms' own characteristics, degree of market competition and regional effects.

Firms' general awareness of CSR can be reflected from their choices among the degree of their knowledge about CSR. Three choices are provided: know CSR, know a little about CSR, and don't know about CSR. Figure 3.1 shows the distribution of the answers from the 1,227 firms, with 44% of the firms reporting that they know what CSR is, 40% claiming they have some knowledge about CSR, and 13% of the firms admitting they do not know CSR[3].

To further evaluate firms' awareness of CSR, we asked the firms to list five CSR-related activities. We group the answers to this open question into 11 categories: (1) providing reasonable salaries for employees; (2) providing employees reasonable retirement and welfare benefits; (3) providing employees with good working conditions, and no child labor; (4) improving relationships with employees through unions, negotiation, and providing care for employees' families; (5) safe production; (6) environmental protection; (7) product quality; (8) activities that serve the interests of the public, such as charitable contributions; (9) paying taxes; (10) providing employment opportunities to the local community and supporting the development of the local economy. The remaining miscellaneous answers are grouped under the category others .

---

[2] http://www.chinacsrmap.org

[3] There are 22 firms which did not respond to the first CSR awareness question, but could list CSR related activities in the second question; there are also 98 firms that marked "No" in the first question but answered question 2. This indicates that firms have subjective views toward whether they know CSR. The statistics below are based on their answers to thesecond the first question.

Figure 3.1

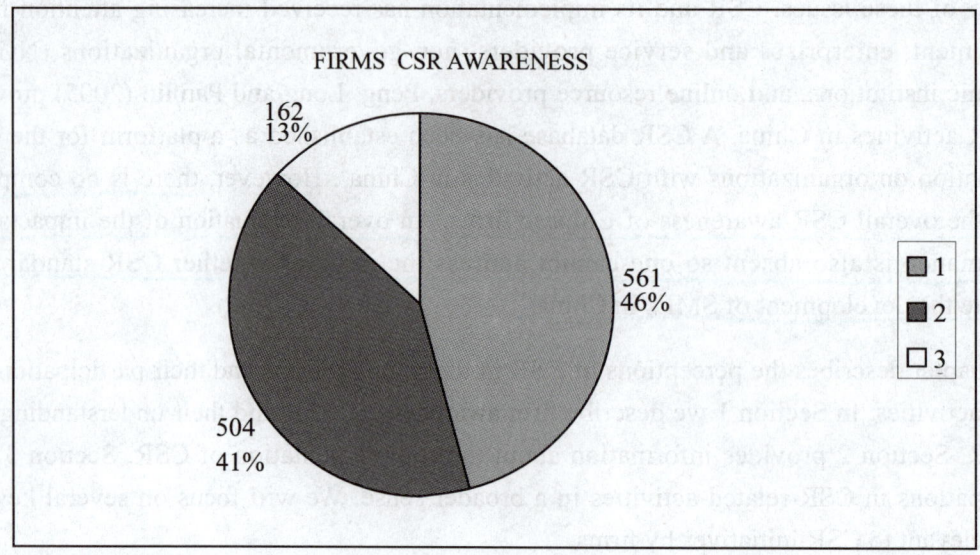

Source: Main Survey

Figure 3.2 shows the distribution of the number of CSR related activities reported by firms for the last three years prior to the survey. This figure indicates that 13.49% of firms filled in 5 activities, 10% complete 4 out of the 5 activities, and another 10.57% complete 3 out of the 5 aspects. No answers were provided by 51.18% of the firms. As only 13% firms admit they don't know what CSR is in Figure 3.1, this implies quite a proportion of firms claiming they at least know a little about CSR, but provide no answer to the question that could prove their real understandings.

Figure 3.2

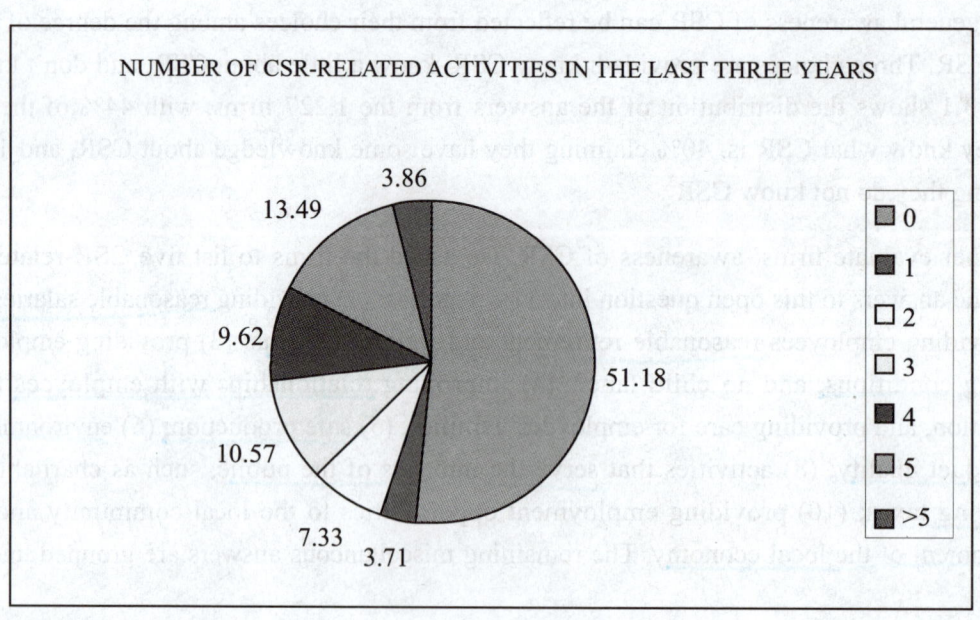

Source: Main Survey

As the number of the listed CSR-related activities just provides a rough idea of CSR awareness, we further inspect the frequencies of the listed CSR activities. Figure 3.3 gives the types of CSR activities reported by firms. This Figure shows that environmental protection is the most frequently mentioned CSR activity, listed by about one-third of the firms. The least mentioned CSR activity is improving employer-employee relationships through union or other channels, listed by only 4% of the firms. Based on frequency, the order of other activities are: activities that serve the interests of the public, paying taxes, providing insurance and welfare, paying reasonable salaries to employees, providing safe production and good working conditions, supporting employment and local economic development, and product quality. This Figure reveals that environmental protection has received most of the attention with regard to CSR awareness. On the other hand, paying taxes is a necessary condition for firms' legal existence, but it is ranked as the third most frequently-mentioned CSR activities. This fact reflects that firms' understanding of CSR could be quite superficial.

Figure 3.3

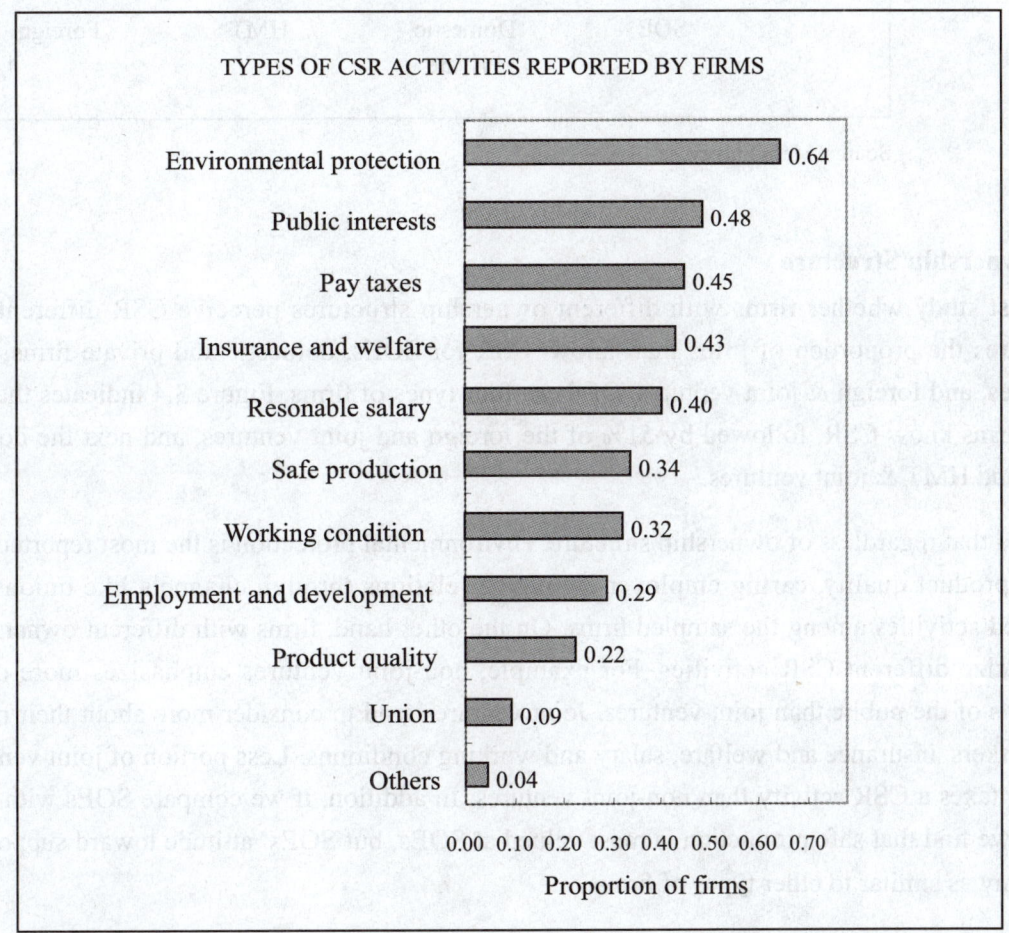

Source: Main Survey

Factors Affecting Firms Knowledge of CSR

After providing a broad picture of firms' awareness of CSR, we further investigate how CSR awareness is related to firm characteristics. We consider the impact of the following factors on CSR: (a) ownership structure, (b) whether a firm is an exporting firm, (c) firm size, (d) education of the management team, (e) degree of market competition and (f) region. The above listed factors (a) to (d) focus on linking firm-specific characteristics to CSR awareness, while factors (e) and (f) look at firms' external environment. Of all environmental factors, we investigate market competition and regional competition in particular.

Figure 3.4

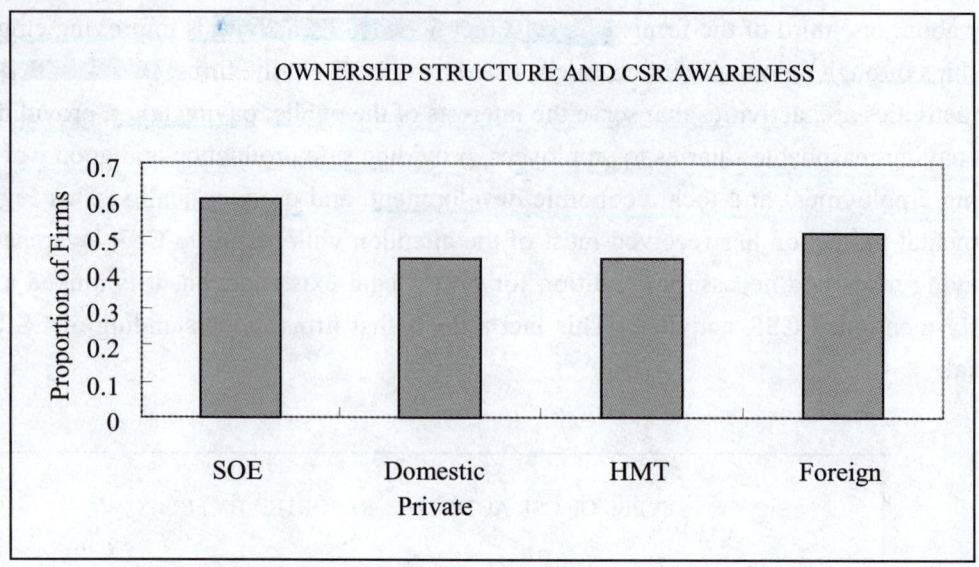

Source: Main Survey

(a) Ownership Structure

We first study whether firms with different ownership structures perceive CSR differently. Figure 3.4 compares the proportion of firms that 'know' CSR for SOEs, domestic and private firms, HMT & joint ventures, and foreign & joint ventures. Of these four types of firms, Figure 3.4 indicates that over 60% of SOE firms know CSR, followed by 51% of the foreign and joint ventures, and next the domestic private firms and HMT & joint ventures.

We find that regardless of ownership structure, environmental protection is the most reported CSR activity, while product quality, caring employer-employee relations through channels like unions are the least reported activities among the sampled firms. On the other hand, firms with different ownership structures emphasize different CSR activities. For example, non-joint ventures emphasizes more on serving the interests of the public than joint ventures. Joint ventures tend to consider more about their responsibilities for workers insurance and welfare, salary and working conditions. Less portion of joint ventures consider paying taxes a CSR activity than non-joint ventures. In addition, if we compare SOEs with other types of firms, we find that safe production is most valued at SOEs, but SOEs' attitude toward supporting the local economy, is similar to other types of firms.

(b) Exporting and CSR awareness

The next factor we consider is whether a firm is an exporting firm. An exporting firm might be more aware of its social responsibilities, as it needs to meet international standards which often require evidence of firms' CSR. The firms in this sample confirm this expectation. There are 51% of the exporting firms that know CSR, compared with 42% firms that know CSR in non-exporting firms. While both types of firms view environmental protection and serving the interests of the public as the most important CSR activities, exporting firms pay more attention to responsibilities to its workers through providing them with insurance and welfare, reasonable salaries and good working conditions.

(c) Size

Larger firms may have more incentives to engage in CSR activities for the following reasons. First, they are more visible to the public and care more about their images. Actively participating in CSR activities can effectively improve a large firm's image before the public hence bring long-term benefits towards its growth sustainability. The 5 12 earthquake in 2008 provides us a chance to observe such an effect. Enterprises which immediatly donated generous funds were walmly welcomed by the public, while those large enterprises who were deemed less active faced tremendous pressure from the public. Such contrast implies that the expectation from the public tend to force enterprises pay more and more attention to the CSR related activities. Secondly, large firms may be required to provide reports on CSR related activities to the government or to their customers, which forces them to be more aware of CSR. In this study we measure the size of a firm by the number of employees. Firms are defined as "small" if they have less than 500 employees, as medium if the employee number is between 500 and 2000, and as large if firms have more than 2000 employees. Figure 3.5 indicates that compared with small firms, medium and large firms are more aware of CSR. As large firms take only 12% of the sample based on this definition, we redefine large firms as those with more than 1000 employees. Now the pattern is clearer: the larger the firm, the more CSR aware it is (Figure 3.6). If we look at the proportions of reported CSR activities from firms of different sizes, we can clearly observe that large firms are more aware of CSR than firms of smaller sizes.

Figure 3.5

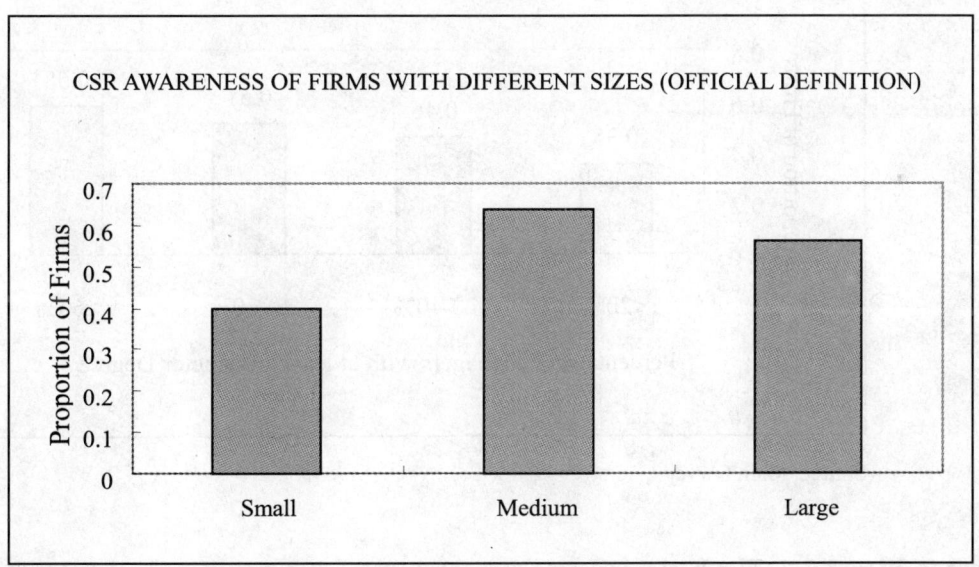

Source: Main Survey

(d) Education of the management team

The education level of the management team could be correlated with CSR awareness, as better-educated managers tend to have more chances to know CSR. We use the proportion of managers with at least Bachelor's degree in a firm to approximate the education level of the management team. If none of the managers holds at least Bachelor's degree, this proportion is 0; if all managers hold Bachelor's degree then this proportion is 1. We then group firms into four categories based on this proportion: 0-20% group, 20-40% group, 40-60% group, and >60% group. We depict the correlation of education level and CSR

Figure 3.6

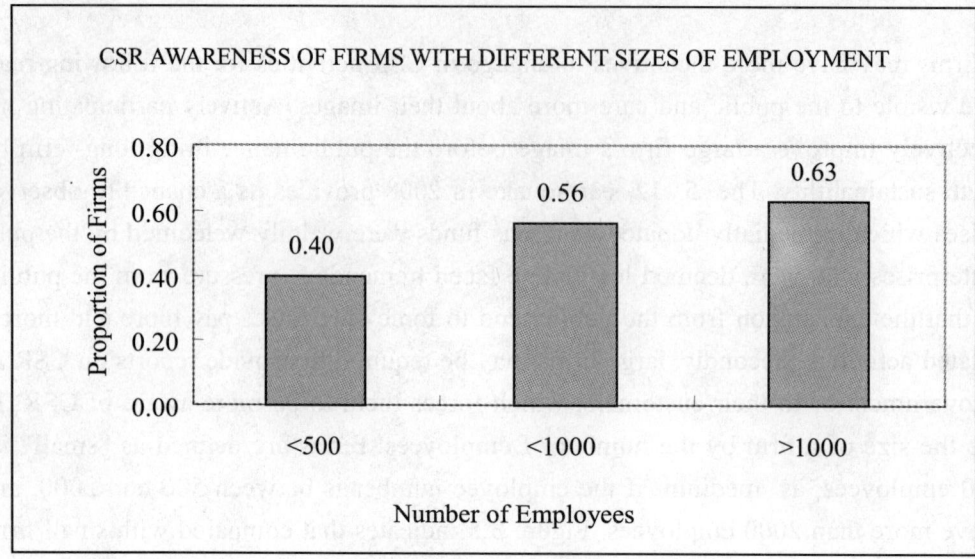

CSR AWARENESS OF FIRMS WITH DIFFERENT SIZES OF EMPLOYMENT

Source: Main Survey

Figure 3.7

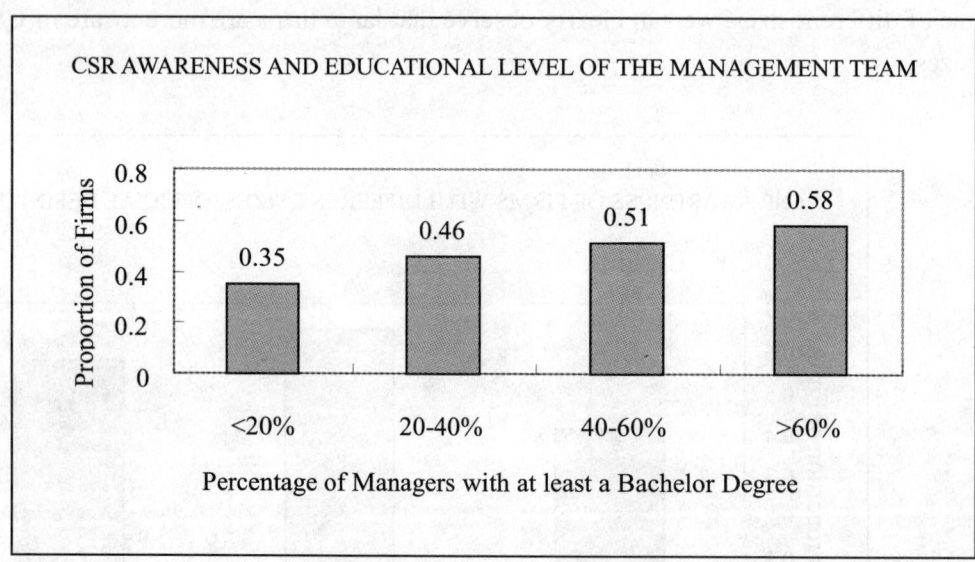

CSR AWARENESS AND EDUCATIONAL LEVEL OF THE MANAGEMENT TEAM

Source: Main Survey

awareness in Figure 3.7. The horizontal axis represents the education level and the vertical axis reports the proportion of firms that know CSR. In the group that less than 20% of the managers hold at least Bachelor's degree, only 35% of them know CSR. In contrast, 58% of firms know CSR when more than 60% of the managers hold at least Bachelor's degree. This pattern provides evidence that better-educated management is beneficial for firms' CSR awareness.

(e) Market competition

If actively participating in CSR activities can help firms to establish and maintain a good image in front of the public, firms may choose to engage in CSR activities to increase their competitiveness. We therefore examine how CSR awareness varies when firms face different degrees of market competition.

Figure 3.8 provides the respondent s subjective ranking of the degree of market competition they face. There are 905 firms which believe they face fierce competition, 267 think they face moderate market competition and only 18 firms believe they face very low competition. Of those firms facing fierce market competition, 46% report they know CSR, 41% of the firms facing moderate competition know CSR, and 9 out of the 18 firms facing very low competition report that they know CSR. The reported CSR activities also show that firms facing fierce competition report larger proportions of all CSR activities than firms facing moderate competition. In particular, firms facing fierce competition more frequently mention providing reasonable insurance and welfare, providing reasonable salary and safe production for their employees as their social responsibilities.

Figure 3.8

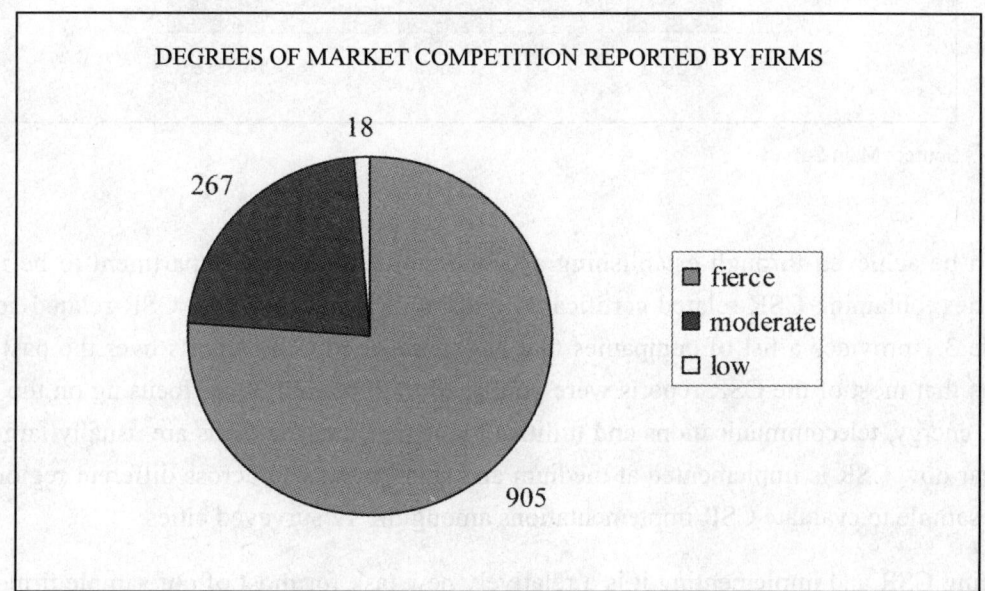

(f) Region

As regional differences in economic development are considerable, one may wonder whether there exist regional differences for CSR awareness. Using the standard in Chapter 2, we divide the 12 cities into coastal, central and western regions. Figure 3.9 indicates that the central region has the largest proportion of firms knowing CSR, following by the coastal region with 47% of the firms knowing CSR. Just above one third of firms in the western region knows CSR, which makes the western region the least CSR-aware region.

To sum up, even though CSR is a relatively new concept to enterprises in China, it has spread quickly to firms with different backgrounds. In the sampled firms, only 13% of the firms admit they do not know what CSR is. We also observe that a firm with one or more of the following characteristics tends to be more aware of CSR: it is a SOE, or an exporting firm, or a large firm, or a firm that operates in a competitive market, or a firm with a better educated management team.

3. 2   CSR Implementations

If a firm considers CSR as part of its long-term development strategy, then the implementation of such

Figure 3.9

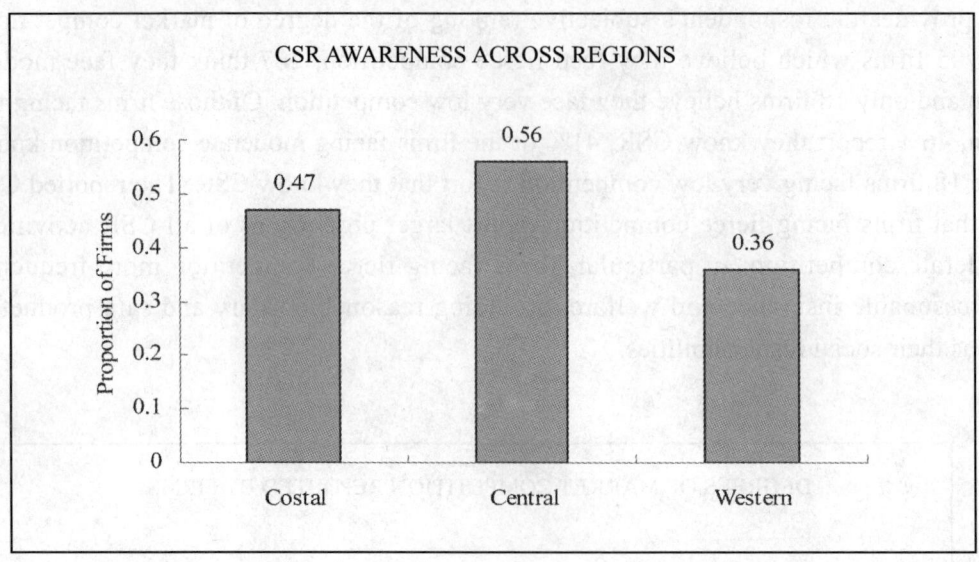

Source: Main Survey

strategy can be achieved through establishing a CSR plan, setting up a department to be in charge of CSR activities, obtaining CSR-related certificates, and publishing reports on CSR-related activities and so on. Table 3.1 provides a list of companies that have published CSR reports over the past years. This Table shows that most of the CSR reports were published in 2005 and 2006, focusing on the automobile, electronics, energy, telecommunications and utilities industries, and the firms are usually large. However, it is not clear how CSR is implemented at medium and small firms and across different regions of China. We use the sample to evaluate CSR implementations among the 12 surveyed cities.

Understanding CSR and implementing it is a relatively new task for most of our sample firms. Only 13% of firms currently have CSR plans, another 39% consider themselves in the process of making such a plan, and the remaining 48% of the firms admit they do not have any CSR plans (Figure 3.10). Even fewer firms have CSR certifications. 104 out of the 1227 respondent firms report that they have CSR certifications, but when being asked about what kind of certificate(s) they have obtained, only 75 firms provide valid answers, taking about 6% of the sample.

On the other hand, among those reporting CSR plans, the number of firms implementing CSR has grown rapidly in recent years. There are 154 out of the 158 firms that report the years they set up their CSR plans. In this group, only 38 firms established CSR plans before 2000. In the year 2000, however, 15 firms established their CSR plans. While year 2001 has fewer firms (8 of them) establishing CSR plans, around 20 additional firms set up their CSR plans in each of the subsequent years. The year 2006 saw 21 firms establishing plans, but as the survey was carried out in the middle of 2006, we would expect more firms to make plans for CSR by the end of that year.

3. 3 Participation in Socially Related CSR Activities

If a firm considers its social responsibilities an important part of its development strategy, then we should be able to observe that firm actively participating in CSR-related activities, through its interactions with

Table 3.1

COMPANIES AND CSR REPORTS*

Company	Sector	Reports
Ford China	Automobile	CSR Report 2003-2005
Haier	Electronics	Environmental Report 2005
TOSHIBA China	Electronics	CSR Report 2005 2006
SONY China	Electronics	CSR Report 2006
Shell(China)	Energy	Sustainability Report 2005
PetroChina	Energy	Environment and Health Security Report, 2000 - 2005
CNOOCSHELL	Energy	Quarterly Monitoring Report the Environment & Social Management Plan
CNOOC	Energy	Annual Philanthropy Report 2005
PingAn Insurance	Finance	Corporate Citizen Report 2004-2006
SPDB	Finance	CSR Report 2006
COSCO	Logistics	Sustainable Development Report 2005
BaoSteel	Metals	Environmental Report 2003 2004
CHALCO	Metals	Sustainability Report 2005
Alcoa	Metals	Sustainability Report 2005
Pfizer	Pharmacy	Special Issue of Pfizer CSR Initiatives 2006
Zhejiang Mobile	TeleCom	Corporate Citizenship System Report 2005
JX Mobile	TeleCom	CSR Report 2006
China Mobile	TeleCom	CSR Report 2006
State Grid	Utilities	CSR Report 2005 2006
SY Water Supply	Utilities	CSR Report 2005.

Source: China CSR Map Database,
http://www.chinacsrmap.org/Page_Show.asp?Page_ID=181

the public, with the government, with its suppliers and its customers, with its employees, and with its peers through joining business associations. We therefore describe CSR-related activities for the sampled firms from these perspectives.

Figure 3.10

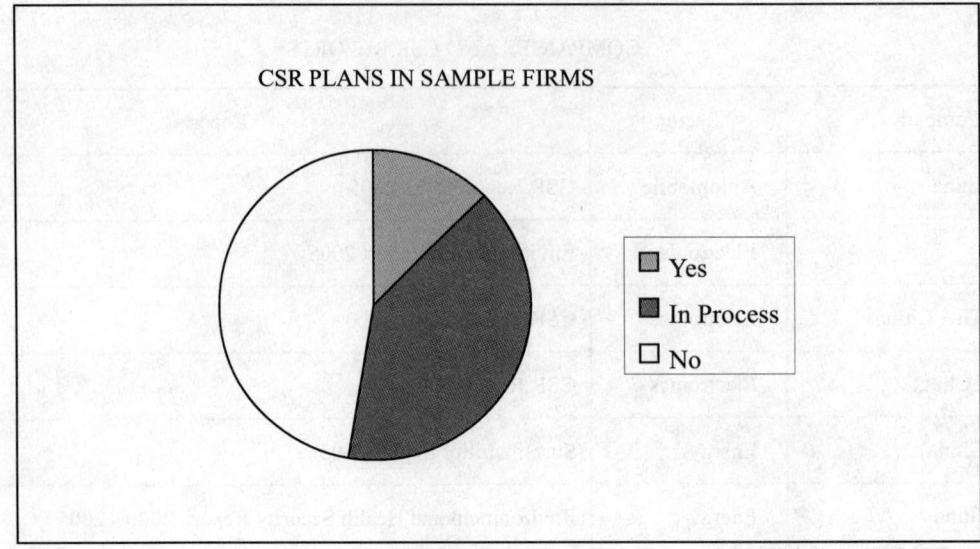

Source: Main Survey

As shown in Section 3.2, sample firms consider serving the interests of the public as the second most important CSR activity. Such activities can taken the form of donations, initiating donor activities, and joining organizations that focus on charities and donations. Our sample shows that firms participate in such activities mainly through providing donations. Two thirds of the sample firms reported that they donated in the past three years. Figure 3.11 provides the distributions of the amounts of the donations made over that period. There were 41% of the firms reported zero donations, 40% made donations of less than 0.1 million RMB, another 13% donated more than 0.5 million RMB. One needs to notice that firms may exaggerate their donations. One piece of evidence is about 8% of firms reported they made donations but in fact reported zero donation amount.

The frequencies of charitable and donor activities are presented in Figure 3.12. Now we observe 72% of firms reported they made no donations, and overall, 90% of firms made no more than 3 donations over the

Figure 3.11

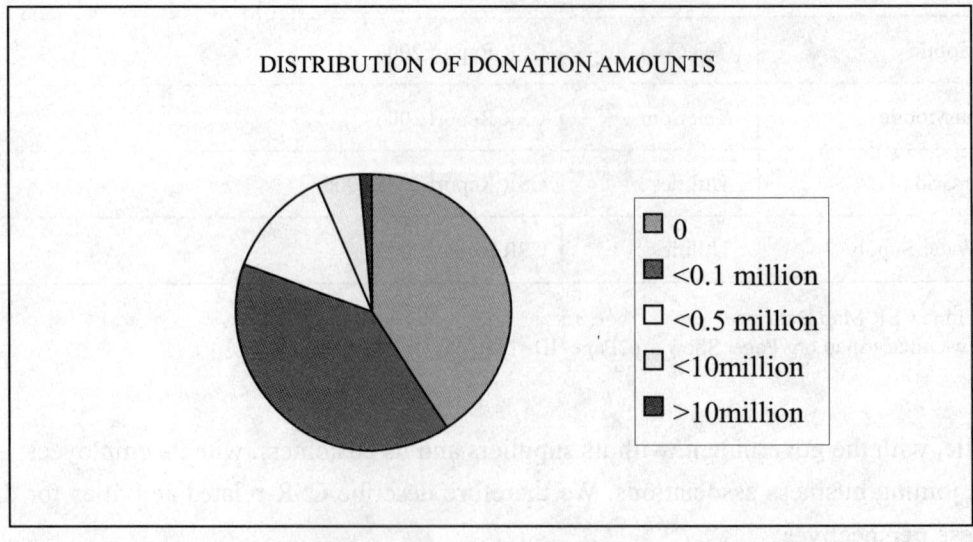

Source: Main Survey

past three years. The survey also shows that only 7% of firms have joined public-welfare organizations like the Red Cross Society of China. The behavior of the sample firms reflects that enterprises has started to consider donations as a way to take their social responsibilities.

Figure 3.12

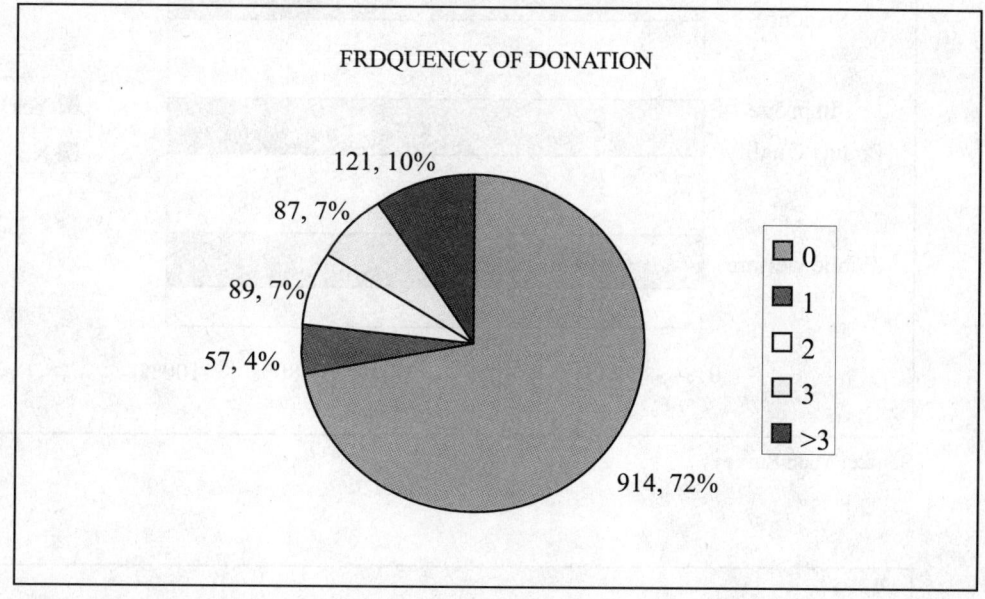

Source: Main Survey

Joining business associations is another possible channel for firms to participate in CSR related activity. Over seven hundred firms have joined business associations, accounting for 60.4% of the sampled firms. Business associations can help firms to improve their social responsibility awareness in various ways. The first channel is to organize firms to take part in activities focusing on improving public welfare, as 364 of the 766 firms indicate that their industry associations has organized such activities in the past three years. In addition to activities serving public welfare, industry associations can help firms by providing specific services to improve product quality, helping firms to set up industry product quality standards, and promoting fair competition. Over 60% of the business associations helped firms in these ways (Figure 3.13). Overall, sample firms welcome such services provided by business associations. Over 90% of the member firms believe industry associations help them to improve their product quality and appreciate the positive effects of business associations in improving the development of sustainability. About 85% of the member firms feel industry associations can improve the fairness of competition (Figure 3.14). This evidence suggests that helping firms to join business associations can be a practical method to improve implementation of CSR.

We then inspect firms' attitude towards their suppliers, towards contracts and advertisements, and towards the supply of product information based on their subjective evaluations. Many firms (67%) indicate that they have clear procedures for collecting feedbacks from their suppliers, customers and other interest groups; only 14% firms admit they don't have such regulations (Figure 3.15). As to whether they have clear procedures for making contracts and advertisements, 65% claim they have such rules and procedures and only 9% do not have them (Figure 3.16). Finally, over 80% firms believe they have provided clear

Figure 3.13

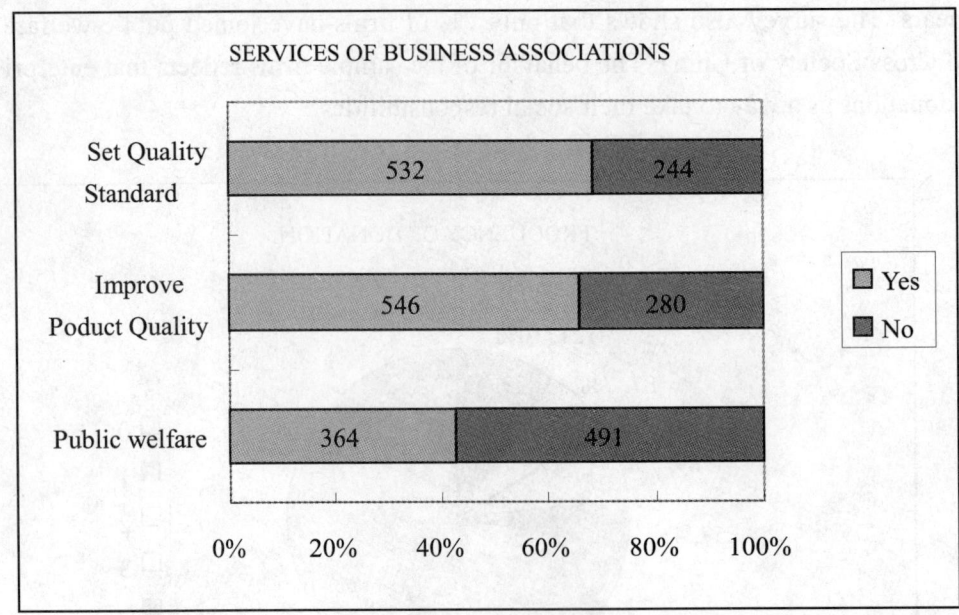

Source: Main Survey

Figure 3.14

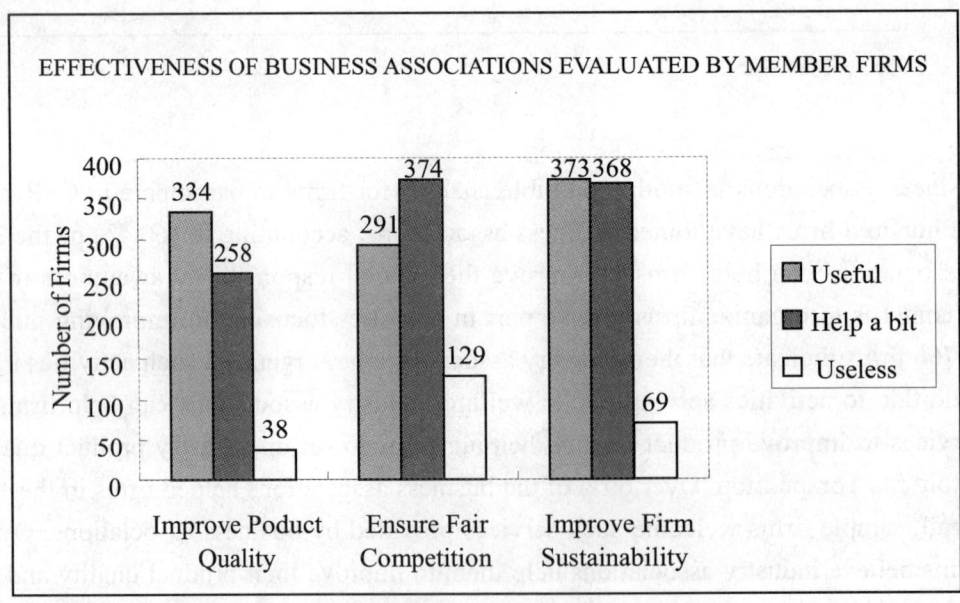

Source: Main Survey

product information, and only 5% of firms report they fail to do so. However, we need to notice that if the category "in process" and "no" are combined, 35% of the sampled firms do not have clear procedures for contracts and advertising, and 33% firms do not collect feedbacks systematically. Therefore, there is still room for improving CSR implementations.

3. 4 Summary

In this chapter we describe the CSR awareness of firms and their participations in CSR activities. Even though CSR is a new concept, sample firms catch up very quickly on CSR awareness and participations

Figure 3. 15

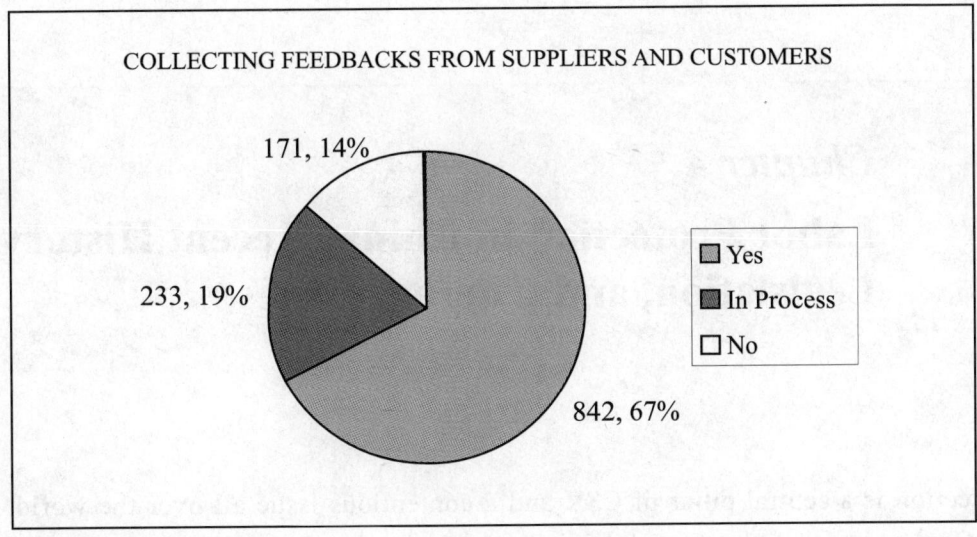

COLLECTING FEEDBACKS FROM SUPPLIERS AND CUSTOMERS

171, 14%

233, 19%

842, 67%

- Yes
- In Process
- No

Source: Main Survey

Figure 3. 16

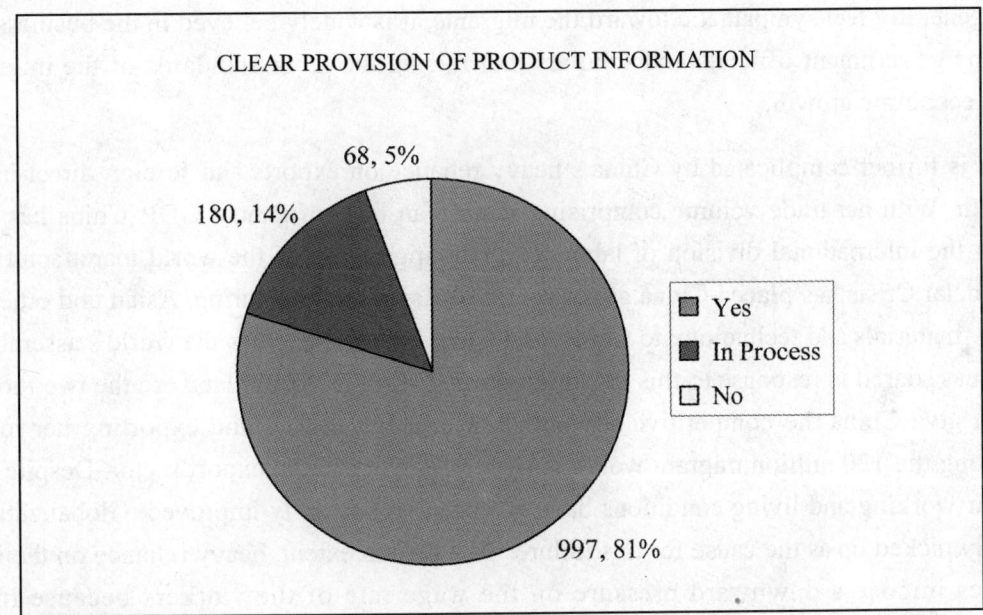

CLEAR PROVISION OF PRODUCT INFORMATION

68, 5%

180, 14%

997, 81%

- Yes
- In Process
- No

Source: Main Survey

in the 21st century. We observe that if a firm is a SOE, or an exporting firm, or a large firm, or a firm that operates in a competitive market, or a firm with a better-educated management team, it tends to be more aware of its social responsibilities. We also observe that implementation of CSR mainly works through providing donations, joining organizations that serve the public interest, and joining business associations. These evidences suggest that through creating an institutional environment of fair competition, providing better education for citizens, taking a proactive attitude toward meeting international standards, and helping firms to join business associations can improve the awareness of CSR among Chinese firms.

Chapter 4
Labor Protection in China: Recent History, Legislation, and Current Issues

Labor protection is a central pillar of CSR and a contentious issue all over the world. China is no exception. On the one hand, the general public has an increasing demand for better labor protection; but on the other hand, labor protection is often compromised in the interests of faster economic growth. The working and living conditions of some 140 million migrant workers are at the center of the debate. While the public generally feel sympathetic toward the migrants, it is widely believed in the business community and by some government officials and scholars that raising the labor standards of the migrant workers would hurt economic growth.

The debate is further complicated by China s heavy reliance on exports and foreign direct investment to drive growth. With her trade volume comprising more than 60% of annual GDP, China has been deeply involved in the international division of labor. The reconfiguration of the world manufacturing after the Asian Financial Crisis has placed China at the center of Asian manufacturing. Asian and other economies provide raw materials and technology to China, and China herself becomes the world s assembly line. FDI into China has soared in response to this reconfiguration. Cheap labor and land are the two most important factors that give China the competitive advantage in drawing in FDI and exporting her manufactured goods. Among the 120 million migrant workers, over 60% work in the export sector. Despite government efforts, their working and living conditions have not been significantly improved. Globalization has been conveniently picked up as the cause for this failure. To a certain extent, heavy reliance on the international market does impose a downward pressure on the wage rate of the workers because international competition brings down wage rates toward those of the poorest country. However, this negative effect of globalization may be outweighed by a positive effect of itself in that it exposes the working conditions in China under scrutiny by consumers and civil society organizations in the importing countries. To the extent that people in the importing countries regard labor standards as part of their satisfaction from their consumption of goods, this exposure will enhance labor standards in Chinese exporting firms.

The debate is no better exemplified than in the one surrounding the new *Labor Contract Law* that will take effect on January 1, 2008. The initial drafts of this law defined it as a law for the protection of labor. However, the final version has been much softened after several rounds of deliberations involving interest group lobbying as well as public discussions. As a result the *Labor Law* has become one that balances the interests of the employees and those of the employers.

This chapter will first review the history of employment and labor protection in China. Before entering the

21st century, labor protection in China was heavily linked with employment in SOEs. Privatization of SOEs in the 1990s thus led to serious erosion of labor protection. This chapter will provide a brief review of the erosion and of rebuilding of the social safety net in urban China. Then major issues in labor protection legislation will be discussed. The next chapter will provide statistics on labor protection based on national and survey data.

4.1   Employment in China since the 1990s

Before privatization began in the 1990s, the Chinese labor market was severely segmented. At the bottom of the segments were peasants who did not have any form of institutionalized social protection. In the city, employment was divided into parts, one in SOEs, some collective firms, education and government agencies, and the other in all sorts of informal employment segments including private firms, most collective firms, and self-employed people. Those working in the first part enjoyed good retirement and medical plans as well as various subsidies for foods, education and housing while those working in the second part did not have any of these benefits.

The 1990s, however, witnessed a dramatic retrenchment of SOE employment due to privatization. The number of SOEs reached the highest of 113,837 in 1996 (Figure 4.1), but then decreased sharply. By the end of 2004, only 27,477 SOEs remained, less than one fourth of the 1996 number. In the meantime, the number of private firms increased from less than 10,000 in 1990 to more than three million by 2004 (Figure 4.1). Notice that here the number of private firms is based on the narrow definition of private firms, that is, firms that are registered as sole-proprietorships. A broader definition of private firms would also include companies and partnerships firms that have shares owned by natural persons. In addition, there are also collective firms that are neither SOEs nor private firms, but are owned collectively by their employees.

Since the 1990s, employment in SOEs and collectives has been declining. Figure 4.2 present the data for urban employment in SOEs, collective firms and private firms in the period of 1998-2004. Consistent

Figure 4.1

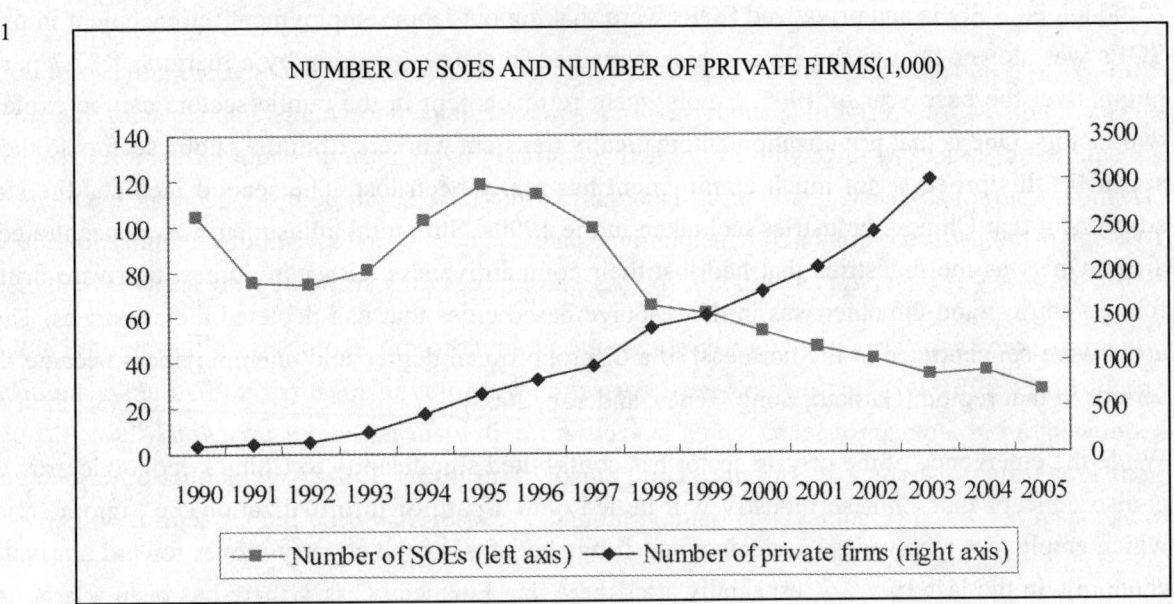

Sources: NBS (1990-2005); NBS (1990-2004).

Figure 4.2

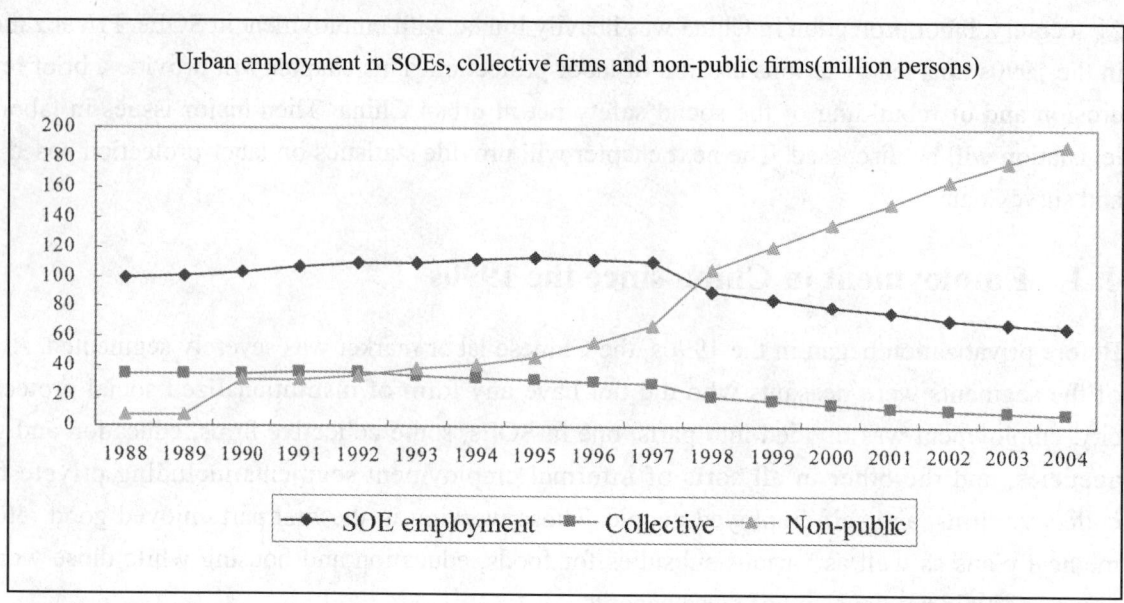

Urban employment in SOEs, collective firms and non-public firms(million persons)

Sources: NBS (1988-2004).

with the trend in the number of SOEs, employment in SOEs increased before 1996, but started to drop after that. The greatest retrenchment happened in 1998 when 20 million people lost their jobs in SOEs. By 2004, the SOE sector had lost 40% of its employment in 1995. The retrenchment in collectives has been smoother, but much deeper. In 2004, their employment was only one fourth of that in 1991, the highest in the 1990s. In the meantime, employment in the non-public sector had increased by 24 times between 1988 and 2004 and the non-public sector had become the largest sector in urban China, employing 71% of the urban labor force. In fact, the non-public sector became the largest sector as early as 1998.

The conventional wisdom is that employment retrenchment in the public sectors was a result of privatization. However, a recent study by Huang and Yao (2006) finds that in the period 1995-2001, privatization had actually worked to reduce the speed of employment retrenchment in the SOE sector. Although both SOEs and privatized SOEs were shaking out labor, employment retrenchment in privatized SOEs was slower than in the firms which remained in state-ownership by a margin of 17.7 percentage points over the base year of 1995. Employment retrenchment in the public sectors can be explained by two factors. One is that privatization automatically transfers workers from the public sectors to the private sector. In this process, not much employment has really been lost. The second factor is the structural adjustment that Chinese industries had taken in the 1990s. Structural adjustment was concentrated in two areas. One was the industries that had lost their competitiveness, either to domestic private firms, or to foreign entries; and the other was in the resource-based cities that had depleted their reserves. These two areas were concentrated in the northeast to a disproportional degree and unemployment became the most serious in that region (Garnaut, Song, Tenev, and Yao, 2005).

While the emergence of the private sector has contributed significantly to China's economic growth, there is also concern that Chinese industry will be led onto a path of informalization, i.e., into a situation in which employees receive less protection and fringe benefits, as the country moves toward a private-based economy. In the last 15 years, especially after the Asian Financial Crisis, there has been a large influx of rural migrant workers into cities (Figure 4.3). There has been a tendency for firms to replace urban workers

Figure 4.3

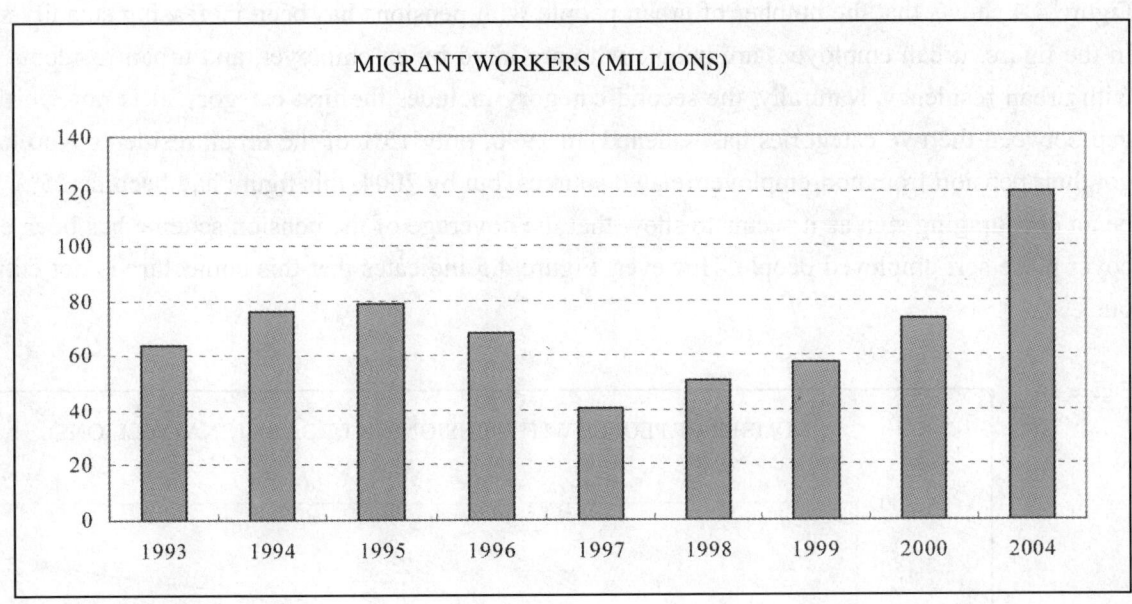

Source: MoA (2005).

by rural migrants who ask for less fringe benefits as well as lower wages. Even if the substitution of urban for migrant workers is not serious, many people who have lost their jobs in the SOEs (*xiagang*), and are being constrained by their lack of proper skills, have to find new jobs that often carry less fringe benefits. Indeed, there has been serious erosion of social protection in urban China since the 1990s. The next section will provide some summary statistics on this process of erosion.

4. 2   Erosion and Rebuilding of the Social Safety-Net

Before privatization began in 1992, employment was concentrated in SOEs and workers enjoyed a relatively high standard of protection provided by individual enterprises. However, this enterprise-based system began to meet serious challenges in China s new mixed economy in the 1990s. The emergence of private firms has intensified market competition and forced many SOEs into financial problems. Many SOEs were not able to pay pensions to their retirees or the medical expenses of current employees. In addition, most of the *xiagang* workers lost their health insurance and many of them had their pension payment interrupted. The 1990s thus witnessed a dramatic downturn in the coverage of the social safety-net.

The Chinese government has been fully aware of the problem. At the end of the 1990s and early 2000s, the government began pension and medical care reforms and established a three-tier minimum-living support system for redundant workers. The pension reform has transformed the pay-as-you-go and enterprise-based system to a mixed and public pooling system. Under this new system, individual employees have an individual account and a public pooling account. Individual employees pay 8% of their wages to their individual accounts, and their employers pay an extra of 3%. In addition, employers contribute 20% to the public pooling account. The most serious problem facing the new system is its transition from the old system. Since the individual account is new, retiring workers do not have sufficient funds in their individual accounts and the government has to step in to subsidize the pension system.

Figure 4.4 shows that the number of urban people with pensions has been increasing steadily since 1990. In the figure, urban employees are people who are hired by an employer, and urban residents are people with urban residency. Naturally, the second category includes the first category. It is noteworthy that the gap between the two categories has widened. In 1990, only 15% of the urban residents who had pension got their pension from non-employer related sources, but by 2004, this figure had become 25%. This could be an encouraging sign as it seems to show that the coverage of the pension scheme has been extended to cover more self-employed people. However, Figure 4.5 indicates that this conjecture is not entirely borne out.

Figure 4.4

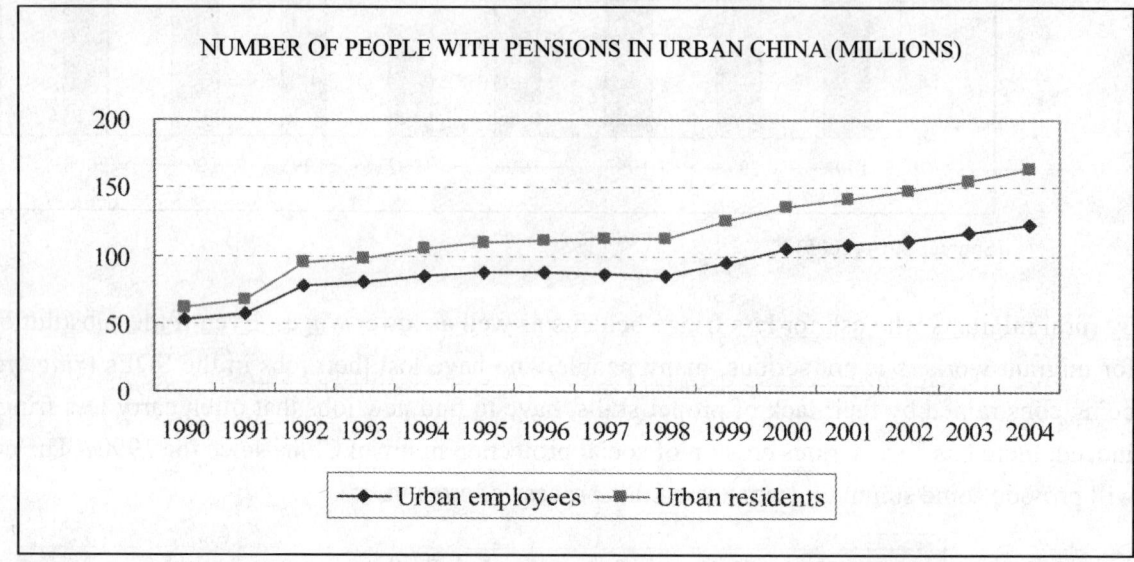

Source: MLSS (1990-2004).

Figure 4.5

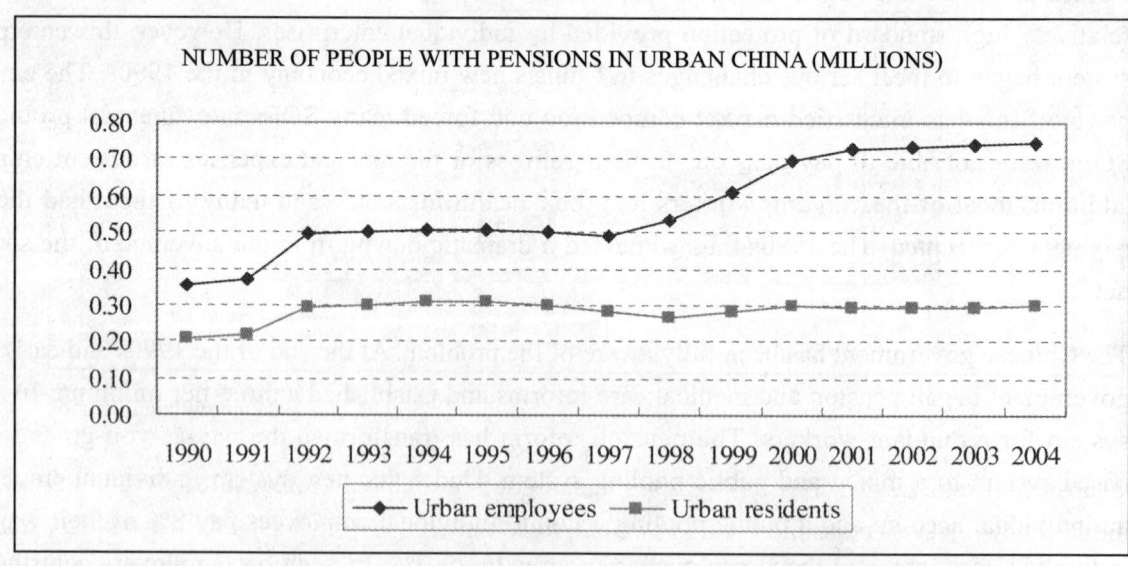

Notes: The lighter line is for the ratio of urban residents, which is defined as the number of urban residents having a pension divided by the total urban population. The darker line is for the ratio of people who had paid jobs, which is defined as the number of employees having a pension divided by the total number of people in formal establishments including SOEs, collective firms, companies with mixed ownership, foreign invested firms, and sole proprietors.

Source: NBS (1990-2004), MLSS (1990-2004).

The figure shows that while job related pension coverage was stagnant in the early 1990s, it increased dramatically from 50% to 70% in the second half of the 1990s. This was the period when the new pension system was established and which had a real effect in boosting social protection. However, the effect seems to have leveled out in more recent years as coverage has stabilized at around 74%.

The whole picture of pension coverage in urban China has not been encouraging. It increased gradually from a mere 20% in 1990 to 31% in 1995, and then fell down to 27% in 1998. Since 1998, there has been slow recovery, but the coverage in 2004 only reached 30%, still falling short of that in 1995. That is, the increase of pension coverage in urban China before 1998 had not caught up with the population growth in the cities. In other words, most of the new urban residents did not have pensions. Urbanization transformed many suburban rural residents into urban residents, but this fast pace of transformation has not been matched by the expansion of social protection. After 1998 when the new pension system began to take effect, the rate of expansion finally surpassed the growth of the urban population. However, it is still a daunting task for local governments to provide protection for the rural residents who have lost their land in the rapid expansion of the cities.

The good news, however, is that there is a general consensus in favor of the new pension system in both policy and academic circles as well as in society at large. However, medical care reform has not progressed as well as pension reform.

Before the medical care reform, urban residents got healthcare insurance from several sources. One was government-sponsored health care. This was for government employees, personnel in government-sponsored organizations, and university teachers and students. It started in 1952 and a large portion of government employees are still covered by this program today. The second was enterprise-sponsored health care, which was designated for employees in SOEs. It started in 1951 and by 1990, 95.64 million people were covered by this program spending a total of 18.2 billion RMB (at current prices. Liang, 2006). The third was cooperative health care. The share of the population taking this form of health care was small, but has been increasing in recent years. The fourth was commercial insurance plans. There were also other kinds of public health care that were sponsored by enterprises and government agencies.

The health care reform was announced in 1997 and introduced gradually afterwards. The major aim of the reform was to transform the enterprise and government-based system to a private-public mixed system. Individuals are given a private account with a certain amount of money in it. This account is used to pay for out-patient hospital visits. If one's expenses exceed the yearly allowance in this account, people have to pay themselves for out-patient visits. On the other hand, they can save any surplus in the account for the following year. On top of the private account is the public pooling scheme that is only responsible for in-patient hospital treatment. In most provinces, public pooling of both the pension and medical insurance plans has reached the provincial level.

Table 4.1 presents the changes in coverage of the above health care plans between 1993 and 2003. During this period, the coverage of government-sponsored, labor-sponsored, and other public health care plans declined by a total of 58.3 percentage points, and the coverage of the new health care plan, cooperative health care plan, and commercial insurance increased by a total of 40.7 percentage points. As a result, the percentage of people who had no health insurance increased by 17.6 percentage points, from 27.2% in

1993 to 44.8% in 2003.

Table 4.1

CHANGES OF COVERAGE OF HEALTH INSURANCE IN URBAN CHINA (% OF PEOPLE)

	1993	1998	2003	Change in 1993-2003
New health care plan			30.4	+30.4
Govt.-sponsored health care	18.2	16.0	4.0	-14.2
Labor-sponsored health care	35.3	22.9	4.6	-30.7
Cooperative health care	1.6	2.7	6.6	+5.0
Other public insurance plans	17.4	10.9	4.0	-13.4
Commercial insurance	0.3	4.3	5.6	+5.3
Without any insurance	27.2	44.2	44.8	+17.6

Source: Wang (2005).

Consistent with the decline of health insurance coverage, Figure 4.6 shows that out-of-pocket expenditure on health care has climbed fast in total household expenditure in cities since 1990 and in the countryside in the last 25 years. The growth has been more significant since the early 1990s. The demand for health care has not become a necessity for many Chinese people, so its income elasticity could be larger than one. It follows that the increase of the share of health expenditure could be a result of increased income. However, Figure 4.7 shows that the burden of health expenditure has been shifted from the government and health insurance to individual households in the last 25 years. The figure compares the share of government expenditure and expenditure by private individuals and non-government bodies with the share of out-of-pocket payments in the whole country. Government expenditure is the expenditure coming from government budget, and social expenditure comes from health insurance plans. In the twenty years between 1980 and 2000, the share of these two kinds of expenditure fell steadily. The decline of government expenditure could be a sign for the health care sector to rely more on independent health insurance schemes. However, the decline of social expenditure renders this possibility invalid. Consistent with the decline of government and non-government expenditure, the share of people's out-of-pocket expenditure increased from 20% in 1980 to 60% in 2000. It is encouraging to find, however, that the decline of government share has been stopped since 2000, and the share of social expenditure has been increasing and the share of out-of-pocket payment has been decreasing since then. It seems that the medical care reform is playing a positive role in reducing the burden on individuals. If this is true, then the critics of the reform need to reconsider their arguments against the reform.

The deterioration of social protection has been most serious for workers made redundant. In addition to providing training, the government has also established a three-tier system to provide minimum living guarantees to those workers. The first tier is enterprise-provided benefits. To minimize social unrest and

Figure 4.6

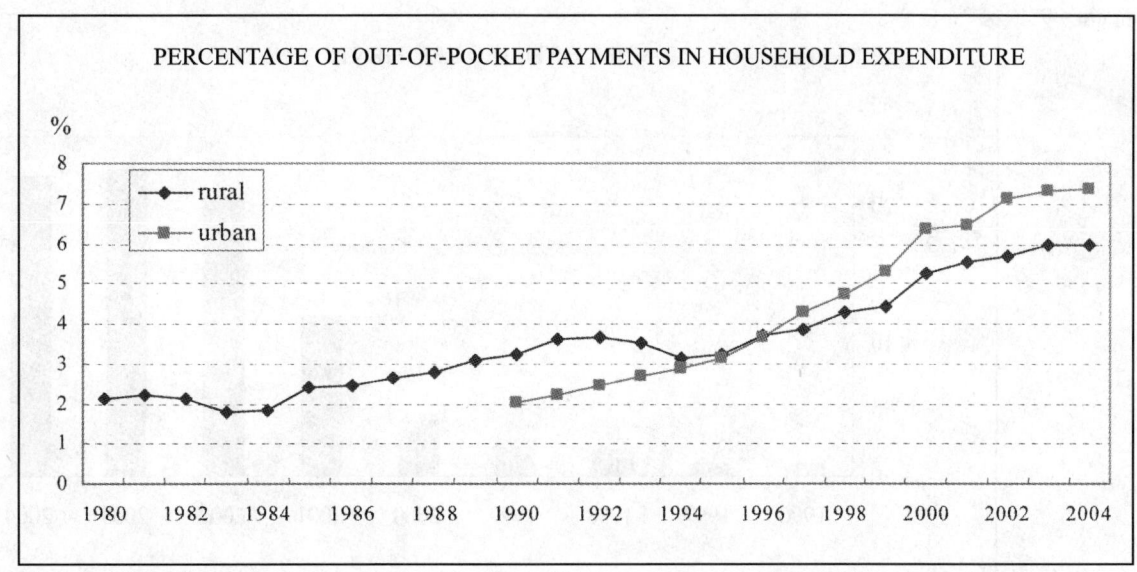

Source: Li (2006)

Figure 4. 7

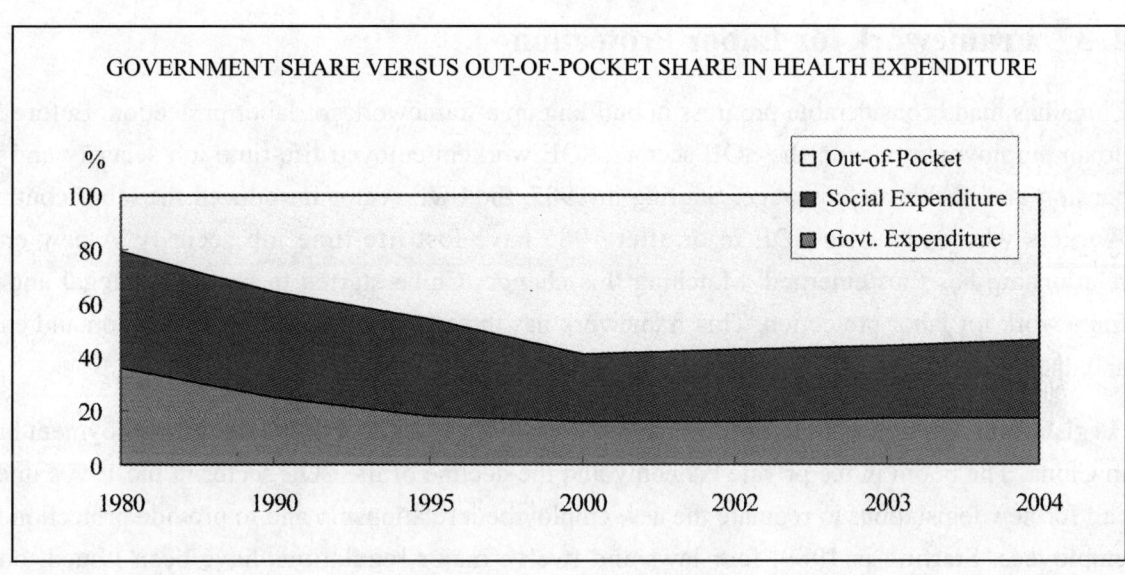

Source: Li (2006)

the government's burden, enterprises are advised to first provide internal retirement to redundant workers. Internal retirement means that the worker has not reached the official retirement age so he is not qualified to get pension payment; instead, the enterprise pays him a minimum living wage. The second tier is *xiagang* and unemployment benefits jointly provided by the government and enterprises. In the case of *xiagang*, both the government and the enterprises pay; in the case of unemployment, the government or the unemployment insurance fund pays. The third tier is the minimum-living income support, or *dibao* in Chinese, provided by the government to low-income urban residents. This program started in 1996. The number of its recipients increased from merely 850,000 in 1996 to more than 22 millions in 2004 (Figure 4.8).

Figure 4.8

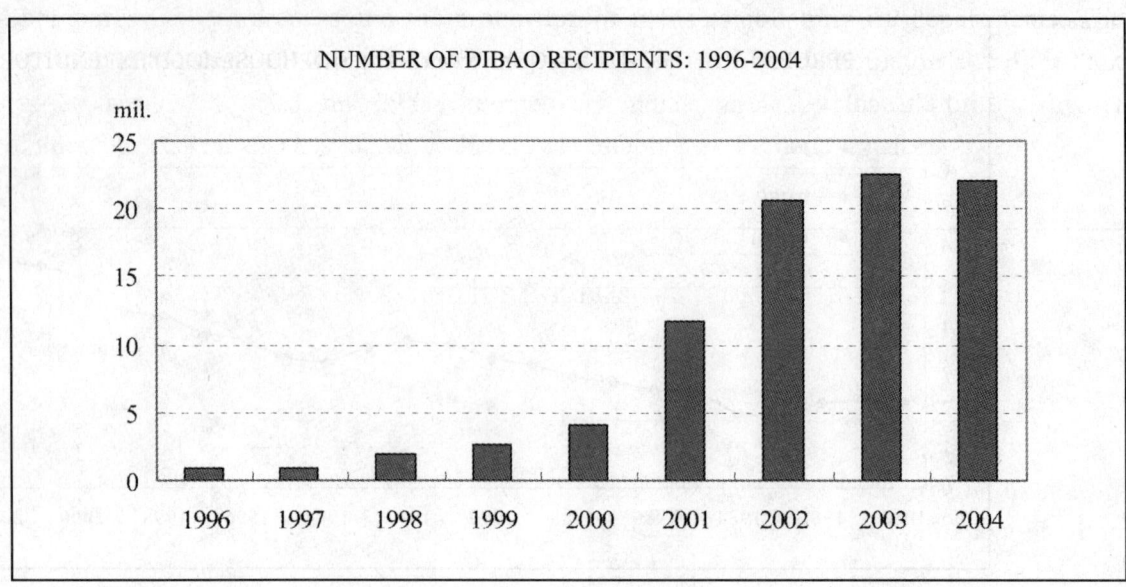

NUMBER OF DIBAO RECIPIENTS: 1996-2004

Source: MLSS (1996-2004)

4. 3   Framework for Labor Protection

China has made considerable progress in building up a framework for labor protection. Before 1985, most urban employment was in the SOE sector. SOE workers enjoyed life-time job security and reasonable pension and healthcare coverage. Starting in 1985, the SOE sector introduced the labor contract system. Workers who entered an SOE in or after 1985 have lost life-time job security. A new employment relationship has thus emerged. Matching this change, China started to build up a legal and regulatory framework for labor protection. This framework has three layers: legislation, inspection and enforcement, and dispute arbitration. The following is a concise description of these three layers.

Legislation. After the ending of life-time job security in 1985, a new chapter of employment has emerged in China. The boom in the private economy and the decline of the SOE sector in the 1990s intensified the call for new legislations to regulate the new employment relationship and to provide protection to ordinary employees. Starting in 1989, four laws and twelve major regulations have been issued, one is under review:

(1) Laws passed by the NPC:
    The Union Law (1992)
    The Labor Law (1994)
    Law for Prevention of Work-related Diseases (2001)
    Law of Work Safety (2002)
    The Labor Contract Law (2008)

(2) Regulations issued by the State Council
    Regulations for Work Protections for Female Employees (1988)
    Regulations for Enterprise Labor Dispute Settlements (1993)
    Revision of Working Hours (1995)

(3) Regulations issued by ministries

Tentative Stipulations for Labor Management in Private Enterprises (MOL, 1989)

Tentative Stipulations for Wage Payments (MOL, 1995)

Announcement on Several Issues in the Implementation of Labor Contracts (MOL, 1996)

Tentative Methods for Collective Wage Negotiations (MLSS, 2000)

Stipulations for Forbidding Child Labor (MLSS, 2002)

Directive Suggestions for Establishing and Improving the Tri-party Coordination Mechanism in Labor
Relations (MLSS, NLU, ACFOE, 2002)

Stipulations on Collective Contracts (MLSS, 2003)

Stipulations on the Minimum Wage (MLSS, 2004)

Regulations for Labor Protection Inspections (MLSS, 2004)

The central pillar of the above laws and legislation is the *Labor Law* and the *Labor Contract Law*, which lay the foundation for labor protection. The *Labor Law* covers a wide range of areas for which principles are laid out for labor protection. Major areas include the term of contracts, working hours, wages, working conditions, termination of contracts, protection of woman workers, child labor, and collective wage negotiations. Other laws are supplements to this law. The *Labor Contract Law* extends the *Labor Law* by making specific requirements for labor contracts.

Inspection and enforcement. Each local government has set up an inspection and enforcement team in its labor department. The team has the authority to inspect firms and issue orders of fines and corrections if wrongdoings are found. It gets information from two sources. One is its regular and random inspections, and the other is information provided by informants or complaints raised by employees.

Arbitration. There are three levels of arbitration. The lowest is the arbitration committee at the firm level. The committee is comprised of representatives from the management, the union, and the employees. The second level is the arbitration agency in the local government, and the highest level is the court. A case in dispute is supposed to first go through the firm arbitrage committee, and if no agreement is reached, the unsatisfied party can take the case either to the government arbitrage agency (often in the labor department of local government) or to the court.

4. 4   Issues with the Legal Framework

The above framework has laid down a foundation for protecting the rights of employees. However, this does not mean that the framework is perfect. The fact that China does not have representative democracy does not mean that there is no interest group politics. The laws passed by the NPC are the results of compromises among different social and economic groups. In the case of laws involving labor protection, noticeably, the *Labor Law* and the *Labor Contract Law*, the compromise is between employee rights and employers' discretionary power. It is interesting to find that the latter is often disguised and argued for by the drive for economic growth. This is nowhere more evident than in the stated purposes of the *Labor Law*. At its outset, the law states that it is enacted to protect the legal rights of workers, regulate labor relations, establish and maintain the labor institutions that are suitable for the socialist market economy, and promote economic development and social progresses. (Article 1) That is, the law gives equal weight to the protection of employees legal rights and the promotion of economic growth. It establishes the market mechanism for labor relation adjustments with the basic means of legalized minimum standards and contractual freedom." (Guo, 2006)In an economy with abundant labor supply, the "minimum standards" are not in employees favor.

This can be shown by the asymmetric rights that the *Labor Law* gives to the employer and the employee regarding the termination of an employment contract. The law gives more discretionary power to the employer than to the worker. There are only limited cases in which a worker can terminate an active contract. These are when the contract is still in the trial period, when the employer uses coercive means to force the worker to work, and when the employer has not paid or provided working conditions by the agreements set in the contract (Article 33). However, the employer has more freedom and discretionary power to decide whether it would like to fire a worker. In addition to the cases in which a worker has seriously violated the regulations of the company or brought large losses by neglect (Article 25), the employer, with a 30-day advance notice, can also fire a worker if he/she cannot perform the original work after he/she ends his/her treatment for a serious illness or work-related injury, or if he/she cannot perform his/her work even after training or changing of his/her posts, or if the contract cannot continue because the worker and the employer cannot agree with each other to the necessary changes for the contractual terms obligated by changes in external conditions (Article 26).

In addition, the *Labor Law* does not provide guidance for the term of labor contracts. In the last ten to fifteen years, there has been a clear trend of replacing long-term workers by short-term workers in Chinese industries (Guo, 2006). The *Labor Contract Law* makes some progress in this regard by requiring the employer to give an employee a permanent contract after there have been two short-term contracts. Whether this will significantly change the situation, however, is still unclear. It is likely that it will only benefit employees with higher levels of human capital but will not have much effect on people with lower levels of human capital. This latter group of people can be easily replaced by other people waiting for a job. So one way for employers to avoid the law is to hire these people for two short terms and then fire them. Only people whose human capital is not easily dispensable can get a permanent contract. To protect the rights of people in the bottom segment of employment, a better method is to increase the costs of layoff and termination of contracts. This will provide the employee a clear legal claim as well as increase the employer's incentive to offer longer-term contracts (Guo, 2006).

When it comes to labor disputes, the *Labor Law* sets a rigorous grievance procedure that is prone to discourage workers from using the law to protect their rights. If a worker has a complaint, he/she needs first to take the case to the arbitration committee within the company. He/She can take his/her case to an external arbitration office or the court only if he/she is not satisfied with the settlement offered by the internal arbitrage committee. Under the *Labor Law*, the internal arbitration committee should be comprised of people representing the employees, the labor union, and the company, and should be chaired by a person from the labor union. However, due to the reasons that will be discussed shortly, the role of the labor union is often more tilted toward the employer than toward the employees. This could create a fear among the employees that they could be retaliated against if they brought their cases to the internal arbitrage committee. Since they cannot bring their cases to the government arbitrage office or to the court without passing through the internal arbitrage committee, employees may just opt for not bringing up their cases at all.

The external arbitration office also has a deficiency (Guo, 2006). It is now purely a branch of government without any participation by the workers or their unions. As economic growth is always the top priority on local government agendas, the arbitrage office often yields to the interests of the companies.

The most serious defect of the current framework, however, is the lack of rigorous implementation. Although they are not perfect, the laws can provide substantial protections to employees once they are rigorously implemented. But the reality is not encouraging. The labor department is designated for the implementation of labor-related laws. But it has limited power to enforce them because as a part of the government it has to bend to the government s urge for economic growth even at the expense of labor and the environment. When it deals with labor violations, the labor department only has the right to fine the violators. More severe punishments such as suspension of business have to be approved by other government agencies. However, some of the violations are so severe that criminal charges can be applied to (See Box 4.1 for a related example). The lack of strict implementation reflects a belief that the law is too progressive for China today and is not meant to be implemented rigorously. The erosion of respect for the law can have a lasting negative effect on the construction of a law-based society in China.

Lastly, the role of the labor union is constrained by the law and collective bargaining is not emphasized. It is required by the *Union Law* that part of the funding of the labor union come from the company. In practice, the salary of the union chairman is paid by the company. Under this circumstance, it is very difficult for the union to act independently. In reality, labor unions are often either an employee club that organizes extra-work activities, or a labor management office of the company whose aim is to make sure that employees conform to the goals of the company. In the *Labor Law*, collective bargaining is stipulated as a neutral device to regulate the employment relationship, not a means to guard the rights of the employees. As a result, collective bargaining is either absent or becoming symbolic. The most serious problem, however, is that the *Union Law* does not stipulate explicitly that strikes are a legal means for workers to improve their benefits. In practice, strikes are effectively not permitted. Yet strikes are the last resort for workers to bargain with the employer. Without a law backing this right, workers are put in a very disadvantageous position.

In summary, the current Chinese legal framework clearly puts labor protection subordinate to economic growth. The related laws put limits to employees ability to protect their rights in the market, and the implementation of these laws is weak. All these are being done in the name of advancing the common good, which is economic growth in most circumstances. However, it is unclear that economic growth will be a common good for everyone when the rights of a significant portion of the population are sacrificed.

Box 4. 1

Enforcement of the *Labor Law*

GDP growth is the most important objective for local governments although the central government also attaches important value to social harmony in which the protection of labor rights is one of the key elements. In addition, many business owners have gained political power in local politics by joining the local people s congress or people s consultation conference. This has seriously weakened the enforcement of the *Labor Law*. As one government official in a sample city's labor department

---

put it frankly in an interview with the research team, these people have become obstacles to the implementation of the *Labor Law*. An incident of the use of child labor in another sample city illustrates this. The city s labor department received information that a silk factory in the county was hiring child laborers. The department called the county government and wanted to inspect the factory, but was rejected because the factory owner was a representative in the county s people s congress. The case was suspended until a serious accident happened in the factory. A girl was so tired that she ducked into the hot water that she was using to wash silk. She was seriously burned. Even at this point, the inspection team was stopped by the factory at its door, and the factory owner was arranging for the rest of the children to escape.

The pursuit of economic growth is taking a toll through the sacrifices of ordinary workers. The collusion between local governments and business elites is reinforcing it. Because of all this, the implementation of the *labor law* in the interviewed four cities has been half-hearted.

4. 5   Major Issues of Labor Protection at the Factory Floor

The working conditions and treatment of workers are contentious issues in current public discourse. To many people, China as the "world factory" is becoming the world's largest "sweat shop". Often, debates become emotional rather than rational. However, the issues cannot be simply brushed away. To a large extent, solving these issues can lead to the improvement of a firm s competitiveness in domestic and international markets. This is particularly true for companies that export their goods to international markets because government regulations and popular pressures in the importing countries are increasingly demanding higher labor standards in the production of the goods they buy. In fact, it is often the case that it merely amounts to abiding by the current legal requirements for companies to observe basic labor standards, yet violations of the law are common. Long working hours are but one such violation, and workers may tolerate it as long as they are properly paid for the extra hours. The more serious issues are with wage arrears, informalization of the workplace, and workplace safety.

Wage arrears. Wage arrears are the most common problem faced by migrant workers. Many of them end up with nothing going back home at the end of the year. According to the estimate of the National Labor Union, the total amount of wage arrears owed to migrant workers had accumulated to about 100 billion RMB by the end of 2004, more than 1000 RMB per migrant worker. This figure was confirmed by statistics from provinces and cities. For example, in the first two months of 2005, the Zhejiang provincial government helped 153,000 migrant workers recover a total of 140 million RMB of wage arrears (Zhejiang Online, 2005). An inspection conducted by the Shenzhen municipal government at the end of 2003 showed that 653 out of the 2838 inspected companies had a total amount of wage arrears of 100 million RMB for about 100,000 workers (IILI, 2006). The problem was so severe that Premier Wen Jiabao personally stepped in to recover the wage arrears of a woman migrant worker. However, the problem has lingered on despite government efforts. The reasons are of two fold. One is that workers, migrant workers in particular, are in a very weak position in bargaining with the employer. The law regarding wage arrears is lax. The most severe punishment now is fining, but no criminal punishment is implied. Migrant workers are a marginalized group in the city, and in many cases they do not know where to find help from the government. The second reason is related to government regulations for the construction business. About 80% of the wage arrears happen in construction companies. A survey conducted by the Beijing municipal government found that 3 billion RMB of wage arrears were found for 700,000 migrant workers in Beijing's construction business in 2004. That is, a worker on average owned more than 4000 yuan of unpaid wages (IILI, 2006), much higher than the average in all industries. It is a rule in the construction business that a construction company has to pay in advance most of the cost of the project. This rule originates in the real estate business. Many of the developers do not have sufficient fund to start a project, but instead rely on advance sales of the property to raise enough money. The result is that the construction company only pays part of the wages to its workers before the construction is finished, and leaves the rest to the end of the project. If the developer has not sold enough apartments or office space, the construction company ends up with insufficient funds to pay its workers. The government has tried to tighten up the regulation on the real estate business by banning advance sales, but the implementation of this policy has been unsuccessful. The real estate business is a powerful sector in the economy and it has various ways of influencing the government.

Informalization of the workplace. The most serious problems are the loss of pension and health care benefits and the replacement of long-term labor contracts by short-term contracts. These two problems are often interlinked, that is, it is the people having short-term contracts, noticeably rural migrant workers and urban laid-off workers that do not have pensions and health care benefits. Section 4.2 showed that the number of urban people working in the formal sector who had pensions increased steadily in the last decade and that the percentage had stabilized at around 80%. It is mostly the migrant workers and urban people working in the informal sector that do not have pensions.

There are several potential reasons for informalization. One is the rise of the private sector and structural adjustments in the SOE sector. In the 1990s, massive structuring adjustments happened in the SOE sector. The aim of these adjustments was to get rid of excessive capacity and obsolete technologies. Many SOEs went deeply into debt because of the lack of R&D investment and competition from the private sector. In addition, some resource-based cities had depleted their resource reserves and their industries had to go through a painful transformation. All these things contributed to massive unemployment in the 1990s. The private sector has played the most significant role in absorbing the unemployed workers. Indeed, it has become one of major contributors to the Chinese economy (IFC, 2000). However, most private firms are small and in their early stages of growth, and informal employment prevails. It is not so much that private firms should be blamed; rather, informalization of this kind is a by-product of the economic transition.

The second potential reason for informalization is China s deep integration into the world market. With its imports and exports accounting for more than 60% of its GDP, China is the most internationally dependent large economy. Since joining the WTO, China has also been becoming one of the most open economies in the world (Sally, 2006). Among China's exports, 60% are processing trade, which means that China's exports face fierce competition from all over the world. To remain competitive in the world market, firms have to keep down every kind of cost including workers' salaries and benefits.

The third potential reason is related to government policies. Currently, there is only one uniform policy for pensions and there are limited options for health care insurance. For pensions, as explained in Section 4.2 it is uniform across the country that individuals pay 8% of their wage payroll, and the firm pays 20% of its total wage payroll. Individual payments go into the individual account. Of the firm payment, 3% goes to the individual account, and the rest, 17%, goes to the public pooling account. This rule is unrealistic for migrant workers because of two policies adopted by most local governments. The first of these policies is that migrant workers cannot easily carry their pension payments with them if they move from one province to another. It is often the case that they can only bring with them their own payments (that is, the 8% part) and have to leave the rest behind. This means that they have to start their pension payments again in the new province. As a result, the payments that their employers made for them in the old province are lost. The other policy is that migrant workers cannot begin to draw their retirement benefits until they turn 60 years old, even if they stay in one province in their whole working life. This is impractical because not many migrant workers can afford to plan to work in one province for their whole working life. On the surface, the current pension rules aim at helping migrant workers, but in reality, they are exploiting them and their employers to subsidize urban workers.

The limited choices of health care plans have also contributed to the low rate of health insurance coverage. Recently there has been a hot debate on China s urban health care system. The debate started with a report released by the Development Research Center in early 2005. The report calls the new system the rich s club and believes that the reform was basically a failure (DRC, 2005). The debate soon became a hot topic over the Internet as well as in newspapers. It has also unfortunately become quite ideological with the two sides of the debate being divided on the issue of whether government should dominate in the provision of basic health care services. In reality, the issues at hand could be more technical than as fundamental as the debate seems to imply. For one thing, increasing the scope of choice will probably solve the problem of coverage. The city of Changchun provides a good example in this regard (see Box 4.2). In March 2006, the city started a new initiative to increase health insurance coverage among its residents. With two technical innovations, i.e., family-based participation and a simplified payment procedure, it is expected that this new initiative would substantially increase health insurance coverage in the city.

Workplace safety. China s rapid economic growth has a heavy price tag in terms of workplace safety. The rate of work-related deaths is about 1 person per 100 million RMB (Xinhua Network, 2005). The situation is worse in the coal mining industry. The death rate in China is 3 persons for 1 million tons of coal output, whereas it is 0.3 in Poland and South Africa, and 0.03 in the United States. China s coal output comprises 31% of the world total, but China's coal mine deaths comprise of 79% of the world total (Xinhua Network, 2005). The chief of the Bureau of Workplace Safety, Mr. Li Yizhong, gave five reasons for the high death rates in China's mining industry; two of them were related to neglect by employers (Xinhua Network, 2005). One was that employers do not observe safety procedures in production. For example, American coal mines have to extract the gas before they start to excavate coal, but in China, extracting the gas is done simultaneously with excavating coal. The other reason was that most miners come from the countryside and do not have enough safety training before they begin to work. In fact, lack of training is not confined to the mining industry. It is estimated that 1.4 billion rural migrant workers are working in the industry and this figure is increasing at the rate of 12 million more each year. Besides, there is still a huge reserve of labor in the countryside waiting to find jobs in the industry. The large supply of migrant workers has worsened their bargaining position and can easily lead to neglect of their safety.

4. 6 Summary

The last two decades have witnessed a declining trend in labor protection in China. While there have been declines in the SOE sector as a result of structural adjustments, it was in the newly emerged sectors, noticeably the private and exporting sectors, that labor protection became the most serious issue. Therefore, it is not so much about the decline of labor protection; rather, labor protection has become an issue because of the rise of the private sector and China s emergence as the global factory. The private and export sectors are China s two most important growth engines. Low labor standards may help these two sectors survive in the short run, but will hurt their competitiveness in the long run. Low levels of labor protection at the firm level drives away people with good human capital and thus lowers the long-term competitiveness of firms. In addition, labor standards are becoming a source of competitiveness in the international market as the consuming countries are demanding higher and higher labor standards in the products that they import. However, not all firms have been ready to explore their competitiveness through higher levels of labor protection.

The issue has been compounded by the drive by local governments to achieve instant economic growth. It is well known that in China political promotion is based on a tournament system (Zhou, 2007). Those who have achieved faster economic growth in their jurisdictions are usually promoted faster than others with slower economic growth. Age is an important factor in this tournament game. There are explicit and implicit rules specifying certain age brackets for certain ranks of office. As a result, short-term performance becomes the key for an official to embark on a fast track in his/her political career. It is thus not surprising that many local governments prefer to exchange labor and environmental protection for faster economic growth. The Hu Jingtao-Wen Jiabao government has set the goal to achieve a "harmonious society" in China. Harmonizing the relationship between labor and capital is one of the keys to a harmonious society. There are some signs that the new goal is beginning to introduce changes to labor protection. For example, some local governments have begun to take stringent measures to punish companies that do not pay their workers in time. However, more changes are needed.

Box 4.2

Changchun Gears up to Increase Health Insurance Coverage

Changchun is the capital of Jilin province in northeast China. It is an old industrial city, but has lagged behind in recent years. The municipal government started a new plan to increase health care coverage in the city in March 2006 (Changchun Municipal Government, 2006). The target of the plan is people who are not covered by employment-based health care plans. The new plan is very pragmatic in its aims. It only covers major illnesses that require hospitalization. The premium is low, but the benefits are reasonable. For example, the premium for people between 18 and 50 years

---

old is only 240 yuan per year, but the benefit is up to 70% reimbursement for the highest bracket of expenses of 10,000-30,000 yuan.

There are two important innovations in the plan. First, it adopts a family-based participation scheme. That is, if a person wishes to join the plan, he/she has to enroll his/her whole family. This method can be quite effective in solving the problem of adverse selection. Second, it simplifies the payment procedure for medical expenses. In many cities, the patient has to pre-pay all his/her medical expenses and then take the receipts to get reimbursement from the city health insurance bureau. This practice has two disadvantages. The obvious one is that it increases the transaction costs of the patients wasting their time and money in travel and queuing before the reimbursing window. The other is not so obvious but no less severe in its social impact. The practice gives away the supervising function of the insurance bureau to the hospitals. There are loud complaints among the public that hospitals are charge ridiculously high prices for their services and medicines. The current practice is forcing the patients to monitor the prices that they receive, which is hardly feasible. Changchun only asks the patients to pay their share and the rest is pre-paid by the hospital and later reimbursed by the insurance bureau. This enhances the role of the insurance bureau in monitoring the medical expenses. For example, if it finds an expense is too high, it can refuse to reimburse the hospital.

There is still room for improvement in Changchun's new initiative, though. Family-based participation can solve the adverse selection problem if individual health is evenly distributed across families. However, it may discourage some marginal families   for example, families with relatively healthy elder members — from joining the plan. One improvement could be allowing for cost pooling within the family. This will have the added benefit of raising the incentive for families to join because healthier family members can subsidize less healthy members.

Chapter 5
Labor Protection in Sample Firms

This chapter provides an analysis of labor protection mainly based on data collected from the main survey. Major topics to be covered include: labor contracts, working hours and wage payments, pensions and medical insurance, workplace safety and amenities, labor disputes and settlements, and labor unions and collective bargaining. The analysis will focus on the factors that affect firms' performance in the above aspects. The factors that were discussed in Chapter 1 affecting general CSR performance all influence labor protection in a firm, but different factors may have different degrees of impact. Therefore, we will not give all the factors equal treatment; rather, we will focus on several key factors that are the most pertinent to the aspect of labor protection under discussion.

Labor protection is a sensitive issue, so the main survey may not reflect the true situation on the ground because questionnaires were completed by firm management which might not be objective. To check the validity of the results based on the main survey, data collected in the individual survey will also be used to supplement the analysis.

5. 1   Labor Contracts

Labor contracts have become a major regulatory tool for the Chinese government to protect employees as well as a private means for employees and employers to protect their legal rights in the employment relationship. This is so despite the fact that China s *Labor Law* is largely neutral toward the employment relationship (see the analysis in the last chapter), because labor is in an inferior position in most cases. Although the enforcement of the labor contract is far from perfect when a dispute happens, signing a contract still provides some support for an employee when disputes go to arbitration or court settlement because he/she is usually the weak party in a conflict with corporate power. However, the national situation is not favourable in terms of the rate of contracts signed. A survey by the NLU found that by September 2005, among the 118.8 million employees in enterprises that had labor unions, only 48.6% had signed a labor contract (NLU, 2006). In non-state SMEs where labor unions are seldom found, the situation is much worse. A survey on 2150 firms in 16 provinces by an inspection team of the NPC, also carried out in September 2005, found that less than 20% of the employees in non-state SMEs had signed a contract with their employers (IILI, 2006). The situation is much better in SOEs and FDI firms. The same NPC survey found that 98% of employees in SOEs and 90% of employees in FDI firms in the city of Tianjin signed contracts, but only 65% of employees in private firms did so (IILI, 2006).

Coverage of Contracts in Sample Firms

The main survey seems to provide a better picture than the national scenario described above. Among the 1,254 firms that provided valid answers, 79% said that they had signed labor contracts with all their white-collar workers, and 77% said that they had signed contracts with all their blue-collar workers. The best performers were foreign-invested firms; 87% of them had contracts with their blue-collar workers. SOEs and HMT-invested firms followed with proportions of 86% and 80.6%, respectively. Domestic private firms had the lowest rate of 73.8% (Figure 5.1). Comparing these figures with those obtained by the national studies, one finds that the bias mainly came from the reports of domestic private firms in the main survey where there seems to have been some window dressing . However, the order among the four kinds of firms is still meaningful and consistent with casual observation.

Figure 5.1

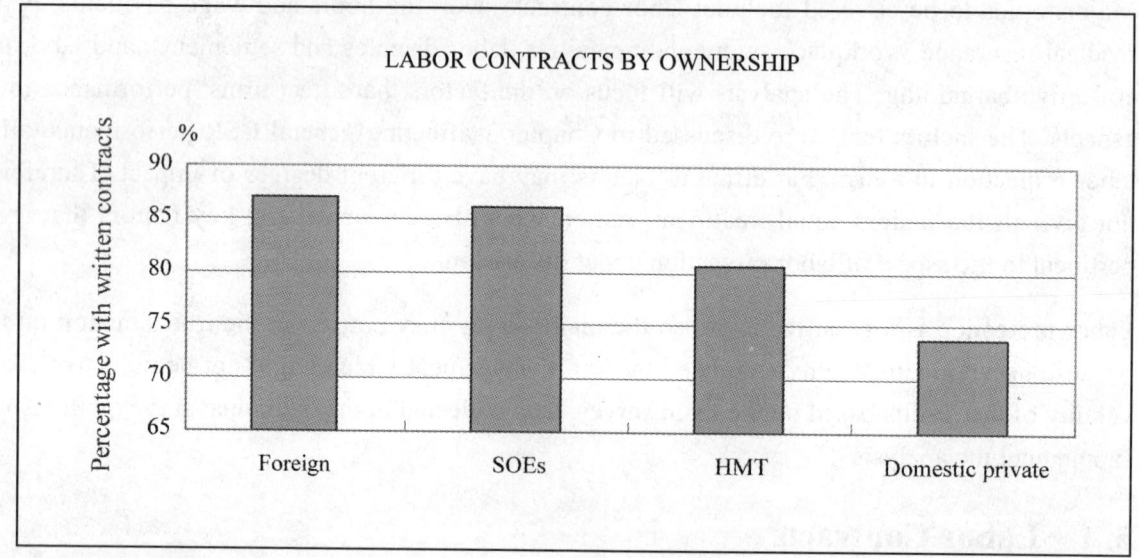

Source: Main survey.

The difference between exporting and non-exporting firms was small; 79% of the former and 75% of latter had written contracts with all of their blue-collar workers. The differences among different sizes of firms were large, though. While 94% of the large firms had contracts with their blue-collar workers, 87% of the medium firms and 74% of the small firms had them.

Regional variations were also large. Figure 5.2 provides a ranking of the cities. Except Shiyan and Xi'an that outperformed their regional peers, coastal cities generally did better than inland cities. The better performance of Xi'an may be explained by its heavier presence of SOEs and FDI firms and scantier presence of domestic private firms, the superb performance of Shiyan as the top performer among all the 12 cities is much harder to explain. Its share of domestic private firms was larger than that in the whole sample, and it had a very small number of FDI firms (Table 2.5). The better performance of the four coastal cities was unlikely to be associated with more SOEs or exports because Hangzhou, Shunde and Wujiang did not have many SOEs and Beijing did not have a large number of exporting firms. It was more likely to be associated with their having more FDI firms and more exposure to information and public demands.

Figure 5.2

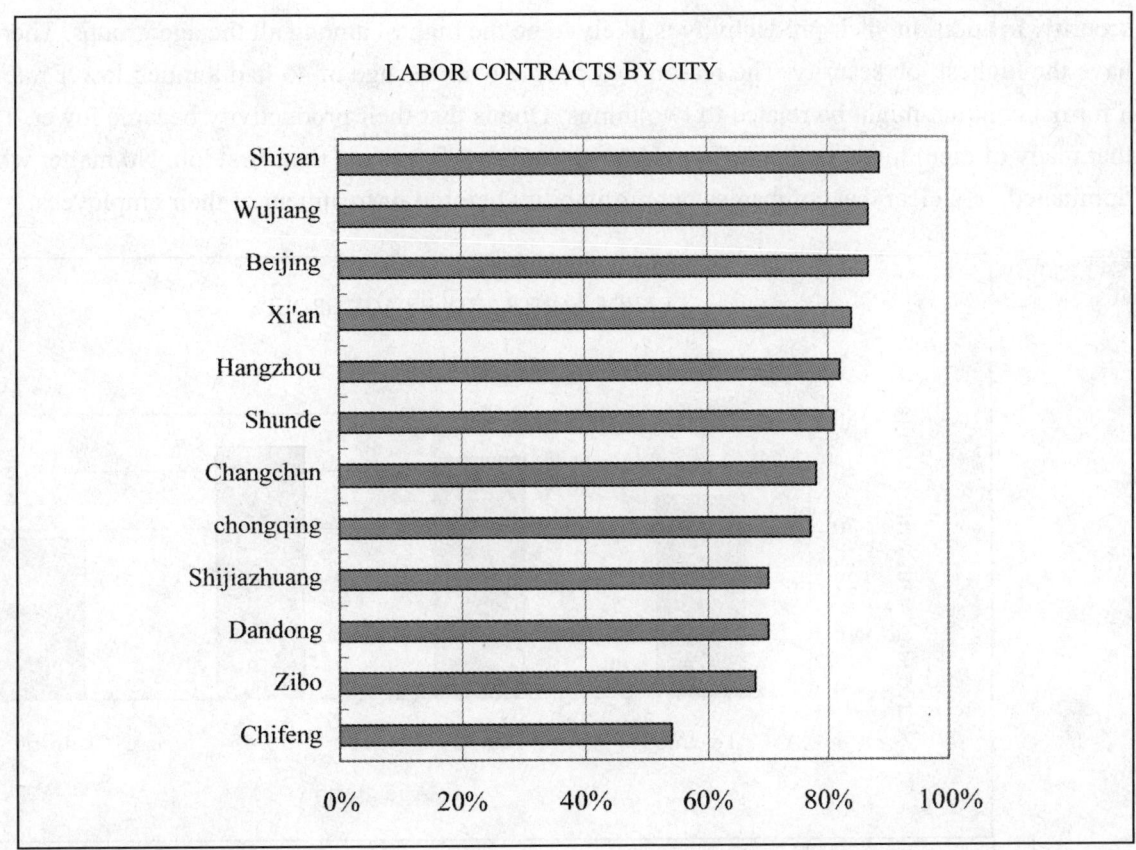

LABOR CONTRACTS BY CITY

Source: Main survey.

The individual survey provides a quite different scenario from the one provided by the main survey, but is more consistent with the national data. The number of respondents who worked in the manufacturing sector and had a written contract in their last job was only 52.8%, much less than what was found for the domestic private firms in the main survey. This shows that one needs to take caution when interpreting the figures provided by the sample firms. Although it was clearly stated on the cover page of the questionnaire that the survey results would be kept strictly for academic purposes and no individual information would be released in any form, the firm management might still be worried about the image of the firm and even some legal liabilities, so it might be inclined to give exaggerated figures. We will therefore take more information from the individual survey whenever we believe that distortions exist in the answers to the main survey.

Factors Affecting Written Contracts

From the results of the individual survey, male workers had a slightly higher percentage signing a formal contract than female workers, but the gap was only two percentage points. It seems that the gender gap is small even if it exists. However, there were significant and interesting variations among people in different age groups (Figure 5.3). The percentage of people with a written contract increased from 35.5% in the 18-25 group to 45.3% in the 36-45 group, but dropped sharply to 28.3% in the 46-60 group. Young people do not have much work experience so companies do not offer them a formal contract. On the other hand, young people themselves may have a low desire to sign a contract because job flexibility is more important than job security to them. People in their prime age have more experience and a greater desire for job security. In addition, their productivity is likely to be the highest among all the age groups. Therefore, they have the highest job security. The reason that people over the age of 45 had a much lower rate of signing a formal contract might be related to two things. One is that their productivity became lower. The other is that many of them might be laid-off workers whose last job was not their first job. No matter which reason dominated, it is clear that companies put profitability before fair treatment of their employees.

Figure 5.3

Source: Individual survey.

Figure 5. 4

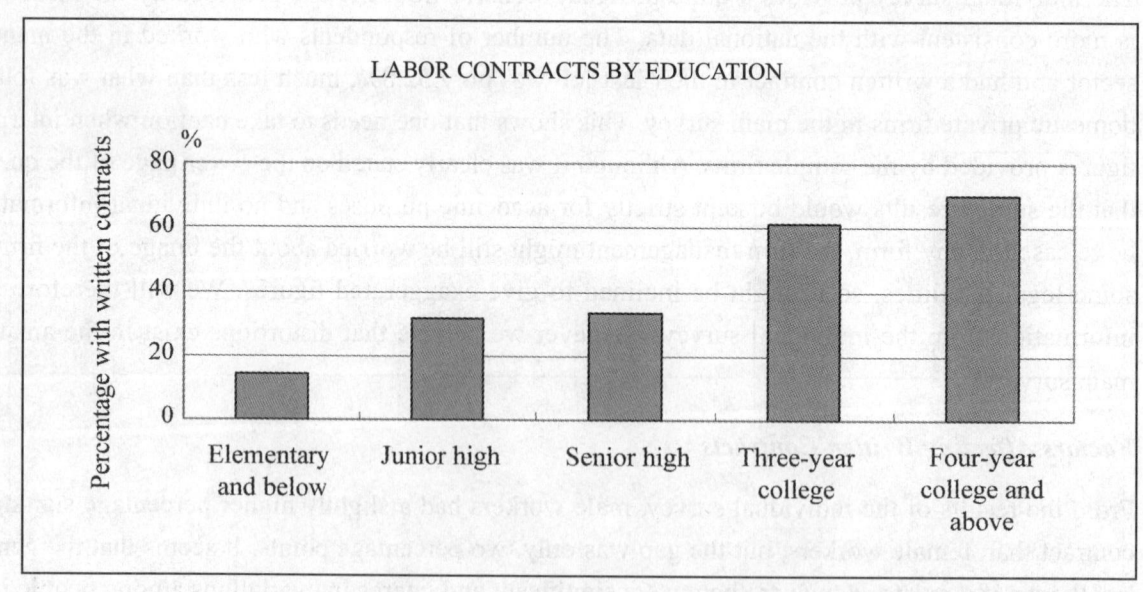

Source: Individual survey.

There was a clear pattern that people with higher educational attainments were more likely to sign a formal contract (Figure 5.4). From the company s point of view, people with higher educational attainments are more valuable so it wants to use a formal contract to retain them. On the other hand, people with higher educational attainments are more conscious about their legal rights and are more likely to use a formal contract to protect them. Figure 5.4 shows two large jumps in the rate of formal contracts. One was between people with an education at or below the level of elementary school and people who had finished junior high, and the other was between people with a senior high school diploma and those with a three-year college degree. Junior high school education gives a person the basic ability to learn the necessary skills required for a factory floor worker, so it is a hurdle for a formal job. A three-year college degree allows a person to become a white-collar worker.

There were significant variations among people working in different sectors. Figure 5.5 ranks the sectors by their percentages of people with written contracts. The manufacturing sector had the highest percentage: 52.8% of the people working in this sector had a written contract. It led the second highest, the trade sector, by 16.6 percentage points. Construction, hotels and catering, and transportation had a smaller percentage than the average for the whole sample. The better performance of the manufacturing sector is linked with its higher demand for elevated human capital than the other sectors.

Firm size was another significant factor that affects the rate of formal contracts (Figure 5.6). For people working in firms smaller than 50 persons, only 22.9% signed a formal contract. The number jumped to 46.7% among people working in firms with 51 to 500 persons. In larger firms with 501 or more workers, the rate of contract signing was above 60%. There are several reasons for larger firms to achieve a better record. First, larger firms have a longer planning horizon than smaller firms so they want to retain experienced workers. Second, larger firms are under more supervision from the government because it is easier for the government to monitor larger firms and their failure to follow government regulations has a larger impact on the society than small firms. Third, the reputation risk is higher for larger firms for not following government regulations because reputation is more important for them than for small firms.

Figure 5.5

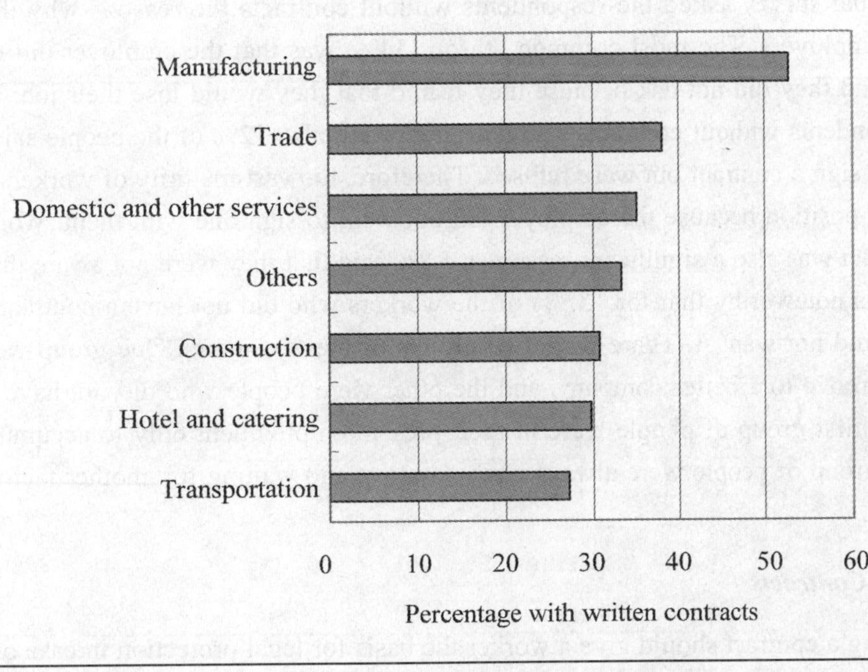

Source: Individual survey.

Figure 5.6

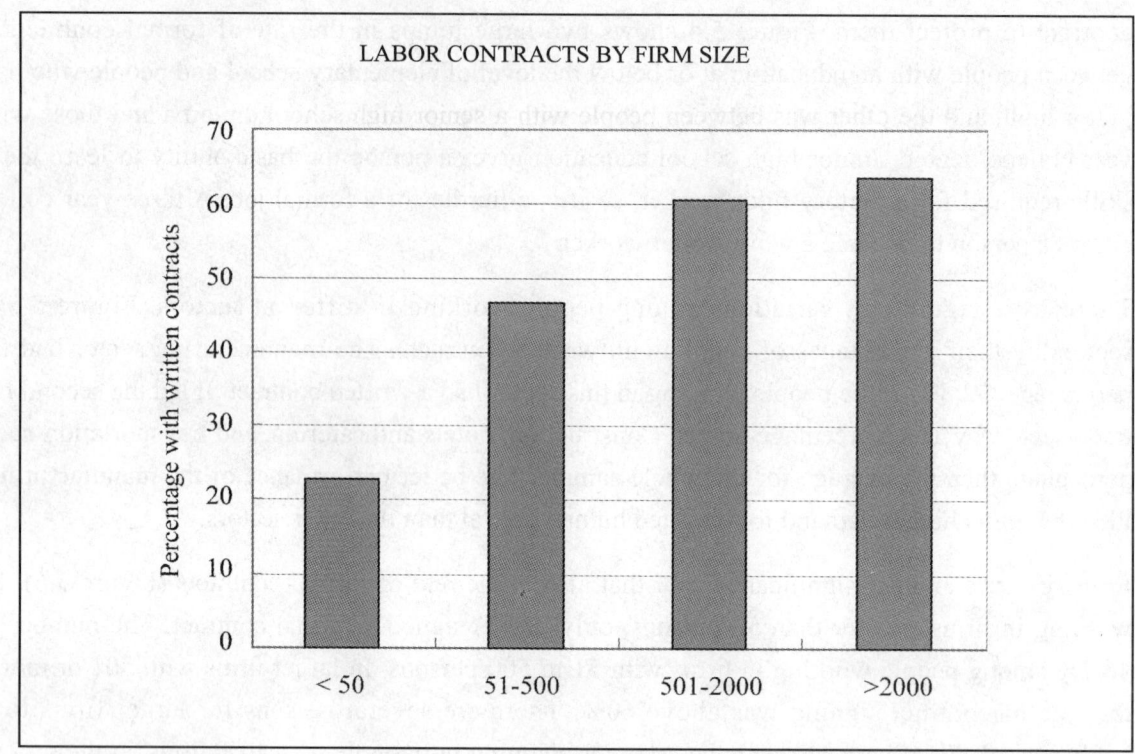

Source: Individual survey.

Finally, there was a significant gap between local workers and migrant workers: 47.4% of the local workers signed a contract, but only 31.0% of the migrant workers did so. Although discrimination could be a reason for this large gap, one has to notice that migrant workers have lower educational levels but higher mobility rates than local workers. Whatever the reason, however, the gap shows that migrant workers are in a disadvantageous position when circumstances come to require the contract to back up their claims.

The individual survey asked the respondents without contracts the reasons why they did not sign one with their employers. The most common reason (54%) was that the employer did not ask them to sign a contract and they did not ask because they feared that they would lose their job. Fifty-four percent of the correspondents without contracts said so. There were also 12% of the people said that they asked the employer to sign a contract but were refused. Therefore, the vast majority of workers that had no contract were in that position because the employer did not want to sign one with them. Workers own ignorance of the contract was also a significant reason as 5.8% said that they were not aware that they should sign a contract. It is noteworthy that for 13.1% of the workers who did not have a contract it was because they themselves did not want it. There were two groups of these workers. One group were people with high potential to move to a better company, and the other were people who did not have firm-specific human capital. The first group of people were in their present employment only to accumulate experience, and the second group of people were always ready to move and waiting for another factory to offer a slightly higher wage.

Contents of Contracts

While signing a contract should give a worker the basis for legal protection in case of dispute, there is no guarantee that the terms of the contract are always in the worker s favor. As Chapter 3 showed, the *Labor*

Figure 5. 7

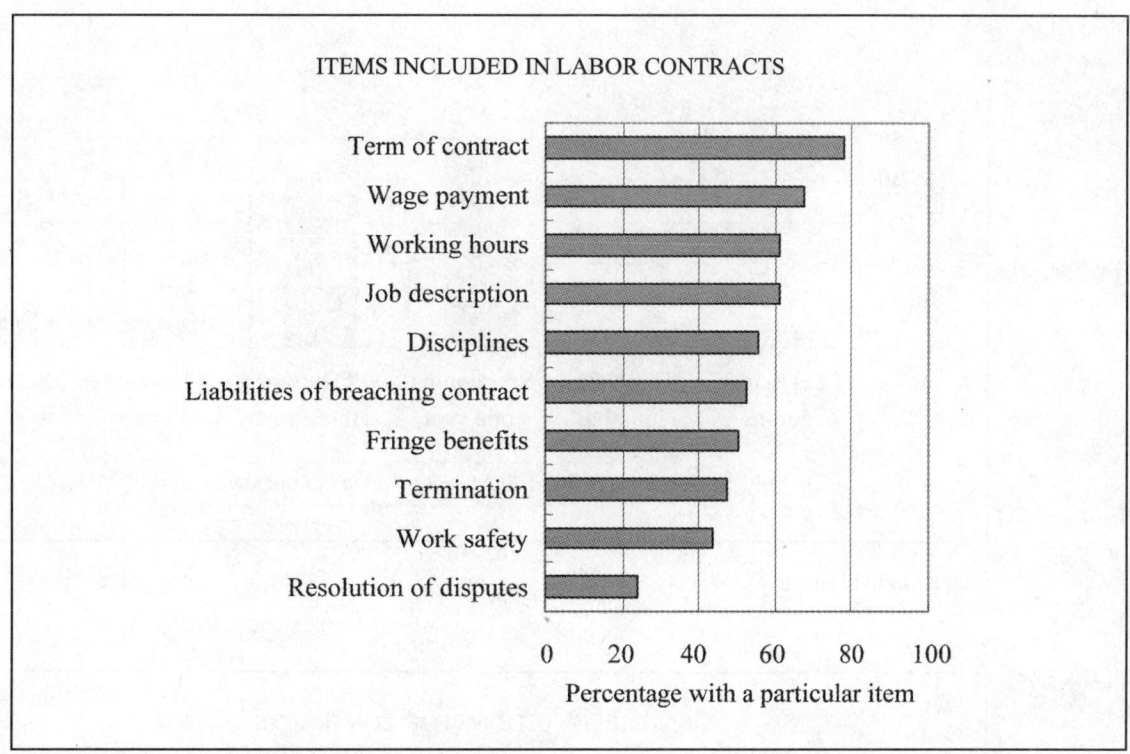

ITEMS INCLUDED IN LABOR CONTRACTS

Source: Individual survey.

Law is neutral and even provides more discretionary power to the employer in some critical aspects (such as termination of contract). The individual survey asked the respondents whether their contract with their previous employer, if there was one, had a particular item. Figure 5.7 ranks the items mentioned by the correspondents by the percentage of contracts that had a specific item. It is clear that items related to the hard terms , e.g., the term of the contract, wage payments, working hours, job description, and discipline, were more frequently included in a contract than items related to "soft terms", e.g., fringe benefits, contract termination, work safety, and resolution of disputes. The low frequency of the soft items points out the weak position of the worker because they are more related to the protection of his extra rights.

Even among the "hard items", the terms were not always in the worker's favor. Take the length of the contract as an example that has a lot to do with a worker s job security. The majority of the contracts, 67.4%, were for between six months and three years, and 7% of them were for less than six months (Figure 5.8). That is, job security was low for people covered by the individual survey. There were variations across sectors and firm size, but the most significant were between local and migrant workers. Figure 5.8 shows the distribution for local workers was more towards longer terms of contract than that for migrants. The concentration for migrant workers was between six months and one year, but the concentration for local workers was between one year and three years. In particular, there were significantly fewer contracts for migrant workers that were for more than three years. The percentage for migrant workers was only 6.4%, but the figure for local workers was 23.8%.

The individual survey also found that employers set preconditions before employees could begin working. Forty percent of respondents said that their previous employer set preconditions. Figure 5.9 ranks the preconditions mentioned. The most common precondition – 59.5% of the correspondents mentioned it –

Figure 5.8

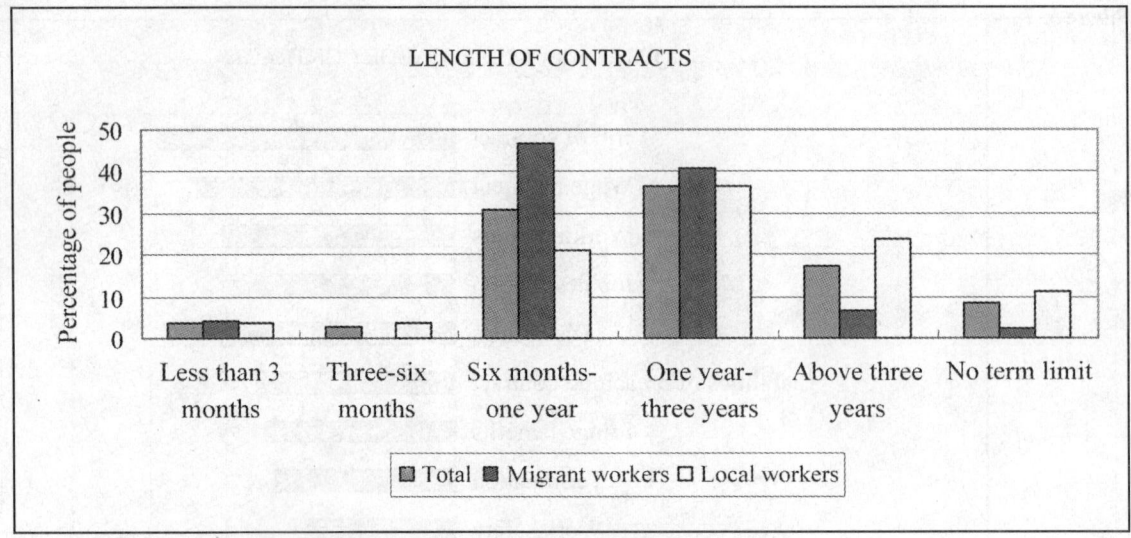

Source: Individual survey.

Figure 5.9

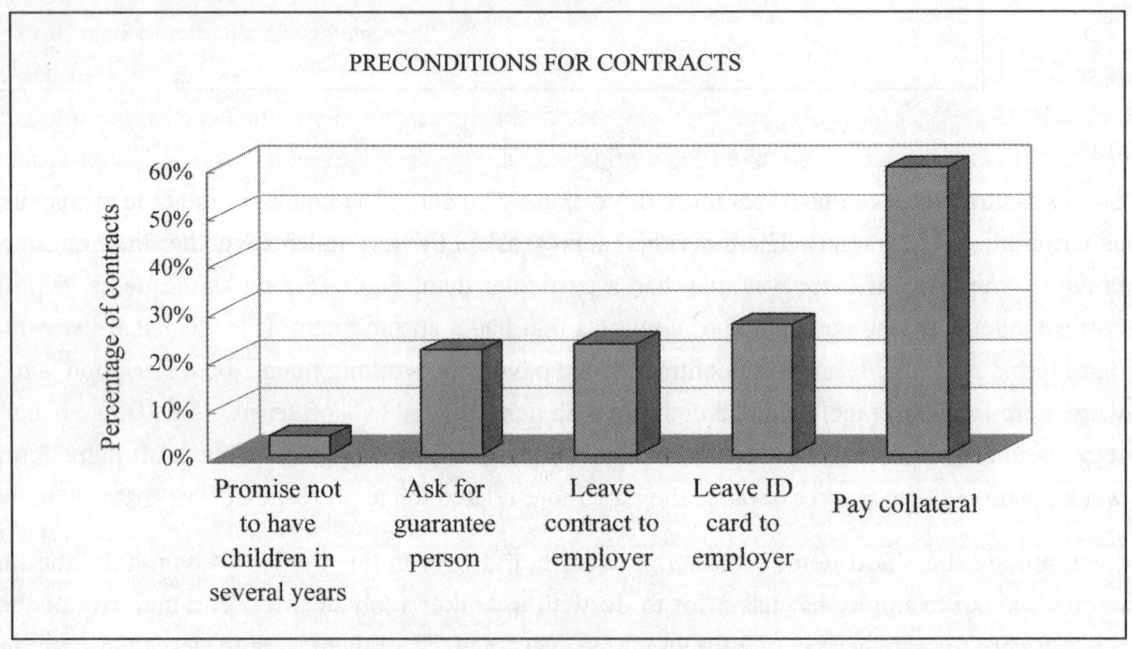

Source: Individual survey.

was a requirement for up-front or installment payments as collateral. When installments were used, they were usually deducted from the worker's salary. Other preconditions included requiring the worker to deposit his/her resident ID card or other identification documents to the employer, to leave the contract document with the employer, and to find someone to act as a guarantor. There were a small number of female correspondents who said that their employer required them not to have children for a certain period of years.

Termination of Contracts

The main survey asked questions about the conditions for the termination of contracts. Twenty-eight percent of the sample firms only gave a short notice of seven days when they wanted to fire a worker. Another 12% gave two weeks, 41% gave one month, and 19% more than one month. Domestic private firms were more likely to give very short notice than the other types of firms: nearly one third of these firms gave only one-week's notice. They were followed by HMT-invested firms (19%). By contrast, only 14% of SOEs and foreign-invested firms gave only one week's notice. On the other hand, more than one third of SOEs and foreign-invested firms gave more than one month's notice while the corresponding percentages for HMT-invested and domestic private firms were only 22% and 15%. Foreign-invested firms were the most generous in terms of the compensation offered to the fired worker. Fifty-seven percent of them offered more than one-month salary. HMT-invested firms and SOEs were slightly less generous: half of the HMT-invested firms and 48% of the SOEs offered more than one-month salary. In contrast, only 29% of domestic private firms did so and one third offered compensation of less than 20% of a month's salary. It is interesting to find that 31% of the SOEs also followed this practice. As a contrast, only 16% of the foreign-invested firms and 21% of the HMT-invested firms did so. Compensation to fired workers seemed to be a question of norms. It is a norm for foreign and HMT-invested firms to offer at least a month's salary to compensate the fired worker, whereas domestic firms do not have such a norm.

5. 2   Working Hours and Wages

It is widely believed that workers in Chinese private firms work for long hours. Long working hours have both immediate and chronic adverse effects on workers' health. In the short run, fatigue can significantly increase the risk of accidents at work; in the long run, extended working hours may causes illness. However, for many workers, especially migrant workers, health may not be as pressing an issue as getting more income. Therefore, the more serious issue may be whether workers are getting properly paid for their long working hours. The *Labor Law* has detailed regulations for working hours and overtime wage rates. These include: workers should work for no more than 8 hours in a day, and no more than 44 hours a week; workers should get at least one day off a week; overtime cannot exceed 3 hours in a day, and 36 hours in a month; and overtime wage cannot be less than 150%, 200%, and 300% of the normal wage for a week day, a weekend day, and a national holiday, respectively. This section will use these requirements as the standard to judge the performance of the sample firms in the main survey and the situation reported by the correspondents in the individual survey. Again, information provided by the main survey may not accurately reflect the true situation. We will check these results with the information obtained from the individual survey.

Working Hours

Among the sample firms, the number of working days in a week was concentrated around five to six days. Forty-six percent of them reported that their workers worked for five days, and forty-three percent of them reported six days. There were also 10% which reported seven days, and the rest reported less than five days.[1] The average working days were 5.6 days, and the average working hours were 45.6, above the national standard of 44 hours. However, the 10% of firms reporting seven working days had apparently violated the national standard for at least one day of rest a week, and the 43% firms with six working

---

[1] A small number of firms reported fractions of working days. Whenever that happened, a fraction of a day was counted as one full day.

days had violated the national standard of no more than 44 working hours per week. That is, more than half of the sample firms had exceeded the national standards for working hours. One implication of this high reported rate of violation is that legal consequences of violation are minimal since the firms did not attempt to hide the information. From the research team s interviews with the city labor department, it is also clear that the department did not pay as much attention to long working hours as to other violations such as wage arrears and hiring workers without formal contracts. The implicit consensus seems to be that as long as workers are being properly paid, long working hours are acceptable. Since the wage rate is low, even workers themselves may not oppose long working hours as long as they are paid properly. The next subsection will study closely the relationship between working hours and wage payments.

Figure 5. 10

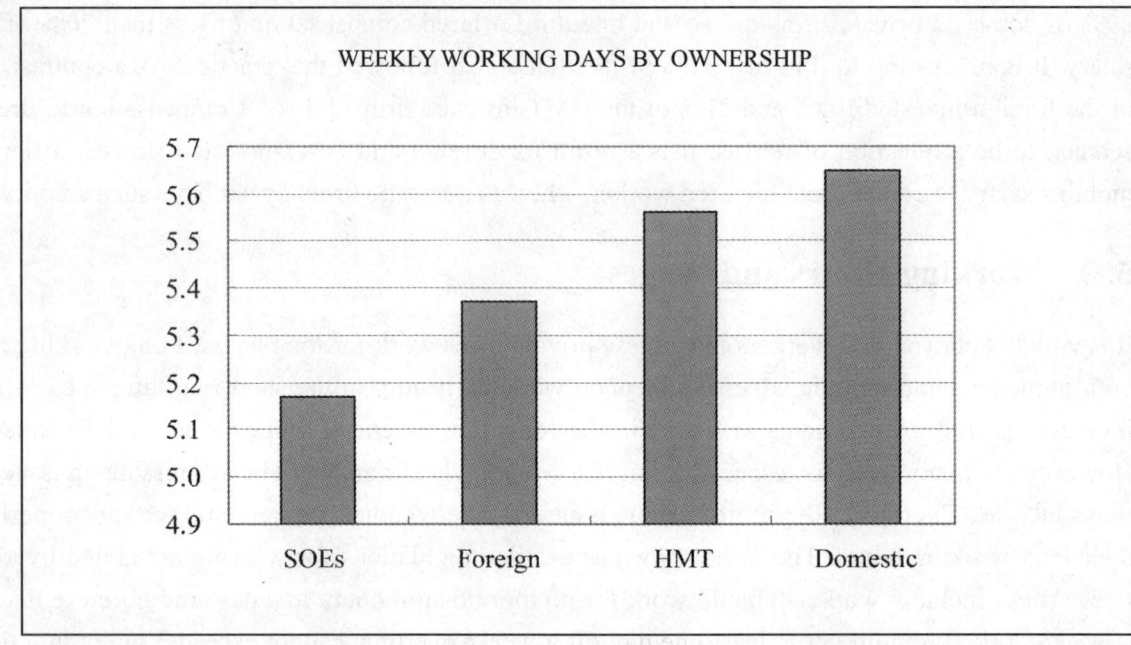

Source: Individual survey.

There were significant variations among firms of different ownership (Figure 5.10). SOEs had the lowest number of working days, foreign and HMT-invest firms were next, and domestic private firms had the highest. This ranking is not surprising in terms of the degree of competition, government regulations and public pressures that the four types of firms face. Their size may also play a role (see below). The difference between SOEs and domestic private firms was 0.49 days, or 3.9 hours assuming that an 8 hour working day. Apart from domestic private firms, other types of firms on average did not exceed the national standard of 44 working hours in a week. Domestic private firms on average exceeded the national standard by 1.6 hours.

As a check of the accuracy of the information provided by the sample firms, the main survey asked the sample firms to give the working days and hours in other firms in the same industry. SOEs were the most honest in this regard because the average of their own weekly working hours was about the same as the average weekly working hours in other firms (in fact, the former was 0.4 hours more than the latter). For all the other three types of firms, the average of their own weekly working hours was less than the average for other firms by 1.8 to 1.9 hours. Although it is small, this gap is still indicative of possible under-

Figure 5.11

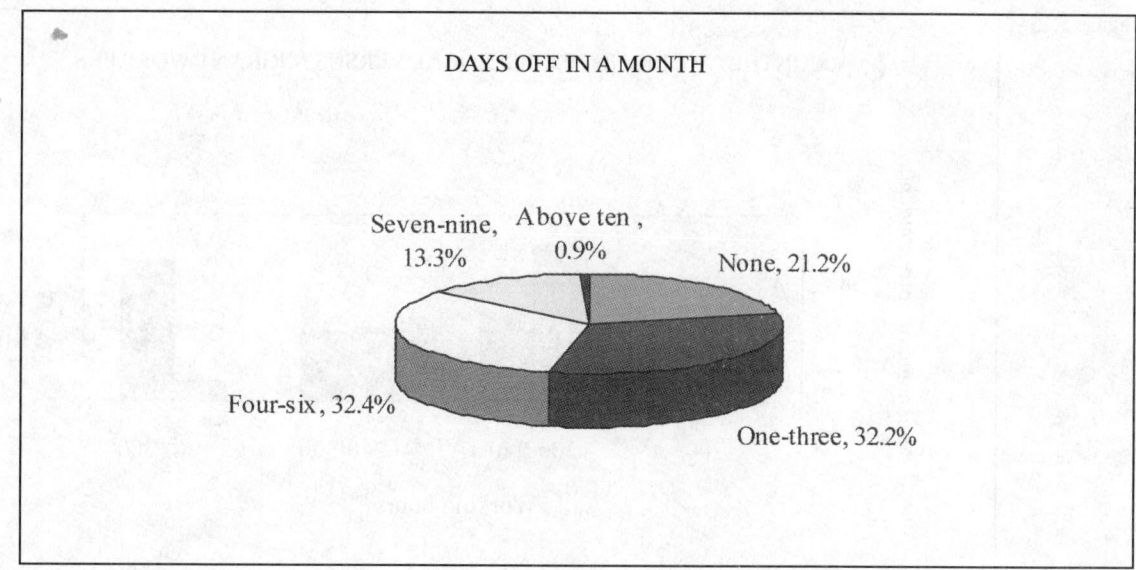

DAYS OFF IN A MONTH

Seven-nine, 13.3%

Above ten , 0.9%

None, 21.2%

Four-six , 32.4%

One-three, 32.2%

Source: Individual survey.

Figure 5.12

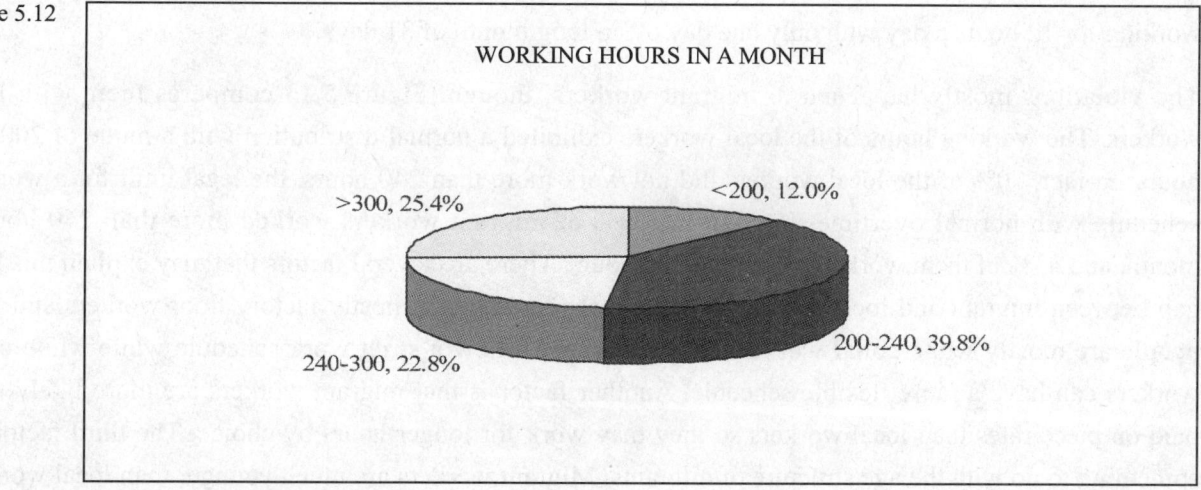

WORKING HOURS IN A MONTH

>300, 25.4%

<200, 12.0%

240-300, 22.8%

200-240, 39.8%

Source: Individual survey.

reporting on the part of non-state firms.

The individual survey reveals a more serious situation in private firms (Figure 5.11). More than one fifth of the respondents said that they had not had a single day off in a month, and about one third said that they had one to three days, which means that more than half of the respondents worked more than six days a week. Figure 5.12 presents a more detailed picture in terms of the working hours in a month. By the national standard, 200 working hours in a month can be regarded as a normal schedule without overtime working, 240 hours can be regarded as a schedule with normal overtime working, and above 240 hours violates the law. In this regard, only 12% of the correspondents reported a normal working schedule without overtime, and 39.8% reported a working schedule with normal overtime. The rest 48.2% reported working hours over the legal limit. In particular, one fourth of the correspondents reported more than 300 hours, which means that they worked 12 hours a day if they took one day off in a month. There were

Figure 5.13

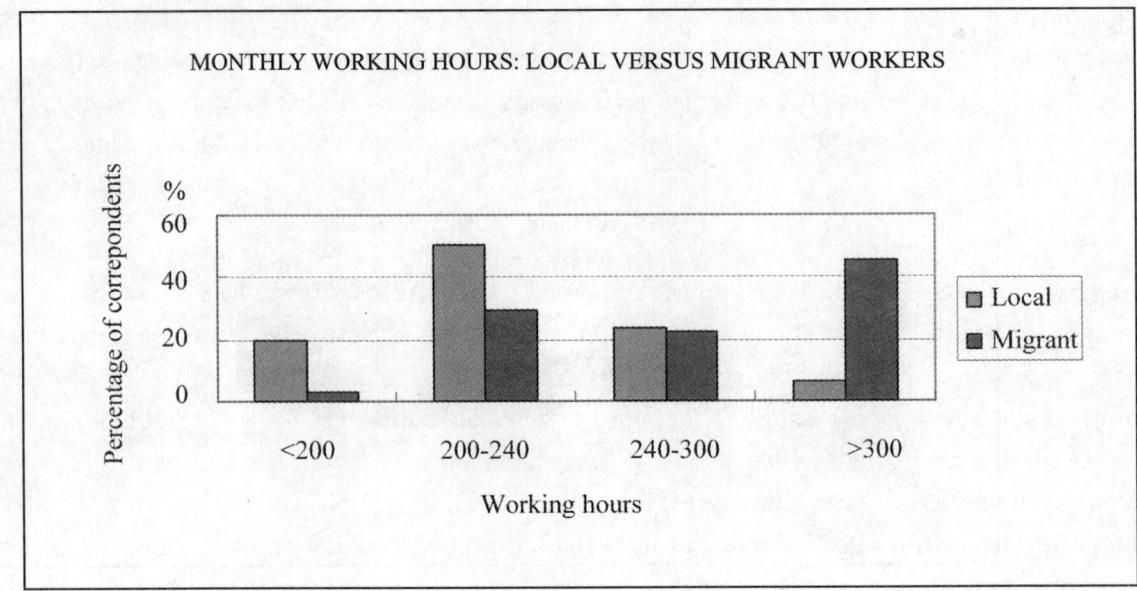

also 6.3% of the respondents who reported 360 working hours or more in a month. This is equivalent to working for 12 hours a day with only one day off in long month of 31 days.

The violations mostly happened to migrant workers, though. Figure 5.13 compares them with local workers. The working hours of the local workers exhibited a normal distribution with a mode of 200-240 hours. In fact, 70% of the local workers did not work more than 240 hours, the legal limit for a working schedule with normal overtime. In contrast, 68% of migrant workers worked more than 240 hours a month, and 45% of them worked more than 300 hours. There are several factors that may explain this large gap between migrant and local workers. One is that migrants are mostly factory floor workers and local people are mostly white collar workers. Floor workers follow a strict work schedule while white collar workers can have a more flexible schedule. Another factor is that migrant workers are more likely to be paid on piece rates than local workers so they may work for longer hours by choice. The third factor has something to do with the age structure of migrants. Migrant workers are much younger than local workers, so they may be more able to work long hours. In addition, many of them are not married, and even if they are married, they do not bring their families with them. This can also contribute to their longer working hours because they do not need to take care of a family as local workers have to do. Lastly, discrimination against migrant workers can also be a reason. Migrant workers are not well organized, and do not have local social networks to provide assistance. Besides, their options are very limited. These factors lead to weak bargaining power that the employer can take advantage of.

Salaries

The wages of workers in the sample firms were low. The average monthly salary was 1255 yuan for white-collar workers and 1037 yuan for blue-collar workers. The median monthly salary was only 1080 yuan and 950 yuan for those two groups of workers, and the minimum salaries for them were only 300 yuan and 400 yuan, respectively. The average hourly wage of blue-collar workers was 5.6 yuan, and the median was 3.7 yuan.

Both the main survey and the supplementary individual survey found that long working hours were common. However, it would not be as serious if long working hours were properly compensated for. Sadly this was not the case among the sample firms. Figure 5.14 plots monthly average salary reported by individual firms against monthly working hours for blue-collar workers. Monthly working hours are obtained from firm-reported weekly working days and daily working hours. . Several firms with monthly working hours of less than 100 or monthly salaries of more than 6000 yuan are not included. A simple linear regression shows that an extra working hour reduces a blue-collar worker's monthly salary by 1.7 yuan, and this effect is statistically significant at the 1% significance level.

Figure 5. 14

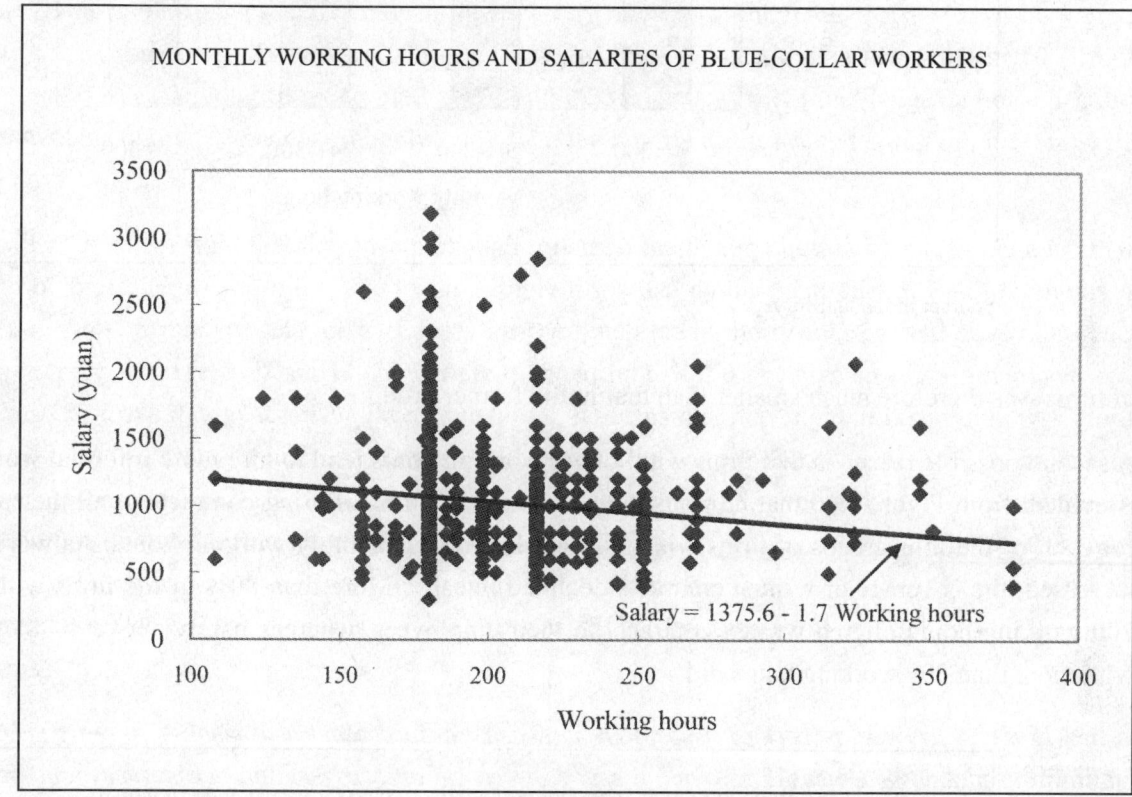

Note: firms with a monthly working hours less than 100 hours or monthly salaries of more than 6,000 yuan are not
        included.
Source: Main survey.

This significant negative correlation between working hours and salaries is caused by the fact that the hourly wage was lower in firms that required more working hours. In Figure 5.15, firms are grouped into four categories according to their monthly working hours. It is clear that firms with shorter monthly working hours offered higher hourly wages. Firms with less than 200 working hours offered a salary that was more than twice as much as that offered by firms with more than 300 working hours. There may be several reasons for this negative correlation between hourly wages and monthly working hours.

One reason is that firms with longer working hours were more labor-intensive than firms with shorter working hours. Among the sample firms, those with monthly working hours of less than 200 had a capital stock (at book value) per worker of 22,000 yuan, whereas those with monthly working hours more than 300 had a per-capita fixed capital stock of 12,700 yuan. The marginal product of labor in the latter group

Figure 5.15

Source: Individual survey.

of firms was therefore much smaller than that in the former group.

A second possible reason is that firms with longer working hours tend to hire more informal workers. This is evident from Figure 5.16 that presents the percentage of firms offering contracts to all their employees for each of the four groups of firms with different lengths of monthly working hours. As working hours increased, the coverage of written contracts declined linearly. More than 80% of the firms with less than 200 working hours offered written contracts to their employees, whereas barely above 40% of the firms with more than 300 working hours did so.

Figure 5.16

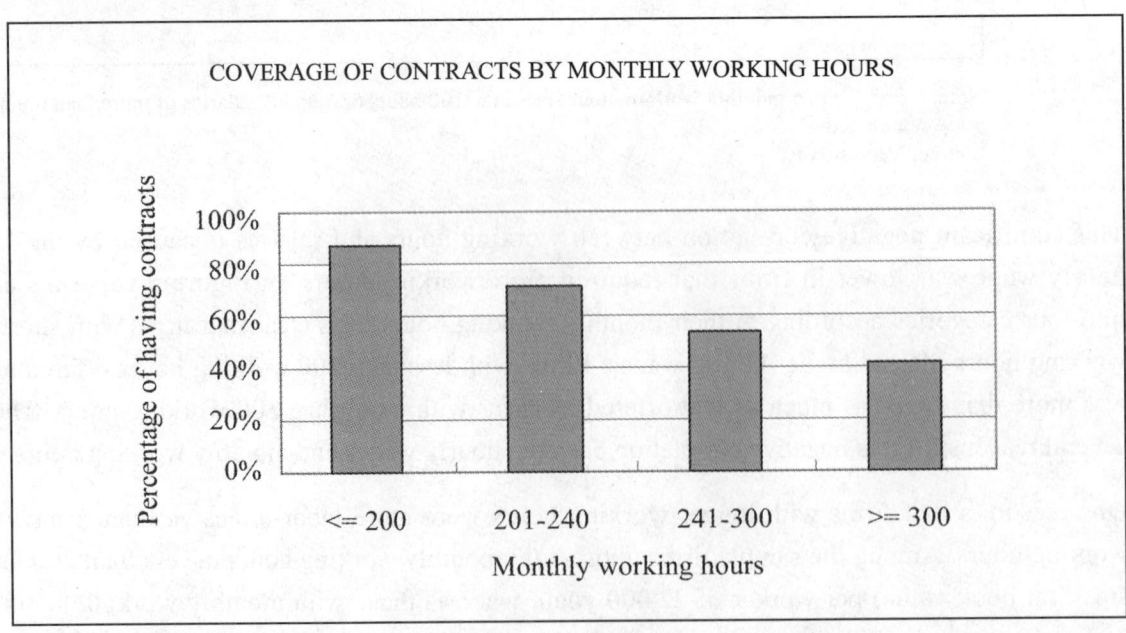

Source: Individual survey.

A third reason is that workers in firms with more working hours were more likely to have less education than workers in firms with less working hours. There could be a self-selection process by which people with less education chose to work in firms that demanded longer working hours because they might want to compensate for their low ability by longer working hours. The main survey did not have detailed data on workers' education. One proxy for it is the share of migrant workers because most migrant workers have low educational attainments. In this regard, the difference between the group of firms with the shortest monthly working hours and the group of firms with the longest working hours was evident. While 60% of the firms in the first group had less than 20% migrant workers and less than 5% of them had more than 80% of migrant workers, only 42% of the firms in the second group of firms had less than 20% of migrant workers, but 21% of them had more than 80% of migrant workers.

It is tempting to believe that it was domestic private firms that tended to have longer working hours and pay smaller hourly salaries. Figure 5.17 shows this is not entirely true, especially among firms with very long working hours. The figure compares the share of each type of firm in the whole sample, in the group of firms with more than 200 monthly working hours, and in the group of firms with more than 300 monthly working hours. SOEs had a smaller presence in both groups of firms than in the whole sample. Domestic private firms had a larger presence in the group with more than 200 working hours, but had a smaller presence in the group with more than 300 working hours. In contrast, HMT and foreign-invested firms had a larger presence in the group with more than 300 working hours than in the whole sample. Because there were only 19 firms with more than 300 working hours, this contrast may not be statistically significant. However, it is clear from Figure 5.17 that domestic private firms were not particularly worse than HMT and foreign-invested firms in demanding longer working hours.

To have a fuller understanding of the determinants of hourly wages, we run a multivariate regression on the logarithm of blue-collar worker hourly wages using several sets of explanatory variables. The first set of variables includes the number of workers (in logarithm term), per-worker capital stock (book value, in logarithm terms), per-worker sales (in logarithm terms), and the share of migrant workers. These

Figure 5. 17

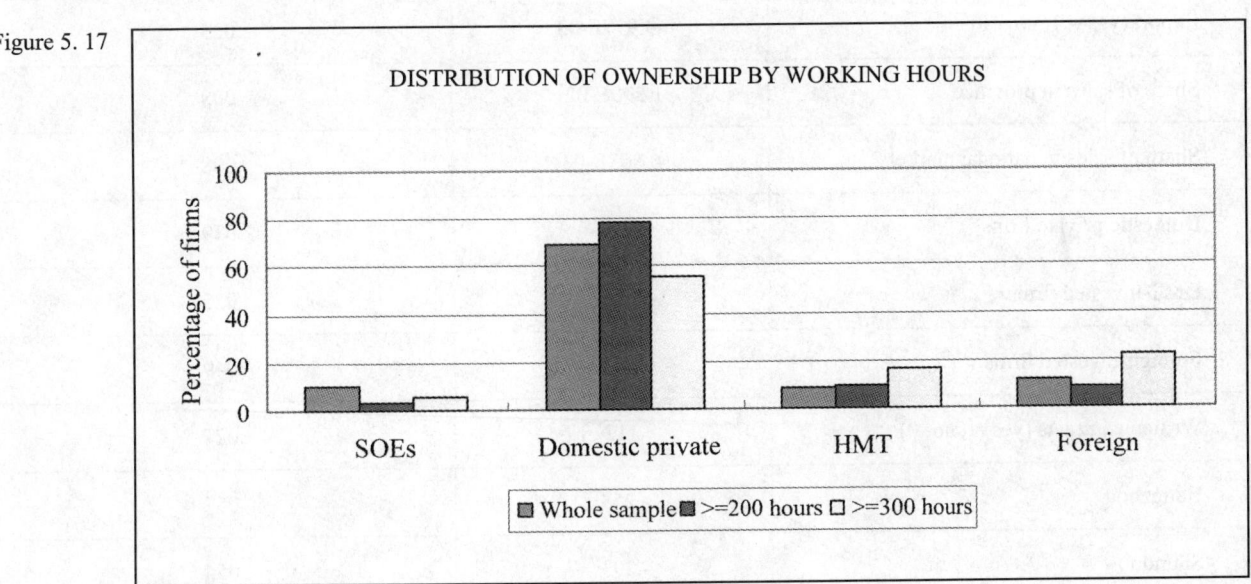

Source: Individual survey.

four variables control the efficiency of labor in a firm. The share of migrant workers is not a continuous variable. In the questionnaire, firms were given five choices for the share of migrant workers: less than 20%, 20-40%, 40-60%, 60-80%, and 80-100%. We number those choices by numbers from 1 to 5, which the variable share of migrant workers takes as values. The second set of variables controls a firm s access to markets and its market power. It includes a dummy variable indicating whether a firm exports, share of sales in the provincial market, and share of sales in the national market. The last two variables are not continuous variables; rather, they take one of the following six values that indicate different ranges of shares: 1 = 0-1%, 2 = 1-3%, 3 = 3-5%, 4 = 5-10%, 5 = 10%-20%, 6 = higher than 10%. The third set of variables controls firm ownership. Using SOEs as the reference group, this set includes three dummy variables indicating, respectively, domestic private firms, HMT-invested firms, and foreign-invested firms. The fourth set of variables consists of only dummy variable indicating whether a firm had signed written contracts with all its workers. The last set of variables is comprised of 11 dummy variables for the sample cities other than Beijing (which is used as the reference). They are meant to capture regional differences in living costs and possible labor market segmentation.

Table 5.1

REGRESSION RESULTS FOR HOURLY WAGES (DEPENDENT VARIABLE: LOGARITHM OF HOURLY WAGES)

Variable	Coefficient	Std. Err.
Constant	1.132***	.108
LN(size)	6.039E-02***	.010
LN(per-worker capital)	5.193E-02***	.011
LN(per-worker sales)	5.689E-02***	.014
Share of migrant workers	-1.534E-03	.010
Export (yes = 1, no = 0)	-9.977E-03	.025
Share of sales in province	1.590E-02*	.008
Share of sales in national market	6.863E-03	.008
Domestic private firms	-.225***	.039
HMT-invested firms	-.183***	.055
Foreign-invested firms	-.151***	.049
Written contracts (yes=1, no=0)	.112***	.027
Hangzhou	-.253***	.057
Shunde	-.293***	.054

Variable	Coefficient	Std. Err.
Wujiang	-.303***	.060
Changchun	-.411***	.062
Dandong	-.556***	.054
Shijiazhuang	-.608***	.055
Zibo	-.467***	.051
Jining	-.493***	.059
Chongqing	-.332***	.054
Shiyan	-.483***	.057
Xi'an	-.458***	.057
Number of cases: 936 R²: 0.391		

Source: Main survey.

The regression is not meant to find out the causality between the explanatory variables and hourly wages. Rather, it is a way to determine the partial correlation between various factors and the wage rate. The results are presented in Table 5.1. The three variables for labor efficiency are all strongly significant. A one percent increase of the labor force increases a firm's average salary for blue-collar workers by 6%, and a one percent increase in its per-worker capital stock and per-worker sales does that by 5.2% and 5.7%, respectively. Exporting does not affect the wage rate, nor does the share of sales in the national market. However, the share of sales in the provincial market does, which means that having market power in the local market brings some benefits to workers. The three kinds of non-state firms all pay their workers significantly less than the SOEs do. The gaps are substantial: domestic private firms pay 22.5% less, HMT-invested firms 18.3%, and foreign-invested firms 15.1%. The order of these figures is consistent with casual observation. The better performance of the SOEs may be caused by their receiving preferential treatment from the government (e.g., low cost bank finance). But it may also be a result of greater concern for protecting workers' rights among SOEs. That is, SOEs may treat their employees with greater formality. Formality protects workers; this is evident from the estimate of the proportion having contracts. If a firm signs contracts with all its employees, its blue-collar workers on average earn 11.2% more than their counterparts in a firm that does not do so. Lastly, there are significant wage gaps between the sample cities. All the 11 cities included in the regression pay less than Beijing. The gap ranges from 25.3% in Hangzhou to 60.8% in Shijiazhuang. The coastal cities pay higher wages than the inland cities, but the difference between the central and western cities is not large.

In summary, the regression finds that worker salaries are positively correlated with firm s size, labor productivity, local market power, and coverage of written contracts. In addition, SOEs pay significantly

Figure 5.18

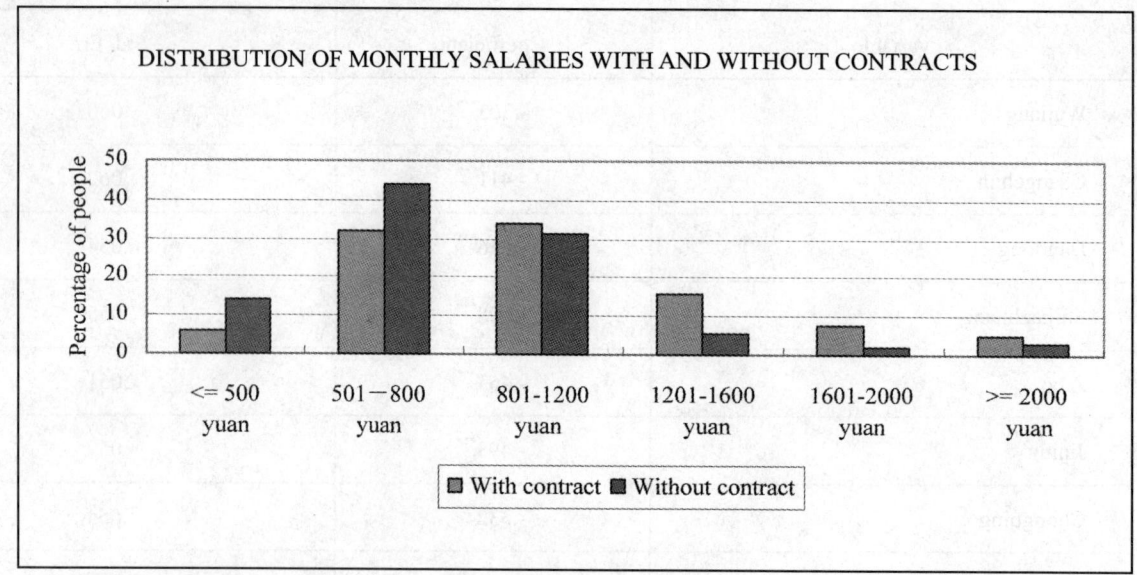

Source: Individual survey.

higher wages than non-state firms do, and coastal cities pay significantly higher wages than inland cities do. The finding that having written contracts increases worker's salaries is particularly encouraging. This finding is also confirmed by the individual survey. Figure 5.18 compares the distribution of monthly salaries for correspondents with or without contracts. It is evident that the distribution of those with contracts indicates that they tend to be higher than for those without contracts. The mode of those with contracts was between 801 and 1200 yuan whereas the mode of those without contracts was between 501 and 800 yuan. In addition, there were a higher percentage of workers with contracts than those without in each of the salary categories higher than 800 yuan.

However, caution is needed when the above conclusion is used to infer policy recommendations. The positive correlation between written contracts and higher wages could be a result of self-selection by firms, that is, they offered written contracts to their workers because they had also decided to offer higher wages to them. In other words, written contracts and higher wages might be simultaneously determined by other factors that are not controlled for in the regression analysis. However, the five sets of explanatory variables cover a fairly large range of concerns and the factors left in the residual term are unlikely to possess high degrees of significance. Even if simultaneity does exist, requiring firms to offer written contracts can still secure higher wages for their employees because the contracts make it harder for firms to evade wage payments. In addition, requiring firms to offer written contracts is likely to raise their awareness of the need to compensate their employees in a proper way. The individual survey offers support for these claims in studying wage arrears, a topic that the next sub-section deals with.

Wage Arrears

Among the firms in the main survey, 15% reported that they had not paid their workers on time at one time or another. Among these firms, the average amount of accumulated wage arrears at the end of 2005 was 600,000 yuan, and the maximum amount was 29.63 million yuan. For comparison, the questionnaire asked the sample firms to give an estimate of wage arrears in other firms in the same industry in the same city. In answering this question, 3.3% of the sample firms said that wage arrears were common in their own industry, 25% said that wage arrears happened occasionally, and the rest said that wage arrears were rare. Adding the shares of the first two answers together, it is apparent that the sample firms reported a higher incidence of wage arrears in other firms than in their own. It is noteworthy that there were no significant differences between the answers provided by firms of different types of ownership. The individual survey found similar results. Twenty-six percent of the correspondents occasionally experienced delays in getting their salaries. The percentage of people experiencing frequent delays was 7%, higher than that reported by the sample firms. Among the one third of respondents having experienced delays, 56% said that the delay was within a month, 31% between one month to three months, and 13% above three months. Among this last group of people, most people eventually got their salaries. Only a small fraction, 3% of the people having experienced delays, said that they did not eventually get their salaries.

Consistent with the national statistics, wage arrears were most common in the construction sector. Fifty-six percent of the correspondents working in this sector experienced wage arrears. The differences among the other sectors were small. Also consistent with the national statistics, migrant workers were more likely to experience wage arrears. While 26% of local workers had wage arrears, the figure for migrant workers was 41%.

Signing a contract helped workers get their salaries on time. Figure 5.19 compares people with and without contracts in terms of the frequency of wage arrears. Overall, the probability of people with a contract to get their salaries on time was higher than that of people without a contract by ten percentage points. The major gap happened with people that experienced frequent delays or did not eventually get their salaries. The percentage for this group of people among workers with a contract was only 3%, but the corresponding figure among workers without a contract was 10.6%. These results provide support to the regression result that signing a contract leads to higher wage payments.

5. 3   Pensions, Medical Insurance, and Workplace Amenities

As shown in the last chapter, the coverage of pension and medical insurance has been increasing slowly nationwide in recent years. The individual survey found that there were only 27.6% of the correspondents

Figure 5.19

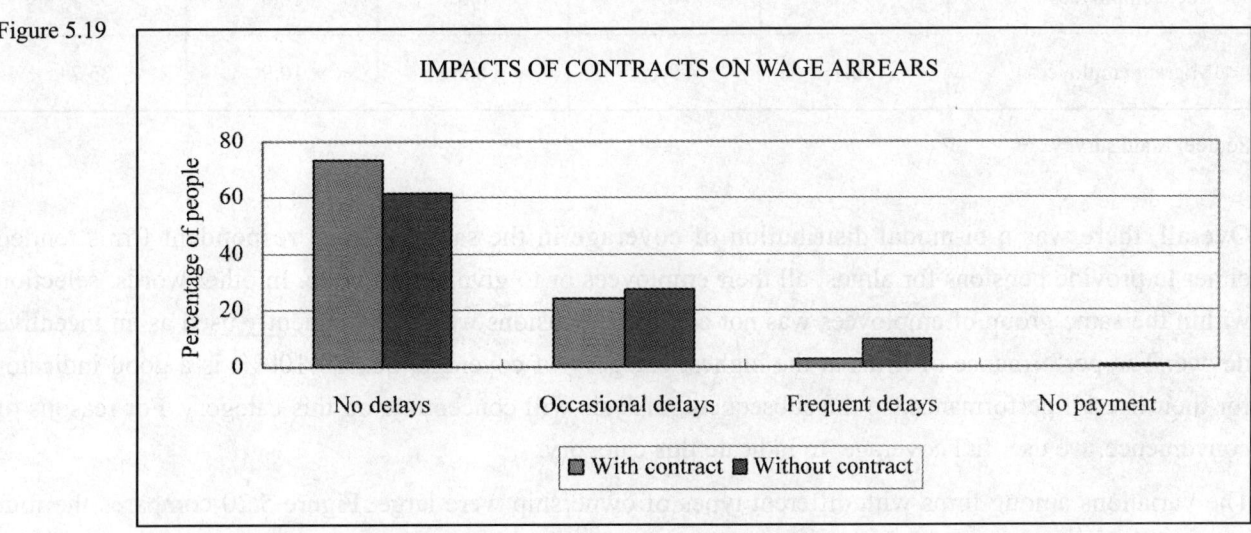

Source: Individual survey.

who had at least one kind of social security insurance. The coverage in the sample firms was also not optimistic. This section presents data for the coverage of pension and medical insurance in the sample firms and analyzes their determinants. It will also deal with workplace safety and amenities in the sample firms. Data from the individual survey will be used to supplement the analysis.

Pensions

In the main survey the respondents were asked to choose an estimation of their pension coverage from five categories: 0-20%, 20-40%, 40-60%, 60-80%, and 80-100%. Table 5.2 presents the results by the type of firm. The best coverage was for white-collar employees, but still only 60.3% of the firms gave their white-collar employees a coverage of 80-100%. The corresponding figure for blue-collar employees was only 47.3%. Local employees fared much better than migrant employees with their gap being 17 percentage points for the highest level of coverage of 80-100%. These figures, however, seem to be higher than what's obtained from the individual survey. For example, only 12% of the migrant workers in the individual survey said that they had at least one kind of insurance, whereas in the main survey, 36.7% of the sample firms said that they provided a pension for most of their migrant employees. Although these two figures are not directly comparable, the large gap between them is still indicative of the possible biases in firms' reports in the main survey. Nevertheless, the structure of the reports may still be meaningful as there were no specific reasons for thinking that a certain type of firm was inclined to give a certain report.

Table 5.2

PENSION COVERAGE IN SAMPLE FIRMS (%)

Coverage / Type of workers	0-20%	20-40%	40-60%	60-80%	80-100%
White-collar employees	17.3	7.0	5.8	9.6	60.3
Blue-collar employees	21.6	9.2	10.8	11.1	47.3
Local employees	19.3	8.4	8.6	10.0	53.7
Migrant employees	36.4	9.1	6.9	10.9	36.7

Source: Main survey.

Overall, there was a bi-modal distribution of coverage in the sample firms: respondent firms tended either to provide pensions for almost all their employees or to give almost none. In other words, selection within the same group of employees was not common; pensions were not frequently used as an incentive device. The performance of firms at the highest category of coverage, i.e., 80-100%, is a good indicator for their overall performance, so the subsequent analysis will concentrate on this category. For reasons of convenience, we use full coverage to indicate this category.

The variations among firms with different types of ownership were large. Figure 5.20 compares the four types of firms in terms of the percentage of firms that offered full coverage for white-collar and blue-collar employees. The ranks for both types of employees were the same: SOEs performed the best, foreign-invested firms were next followed HMT-invested and domestic private firms. The gaps between SOEs and the three other types of firms were large. SOEs surpassed foreign and HMT-invest firms by 15 percentage points, and domestic private firms by 40 percentage points for white-collar workers. The gap between white-collar and blue-collar workers was about the same for each type of firm.

Figure 5.21 further compares the four types of firms in terms of their treatment to local and migrant workers. Again, SOEs performed the best for both local and migrant workers. The figure orders the four types of firms by their treatment to local workers. In this case, HMT-invested firms were ranked before

Figure 5.20

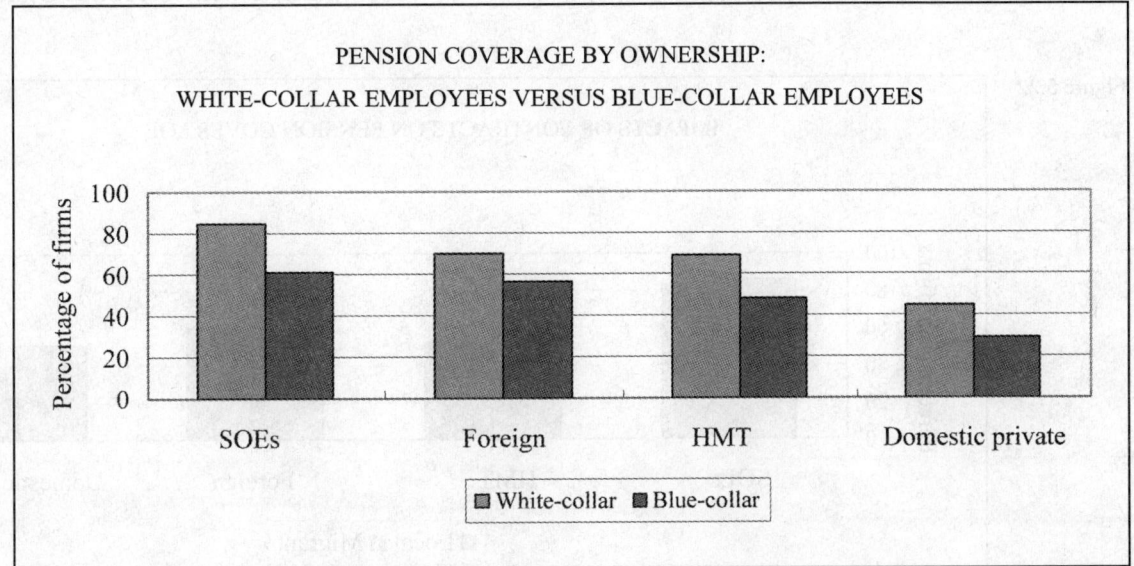

Note: The measure is the percentage of firms that offered full coverage to the specified types of employees.
Source: Main survey.

Figure 5.21

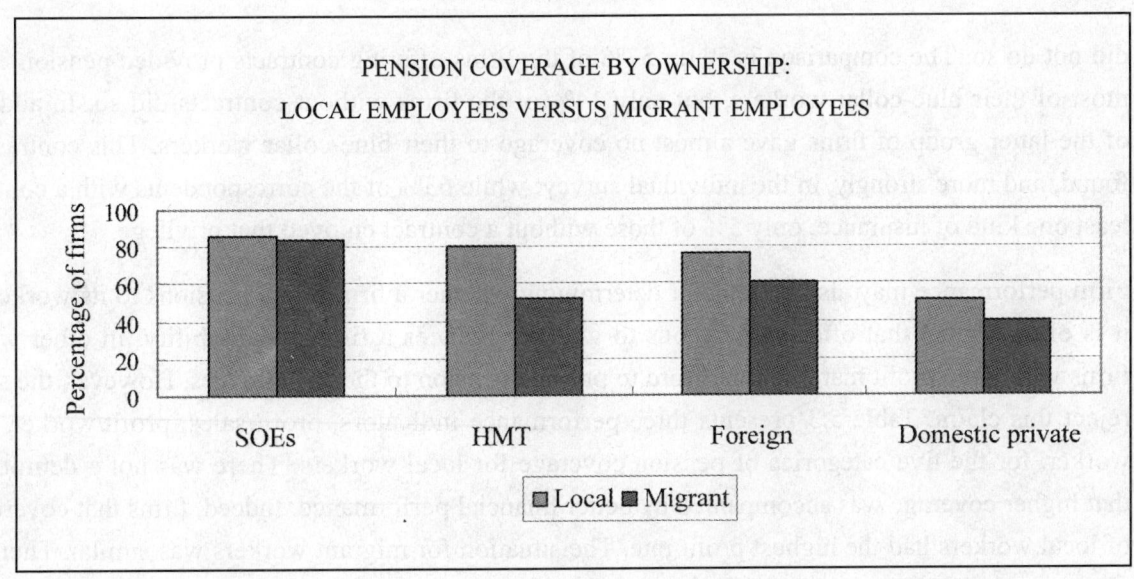

Note: The measure is the percentage of firms that offered full coverage to the specified types of employees.
Source: Main survey.

foreign-invested firms. However, foreign-invested firms treated migrant workers better than HMT-invested firms. Domestic private firms again performed the worst. Another major difference between SOEs and the other types of firm was that SOEs treated local and migrant workers almost the same while the three other types of firm all treated local workers better than migrant workers.

Firm size was another factor determining coverage. Eighty percent of large firms offered full coverage to local workers, and 63% of them offered full coverage to migrant workers. The corresponding figures for median firms were 70% and 53%, and those for small firms were only 44% and 30%.

Written contracts played a significant role in determining whether a firm offered pension coverage to its workers. Figure 5.22 compares firms offering most of blue-collar workers written contracts and those that

Figure 5.22

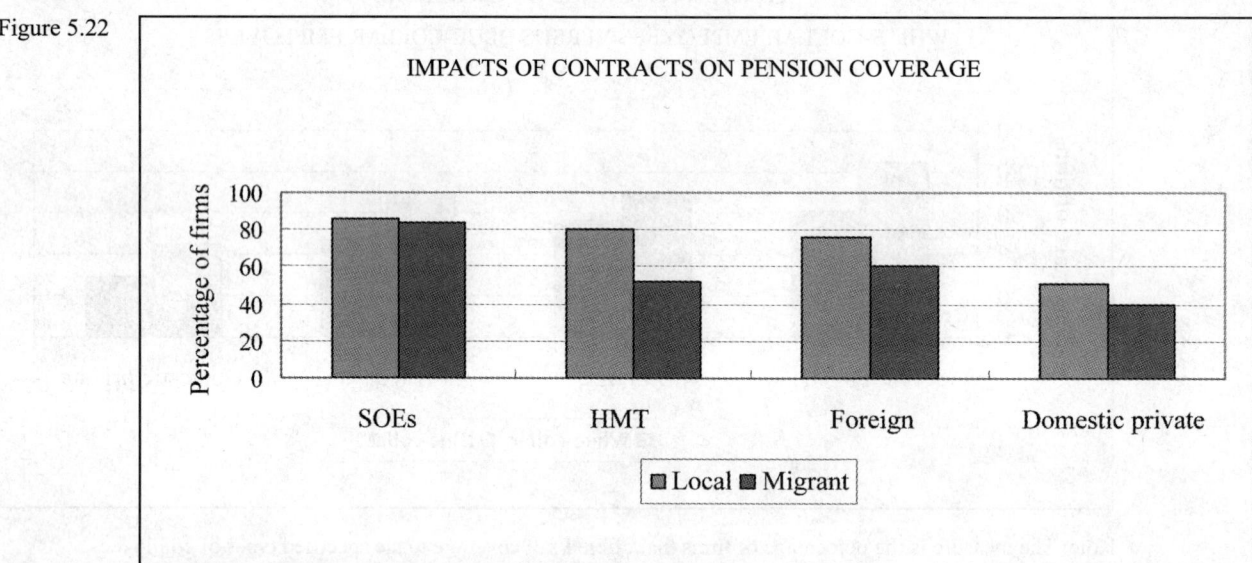

Source: Main survey.

did not do so. The comparison is stark: 57% of the firms offering contracts provided pension coverage to most of their blue-collar workers, but only 14% of the firms without contracts did so. In addition, 43% of the latter group of firms gave almost no coverage to their blue-collar workers. This contrast was also found, and more strongly, in the individual survey: while 63% of the correspondents with a contract had at least one kind of insurance, only 5% of those without a contract enjoyed that privilege.

Firm performance may also be a factor determining whether a firm offers pensions to its workers. Indeed, it is often argued that offering pensions to workers reduces a firm s profitability; in other words, only firms with large profit margins can afford to provide pension to their employees. However, the survey data reject this claim. Table 5.3 presents three performance indicators, profit/sales, profit/worker, and sales/worker, for the five categories of pension coverage for local workers. There was not a definitive pattern that higher coverage was accompanied by better financial performance. Indeed, firms that covered 60-80% of local workers had the highest profit rate. The situation for migrant workers was similar. Therefore, firm performance is not a significant factor determining a firm's pension coverage. The much better pension coverage within SOEs also lends a strong support to this claim because SOEs had low profit margins.

Table 5. 3

FINANCIAL PERFORMANCE OF FIRMS WITH DIFFERENT DEGREES OF PENSION COVERAGE FOR LOCAL WORKERS

Coverage	Profit/sales	Profit/worker (1,000 yuan)	Sales/worker (1,000 yuan)
< 20%	3.82%	2.127	44.001
20-40%	3.71%	1.731	37.309
40-60%	5.64%	2.383	49.880
60-80%	5.79%	2.492	48.106
80-100%	0.04%	2.392	49.560

Source: Main survey.

Variations among the sample cities were large, though. Figure 5.23 ranks the 12 cities by the percentage of firms offering full coverage to their local employees and it also presents the percentage of firms offering full coverage to their migrant employees. The cities can be divided into two groups. Beijing, Shiyan, Hangzhou, Shunde, Xi'an, and Changchun were in the first group. More than 60% of firms in this group offered full coverage to local workers, and more than 40% offered the same to migrant workers. Wujiang, Chongqing, Dandong, Jining, Zibo, and Shijiazhuang were in the second group. In Jining, barely 20% of its firms offered full coverage even to local workers. Less than 60% of their firms offered full coverage to local workers, and less than 40% of their firms offered the same coverage to migrant workers. It is noteworthy that Beijing had the most unequal treatment between local and migrant workers. The gap between those two types of workers was almost 30 percentage points. In contrast, Changchun had the smallest gap. However, as argued in Chapter 3, paying for pensions may not be in the interest of migrant workers. So a larger gap between local and migrant workers may not be interpreted as discrimination against migrant workers.

The ranking of cities in Figure 5.23 cannot be explained by firm ownership because for one thing, Shunde barely had any SOEs and for another, Shijiazhuang had a fair number of SOEs (Table 2.5). Exporting seems not to be a reason either because Shunde and Wujiang both export a lot but the gap between them was about 20 percentage points. Regional differences also cannot be a reason because two western cities, Shiyan and Xi'an, were ranked very high. Firm size could be a reason. While firms in Beijing were relatively small (with an average size of 405 workers in 2005), firms in Shiyan, Shunde, Xi'an, and Hangzhou were relatively large, with their average size being, respectively, 969, 1383, 1260, and 740 workers in 2005. On the other hand, the average size in Zibo, Dandong, Shijiazhuang, and Jining was only 632, 316, 616, and 250 workers, respectively. However, even size cannot fully explain the regional variations. Beijing is a case in point. Different degrees of government enforcement must have played a role.

The main survey did not provide information on pension coverage outside the enterprise. The city

Figure 5.23

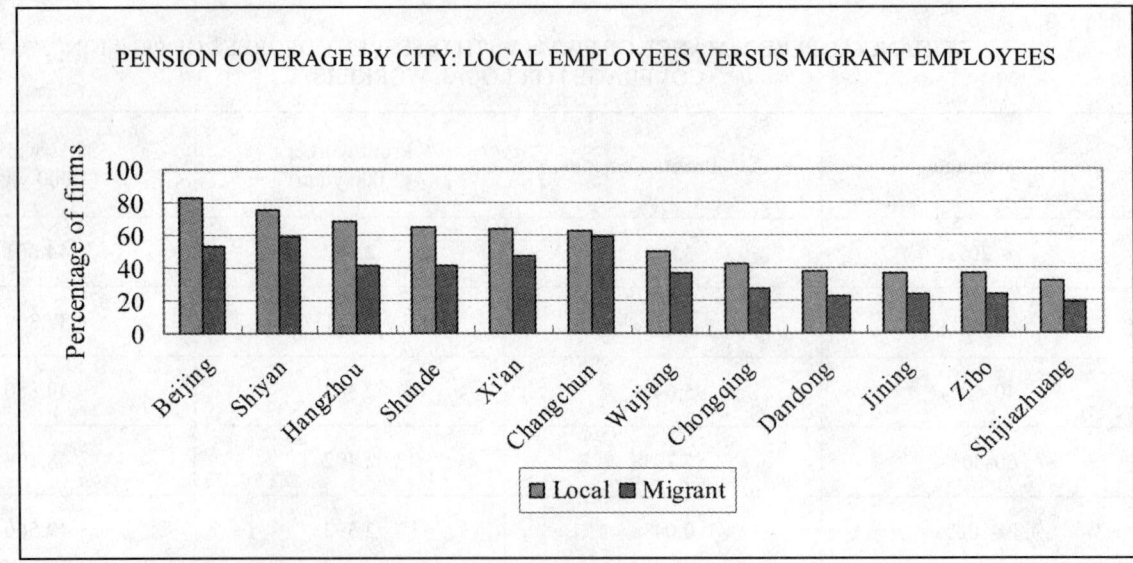

PENSION COVERAGE BY CITY: LOCAL EMPLOYEES VERSUS MIGRANT EMPLOYEES

Note: The measure is the percentage of firms that offered full coverage to the specific types of employees.
Source: Main survey.

survey obtained data for the city-wide coverage. It is quite possible that the coverage within the formal establishment of the enterprise and the coverage outside it are very different. The share of employment in the formal establishment and the government s efforts in expanding the coverage in the informal sector are the two most important factors in determining the gap. Table 5.4 lists the coverage for each sample city in each year in the period 2001-2005. There are two features that are worth discussion.

Table 5. 4

CITY-WIDE PENSION COVERAGE IN THE SAMPLE CITIES (%)

City	2001	2002	2003	2004	2005	Increase of 2005 over 2001
Beijing	37.9	38.4	39.0	39.6	44.0	6.1
Hangzhou	15.6	25.8	29.7	32.1	35.5	18.9
Wujiang	30.4	33.4	35.4	43.4	49.8	19.4
Shunde	36.9	37.9	38.3	40.0	41.3	5.4
Changchun	30.3	29.9	31.1	32.6	33.4	3.1
Dandong	43.8	42.8	44.0	45.4	46.7	2.8
Shijiazhuang	32.2	35.6	29.1	39.0	46.7	15.5
Zibo	11.3	11.7	12.9	13.8	11.8	0.4
Jining	5.4	5.7	5.0	5.2	5.9	-0.4
Chongqing	6.1	6.2	6.0	9.0	9.1	3.0

City	2001	2002	2003	2004	2005	Increase of 2005 over 2001
Shiyan	3.9	5.9	5.0	5.3	5.4	1.5
Xi'an	13.1	13.3	13.4	18.5	18.6	5.5

Note: The coverage is calculated as the percentage of people with pensions in the population with local residency.
Source: City survey.

First, there existed a clear regional pattern in which the coastal and central cities have consistently performed much better than the western cities. All the coastal and central cities had a coverage of more than 30% in 2005, higher than the national average (Figure 3.5). In addition, these cities had also achieved much higher growth rates than the western cities in the period of 2001-2005. The fastest growers were Hangzhou, Wujiang, and Shijiazhuang, which had reached double-digit growth in the whole period. However, Hangzhou had a low start in 2001, so its coverage was still low in 2005 compared with the other cities in the coastal and central regions despite its high growth rate. In the western cities, Jining was the worst performer. It not only had the lowest coverage of merely 5.9% in 2005, but also experienced a decline in the period 2001-2005. Xi'an was the only city that reached double-digit coverage among the western cities.

Second, there were considerable gaps between the city-wide coverage and the coverage revealed by the firm survey. Because Figure 5.23 only shows the percentage of firms that provided full coverage to its employees, direct comparison of this figure and the numbers in Table 5.4 is impossible. However, the comparison of the ranking of the cities can still be meaningful. In this regard, two groups of cities are of particular interest for analysis. One group includes the cities where the city-wide coverage was much higher than the within-firm coverage, and the other group includes the cities where the opposite was true. Dandong and Shijiazhuang belonged to the first group. In theory, within-firm coverage should be higher than city-wide coverage unless the coverage for the informal sector is higher than for the formal sector. One explanation for the abnormal records of Dandong and Shijiazhuang is that the sample in each of these two cities overdrew firms with small coverage. However, the sample firms of these two cities were not particularly small, nor did they have a particularly higher percentage of domestic private firms. We will then leave them as two outliers in the sample. For the second group, while it is natural to find that the within-firm coverage is higher than the city-wide coverage, the gap was particularly high in Shiyan and Xi'an. This shows that the formal sector had a much higher rate of coverage than the informal sector in these two cities.

Medical Insurance

The coverage of medical insurance exhibited the same pattern of bi-modal distribution as that for pensions although it was lower than the latter for all types of workers (Table 5.5). In addition, white-collar workers were preferred to blue-collar workers, and local workers were preferred to migrant workers. SOEs again outperformed the other types of firms by wide margins. For example, 85% of SOEs gave all white-collar workers medical insurance, and 76% gave all blue-workers medical insurance, whereas the corresponding figures for domestic private firms, HMT-invested firms, and foreign-invested firms were, respectively, 42% and 33%, 72% and 51%, and 67% and 58%. Again, the better performance of SOEs was not a result of their having larger profit margins. Also consistent with the case of pensions, larger firms and firms offering contracts were more likely to offer medical insurance to their employees. For example, 11% of the firms without contracts offered medical insurance to most of their blue-collar workers, but 50% of the firms with contracts did so.

Table 5.5

MEDICAL INSURANCE COVERAGE IN SAMPLE FIRMS (%)

Coverage / Type of workers	0-20%	20-40%	40-60%	60-80%	80-100%
White-collar employees	29.6	5.3	5.8	8.0	52.3
Blue-collar employees	36.9	6.3	7.2	8.1	41.4
Local employees	30.0	5.7	6.6	8.1	49.6
Migrant employees	45.3	7.7	5.0	8.2	35.8

Source: Main survey.

Figure 5.24

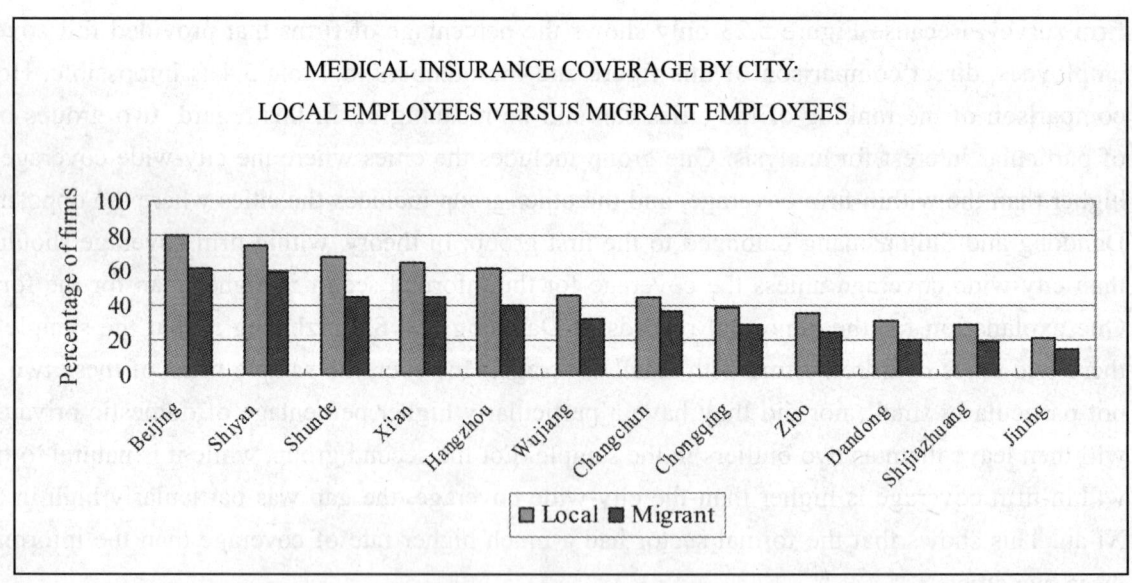

Source: Main survey.

The pattern of regional variations in medical insurance coverage was about the same as that in pension coverage (Figure 5.24). There was only one interchange between the two groups of cities: Changchun dropped from the first group to the second group, and Wujiang moved up to the first group. While pensions may not bring immediate benefits to migrant workers, medical insurance does. It is encouraging to find that the gap between local and migrant workers was smaller for medical insurance than for pension. For example, it dropped to 20 percentage points in Beijing. On the other hand, it is depressing to find that less than 30% of firms in Chongqing, Zibo, Dandong, Shijiazhuang, and Jining offered full coverage to both their local and migrant workers. In the worst case of Jining, barely 20% of the firms did so, and 64% of the firms offered medical insurance to less than 20% of their local employees.

Table 5.6

CITY-WIDE MEDICAL INSURANCE COVERAGE IN THE SAMPLE CITIES (%)

City	2001	2002	2003	2004	2005	Increase of 2005 over 2001
Beijing	19.3	33.7	38.0	41.6	48.7	29.4
Hangzhou	n.a.	21.9	25.2	26.4	28.4	6.5*
Wujiang	7.3	15.1	19.4	26.8	37.3	30.0
Shunde	41.5	43.3	45.6	46.1	48.1	6.7
Changchun	10.2	15.5	20.7	27.8	28.7	18.5
Dandong	18.8	39.5	40.6	46.1	50.5	31.8
Shijiazhuang	n.a.	25.7	26.8	32.7	43.0	18.4*
Zibo	6.4	8.7	10.1	12.6	15.4	9.0
Jining	3.3	4.0	5.7	5.6	6.1	2.8
Chongqing	1.6	2.0	3.9	6.6	7.5	5.9
Shiyan	5.5	6.9	7.3	8.0	8.7	3.2
Xi'an	13.2	16.3	17.2	18.0	19.5	6.3

Note: The coverage is calculated as the percentage of people with health insurance in the population with local residency.
* The increase is for 2005 over 2002.
Source: City survey.

As in the case of pensions, Table 5.6 presents the city-wide coverage of medical insurance in the sample cities. There are several kinds of medical insurance. The figures in Table 5.6 are for the basic medical insurance (corresponding to the new health care plan in Table 4.1. The situation was about the same as that for pension coverage. The coastal and central cities were much better than the western cities. Dandong and Shijiazhuang were still two outliers that had higher city-wide coverage than within-firm coverage. In addition, Xi'an was still the only city in the western region that reached double-digit coverage.

Compared with regular medical insurance, more firms offered accident insurance to their employees. For example, 63% of the sample firms offered most of their white-collar workers accident insurance, and 61% of them offered most of their blue-collar workers the same. It may be more relevant for migrant workers than for local workers to have accident insurance because they are usually less skillful than local workers. Fifty-five percent of firms offered most of their migrant workers accident insurance, nine percentage points lower than for local workers. This gap was much smaller than in the case of pensions and regular medical insurance where a gap of 17 percentage points and 15 percentage points was found, respectively. The better record of accident insurance might be a result of two causes. One is that accident insurance has been made mandatory in many cities and its premium is low (less than 2% of the payroll). The other is that accidents have immediate physical and mental consequences for the victims, which may increase firms' incentive to pay for insurance.

It is said that the low coverage of social security is a result of the workers low awareness. In analyzing this issue, one needs to be careful in distinguishing between wishes and reality. The vast majority of workers want social security: overall, 85% of respondents in the individual survey believed that they needed social security. Only 12% said that they did not need it or were indifferent about it (the rest 3% said they did not know the answer). The difference between migrant and local workers was small: while 88% of the local workers said that they needed social security, 81% of the migrant workers said the same. However, when asked why they did not have social security, the respondents gave mixed answers (Table 5.7). There is one reason, "I requested, but the firm did not want to", that indicates firms' clear rejection of social security to workers. Twenty-three percent of the respondents gave this reason. Another reason was "the firm did not mention it and I did not ask" is a mixture of the employer's rejection and worker reluctance. About half of the correspondents mentioned this reason. Two reasons given show that worker compromised with reality. One is that "current income is low and social security can be postponed", and the other is that "I prefer higher wages than having social security". Thirty-eight and seventeen percent of the correspondents mentioned these two reasons, respectively. These figures support the argument that the low coverage of social security is caused by firms' low willingness and workers' compromises with the reality. The problem, however, is whether the workers do get more current income by sacrificing social security. It is also noteworthy that 17.3% of the correspondents believed that low portability was a cause for their not having social security. People giving this answer were those informed ones who more or less understood the government s social security policy. As suggested in the previous chapter, improving the portability of social security will indeed increase workers willingness to have social security.

Table 5. 7

CAUSES FOR NOT HAVING SOCIAL SECURITY (MULTIPLE CHOICES ARE ALLOWED)

Cause	% of answers
I requested, but the firm did not want to	22.9
The firm did not mention and I did not ask	48.2
Current income is low and social security can be postponed	37.8
I prefer higher wages than having social security	16.9
Social security is not portable	17.3
Social security provides limited benefits	5.6
I did not know much about social security	9.2
I was in the probation period	7.2
Other causes	5.6

Source: Individual survey.

Workplace Safety and Amenities

Safety facilities and training are the two most important factors for workplace safety. Almost all the sample firms in the main survey reported that they provided safety training to workers before they started working. However, the individual survey found that 40% of the correspondents said that they did not receive adequate pre-work safety training. In addition, 20% of them said that there were no safety facilities in their factories, and 38% said that safety facilities were inadequate.

Forty-five percent of the sample firms reported that there was at least one work-related accident in 2005. The average number of accidents in those firms was 4, and the maximum was 256.[2] The city survey obtained the number of work-related accidents in each city. However, the quality of information varied from city to city. Chongqing, Zibo, and Xi'an reported 2,117, 4,861, and 7,621 accidents in 2005, but Wujiang, Shunde, and Dandong only reported 7, 17, and 42 accidents. Unless the first group of cities did not exaggerate their figures (which is probably true), then the reports of the second group of cities must be biased downward.

Most firms, 85% of them, said that there were enough toilets in the factory, but the rest 15% believed that there should be more. However, only 21% of the sample firms had a clinic and only 5.7% of them had a daycare center. Most firms gave one or two hours for the lunch break. Forty-four percent gave one hour, and forty-nine percent gave two hours. There were eight firms that did not give any time for lunch, but there were also 87 firms that generously gave three hours. It seems that the length of lunch time was more an issue of custom than that of generosity, though. Although SOEs were the most "generous" by providing an average of 1.74 hours for lunch, domestic private firms also provided an average of 1.51 hours, whereas HMT and foreign-invested firms gave 1.35 and 1.17 hours on average, respectively. When a firm had a short time for lunch, it was more likely to provide lunch inside the factory. While 74% of SOEs had employee canteens, 84% of the domestic private firms and HMT-invested firms and 86% of the foreign-invested firms had the same.

Most sample firms provided job-related training for their workers. Eighty-five percent of them had a training plan, and the average number of training sessions was 5.6 a year. However, spending on training was small. Ninety-two percent of the sample firms spent less than 3‰ of their sales revenue on training in 2005. Since the median sales revenue was 50 million yuan in the sample, this means that at least half of the firms spent less than 150,000 yuan on training in 2005. Among other things, the turnover rate of employees was a significant factor affecting a firm's spending on training. Figure 5.25 presents the average job tenures of white-collar and blue-collar workers for firms of different amounts of training spending. It is evident that the amount of training spending was positively correlated with the average job tenures of both types of workers. Training has a cumulative effect only for individual workers, so a higher turnover rate reduces the benefits accrued to the firm. Therefore, it is natural to find a positive correlation between the average length of job tenure and the amount of spending on training.

---

[2] This figure seems too large. It might be the case that the correspondent of this firm misunderstood the question and put the number of people hurt instead of the number of accidents as the answer.

Figure 5.25

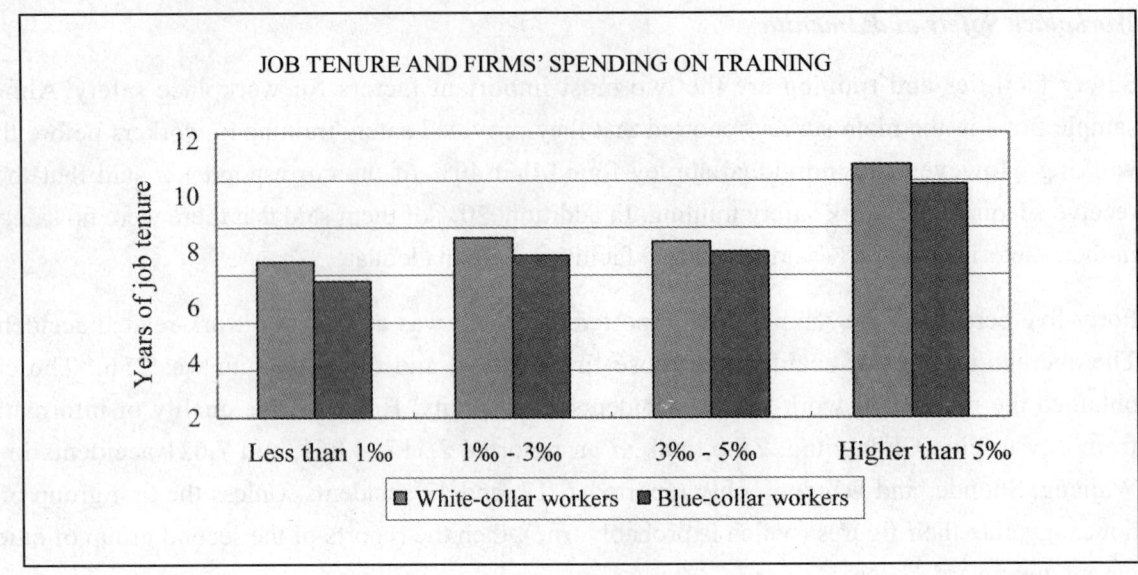

Source: Guo (2006).

5. 4   Labor Disputes and Settlements

Disputes

Before *The Labor Law* came out in 1994, the State Council issued *Regulations for Labor Dispute Settlement* in 1993. In the same year, the Ministry of Labor issued three regulations to establish procedures for labor dispute arbitration. A major feature of the procedure is that each enterprise and each level of the government should set up a labor dispute arbitration committee. These regulations laid the foundation for labor dispute settlement in a new age of market-based employment relations. Figure 5.26 presents the growth of the number of registered labor disputes in China in the period of 1987-2005. It is clear that 1993 and 1994 were turning points for the growth of registered labor disputes received by labor dispute

Figure 5.26

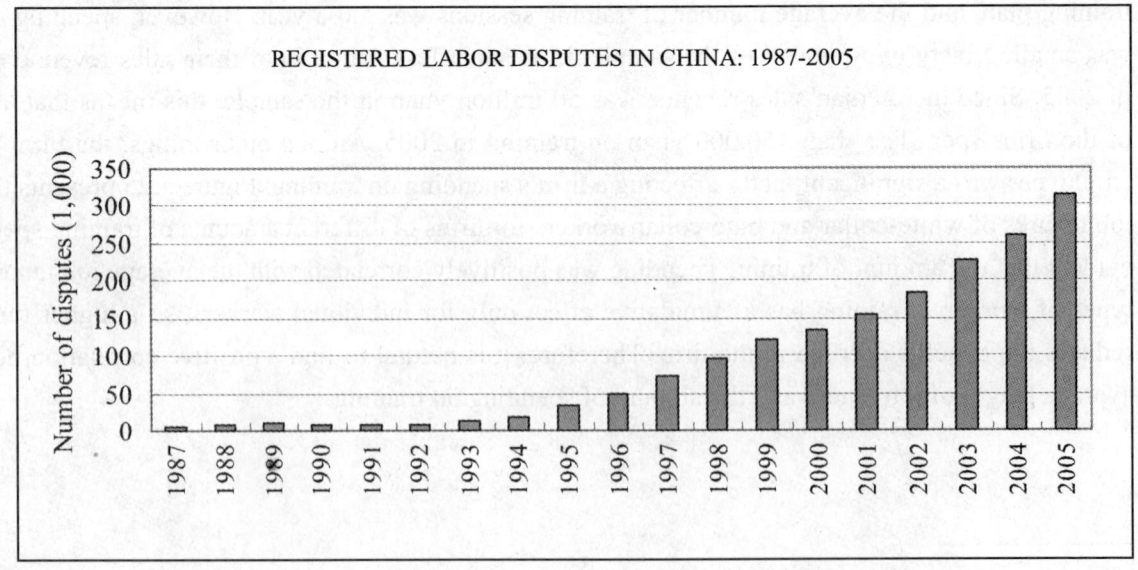

Source: Guo (2006).

arbitration committees at various levels. In 2005, a total of 314,000 labor disputes were registered with and settled by the arbitration committees involving 744,000 people. These figures should be taken as the lower bound of the real number because many disputes do not go through the arbitration committee.

Among the sample firms, 22% had at least one labor-related dispute in the period 2004-2006. The average frequency of disputes in the whole sample was 0.69. This was a very low rate. The individual survey found that 53% of the respondents had at least one dispute with their employer. Although the main survey asked about disputes in the three years prior to the survey and the individual survey asked about any dispute in a worker's work life, the contrast between the above two results still indicates that disputes were under-reported by the sample firms. Under-reporting on the part of firms is understandable for the apparent reason that disputes damage the reputation of a firm. However, another possible reason is a different perception by the firm and the worker over what constitutes a dispute. When a worker thinks that he is underpaid in a month, the firm may believe that the worker has got what he deserves. So the worker may think that there is a dispute, but the firm does not think so.

The individual survey provided information on the types of issue involved in labor disputes. Sixty-two percent of the disputes were about salaries, 31% about working hours, 30% about fringe benefits other than social security, 16% about social security, and 10% about workplace safety.[3] It is apparent that issues related to a worker s immediate work and payment conditions were the most common reasons for disputes. This shows that the most urgent task for labor protection is to monitor working hours and make sure that workers are being properly paid. On the other hand, it also shows that there is still a long way to go in raising worker awareness of other aspects of labor protection, noticeably, social security and workplace safety.

Settlements

In terms of the means for resolving disputes, the main survey gave five alternatives for respondents to choose from: firm management, the labor union, government arbitration agency, other government agencies, and the courts. Firms were allowed to make multiple choices. The percentage of firms that chose each of the above means was 60%, 43%, 40%, 11% and 9%, respectively. The heavy involvement of the firm management might be related to the legal requirement for a dispute to go through the grievance procedure inside the firm before the plaintiff can take it to an external arbitration agency. The large presence of the labor union was a favorable sign that unions were playing an active role in settling labor-related disputes. Because a dispute cannot reach the external arbitration agency or the courts before it goes through the grievance procedure inside the firm, we can infer that about 60% of the disputes (i.e., the sum of the last three figures), were resolved outside the firm by either government agencies or the courts. The actual figure might be smaller because some cases could reach both government agencies and the courts. Between government agencies and the courts, the former were much more often used than the latter. Since going to court is costly and requires specific knowledge, a bigger role for the government labor department, the agency that deals most of the cases, helps lower the barriers faced by the worker. Of course, the drawback is also clear; that is, government agencies may not be as impartial as the court in resolving labor disputes, especially in localities where economic growth is given a paramount priority.

---

[3] Because multiple choices were allowed, the figures do not add up to 100%.

The result of a labor dispute is often not in the worker s favor. The individual survey provided more detailed information on the results of settlements, which were not encouraging. In 29% of the disputes, no conclusion was reached and the worker had to take the status quo. In another 18%, the worker ended up being fired or leaving the firm voluntarily. However, there were also some encouraging signs. For example, satisfactory results were obtained in 31% of the disputes through negotiations within the firm. The percentage of settlements through outside arbitrage agencies or the court was very low, being only 2.6%. These figures were different from those obtained from the main survey. This was not because the main survey included both domestic private firms and other types of firms because even among the domestic private firms in the main survey, 37% used government arbitration agencies and 7% used the courts. The difference might arise because of the different perceptions of disputes held by the firm and the worker. It might be easier for the firm management to remember labor disputes reaching outside arbitrage agencies and the court, whereas the worker remembers all kinds of disputes.

When asked the reasons for not using external arbitration agencies or the courts, the respondents in the individual survey often mentioned high costs and the uncertainty of winning the case. This observation brings us two pieces of information. The first is that the labor department should play a more pro-active role in labor protection. Since the worker is often in a disadvantageous position, it is not a good idea to wait for cases to go through the entire grievance procedure to reach the desk of the enforcement officer. Active inspections and collection of information can significantly improve labor protection. The second piece of information is that the grievance procedure should be made simpler and more transparent to make it easier for the worker to go through. While ordinary means such as the Internet and newspapers are necessary, information dissemination should be more targeted to reach the most vulnerable part of the working class, i.e., the migrant workers. They often do not have access to the Internet; they may not read newspapers either. In this case, door-to-door delivery is needed. For example, the labor department could print small pamphlets introducing the basic concepts of labor rights and the grievance procedure and deliver them directly to the hands of migrant workers.

Government Efforts

Government efforts to protect workers rights have been increasing in the sample cities. Table 5.8 provides the number of labor cases handled by the city labor department in each sample city in each year of the period 2001-2005. Here "handled" means that the labor department finds faults with the role of the employer and rectifies its behavior. The sources of these cases are either departmental inspections or complaints and information provided by employees. The table shows that the growth of cases was high in all the sample cities that provided information except Shijiazhuang (Beijing and Jining did not provide information). Whilst an increase in violations might have contributed to the growth, more government efforts were likely to be the most important factor. This was confirmed by the research team in interviews with the city labor department officials. In recent years, the labor department has become more pro-active in enforcing *The Labor Law* and related government regulations.

Table 5.8

NUMBER OF LABOR CASES HANDLED BY THE GOVERNMENT IN THE SAMPLE CITIES

City	2001	2002	2003	2004	2005	Average annual growth rate (%)
Hangzhou	4,889	5,381	7,617	12,056	12,484	28.4
Wujiang	50	135	138	220	288	65.6
Shunde	145	366	561	535	738	59.8
Changchun	796	860	882	2,015	2,408	39.6
Dandong	831	868	1,061	2,433	1,384	28.2
Shijiazhuang	1,114	894	1,648	1,674	757	2.8
Zibo	850	828	1,111	846	1,893	32.9
Chongqing	1,989	3,454	6,164	9,690	10,860	55.3
Shiyan	61	72	84	95	106	15.8
Xi'an	1,294	3,396	3,182	4,314	3,105	40.9

Note: Beijing and Jining did not provide data. The number for Shijiazhuang number is the sum of cases of violations in wage payments, labor contracts, pension coverage, and medical insurance.

Source: City survey.

About 70% of the violations were over wage payments and labor contracts. The share of wage arrears was between 41% and 47% in the period of 2001-2005, and there was no obvious increasing or declining trend. The share of labor contract violations was between 25% in 2005 and 32% in 2001, that is, there was a weak downward trend. Among other violations, failure to pay pension premiums were the most significant, but its share declined from 22% in 2001 to 9.5% in 2004, and then increased slightly to 12% in 2005. The labor department's strategy of paying attention to labor contracts was well-founded because, as the analysis in this chapter has shown, they play a significantly positive role in protecting worker rights. Clearing up wage arrears has been emphasized by central government as an important element in building a harmonious society, so it is not surprising that the labor department spent a large part of its efforts on it. Figure 5.27 presents the amount of wage arrears cleared up in 2005 in each sample city (Beijing, Chongqing, and Wujiang did not provide data). Xi'an was the champion by clearing up 255 million yuan of wage arrears. Shijiazhuang and Hangzhou did also well by clearing up 102 and 97 million yuan, respectively. In addition, Shunde cleared up 59 million yuan. The amount for other cities was relatively small. However, the ranking in Figure 5.27 may not reflect the efforts spent by the sample cities in 2005. For one thing, the amount of wage arrears cleared up in 2005 might have accumulated in years before 2005, so a better performance in 2005 may be an indicator of a worse performance earlier. The purpose of the figure is simply to provide a sense of the size of cleared wage arrears in the sample.

Figure 5.27

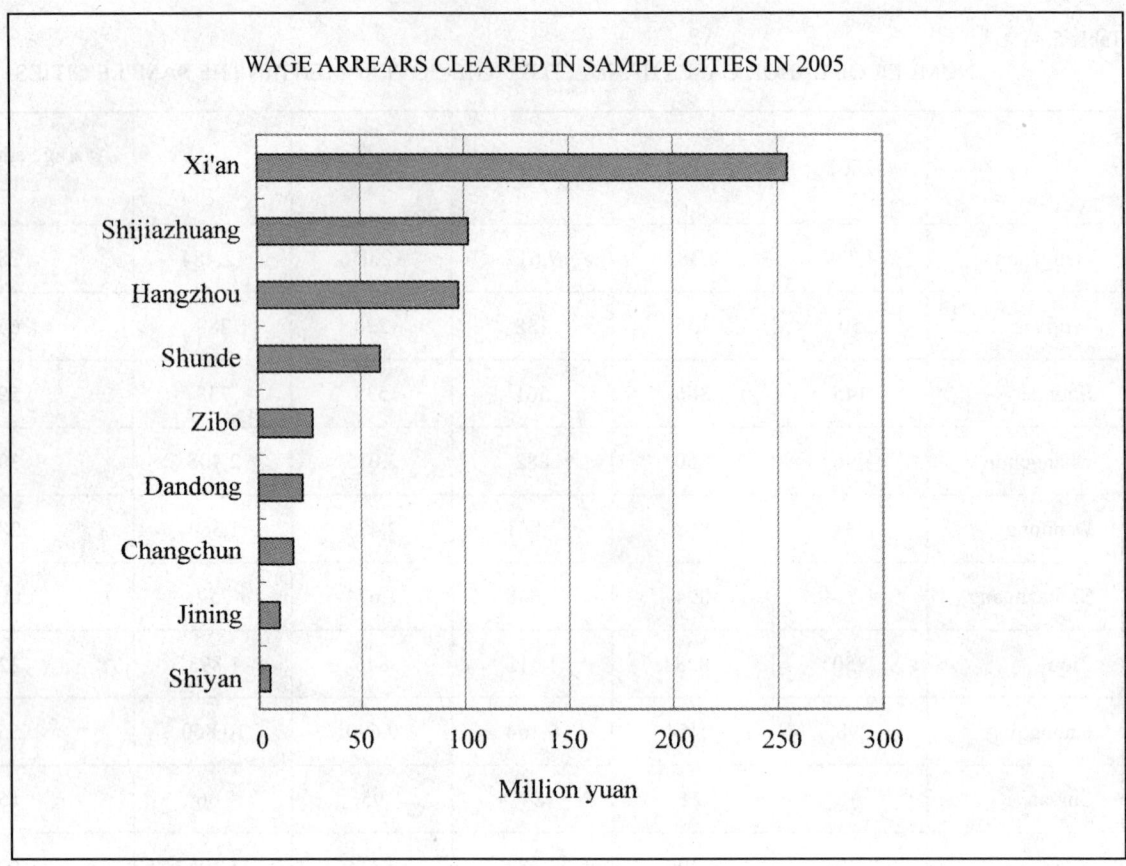

WAGE ARREARS CLEARED IN SAMPLE CITIES IN 2005

Note: Beijing, Chongqing, and Wujiang did not provide data.
Source: City survey.

5. 5   Labor Unions and Collective Bargaining

Labor Unions at the National Level

According to the Bluebook of the National Labor Union for 2005 (NLU, 2006), the major tasks of labor unions in China include protecting workers rights to organize and participate in labor unions, promoting collective bargaining, protecting the economic and political rights of workers, meeting workers cultural needs, participating in labor dispute arbitration, protecting the legal rights of migrant workers, and promoting gender equality. In 2005, labor unions in China made significant accomplishments.

By September 2005, there were 1.174 million grassroots labor unions in China. Compared with a year earlier, the number of unions grew by 154,000. A total of 2.331 million enterprises and other legal identities were covered, reaching a growth of 20.5% over the year before. There were 150.294 million union members in September 2005. This was a growth of 9.7% over 1994. Among the members, 21 millions were migrant workers (NLU, 2006).[4] The growth of labor unions is not confined to domestic firms, but has extended to FDI firms. The most significant development, perhaps, is Walmart s recent move to allow Chinese employees to organize unions. This is the first time that Walmart has allowed labor unions in its gigantic retail empire. Although the quality of the labor unions varies, the growth of labor

---

[4] The figures in this section come from NLU (2006) where not otherwise indicated.

unions, in particular the growth of their membership among migrant workers, will eventually reach a critical point at which they become indispensable for the protection of workers rights.

One important task of a labor union is to promote written contracts for its members. By September 2005, 57.714 million workers in enterprises with labor unions signed contracts with their employers. However, this was only 48.6% of the total number of workers in these enterprises. That is, more than half of the workers did not sign a contract with their employers even if there was a labor union in their enterprise. Therefore, there is still a long way for the unions to go.

As our analysis has shown, the coverage of pension and medical insurance was low in the sample firms. One task of the labor union is to sponsor the labor cooperative pension and medical insurance scheme that serves as a supplement to the government-sponsored pension and medical insurance schemes. In 2005, 38,000 grassroots labor unions sponsored such a scheme. This was a growth of 20.2% over 2004. A total of 8.949 million workers participated in the scheme, an increase of 7.3% over 2004. Among them, 6.208 millions participated in medical insurance, 3.012 millions in pension insurance, and 2.724 millions in accident insurance. In 2005, 868,000 people received a total of 550 million yuan in benefits from the three kinds of schemes combined.

Labor unions also participated in the monitoring of workplace safety. By September 2005, the grassroots labor unions had established 223,000 workplace safety monitoring committees, covering 60.161 million workers. These committees received 34,000 cases of complaints in 2005. The NLU has also been actively involved in promoting safety education among workers. For example, it organizes the nation-wide An-kang Competition of Safety Knowledge each year. In 2005, 65 million people in 150,000 enterprises participated in the competition.

Labor unions provide help for poor, unemployed, and socially or economically disadvantaged workers. Labor unions at or above the county level have established 2,229 help centers. In 2005, they provided financial subsidies for 1.18 million low-income people, 129,000 people with urgent medical needs, and 226,000 people for their children's education. They also provided 39,000 people with start-up loans, 845,000 people with job connections, 725,000 people with employment training, 372,000 people policy consultation, and 50,000 people legal consultation. These figures are not large but they are signs that labor unions are improving their public relations.

The labor union in China was for a long time a semi-government organization. Its tasks were to provide sideline welfare to workers. The changing of the employment relationship in Chinese enterprises has called for a change in the role of the labor union so as to become the organizer of the protection of workers rights as its central task. However, the change has been happening slowly due to the concern that independent labor unions would become a force for social unrest. The situation has begun to change since the government acknowledged the government-union-employer three-party coordination scheme (TCS) as a way of harmonizing the worker-employer relationship. Although it is not formally acknowledged, TCS strengthens the labor union's position as the representative of the workers. In October 2005, the NLU held a conference with the MLSS and the All China Federation of Entrepreneurs to discuss the TCS. In their statement at the conference, the three parties made it clear that they would promote the establishment and improvement of the TCS under the guidance of the harmonious society. By September 2005, there were 8,030 TCSs nationwide, an increase of 20.1% over the year before. Eight-two percent of the cities and 71% of the counties have established the TCS. The current problem is that the link between city and county-level labor unions and the grassroots labor unions at the enterprise level is weak. Workers in the same industry share more common interests, but there are still no labor unions by industry. How to involve the grassroots labor unions is an immediate task for the TCS.

Within the enterprise, the workers representative conference (WRC) is an important institution for enabling workers to participate in firm management, especially when it is related to workers welfare. For example, WRC played a significant role in protecting the interests of workers in the process of SOE privatization (Garnaut et al., 2005). By September 2005, there were 432,000 enterprises and other legal identities that established the WRC, covering 82.638 million employees. Among the enterprises registered as companies, 29,000 of them had employee directors on the board of directors, an increase of 4,799 over 2004.

The role of the labor union in labor dispute arbitration has been institutionalized by the establishment of the arbitration committees and the TCS. By September 2005, there were 231,000 arbitration committees at the grassroots level, covering 59.407 million employees. These committees received a total of 193,000 cases and successfully resolved 42,000 of them in 2005. There were also 8,891 regional and industrial arbitrage committees established under the TCS. They received 65,000 cases and resolved 51,000 of them in 2005.

Until recently, providing equal employment opportunities for men and women had been a matter of pride in China. Many studies have shown, however, that the situation has changed and women are being discriminated against in getting jobs. One of the reasons for the discrimination is that bearing and rearing children affect women s productivity. As a correction, the Chinese government has begun to promote an insurance scheme for maternity leave. This scheme requires that an enterprise pays a premium for every worker, regardless of whether they are male or female. The money collected is used to pay the salaries of female workers during their maternity leave. The research team found in the interviews that many enterprises did not understand the scheme and believed that it was unfair if they did not have many female workers of child- bearing age. Despite this, the number of people participating in the insurance scheme has increased rapidly in recent years. In 2000, there were 30.02 million people; and by the end of 2005 53.89 million. In 2005, 600,000 women enjoyed the benefits of the insurance scheme.

In summary, labor unions in China are experiencing a critical transition from being a wing of government to a more independent institution that represents the true interests of workers. This transition has just started. The establishment of the TCS recognizes the labor union as a player independent of the government and the employer. Through the TCS, the labor union begins to play a role in labor dispute arbitrages and collective bargaining. With its linkage with grassroots labor unions being enhanced, the TCS will serve as a vehicle for the labor union to become more independent organizations protecting workers interests.

Labor Unions in the Sample

Among the sample firms, 69% have labor unions. This figure is very close to the national average of 70%

(NLU, 2006). However, there are large variations across ownership, firm size, and city. As expected, SOEs performed the best with 93% having labor unions (Figure 5.28). Foreign-invested were second, and domestic private and HMT-invested firms had about the same share and were ranked last. The gap between firms with different sizes was also large. Among large firms, 85% had labor unions. The corresponding figures for medium and small firms were 75% and 64%, respectively.

Figure 5.28

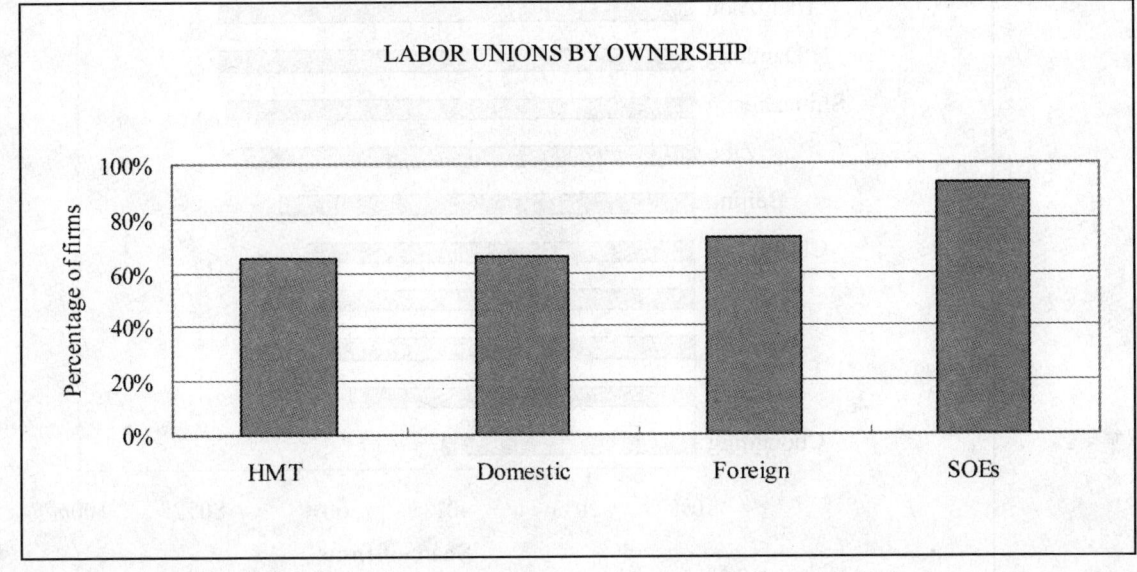

Source: Main survey.

Figure 5.29 ranks the sample cities by the share of firms having labor unions. There was not a clear regional pattern, though. Shiyan, a western city, performed the best having 95% of its firms with labor unions. But another western city, Chongqing, performed the worst with barely 40%. The four coastal cities performed at about the average level except that Hangzhou was ranked no. 3.

The ranking in Figure 5.29 has a lot to do with the share of SOEs and firm size in each city. The sample firms in both Shiyan and Xi'an, the two frontrunners, had a larger presence of SOEs (15% and 22%, being No. 3 and No. 1, respectively), and their average size was relatively large (Xi'an was ranked No. 3 and Shiyan was ranked No. 4). Beijing also had a heavy presence of SOEs (being No. 2 at 17%), but its average firm sizes were relatively small, and ranked No. 9 among the 12 sample cities. The average size of sample firms in Shunde and Changchun was large (ranked No. 1 and No. 2), but their share of SOEs was low: there was only one SOE in Shunde, and the share of SOEs in Changchun was about the level of the sample average (Table 2.5). Therefore, a larger share of SOEs and a larger average size of firms together are the determining factor for more labor unions.

Among the firms with labor unions, 69% were a member of larger regional or industrial labor unions. This ratio is pretty good. It means that the link between grassroots labor unions and higher-level labor unions is widespread. What it does not say anything about is the quality of the link, though.

However, caution is needed for the above numbers because the individual survey provides a quite different picture for domestic private firms. Only 20% of the respondents said that there was a labor union in their

Figure 5. 29

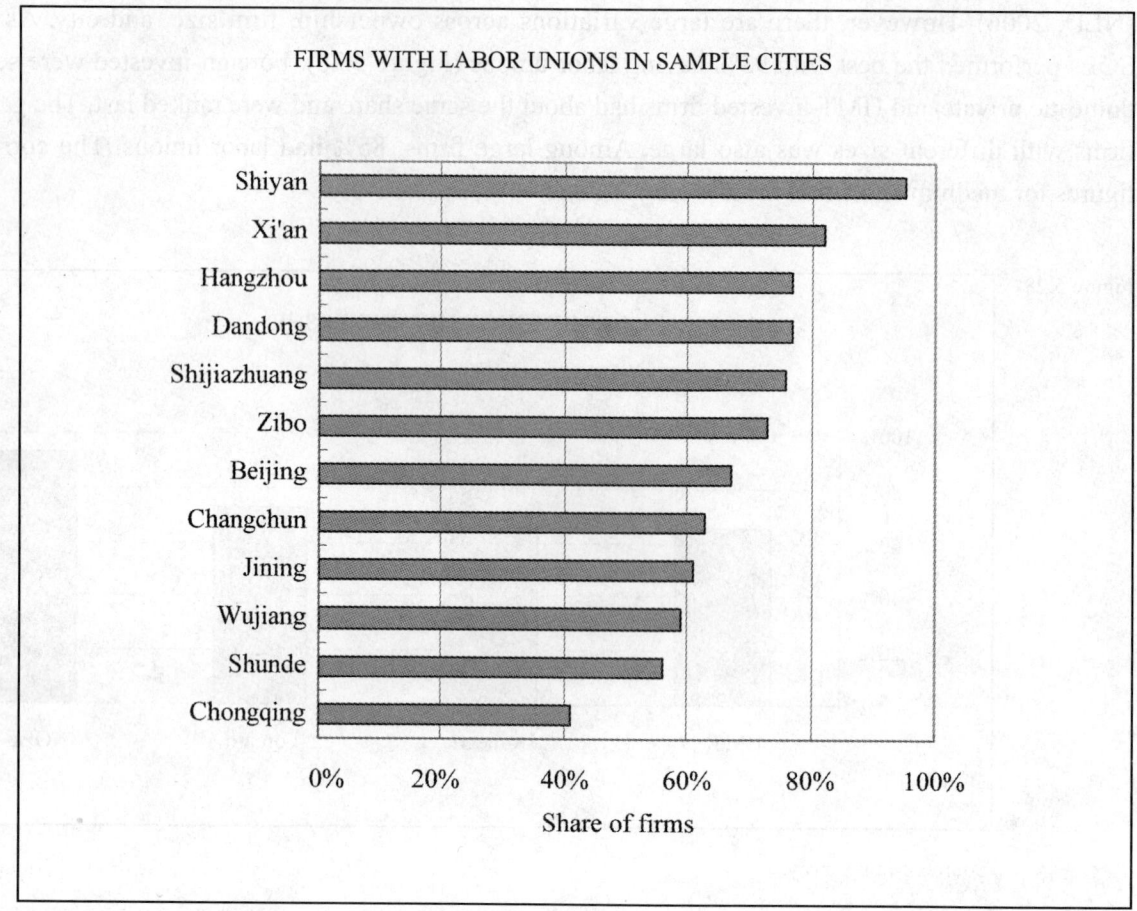

FIRMS WITH LABOR UNIONS IN SAMPLE CITIES

Source: Main survey.

enterprise; 55% of them said that there was not; the rest 25% said that they did not know. It is possible that there is a labor union in firm, but its functions are very limited so workers do not notice its existence. If this reasoning holds and the results of the individual survey are valid, then we have reason to doubt whether most of the labor unions in the domestic private firms in the sample were actually performing their functions. However, as long as workers notice the existence of the labor union, there are a high percentage of them who would give a positive evaluation. In the individual survey, fifty-eight percent of the respondents who worked in a unionized firm believed that the labor union played at least some role in protecting workers' rights. Data from the main survey support this finding.

Benefits of Unionization and Collective Bargaining

There is ample evidence showing that unionization in developed countries raises the wage rates of workers. It is expected that it would benefit the workers also in China. Table 5.9 compares unionized and un-unionized sample firms by monthly working hours, hourly wage, and coverage of pensions and medical insurance. It is clear that unionization pays off for workers. Workers seem to be much better treated in unionized than in un-unionized firms on every indicator. However, the differences for working hours and hourly wages were actually negative, being -5.4% and -1.8%, respectively for unionized versus non-unionized. The effects on pension and medical insurance coverage were very large, the gap being 73.7% and 75.7% higher respectively.

106

Table 5.9

THE EFFECTS OF UNIONIZATION ON WORKERS' BENEFITS

	Monthly working hours	Hourly wage (yuan)	Firms with full pension coverage (%)	Firms with full medical insurance coverage (%)
Un-unionized firms	210.8	5.7	35.4	32.8
Unionized firms	199.5	5.6	61.5	57.3
Gap of unionized over un-unionized	-5.4%	18.0%	73.7%	75.7%

Note: Full coverage for pension and medical insurance means a coverage of 80-100% of the employees in a firm.
Source: Main survey.

There is a possibility that unionization is correlated with other factors that also exert influence on the four welfare indicators, so the effects on working hours and hourly wage may pick up the effects of other factors. However, the large effects on the coverage of pension and medical insurance cannot be easily dismissed. The results of two regressions confirm this assertion. The dependent variables of the two regressions are dummy variables indicating whether a firm had full coverage of pension and medical insurance for local employees, respectively. The explanatory variables are the same as those used in the regression for hourly wages (Table 5.1) plus a dummy variable indicating whether a firm was unionized. Table 5.10 presents the results using the linear probability model for the estimation. The results agree with our previous analysis. For example, larger firms offer better coverage than smaller firms; SOEs do better than the other three types of firms; and firms offering written contracts do better than firms that do not. In addition, except for Shunde and Jining, all the other cities perform worse than Beijing. The most interesting result in terms of the current concern is that unionization pays off: its marginal effect is to raise the probability of a firm having full pension coverage by 11.4%, and to have full medical insurance coverage by 7.55%.

Table 5.10

REGRESSION RESULTS FOR PENSION AND MEDICAL INSURANCE COVERAGE

Variable	Pension		Medical insurance	
	Coefficient	Std. Err.	Coefficient	Std. Err.
Constant	0.260*	.141	0.381***	.145
LN(size)	2.18E-02*	.013	3.34E-02***	.014
LN(per-worker capital)	6.73E-02***	.015	5.34E-02***	.015
LN(per-worker sales)	-1.92E-02	.018	-8.62E-03	.018
Share of migrant workers	-1.56E-03	.014	-1.89E-02	.015

Export (yes = 1, no = 0)	-9.30E-03	.033	-2.94E-02	.034
Share of sales in province	5.70E-02***	.011	1.44E-02	.011
Share of sales in national market	-2.06E-03*	.011	3.55E-03	.011
Domestic private firms	-.233***	.051	-.268***	.052
HMT-invested firms	-.161**	.071	-.197***	.072
Foreign-invested firms	-.135**	.064	-.137**	.064
Written contracts (yes=1, no =0)	.237**	.037	.225***	.038
Unionization (yes=1, no =0)	0.114***	.036	7.55E-02**	.037
Hangzhou	-.138**	.074	-.187***	.076
Shunde	-9.22E-02	.070	-6.22E-02	.072
Wujiang	-.281***	.080	-.373***	.082
Changchun	-.155***	.084	-.366***	.101
Dandong	-.345***	.070	-.438***	.071
Shijiazhuang	-.380***	.072	-.440***	.073
Zibo	-.382***	.067	-.448***	.068
Jining	-.362***	.082	-.499***	.084
Chongqing	-.277***	.071	-.345***	.074
Shiyan	-7.51E-02	.075	-.118	.076
Xi'an	-.280***	.074	-.292***	.076
Number of cases	893		845	
R^2	0.31		0.32	

Source: Main survey.

Collective bargaining is one of the central functions that NLU is currently promoting for labor unions in China. Among the sample firms, 53% allowed collective bargaining, and 29% had collective contracts. Labor unions played a significant role. Among the unionized firms, 57% allowed collective bargaining, whereas the percentage in un-unionized firms was 47%. The gap was larger in terms of collective contracts: 34% of the unionized firms had collective contracts whereas only 19% of the un-unionized firms did so.[5]

---

[5] It is interesting to find that un-unionized firms also allowed collective bargaining and collective contracts. In these firms, workers might organize temporarily to bargain with the employer.

The difference between large firms and SMEs was large. Forty-seven percent of large firms had collective contracts, but only 28% and 29% of median and small firms, respectively had them. In terms of ownership, SOEs were still the front runner having 37% offering collective contracts. The surprise is that domestic private firms for the first time performed better than FDI firms: 30% of them offered collective contracts, whereas only 21% of foreign-invested and 24% of HMT-invested firms did so. Since domestic private firms did not lead FDI firms on other labor-related issues, their better performance in collective contracts is surprising and not likely to be the result of their own volition, but rather a result of government efforts in promoting collective contracts. From another perspective, this also suggests that local governments have not paid as much attention to FDI firms as to domestic firms.

However, collective contracts have not significantly improved workers' welfare. Table 5.11 compares the performance of firms with and without collective contracts in terms of the four indicators used in Table 5.9. Except that in firms with collective contracts workers worked a slightly smaller number of hours in a month, the two kinds of firms were virtually the same in terms of the four indicators. Comparison made within the group of unionized firms does not find significant differences among firms with and without collective contracts either.

Table 5.11

THE EFFECTS OF COLLECTIVE CONTRACTS ON WORKERS' BENEFITS

	Monthly working hours	Hourly wage (yuan)	Firms with full pension coverage (%)	Firms with full medical insurance coverage (%)
Firms without collective contracts	205.7	5.9	52.2	49.3
Firms with collective contracts	201.2	5.3	52.9	48.3

Note: Full coverage for pension and medical insurance means a coverage of 80-100% of the employees in a firm.
Source: Main survey.

In summary, the above analysis shows that organized labor through the labor union is the key to promoting workers welfare. Although they may not be wholly independent of government or even of the enterprise, labor unions are playing a significant role in protecting workers' rights. On the other hand, collective contracts have not played a significant role. Perhaps, most of the collective contracts have only a nominal value. In contrast, unionization has the real power either to initiate real action against infringements of workers' rights, or to engage workers in organized negotiations with the employer. Either way, workers are under better protection.

It is noteworthy that unionization has much larger effects on workers' fringe benefits than on their working hours and wage rates. This result is understandable. To the extent that more working hours are properly compensated, both the hourly wage rate and monthly working hours are mostly determined by the market, so unionization has smaller effects on them. In contrast, fringe benefits such as pension and medical insurance are required by the government, and it is an enforcement issue to have a firm offering them to their workers. In this regard, workers' own demands can play a significant role. This is why unionization has very large effects on fringe benefits.

5. 6 Summary

This chapter has presented statistics on several important aspects of labor protection for the sample firms and analyzed the causes and correlates for the observed patterns. Data from the individual survey were also used to supplement the analysis. Several significant conclusions can be drawn.

First, labor protection has been strengthened in recent years in the sample cities (except perhaps, in Jining) in terms of pension and medical insurance coverage. Nationwide, the NLU has also been increasing its efforts to promote workers' rights. One important advance emerges from the three-part coordination scheme that recognizes the labor union as a representative of workers interests independent of the government and the employer.

Second, among the factors influencing workers' welfare, firm size, ownership, and written contracts are the most important. Larger firms treat workers better than smaller firms; SOEs treat workers better than domestic private firms and FDI firms; and firms offering written contracts treat workers better than firms that do not. Financial performance of the firm is not a significant factor, though.

Third, fringe benefits are more sensitive than working hours and hourly wage rates to the efforts of government and workers in getting better treatment. Long working hours are likely to be endogenously chosen by workers themselves.

Fourth, labor unions are playing a significant role in promoting workers' welfare despite the fact that they may not yet be fully independent. In contrast, collective contracts have not begun to deliver real benefits to workers.

Policy recommendations from the conclusions are clear. First, the NLU should continue to strengthen the role of labor unions in the TCS. The TCS is an institutionalized platform where labor unions have an independent voice; with their active participation, the independent role of labor unions will be gradually enhanced. Second, the government should continue to place emphasis on written contracts in its enforcement of labor regulations. Contracts raise workers awareness of the need to protect their own rights and alert employers to the legal consequences of reneging on their own promises to workers. Third, the government should pay more attention to workers' fringe benefits because they are more responsive to outside interventions. For working hours and salaries, the most important thing is to make sure that overtime working hours are being properly paid for.

One final discussion on the better performance of SOEs is warranted. SOEs treat workers better than other kinds of firms not because they are more profitable or have higher labor productivity. In fact, Chapter 2 showed that they are the worst among the four types of firms. The only reason that SOEs treat their workers better than other types of firms is that they care more about their workers. One possible reason for this "paternalistic" behavior is that SOEs function more like labor-managed firms than state-owned firms. It is a classic result that a labor-managed firm tends to provide more benefits to its current workforce. However, this reason does not stand the test. One such test is to compare privatized SOEs and domestic private firms. Privatized SOEs have established private ownership, so it is unlikely that they would still behave in a paternalistic fashion. If they perform better in labor protection, it must be for other reasons. Data provided by the main survey do show that in some respects they perform better than domestic private firms though working hours and wages are similar. However, 70% of the privatized SOEs provided full pension coverage and 62% of them provided full medical insurance coverage while the corresponding figures for domestic private firms were 40% and 35%, respectively. These differences were not arrived at because of private SOEs' better financial performance. Their return on capital was 15% and their labor productivity was 35,100 yuan/worker; in contrast, the corresponding figures for domestic private firms were 32% and 47,300 yuan/worker, respectively.

Therefore, privatized SOEs must have inherited from their SOE predecessors some traits other than paternalistic feelings toward their workers. Some tentative suggestions for these traits include better organized labor unions, a better functioning employee representative conference, greater worker awareness, and greater government supervision. Indeed, the first two have been confirmed by our analysis. The last two are also quite possible to hold because workers in privatized SOEs are more familiar with the benefits that they enjoyed in SOEs and privatized SOEs are closer to the government than other private firms. These factors probably are also the factors that lead to the better performance of the SOEs.

Chapter 6
Environmental Standards

Environmental protection is one of the core measures for sustainable development. There are over 100 definitions of sustainability and sustainable development, but the best known is provided by the World Commission on Environment and Developments. This defintion suggests that development is sustainable when it "a meets the needs of the present without compromising the ability of future generations to meet their needs." Environmental issues are defined as "those that have an impact on physical environment and thus on its inhabitants" by IFC (2002). With the rapid economic development of China over the past thirty years, environmental problems like pollution and the ecological damage have gradually become crucial problems for China's sustainable economic development as well as for her international relations. In this Chapter we discuss the situation of environment protection for the sampled firms.

The Chinese government initiated the effort of protecting the environment in 1949. The constitution clearly requires that "The country protect and improve the living environment and the ecological environment, preventing pollution and other kinds of damages to the environment". Since 1949, National People's Congress (NPC) and the Standing Committee of NPC have passed 8 laws for environment protection, and 15 laws for the protection of natural resources. The relevant departments in the State Council, the local People's Congress and local governments have passed over 660 local regulations to effectively implement these laws and the related administrative decrees. China has also established environmental protection standards at the national level as well as the local level. The national environmental standards include national environmental quality standards, national pollutant discharge standards, national environmental sample standards; local environmental standards include local environmental quality standards and pollutant discharge standards. Up to 2005, over 800 national environmental protection standards were released; Beijing, Shanghai, Shandong and Henan have established over 30 local environmental protection standards. The enforcement of the environmental laws has also been strengthened. For example, over 160,000 firms were clamped down for illegally discharging pollutants from 2002 to 2005. Projects on checking the law enforcement on mining environmental protection and on sea environment protection have also been carried out.

In China local governments are responsible for local environment quality, and the ministry of Environmental Protection reports to the State Council for China's overall environmental protection. Up to the end of 2005, there were 3,226 administrative departments in charge of environmental protection. There were 3,854 institutions and over 50,000 staff that monitored the environment and enforced reievant laws. In addition, there were about 167,000 persons engaging in environmental management, supervision, research and education[1].

As government emphasizes environmental protection through establishing laws and initiating specific measures to protect the environment, the awareness of private firms on the importance of environmental protection has increased. As discussed in Chapter 3, environmental protection is the most frequently mentioned CSR-related activity by sample firms. Private firms can respond to environmental issues in a variety of ways. The IFC (2002) report grouped private firms into four categories based on their strategies toward profitability and environmental and social issues: the proactive group that enjoys both profit and protecting the environment, the reactive group that protect the environment but cannot make profits, the minimalist group that generate profit at the cost of the environment, and the unsustainable group that not only damage the environment but also fails to make a profit. Reinhardt (2000) discusses a number of factors that can influence firm response strategy, including the products a private enterprise chooses to produce, the location where they site their business, the degree of competition they face in the market, the employment and labor practices they use, etc. In China other factors, like ownership structure, can also affect firms' strategy toward environment protection, and it is unclear how each of these factors affects firm behavior in tackling the environmental-protection issue.

In this chapter we focus on investigating two issues. One is what is the status quo of environmental protection, and the second issue is what factors may affect the willingness of firms to protect the environment. Section 6.1 describes the status quo in environmental protection; and section 6.2 discusses the potential factors that can influence firm's strategy toward environment protection and finally, as the Law on Cleaner Production was passed on January 1st 2003, but the public knows little about cleaner production, we disscuss cleaner production in section 6.3.

6. 1   The Status Quo of Environmental Protection

How to ensure fast economic growth and to protect environment simultaneously has been a challenging task for the Chinese government. At the country level, the average growth rates for the discharge of waste water and air emissions have risen quickly in recent years. The discharge of waste water increased from 35 billion tons in 1990 to 48.2 billion tons in 2004, with an average growth rate of 2% over the 15 years but 4.9% in 2004. The growth rate for industrial solid wastes is higher. It increased from 0.6 billion tons in 1990 to 1.2 billion in 2004, with an average growth rate of 4.7% and 19.5% in 2004. To take up the challenge, the government increased investment for environmental protection. In 2004, the total investment for tackling pollution reached the highest historical value of 190.86 billion RMB, which was 17.3% higher than 2003 and took 1.4% of GDP in 2004.

Whether we can reach the national targets for environmental protection depends on the performances of all of the enterprises in the country. In this section we inspect the status quo of environment protection among the sampled firms. We first look at the measures firms take to protect the environment, we then investigate environmental compliance rates and environmental / biological labeling, and next we discuss the difficulties of complying with national standards from the perspectives of firms.

---

[1] Statistics on this page are from "The Environmental Protection in China: 1996 – 2005 (White Book)", State Environmental Protection Administration of China.

Measures to Protect the Environment

In this subsection we investigate measures that firms have taken to protect the environment. Such measures include setting up an environmental protection department; planning expenditure for maintaining environment standards and making investments in equipment for reaching national standards. As we cannot directly evaluate the attitudes of firms toward environmental protection, their participations in these activities will provide indirect evidences of how serious they consider enviromental protection.

In 2005, 654 out of the 1,225 firms reported that they have an environmental protection (EP) department. Among these 654 firms, 627 provided the year they set up the EP department. The data shows there are only 35 firms establishing the EP department before the Open and Reform Policy (1978), 285 of the firms set up an EP department between 1978 and 2000, and the remaining 307 firms established their EP department between 2001 and 2006. Another way of looking at the frequency of setting up EP departments is to look at the average numbers. On average only about1.2 EP departments were set up between 1949 and 1977, but this number rises to 12.4 during 1978 – 2000, and increases to 51.17 during 2001-2006, indicating a clear trend in the establishment of EP departments.

From the ownership structure point of view, the proportion of SOEs that had an EP department is 63%, 10% higher than average; domestic private firms take the lowest percentage of 52%, and joint ventures are in between (Figure 6.1). SOEs also distinguish themselves as the earliest firms to set up EP departments in China. Figure 6.2 shows the average year of establishing EP departments, where SOEs on average are about 14 years earlier than other types of firms. The other three types of firm on average had their EP departments by the end of the 1990's, with domestic private firms about half a year later than joint ventures.

Figure 6.1

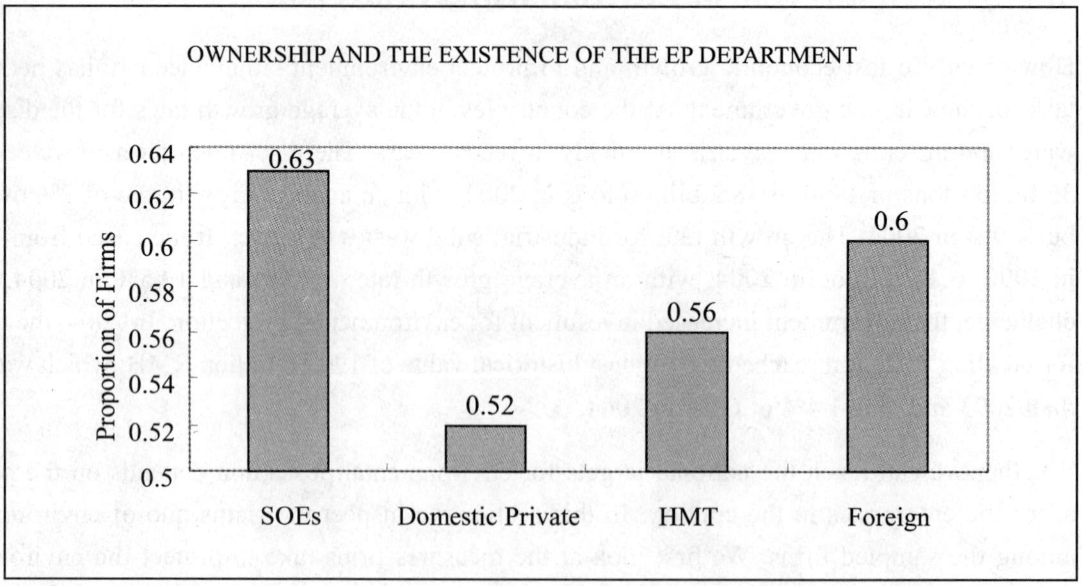

OWNERSHIP AND THE EXISTENCE OF THE EP DEPARTMENT

Source: Main Survey

Figure 6.2

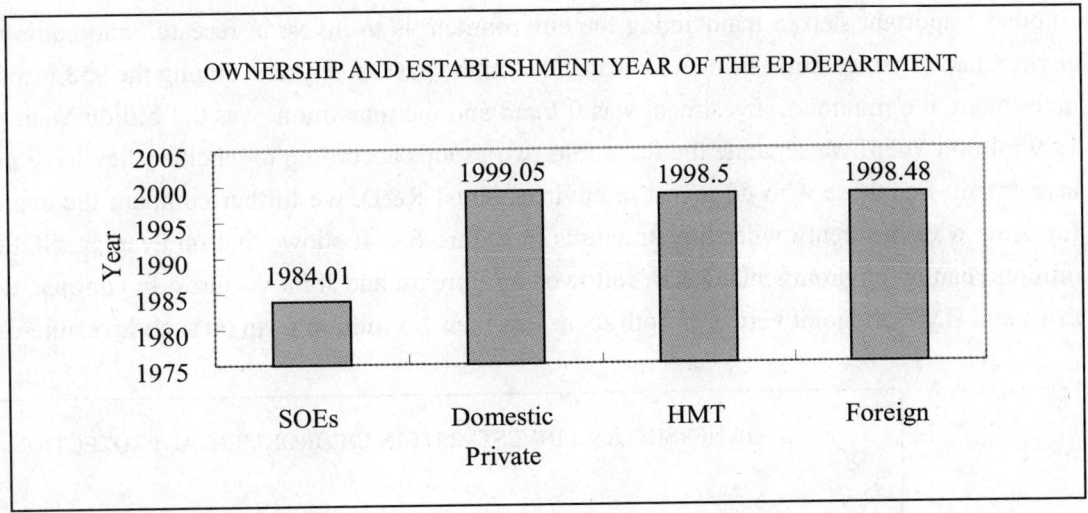

Source: Main Survey

The second perspective we investigate is the expenditure on environmental maintenance. With the strengthening of law enforcement, firms need to maintain their responsibilities for the environment through supervision, auditing, paying regulatory fees and fines, etc. In this sample, among the 948 firms providing information about their environment-related expenditure, the minimum expenditure is 0 Yuan and the maximum is 50 million Yuan, resulting in an average of 0.43 million Yuan; 86% of firms reported such expenditure for 2005, with a minimum of 500 Yuan. From ownership point of view, SOEs on average spent 950,000 Yuan, which is almost twice of that by Foreign & Joint Ventures, three times more than that spent by domestic private firms, and about six times of the spending by HMT & Joint Ventures (Figure 6.3).

Figure 6.3

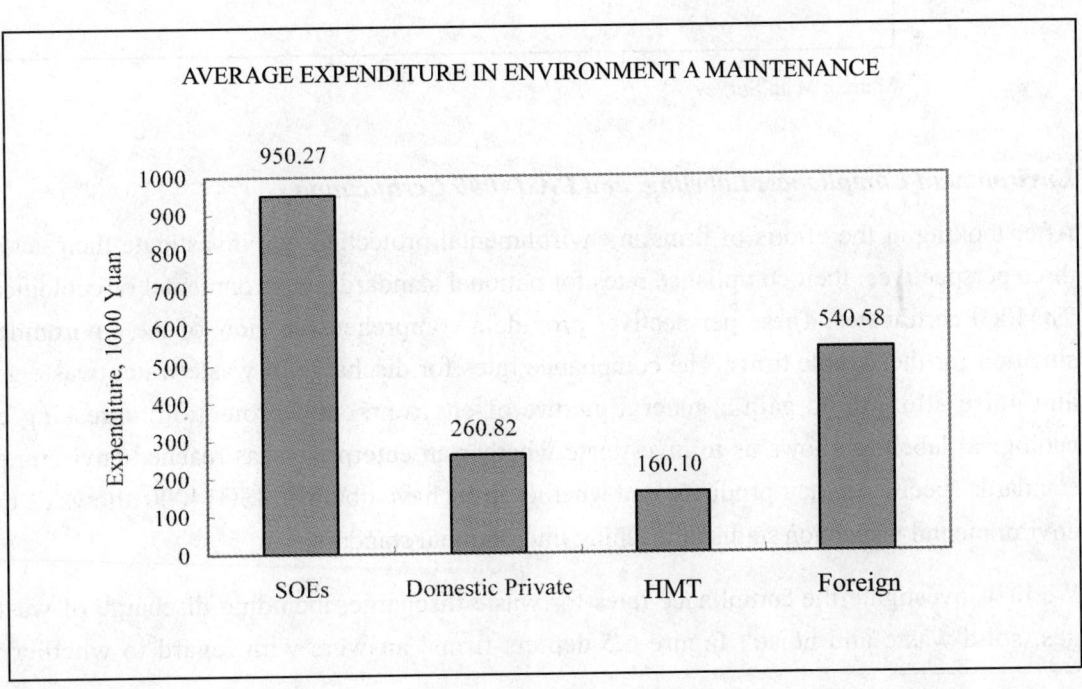

Source: Main Survey

Another important step in maintaining the environment is to invest in research and equipments related to environmental protection. The data indicates that in the past three years, among the 958 firms reporting such investment, the minimum investment was 0 Yuan and the maximum was 0.3 billion Yuan, with a mean of 1.89 million Yuan. We separate the firms into two groups according to whether they have made a non-zero investment. For those who do invest in environmental R&D, we further compare the average investment for firms with different ownership structures in Figure 6.4. It shows that on average, SOEs invested 3.25 million yuan on environmental R&D, followed by Foreign and Joint vectures. In contrast, domestic private firms and HMT and joint verctures both spent less than 1.5 million yuan on such investments.

Figure 6. 4

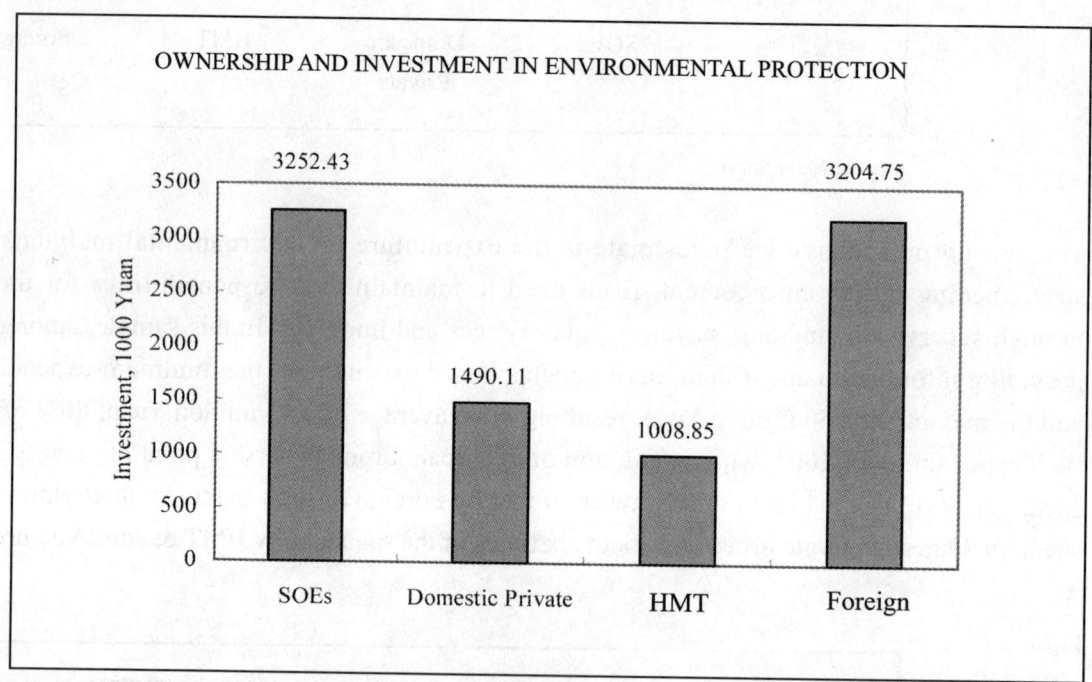

Source: Main Survey

Environment Compliance, Labeling, and ISO14000 Certification

After looking at the efforts of firms in environmental protection, we investigate their achievements from three perspectives: their compliance rates for national standards, environmental or ecological labeling, and ISO4000 certificates. These perspectives provide a comprehensive view of the environmental protection situation for the sample firms. The compliance rates for discharge of waste water, waste gas, solid wastes and noise allow us to gain a general picture of environmental protection; assessing environmental/ ecological labeling allows us to investigate whether an enterprises has reached environmental-protection standards specific to their products, and whether firms have obtained ISO14000 allows us to explore firms' environmental protection status in reaching international standards.

We first investigate the compliance rates for waste discharge, including discharge of waste water, waste gas, solid waste and noise[2]. Figure 6.5 depicts firms' answers with regard to whether they have met

---

[2] Firms were also asked about whether they passed national standards on ecological diversity. But this is a category that much fewer firms provided valid answers. There were over 15% of missing observations, and more than half the firms believed this category was irrelevant to them. Therefore the analysis below does not discuss ecology diversity.

national standards on disposing these wastes. Firms can choose to answer yes, no, and not relevant.[3] For each category, over 60% of firms claim they have passed national standards, and about 25% say that a specific waster category is irrelevant to them. The firms admitting not having reached national standards are few. With regard to solid waste, waste gas and waste water, less than 3% of the firms have not reached national standards; the noise standards are more demanding, but also only 6% firms reported that they failed to pass them. As firms may tend to over-report their compliance rates, we combine their subjective reports on compliances with the firms' evaluations of the degree of difficulty in reaching national standards to get a comprehensive understanding on compliance rates in the subsection on "difficulties".

Figure 6. 5

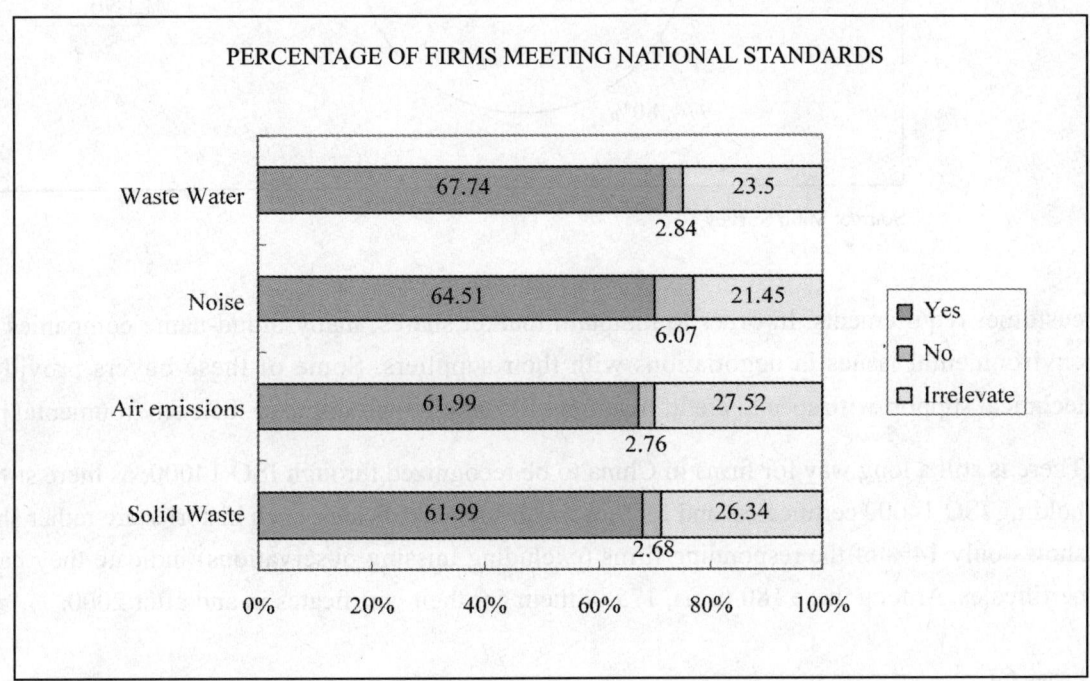

Source: Main Survey

In addition to meeting the requirements for protecting the environment during the production process, firms may be required to meet national environmental standards for their products. In this regard we find that firms put much less effort on product environmental certificates than on dealing with wastes in the production process. There are 35% of firms reporting the existence of national environment standards for their products[4], but only 12% of sample firms are shown to have obtained environmental or ecology certificates (Figure 6.6), and among the 146 firms, only 102 firms provided the date they obtained such certificates.

ISO 14000 is regarded as the most comprehensive and widely known international environmental manage-ment system. For firms in developing countries, registration for ISO 14000 through an internationally well-known accreditation institution provides an entry ticket to markets in the developed countries. With the launching of ISO 14000 in 1996 in China, enterprises started to care about their environmental performances not only with respect to gaining a market advantage, but also in response to

---

[3] The missing values in this section are less than 9% of the sampled firms.

[4] The non-response rate for this question is as high as 17%.

Figure 6.6

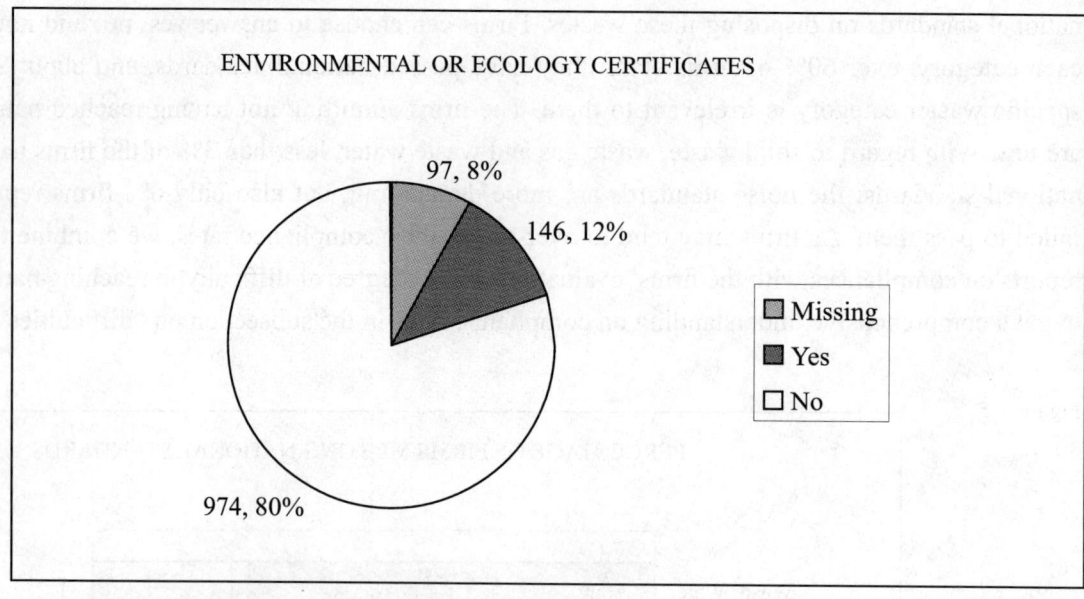

ENVIRONMENTAL OR ECOLOGY CERTIFICATES

97, 8%

146, 12%

974, 80%

Missing
Yes
No

Source: Main Survey

customer requirements. In order to maintain market shares, many brand-name companies have included environmental issues in negotiations with their suppliers. Some of these buyers provide training and technical support with special credit treatment for suppliers to improve their environmental performances.

There is still a long way for firms in China to be recognized through ISO 14000, as there still are few firms holding ISO 14000 certificates, and for those with such certificates, such histories are rather short. Figure 6.7 shows only 14% of the responding firms (excluding missing observations) indicate they have ISO 14000 certificates. Among these 180 firms, 175 of them got their certificates in and after 2000.

Figure 6.7

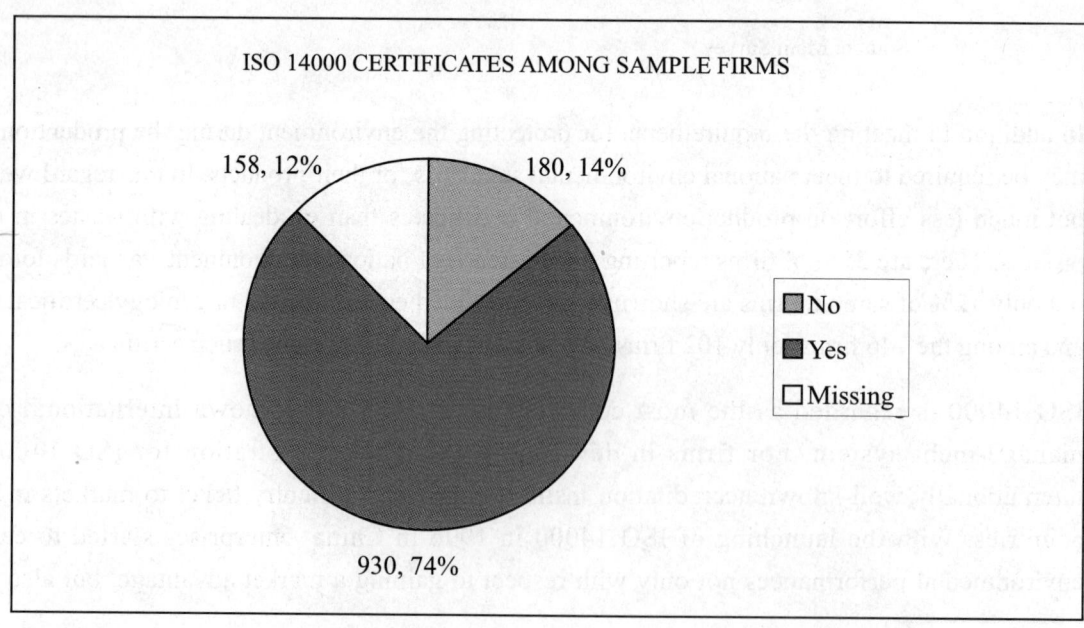

ISO 14000 CERTIFICATES AMONG SAMPLE FIRMS

158, 12%

180, 14%

930, 74%

No
Yes
Missing

Source: Main Survey

From an ownership structure point of view, domestic private firms are in a relatively inferior position compared with other firms (Figure 6.8). Only 12.6% of the domestic private firms hold ISO 14000 certificates, this is almost one third of that for Foreign and Joint Ventures. Therefore, if domestic private firms wish to enter and survive in the international market, much more effort needs to be spent on acquiring ISO 14000 through improved product quality and environmental protection.

Figure 6.8

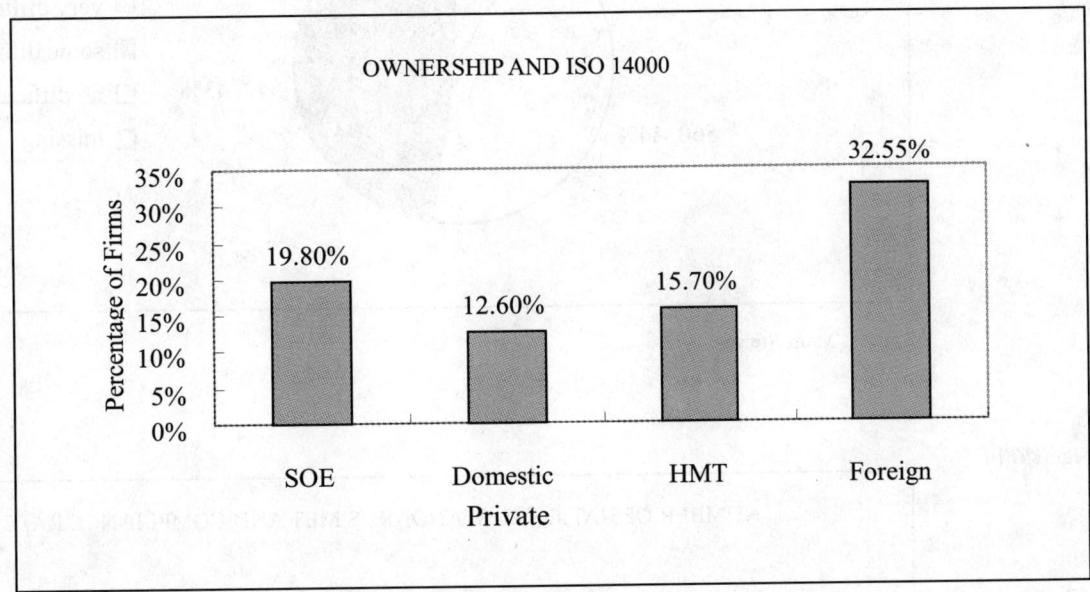

Source: Main Survey

In summary, firms put relatively more effort in reaching national standards to deal with pollution during the production process, but obtaining environmental certificates for their products is still at the initial stage. On the other hand, firms have started to appreciate the importance of environmental protection on products and take a more comprehensive attitude toward environmental protection.

Difficulties

With over 30% firms fail to reach the national standards for waste discharge and 80% firms fail to obtain environmental certificates for their products, environmental protection is still an arduous task for the sample firms. Failing to reach national standards for waste discharge as well as for products can either be because firms have little incentive to do so, or because the standards are too high conditional on the resources they can mobilize for environment protection. Since we cannot directly observe firm incentives, investigating the degrees of difficulty in satisfying national standards will help us to identify factors affecting firm behavior in environmental protection.

We plot the subjective evaluations of degrees of difficulty in meeting national standards for waste discharge in Figure 6.9. 44% of firms report that they do not have any difficulty in meeting the standards, and another 43% of firms feel they have some difficulty but only about 5% say that it is very difficult for them to meet national standards.

Figure 6.9 alone seems to imply that firms are quite optimistic toward their environmental protection tasks, but the comparison of the number of national standards met by firms and the compliance rates gives

Figure 6.9

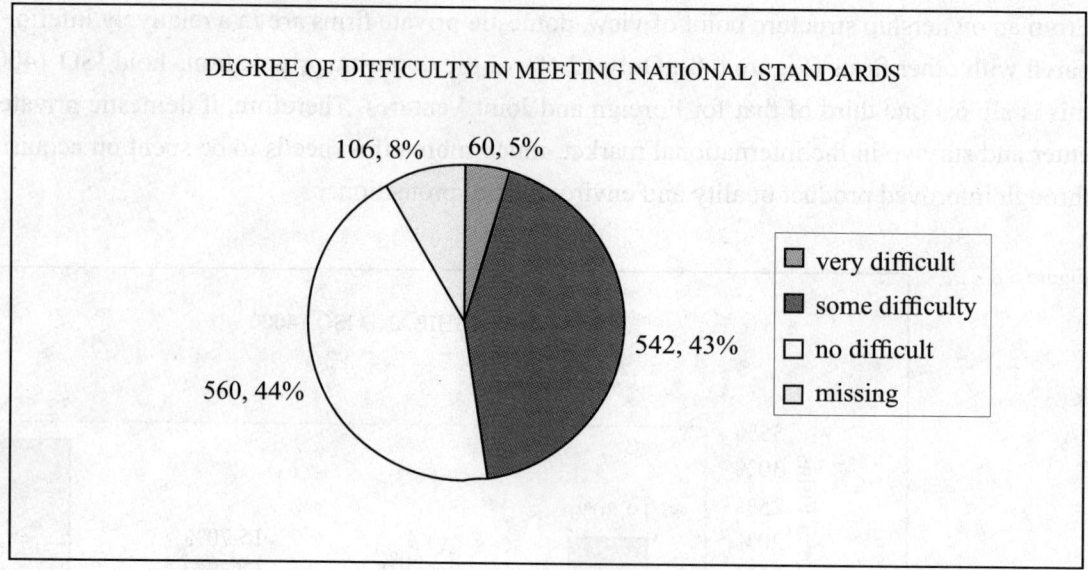

DEGREE OF DIFFICULTY IN MEETING NATIONAL STANDARDS

60, 5% very difficult
542, 43% some difficulty
560, 44% no difficult
106, 8% missing

Source: Main Survey

Figure 6.10

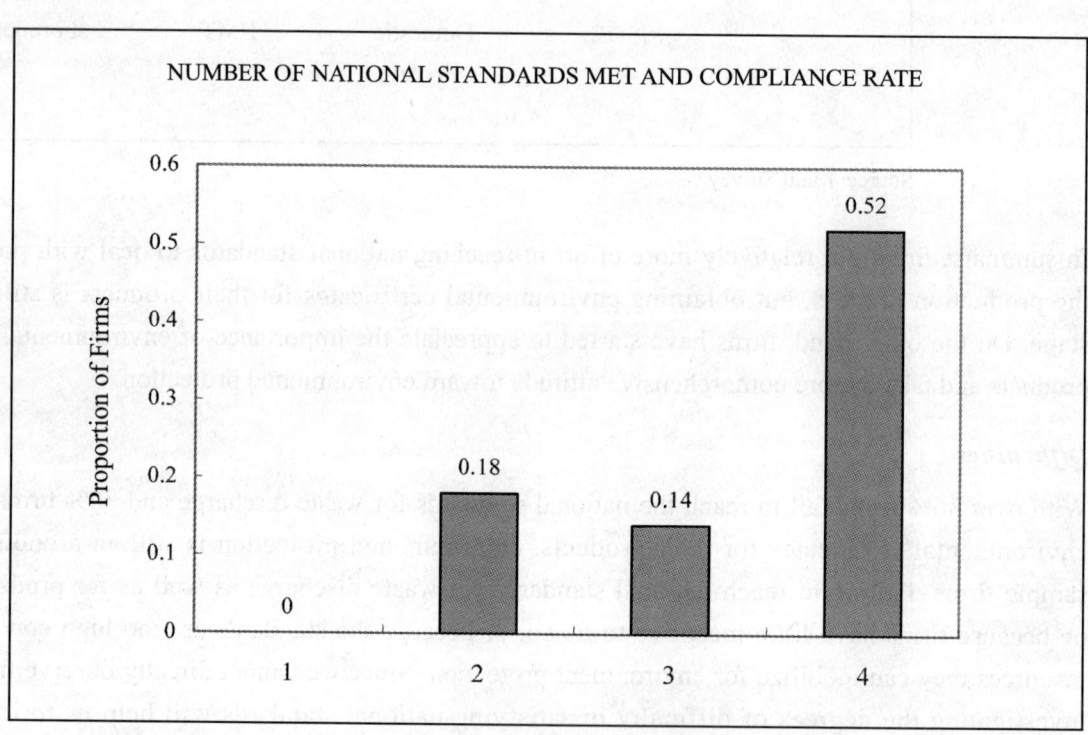

NUMBER OF NATIONAL STANDARDS MET AND COMPLIANCE RATE

Source: Main Survey

a different story. Figure 6.10 provides the adjusted compliance rates by separating firms into four groups based on their answers to whether they pass the national standards on air emissions, waste water, solid waste and noise. A group numbered 1 means only one of the standards is satisfied, and a group numbered 4 means all four standards are met[5]. We group firms choosing 'irrelevant' as automatically satisfying

[5] There were only 6 firms reporting they passed none of the national standards. As the reported compliance rates are already zero we do not include them as a separate group.

the national standards. We calculate a new compliance rate by dividing the number of firms choosing "no difficulty" over the total number of firms in that group. Figure 6.10 shows that the compliance rates defined in this way are lower than those in Figure 6.5. Only 52% of the firms reported passing all four standards believe they have no difficulty in meeting national standards for waste discharge. Among those passing 2 of the national standards, only 18% report no difficulty, and among those passing 3 of the national standards, only 14% report no difficulty. All firms passing national standard believe they had at least some difficulty in meeting the national standard. This information more or less shows firms reporting information consistently, as a higher proportion of those reporting passing all national standards also report no difficulty in meeting national standards. On the other hand, as the adjusted compliance rates are low it indicates that it is still a challenging task for firms to meet national standards on waste discharge.

6. 2   Factors Affecting Firms Environmental Protection Behavior

The earlier discussions indicate that firms do make effort to protect the environment through establishing EP departments, and the majority of them have environmental-related expenditure and investment. How-ever, we also need to notice that these environmental activities vary considerably between firms. For example, while the maximum environmental-related expenditure is 50 million, 134 firms reported zero expenditure, equivalent to 14% of the 948 firms with non-missing observations. Similarly, 122 firms reported zero environmental-related investment, taking 13% of the 958 firms providing related information. What factors influence firm behavior in environmental protection is of policy relevance hence deserving further investigation.

The relationship between environmental protection and profitability was thought to be a trade-off until Porter put forward his hypothesis. Porter (Porter, 1991 and Porter and van der Linde, 1995) proposed that it is possible to create a win-win situation in which social welfare (represented by a better environment) could be accompanied by increased private benefits for regulated firms. The Porter hypothesis emphasizes stringent environmental regulation and argues that such regulation can induce innovatory activities which increase the competitiveness of firms. This argument implies that market competition can influence firm strategies for protecting the environment. In addition to competition, Reinhardt (2000) also discusses a number of factors that can influence firm strategies, including the product a private enterprise chooses to produce, the location where they site their business, and so on. In this subsection we follow the literature in studying the firms' responses for protecting the environment from the perspectives of competition, CSR awareness, region, industry, and government policy.

Competition and Environmental Protection Strategy

The degree of market competition and firms' CSR represented by environmental protection could have significant correlation. For example, at an international forum held at Shanghai in year 2006, it is perceived that enterprise competitiveness mainly comes from firm's CSR as well as firm's comparative advantage in the industry. While this idea has emphasized both CSR and competition, there is no empirical evidence in supporting such an argument. In sample firms, we observe that there is a positive correlation between degree of market competition and proportion of EP departments. We observe that firms in fiercely competitive markets have about a 10% larger proportion of EP departments[6] than those in markets with

---

[6] Since the number of firms in low competition markets is small, we add them into the moderate competition group.

moderate or low degrees of competition (Figure 6.11).

In addition to making greater efforts to protect the environment, firms facing fierce competition also reported more achievements through passing national standards on waste discharge as well as in obtaining ISO 14000 certificates. Figure 6.12 indicates that firms facing fierce competition also reported higher compliance rates than firms in a moderately competitive situation for all the four categories of wastes in general. For solid waste and noise, the patterns are clear: firms facing higher degree of competition are more likely to meet the national standards. Figure 6.13 then demonstrates that 15.65% of firms in high competition markets are reported to have ISO 14000 certificates, 5.1% higher than those in moderate or low-competition markets.

Figure 6.11

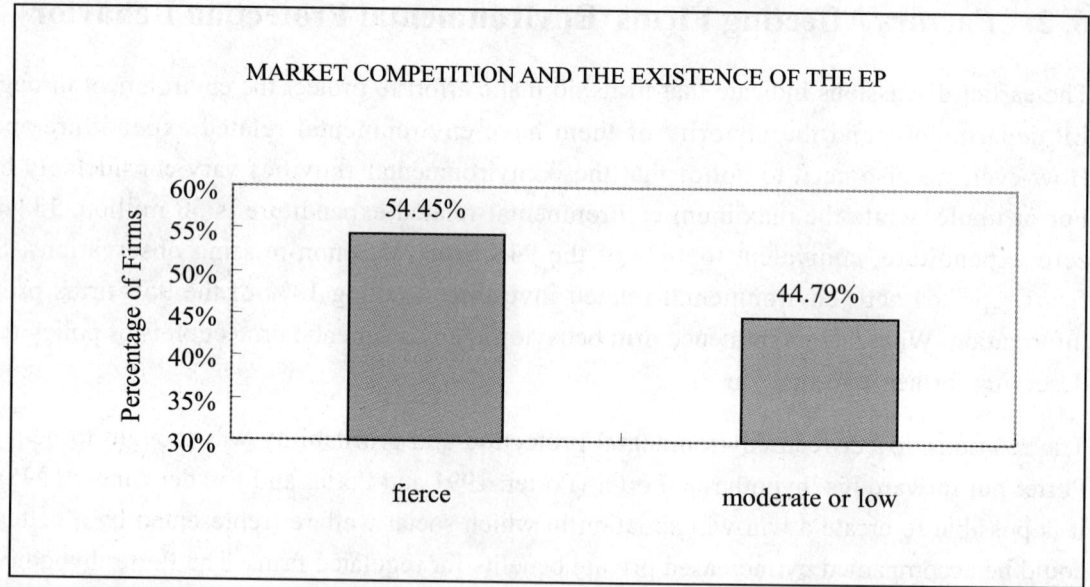

Source: Main Survey

Figure 6.12

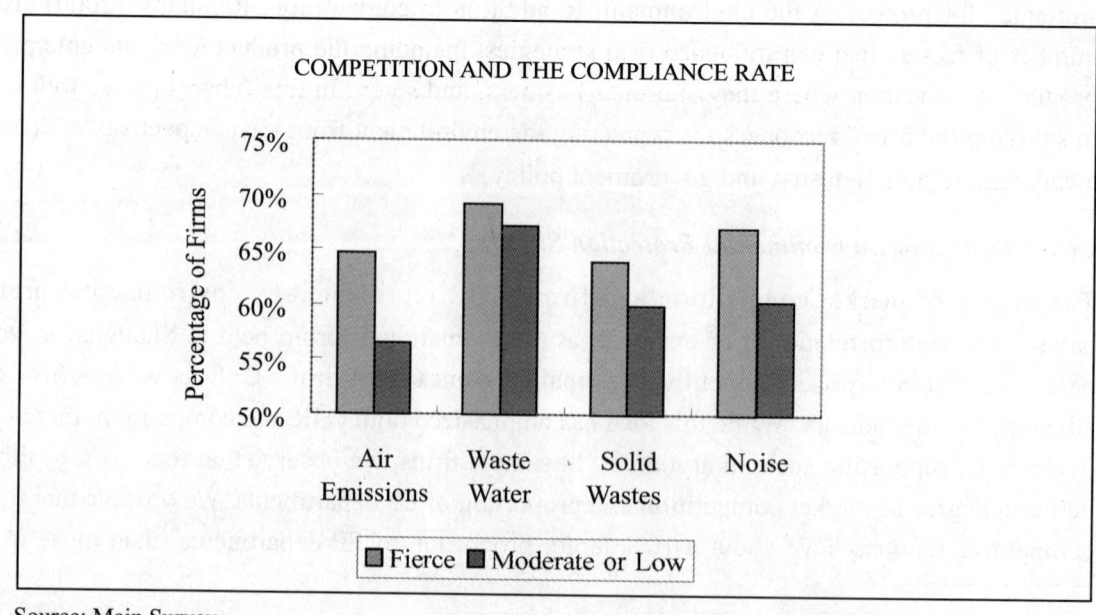

Source: Main Survey

Figure 6.13

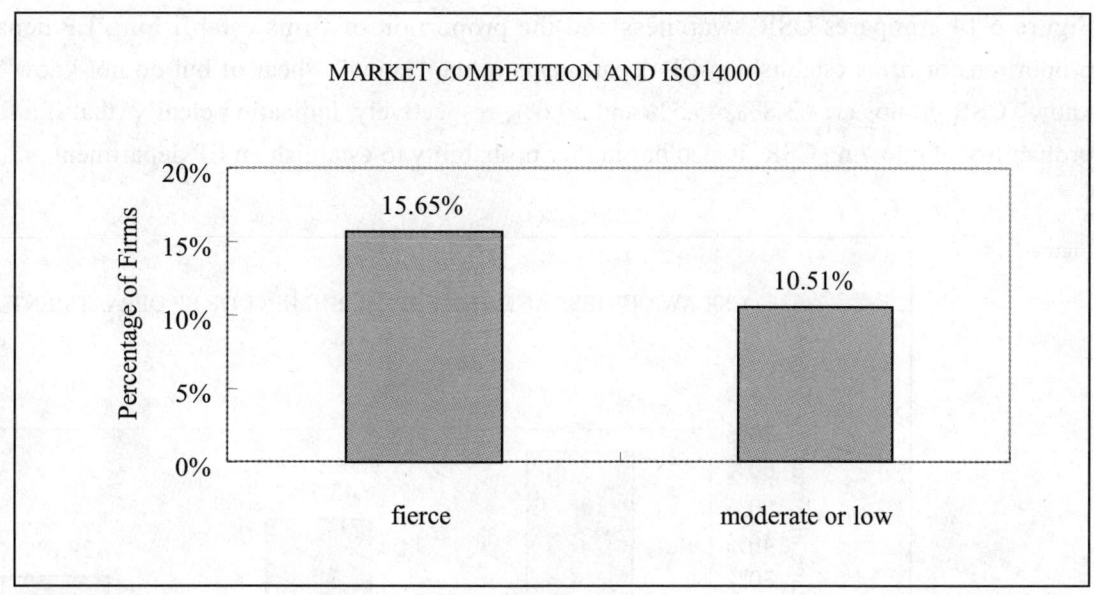

Finally, firms facing different degrees of competition also behave differently in their expenditure on environmental maintenance and investment. As shown in Table 6.1, firms in high competition markets on average spent 0.44 million Yuan on environment-related expenditure, but those in moderate and low competition markets spent 0.34 million on average. On the other hand, one needs to notice that firms facing fierce competition spent less on environment-related investment, as shown in the second column of Table 6.1. This implies that firms facing fierce competition are more interested in satisfying the current environmental standard, possibly by paying fees and fines, than doing more R & D on protecting the environment for the long run. Based on the standards by IFC (2002), these firms do not belong to the proactive group and this needs attention from the government to ensure sustainability in environmental protection.

Table 6.1

COMPETITION AND ENVIRONMENT-RELATED EXPENDITURE AND INVESTMENT

Degree of Competition	Average Expenditure in 2005 (1000 Yuan)	Average Investment in the past three years (1000 Yuan)
Fierce	441.557	1665.53
Moderate or low	344.75	2645.09

CSR Awareness and Environmental Protection Strategy

CSR awareness also has a great impact on firms' environmental protection behaviors. If we divide firms into three groups based on their awareness of CSR, we can observe how CSR awareness affects both firm efforts and achievements in protecting the environment.

Figure 6.14 compares CSR awareness and the proportion of firms establishing EP departments. The proportions of firms establishing EP departments in the "know", "hear of but do not know", and the "not know" CSR groups are 63.8%, 45.5% and 29.6%, respectively, indicating clearly that if a firm has higher probability of knowing CSR, it also has higher probability to establish an EP department.

Figure 6.14

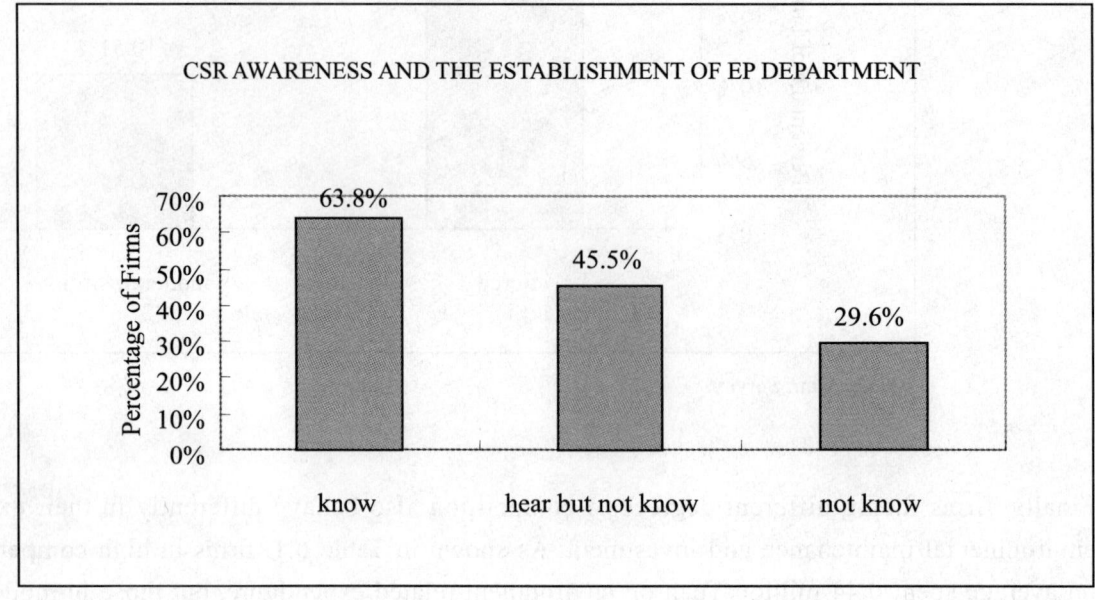

Source: Main Survey

It would also be of interest to compare the proportion of firms obtaining ISO14000 certificates among firms with different degrees of CSR awareness. Figure 6.15 shows that firms that know about CSR are more likely to hold ISO14000 certificates than those who are less familiar with CSR.

Figure 6.15

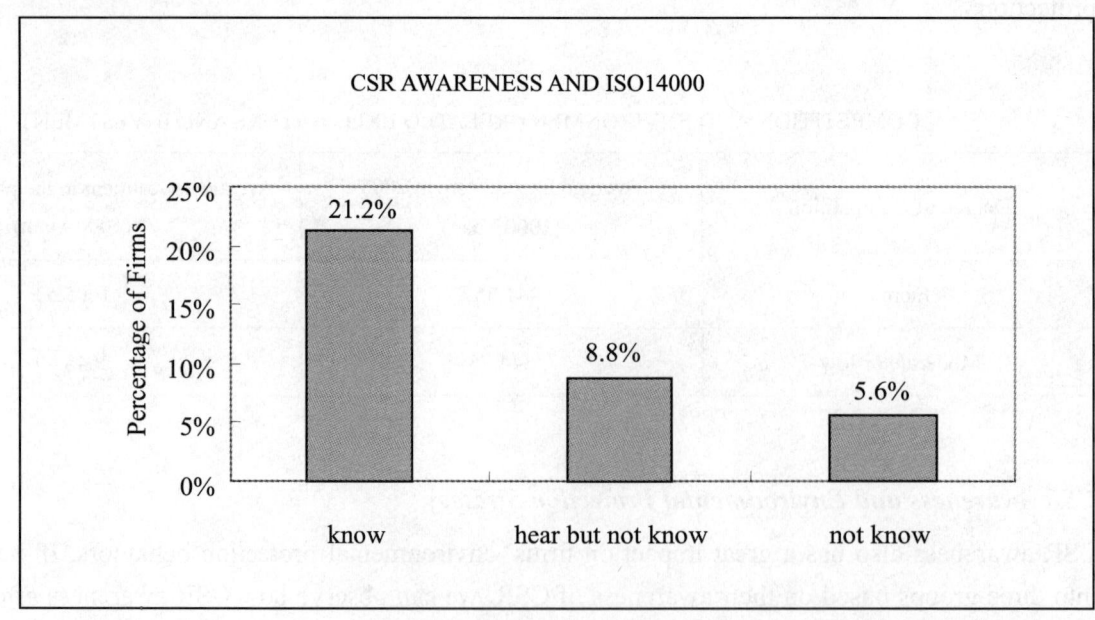

Source: Main Survey

From our observations on degrees of competition and environmental spending, we find that firms more aware of CSR emphasize environment protection in both their short-run and long-run development strategies. This is reflected in their average environmental expenditure and investment. Figure 6.16 and Figure 6.17 unambiguously indicate that firms knowing about CSR spend the most among the three groups and these firms spent more on environmental maintenance in 2005.

Figure 6.16

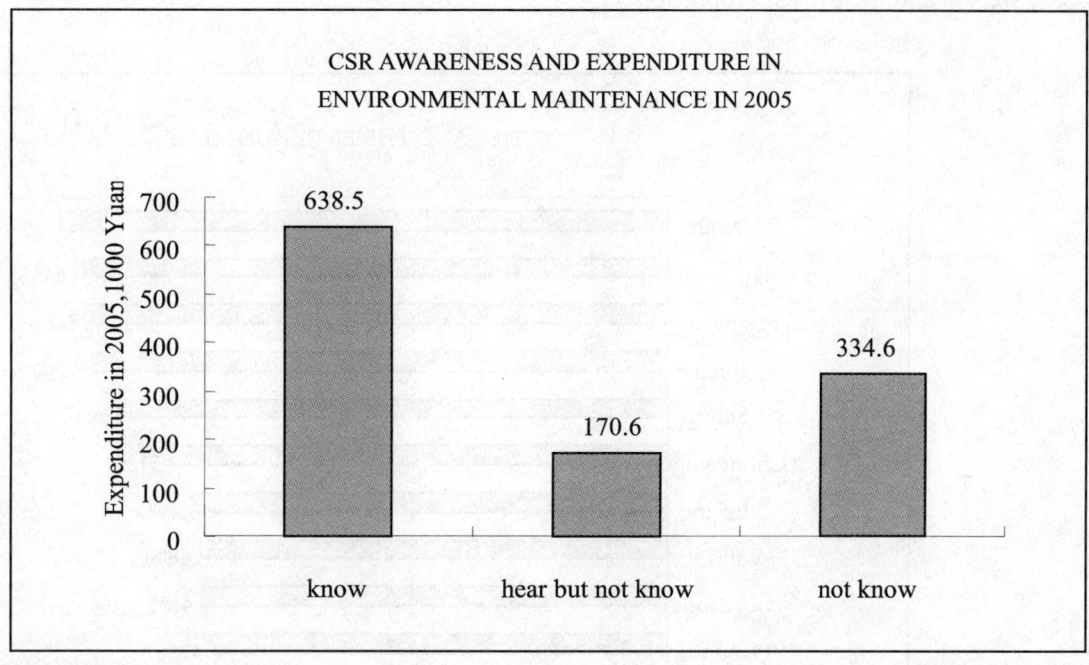

Source: Main Survey

Figure 6.17

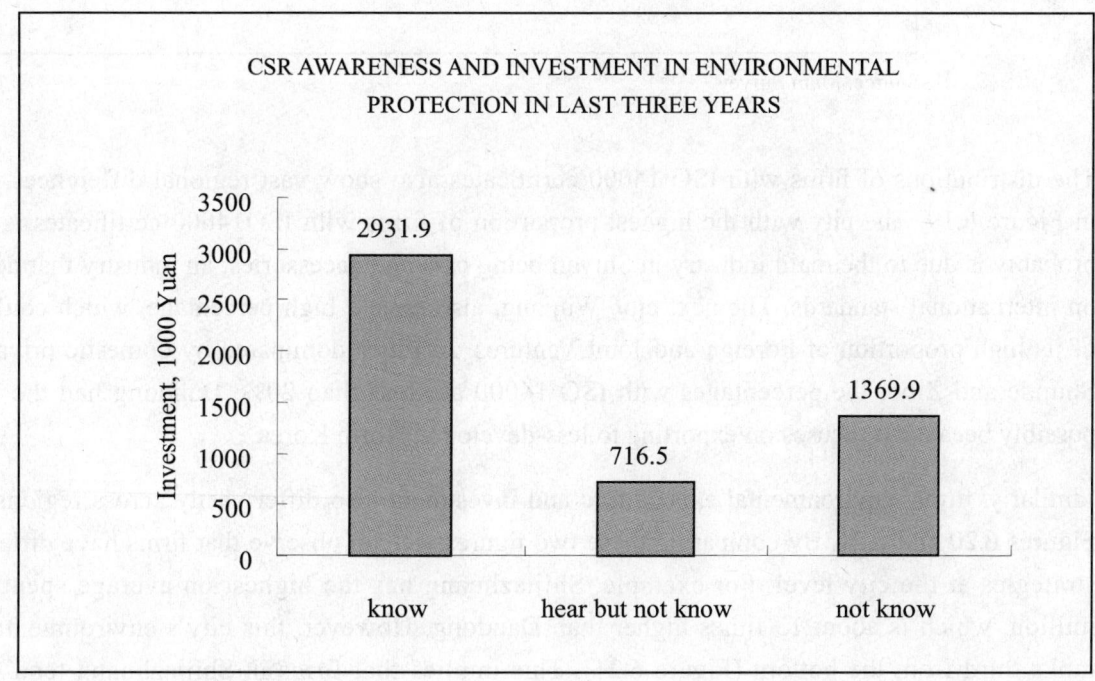

Source: Main Survey

Environmental Protection by Region

As Reinhardt (2000) has indicated, the choice of location can be an important consideration for firm strategies in dealing with environmental protection issues. In this subsection we compare the regional response strategies in terms of cities. Figure 6.18 compares the proportions of firms with EP departments in different cities. We observe this proportion varies considerably across cities, with the highest proportion being 62.4% and the lowest proportion 36%.

Figure 6.18

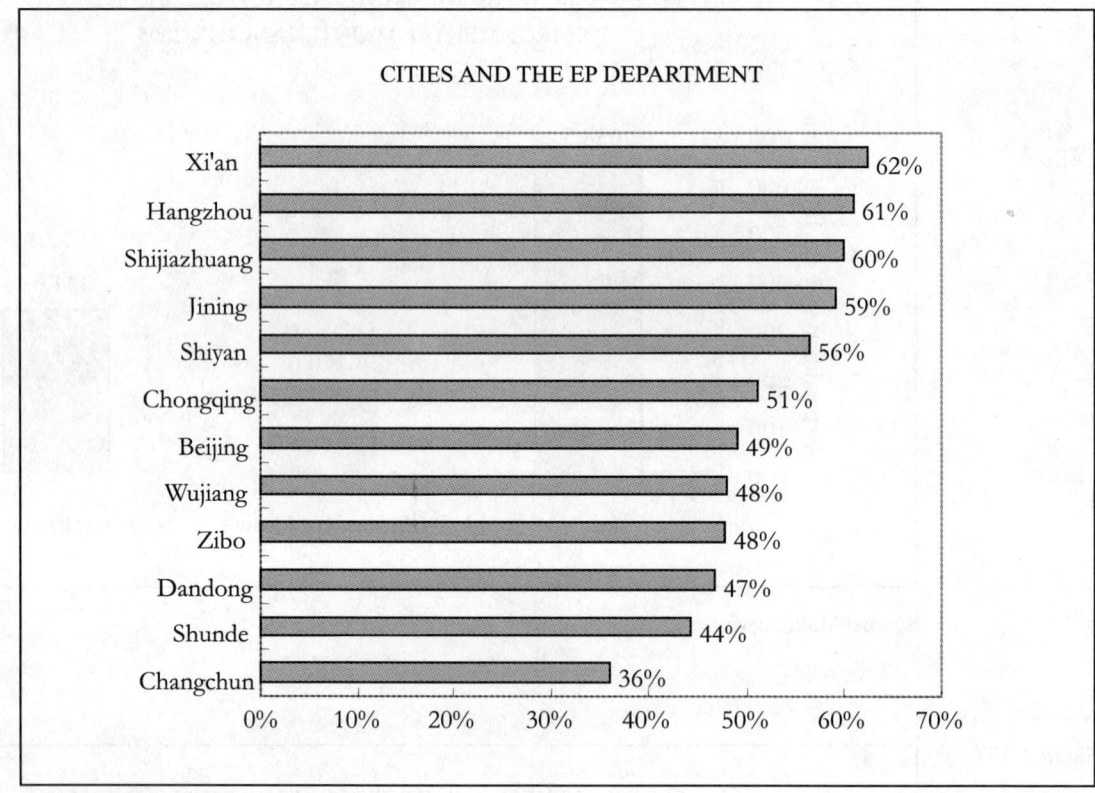

Source: Main Survey

The distributions of firms with ISO 14000 certificates also show vast regional differences, as illustrated in Figure 6.19. The city with the highest proportion of firms with ISO14000 certificates is Shiyan. This probably is due to the main industry in Shiyan being cars and accessories, an industry that depends highly on international standards. The next city, Wujiang, also have a high percentage, which could be because of its high proportion of Foreign and Joint Ventures. At cities dominated by domestic private firms, like Shunde and Zibo, the percentages with ISO 14000 are less than 20%. Dandong had the lowest share, possibly because it focuses on exporting to less-developed North Korea.

Similarly, firms' environmental expenditure and investment also differ vastly across regions as shown in Figures 6.20 and 6.21. By comparing these two figures we can observe that firms have different response strategies at the city level. For example, Shijiazhuang has the highest on average spending of 0.103 million, which is about 13 times higher than Dandong. However, this city's environmental investment ranks third from the bottom (Figure 6.21). This implies that firms in Shijiazhuang tend to emphasize meeting current environmental standards than to think about long-term investment. Wujiang, incontrast,

126

Figure 6.19

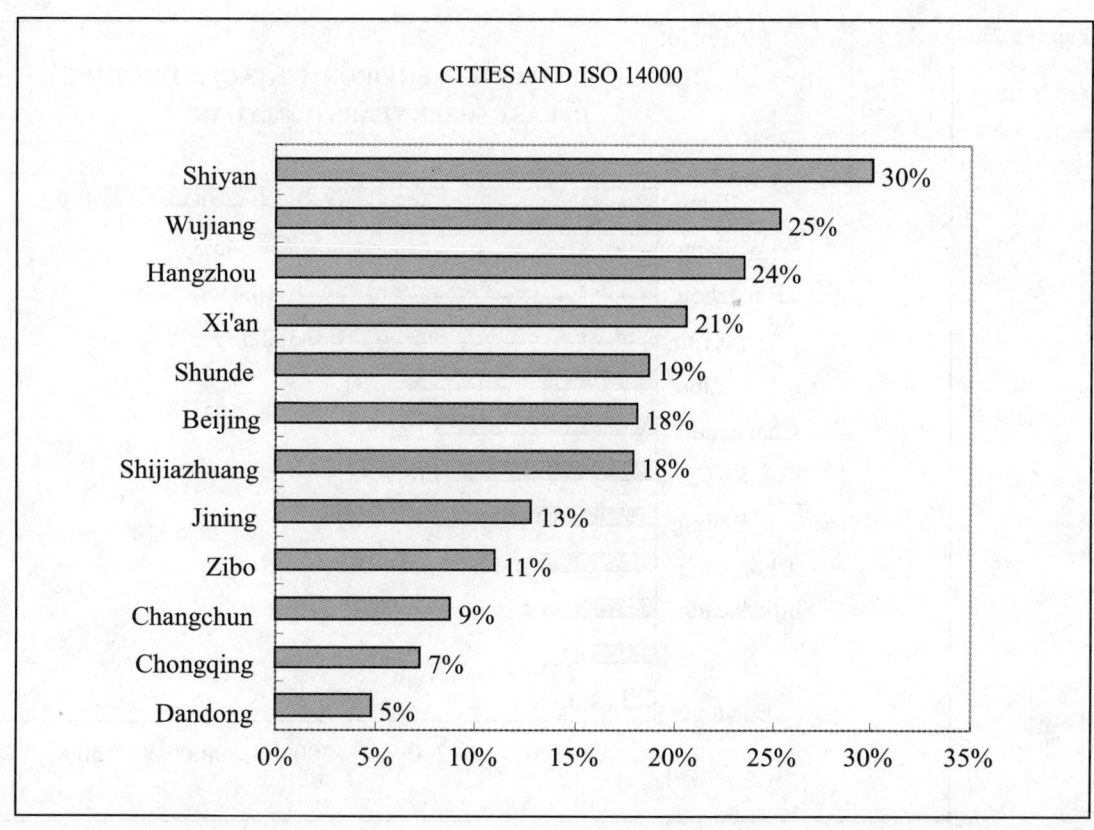

Source: Main Survey

Figure 6.20

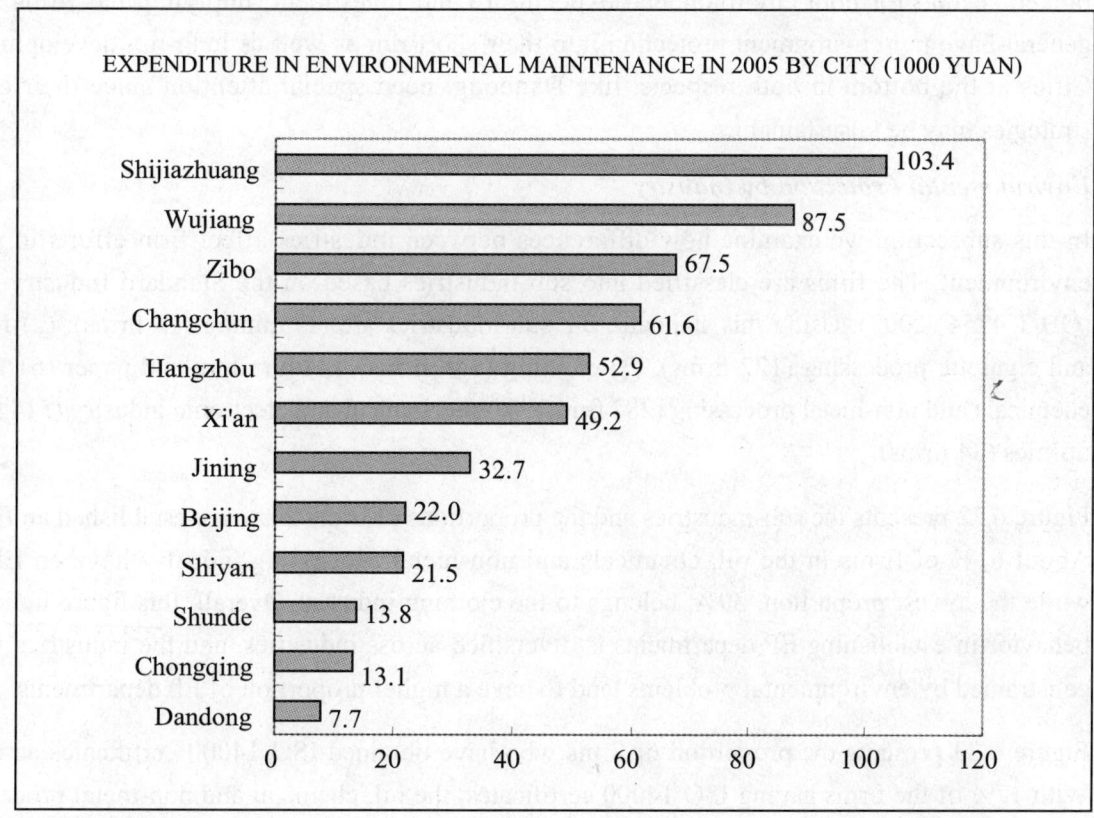

Source: Main Survey

Figure 6.21

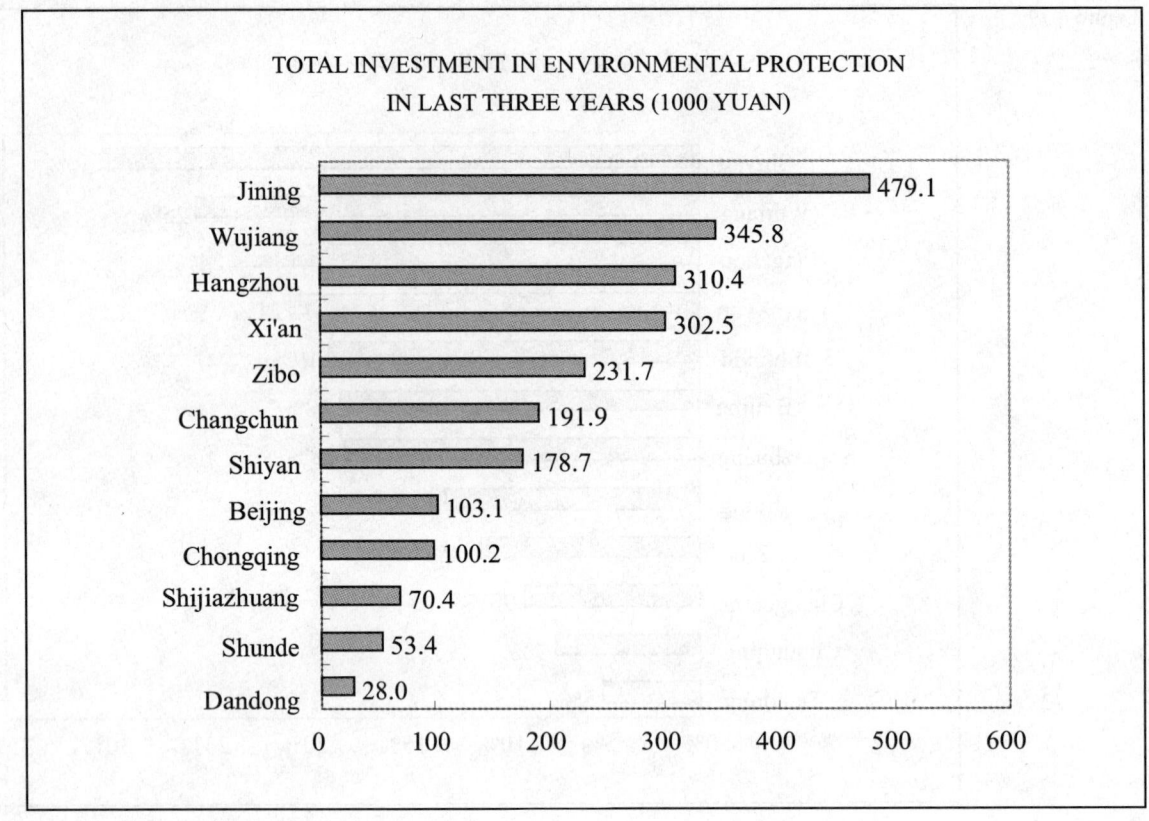

Source: Main Survey

ranked second for both environmental expenditure and investment, implying that firms in this city in general have put environment protection into their short-run as well as long-run development strategies. Cities at the bottom in both respects, like Dandong, need special attention since their environmental strategies may be unsustainable.

Environmental Protection by Industry

In this subsection we examine how differences between industries affect firm efforts in protecting the environment. The firms are classified into sub-industries based on the Standard Industry Classification (GB/T 4754 -2002). Using this standard, the sub-industries are (1) mining (15 firms), (2) food, beverage and cigarette processing (122 firms), (3) clothing (148 firms), (4) furniture and paper (61 firms), (5) oil, chemicals and non-metal processing (287 firms), (6) mechanical and electronic industry (514 firms), and (7) utilities (34 firms).

Figure 6.22 presents the sub-industries and the proportions of firms that have established an EP department. About 61% of firms in the oil, chemicals and non-metal processing industry have an EP department, while the lowest proportion, 39%, belongs to the clothing industry. Overall, this figure indicates that firm behavior in establishing EP departments is diversified across industries, and the industries which is more constrained by environmental problems tend to have a higher proportion of EP departments.

Figure 6.23 presents the proportion of firms who have obtained ISO 14000 certificates across industries. With 17% of the firms having ISO 14000 certificates, the oil, chemical and non-metal processing industry ranks number one on this list while mining has the lowest proportion. This information again indicates

Figure 6.22

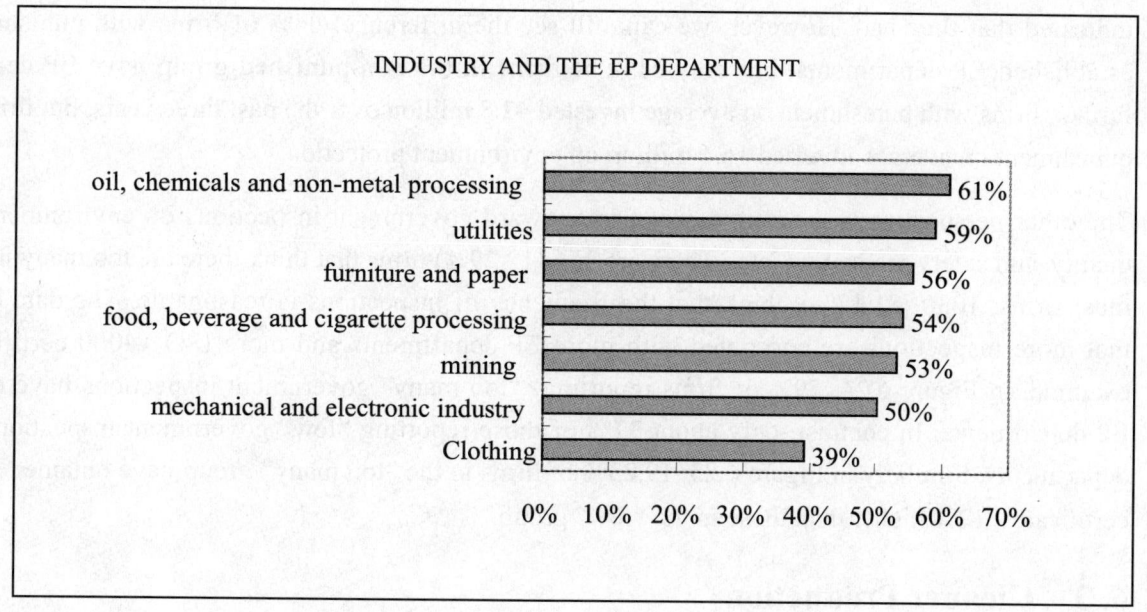

Figure 6.23

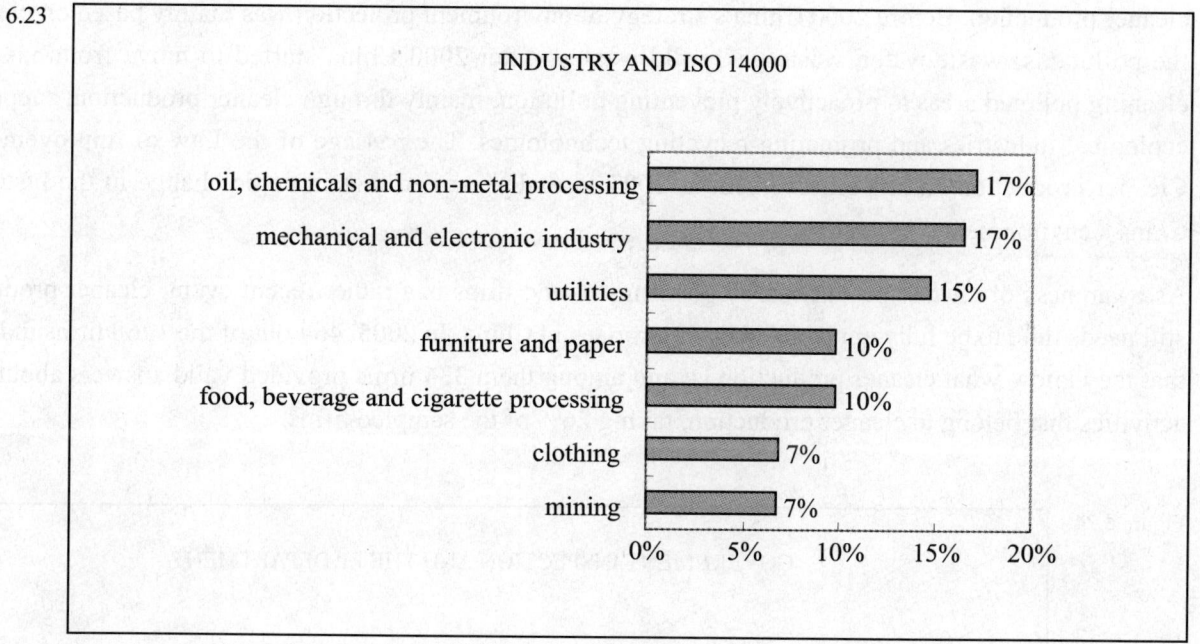

that the specific industry that the firm is in will have an impact on whether or not firms have incentives to get ISO 14000 certificates.

Government Policies and Environmental Protection

Government can influence firm environmental protection strategies through channels like inspections, fines and other types of regulation. In this subsection we focus on evaluating whether government punishment and inspection affect firm behavior in protecting the environment.

When asked about whether a firm has been punished for environmental issues, only 9.4% of firms indicated that they had. However, we can still see the difference: 64% of firms with punishment have established EP departments, but only 51% of firms in the non-punished group have EP departments; further, firms with punishment on average invested 42.8 million over the past three years, but firms without punishment on average invested 16.6 million on environment protection.

The other perspective is the attitudes of firms toward government inspections on environment, product quality, and safety production, etc.. There are 156 (12.29%) firms that think there are too many inspections, most firms, 1030 (81.17%), think that the frequency of inspections is reasonable. The data does show that more inspections are correlated with more EP departments and more ISO 14000 certificates. For example, in Figure 6.24, 59% of firms reporting "too many" government inspections have established EP departments. In contrast, only about 37% of those reporting "few" government inspections have EP departmants. Similarly in Figure 6.25, 19.23% of firms in the "too many" group have obtained ISO 14000 certificates, 12% higher than those in the "few" group.

6. 3 Cleaner Production

A critical change in environmental protection is in the attitudes of government and enterprises toward cleaner production. Before 2000 China's strategy of environment protection was mainly based on cleaning the pollutants: waste water, waste gas, solid wastes. After 2000 China started to move from passively cleaning polluted areas to proactively preventing pollution, mainly through cleaner production, supporting ecological industries and promoting recycling technologies. The passage of the Law of Improvement of Cleaner production and its enforcement in 2003 formally marked this strategic change in the history of China s environmental protection.

As awareness of cleaner production by government and firms is a rather recent event, cleaner production still needs time to be fully appreciated by enterprises in China. In 2005, 464 out of the 1268 firms indicated that they know what cleaner production is, and among them 334 firms provided valid answers about three activities that belong to cleaner production, taking 26% of the sampled firms.

Figure 6.24

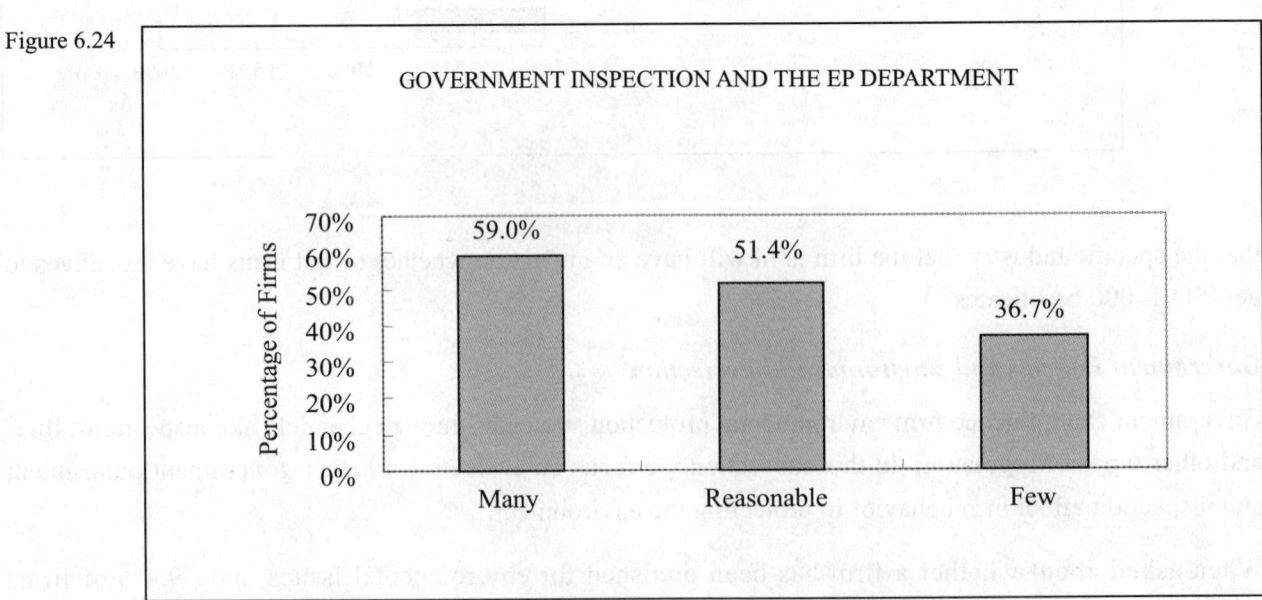

Figure 6.25

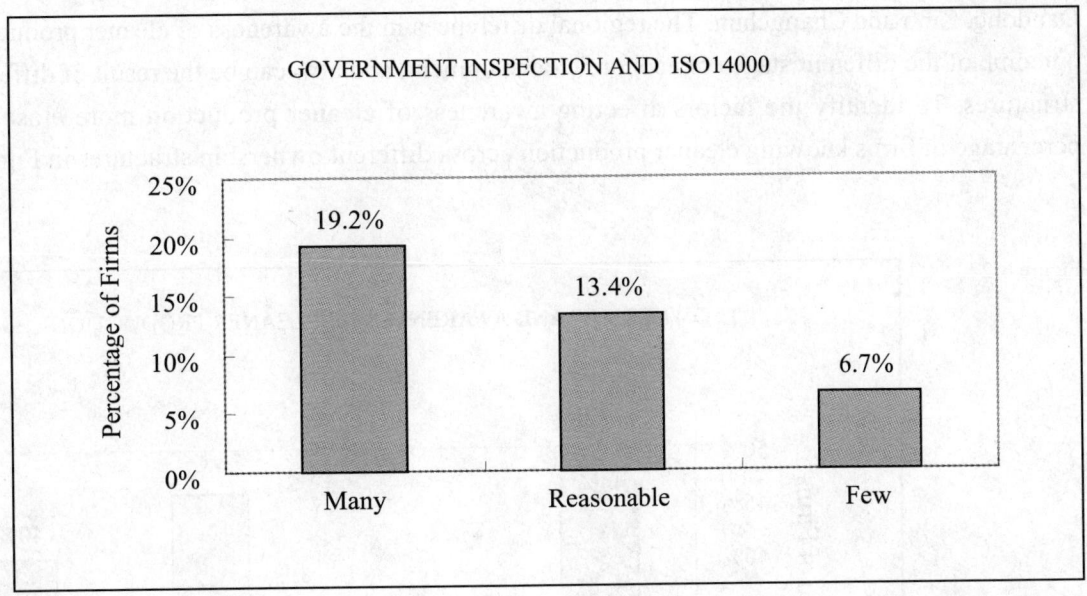

Figure 6.26

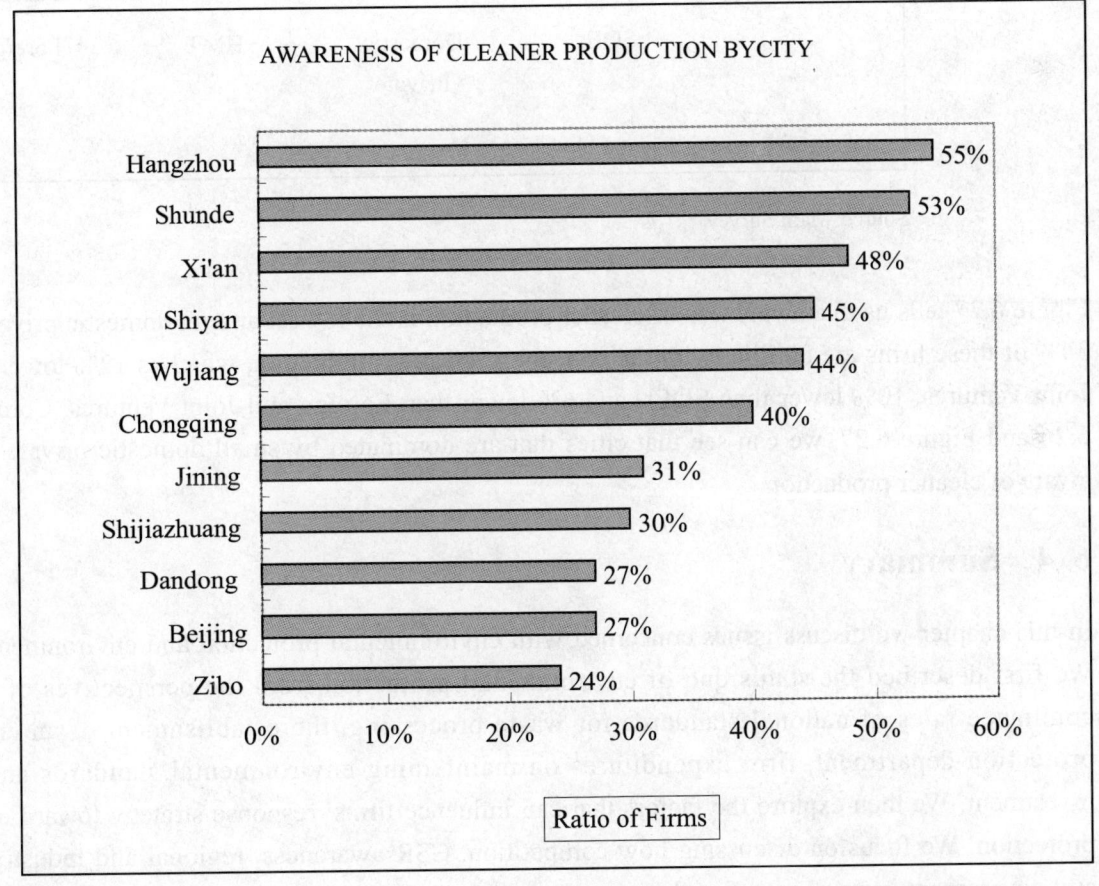

Source: Main Survey

The awareness of cleaner production varies across regions as well as for firms with different ownership structures. Figure 6.26 shows the regional differences. Cleaner production is known only in two cities, Hangzhou and Shunde, by more than half of the firms. The lowest percentages are below 30% for Beijing,

Dandong, Zibo and Changchun. The regional differences in the awareness of cleaner production can be the outcome of the different stages of economic development, and also can be the result of different ownership structures. To identify the factors affecting awareness of cleaner production more closely, we plot the percentage of firms knowing cleaner production across different ownership structures in Figure 6.27.

Figure 6.27

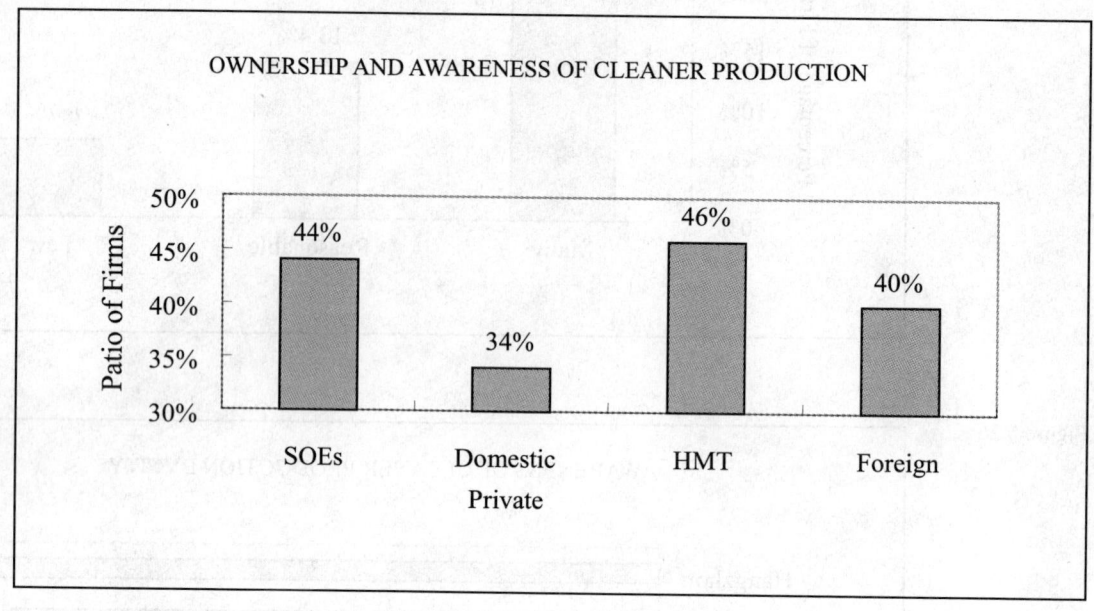

Source: Main Survey

Figure 6.27 tells us that awareness of cleaner production is the lowest among domestic private firms. Only 34% of these firms are familiar with the concept of cleaner production, which is 12% lower than HMT & Joint Ventures, 10% lower than SOEs, and 6% lower than Foreign and Joint Ventures. Combining Figure 6.26 and Figure 6.27, we can see that cities that are dominated by small domestic private firms are less aware of cleaner production.

6. 4   Summary

In this chapter we discuss issues concerned with environmental protection and environmental standards. We first described the status quo of environmental protection from the perspectives of self-reported comliance rates of national standards for waste processing, the establishment of an environmental protection department, firm expenditures on maintaining environmental standards and equipment investment. We then explore the factors that can influence firms' response strategy toward environmental protection. We focus on discussing how competition, CSR awareness, regional and industry differences, and government inspections affect firms' environmental protection behavior.

We find that firms facing fierce competition put more effort into setting up environmental protection departments, in complying with national standards and in making environment-related expenditures, but spent less on environmental-related investment than firms facing moderate and low market competition. Firms which are more aware of CSR, on the other hand, perform better in protecting the environment from all perspectives than firms knowing less about CSR. We also observe large regional differences and industry differences in environmental protection. Putting all these information together, a message for policy-makers is that policies need to pay more attention to regional and industry differences to effectively protect the environment. Furthermore, promoting CSR among private firms and helping firms facing fierce competition to fully appreciate the benefits of protecting the environment will be important steps toward encouraging firms to take environmental protection more proactively.

We also wish to call particular attention to the situation of domestic private firms. They seem to be the weakest link in the course of environmental protection. In general they are small in size and large expenditures on environmental protection are often less unaffordable for them. They are the group that has the least proportion of firms with ISO 14000 and they are least aware of cleaner production. Therefore, it is very important for policy makers to foster mechanisms that provide firms with more incentives to protect the environment and to make them more aware of the business case for taking care of the environment.

Chapter 7
Product Quality

Product quality is essential for the survival and prosperity of a firm. However, according to data collected by Sohu Finance channel, 33% of the CSR-related disputes in China were concerned with product quality and food safety in 2006. The involved companies included famous multinationals like Bosch & Lomb, Dell, and SKII as well as domestic enterprises. While firms can make profits with inferior products in the short-run, such products are detrimental for their long-run sustainability.

One example is the tainted milk event exposed to the public on September 18th, 2008. Worry and fear spread when the public got to know that baby formula was tainted with industrial chemical melamine, leading to the death of four infants and kidney stones to over 50,000 of other. This event was then turned into a crisis for the diary industry when supermarkets cleared products from their shelves, and when Taiwan, Singapore and Japan found tainted dairy goods imparted from China. The development of this event reflects that product quality is not just crucial for the survival of one firm, it can be crucial for the whole industry, for the confidence of the public on China-made brands.

This chapter provides an analysis of product quality and food safety based on data collected from the main survey. The analysis will focus on the factors that affect product quality management, product quality certification, brand name establishment, and quality inspection. Section 7.1 describes the status quo of product quality through self-evaluations by firms and more subjective measures like ISO 9001 accreditation and qualification for national and firm-specific product quality standards. Section 7.2 is concerned with the measures that firms have taken to improve product quality. Section 7.3 discusses factors that can affect product quality and firm efforts in product quality management.

7.1   The Status Quo of Product Quality

In this subsection we describe product quality through several perspectives. The first is the subjective evaluation of product quality. The second is whether the respondent firms have obtained ISO9001 accreditation for their products. Thirdly, we examine whether there are national standards and firm-specific product quality standards, and the last perspective is to look at the degree of danger in products.

Product Quality: Self-Evaluation by Firms

We first investigate the subjective evaluations of relative product quality as compared with other firms in the same industry. Even though subjective evaluations have the shortcoming that firms may tend to underestimate the degree of danger and hazard inherent in their products but over-estimate their product

Figure 7.1

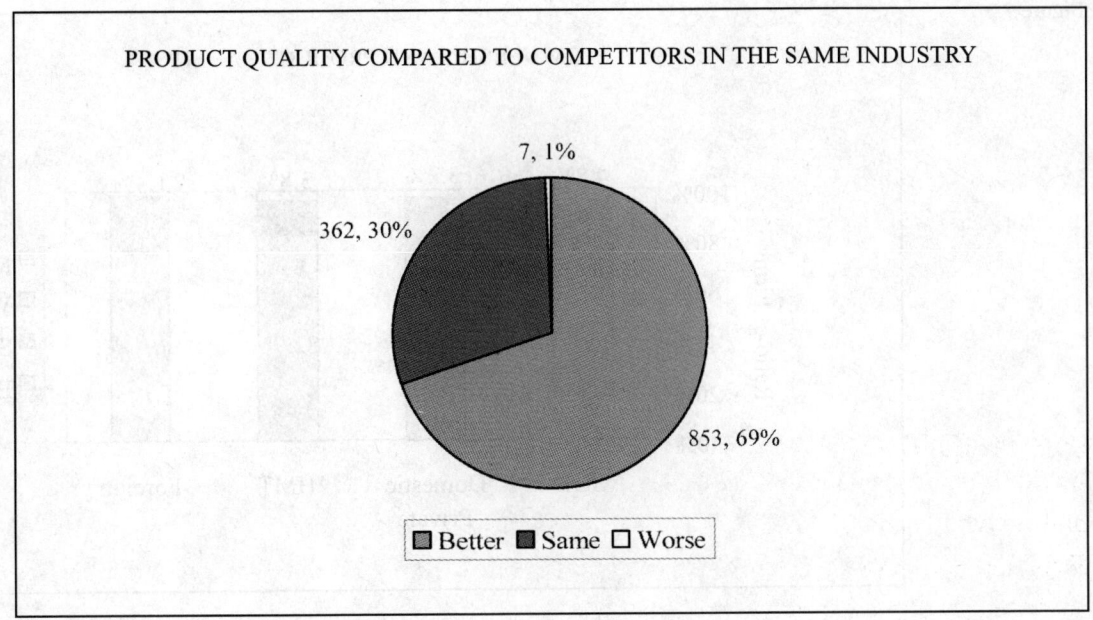

PRODUCT QUALITY COMPARED TO COMPETITORS IN THE SAME INDUSTRY

7, 1%

362, 30%

853, 69%

☐ Better ■ Same ☐ Worse

Source: Main Survey

quality, we should still be able to observe the big pictures as long as firms behave similarly. Figure 7.1 depicts how each firm perceives its own product quality. 69% of the firms are confident that their products are better than those of their peers, 30% of the firms believe that their product quality is similar to that of their competitors. Only 1% firms admit their product quality to be inferior to that of others, implying that over-estimation of the product quality in the remaining 99% firms is an issue. On the other hand, if firms exaggerate their product quality homogenously, the relative product quality is still comparable.

One way to check whether firms have a homogenous attitude toward over-estimation is to study the correlation relationship between market shares of firms with their confidence in their own product quality. As the product quality part of the survey is filled up by production manager but the market share part is filled up by sales manager, we can consider these two pieces of information independently provided. If

Figure 7.2

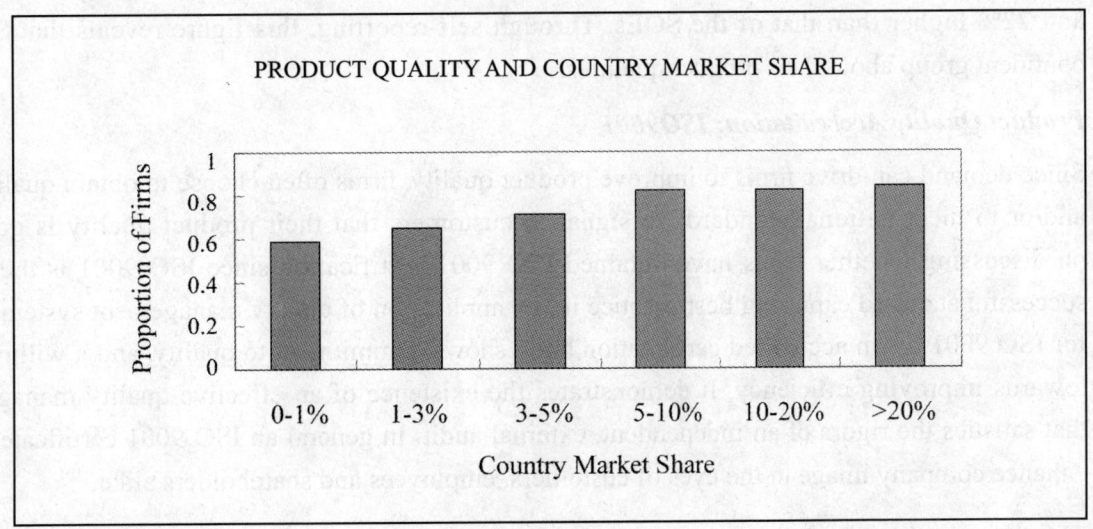

PRODUCT QUALITY AND COUNTRY MARKET SHARE

Source: Main Survey

Figure 7.3

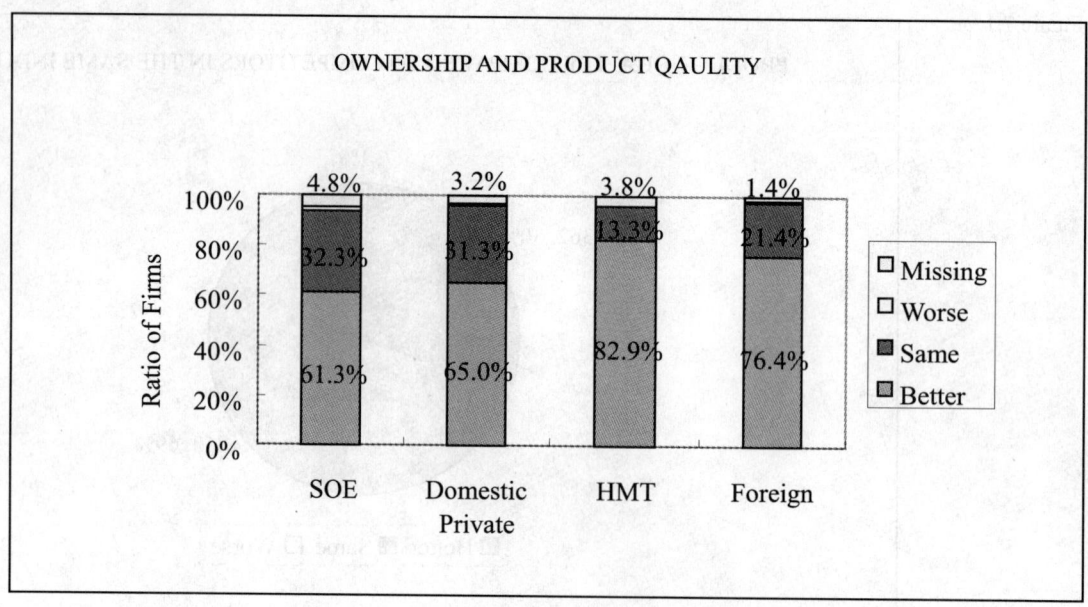

Source: Main Survey

there is a strong positive correlation between the more-objective market shares with the more-subjective evaluations of product quality, then such phenomenon can be considered as supporting homogenous over-estimation of product quality. Figure 7.2 confirms that this is indeed the case. The horizontal axis represents the product country market shares, where we divide all firms into 6 categories based on their reported product market shares. The vertical axis represents the percentage of firms who believe their products are of better quality than those of competitors. This figure suggests that the larger the market share, the higher the percentage of firms who believe their products are of better quality.

Having confirmed that the relative comparison of product quality is meaningful, we then investigate the factors that may affect product quality. Figure 7.3 indicates that higher proportions of joint ventures believe their products are better than those of domestic firms. Among the joint ventures, 83% of the HMT & Joint ventures reported their products are better, 6% higher than that of the Foreign and Joint Ventures, and 22% higher than that of the SOEs. Through self-reporting, this figure reveals that SOEs are least confident group about their product qualities.

Product Quality Accreditation: ISO9001

Since demand can drive firms to improve product quality, firms often choose to obtain quality certificates, and/or to meet national standards to signal to customers that their product quality is good. We focus on discussing whether firms have obtained ISO 9001 certification since ISO 9001 is the world's most successful standard capturing best practice in the application of quality management systems. Registration for ISO 9001 by an accredited certification body shows commitment to quality, and a willingness to work towards improving efficiency. It demonstrates the existence of an effective quality management system that satisfies the rigors of an independent, external audit. In general an ISO 9001 certificate is believed to enhance company image in the eyes of customers, employees and shareholders alike.

The firms in the sample in general recognize the importance of ISO 9001. There are 57.89% of firms registered for ISO 9001 through an accredited certification. This is 25% higher than firm registration for other certifications for product quality. The timing in obtaining ISO 9001 varies. 75% of the certified firms were accredited in and after 2000, indicating that ISO 9001 is a new standard to most Chinese firms. The typical firm certified before 2000 would be an SOE, or an exporting firm of moderate size, whereas after 2000 the majority of certified firms are domestic private firms, or firms focusing on the domestic market, or of small size.

Since ISO 9001 is an international standard, one would expect that non-domestic firms have advantages in appreciating its importance as well as making efforts to obtain it, and also that firms aiming at international markets have stronger incentives to get accredited. This is indeed the case. Near 70% of the Foreign and Joint Ventures obtained this certification, 13% higher than domestic private firms and 10% higher than SOEs (Figure 7.4). For firms focusing on international markets through exporting, 66% of them are certified, 12% higher than non-exporting firms.

Figure 7.4

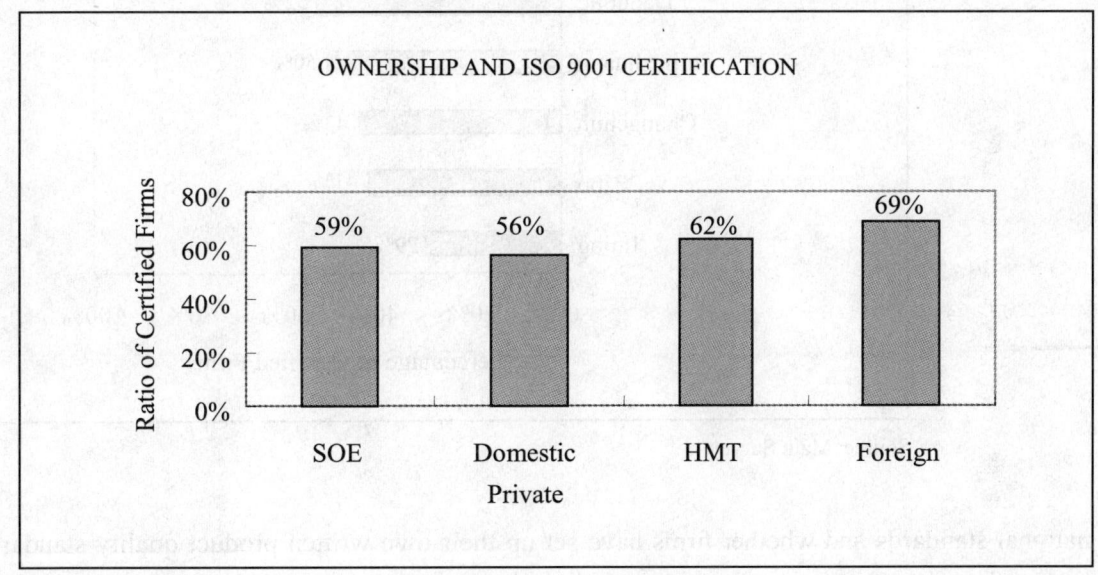

Source: Main Survey

It is interesting to notice that the proportions of ISO 9001 certified firms have quite distinct regional differences. Figure 7.5 presents their differences across cities. Overall, the western region gets similar shares of certified firms as the coastal regions. In particular, Chongqing gets the highest share of 80%, with the majority of firms (over 60%) to be domestic private, small size and non-exporting firms. Xi'an follows Chongqing to be the second highest certified city, but with exporting and non-exporting firms having similar shares. Jining gets the lowest share as it is an inland and less developed region. There are no joint ventures in the sampled firms, and 24% firms are agricultural firms for Jining. The central region gets the lowest share of certified firms as the shares of its four cities, Changchun, Dandong, Zibo and Shijiazhuang, are only somewhat higher than Jining.

Existence of National Standard and Firm-specific Standards

The third perspective from which to inspect the status quo of product quality is to check the existence of

Figure 7.5

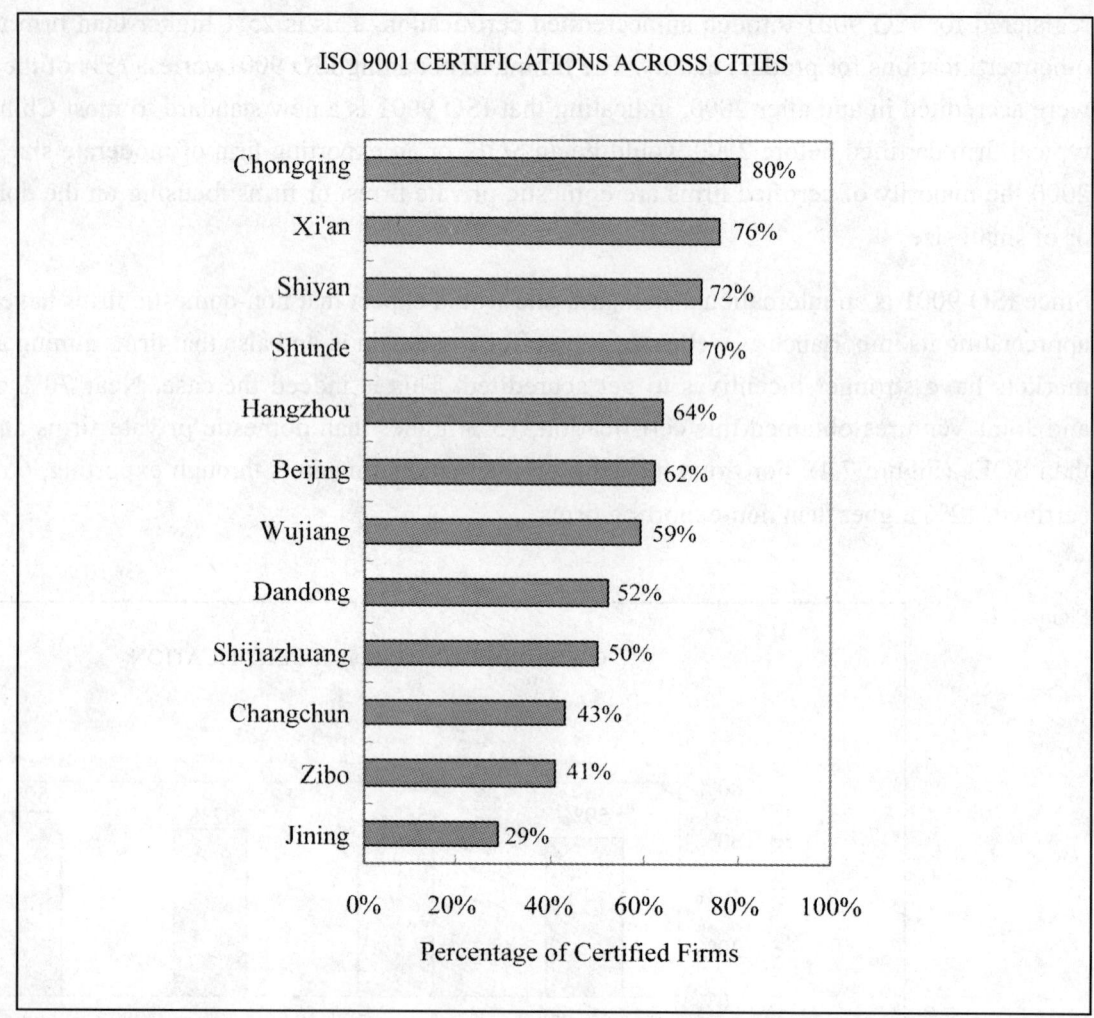

ISO 9001 CERTIFICATIONS ACROSS CITIES

City	Percentage
Chongqing	80%
Xi'an	76%
Shiyan	72%
Shunde	70%
Hangzhou	64%
Beijing	62%
Wujiang	59%
Dandong	52%
Shijiazhuang	50%
Changchun	43%
Zibo	41%
Jining	29%

Percentage of Certified Firms

Source: Main Survey

national standards and whether firms have set up their own written product quality standards. Figure 7.6 groups firms into four categories based on the existence of such standards. The label N indicates a national standard, F indicates a firm standard, 0 represents no related standard and 1 indicates that such standards do exist. For example, label "(N1, F1)" means the product has national standard as well as firm production standards. Figure 7.6 shows that 901 firms report their products have both national and firm-specific standards, 41 firms have only national standards, and there are 98 firms faces neither national standards nor firm-specific standards. Furthermore, for those who have both national and firm-specific standards, 27% of the firms report their standards are higher than national standards, and the rest 73% firms believe their product quality standards are as stringent as those of national standards. We use whether firm product quality standards are higher than national standards as a proxy for firms' product quality in later analysis about factors affecting firms product quality.

Product Safety

As products can be beneficial as well as potentially hazardous to the environment and people, it is necessary to investi-gate the flip side of product quality, that is, the hazard or danger level of their products. When being asked about the potential hazard degree of their products, 65% of the firms believe their products have no hazards, another 29% of firms think the hazard degree of their products is very low, only 6% of firms admit that their product is moderately hazardous or very dangerous (Figure 7.7).

Figure 7. 6

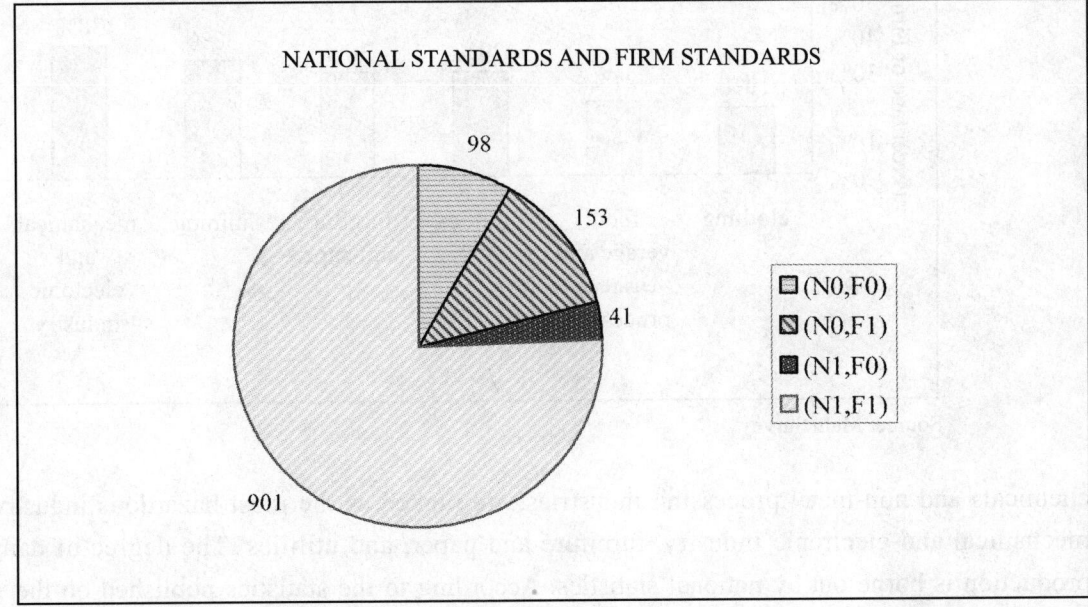

NATIONAL STANDARDS AND FIRM STANDARDS

Legend:
- (N0,F0)
- (N0,F1)
- (N1,F0)
- (N1,F1)

Source: Main Survey

Figure 7. 7

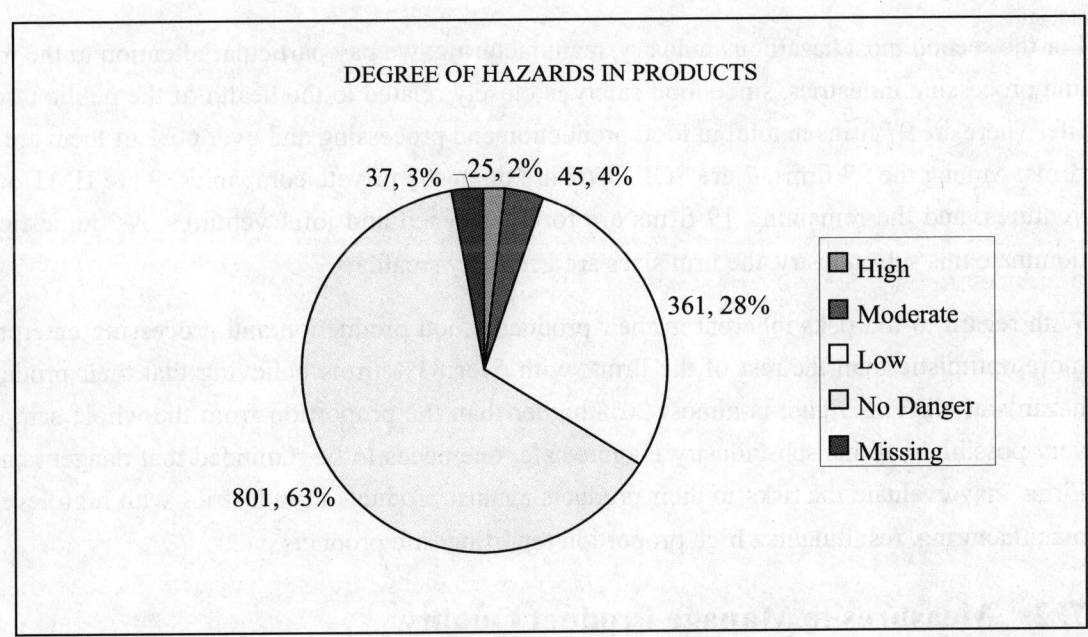

DEGREE OF HAZARDS IN PRODUCTS

Legend:
- High
- Moderate
- Low
- No Danger
- Missing

Source: Main Survey

Intuitively, product hazards are closely related to the industry to which the product belongs. Figure 7.8 provides the proportion of firms choosing at least some level of hazard for their products across industries surveyed in this sample. With 46% of firms indicating their products have at least some hazards, oil,

Figure 7. 8

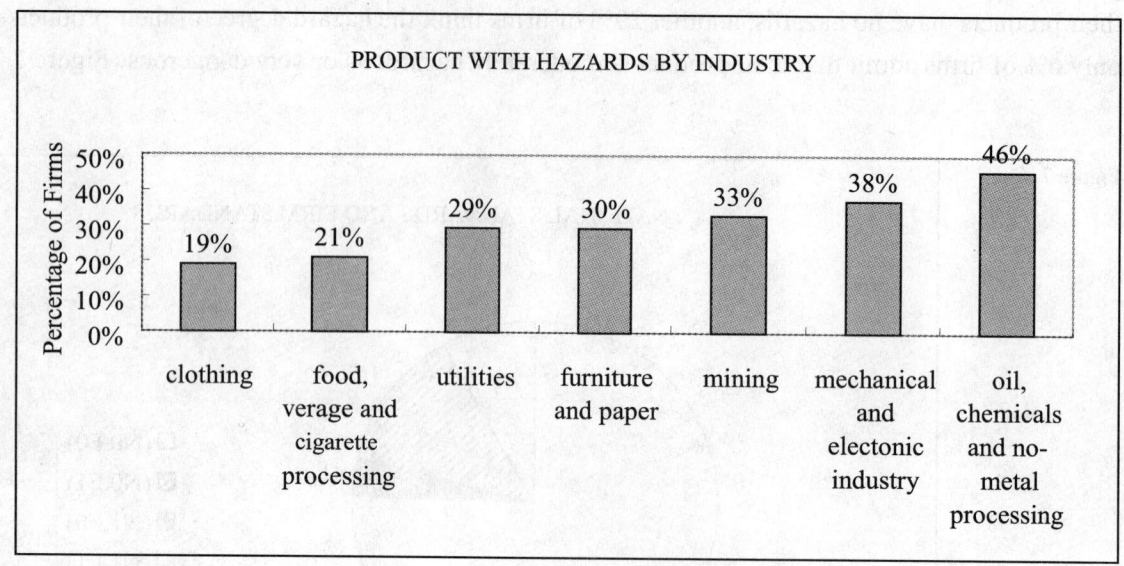

Source: Main Survey

chemicals and non-metal processing industries, are ranked as the most hazardous industry followed by mechanical and electronic industry, furniture and paper, and utilities. The degree of danger in mining production is borne out by national statistics. According to the statistics published on the website of the State Administration of Work Safety[1], there were 12065 safe production accidents in commerce and mining firms causing 14382 deaths in 2006. In particular, there were 2945 accidents in coal-mining and 4746 lives were lost, taking about 33% of all the deaths in commerce and mining firms[2].

For the second most hazardous industry, manufacturing, we pay particular attention to the food production and processing industries, since food safety is closely related to the health of the public through everyday life. There are 97 firms in total in food production and processing and over 60% of them are non-exporting firms. Among the 97 firms, 7 are SOEs, 62 are domestic private companies, 9 are HMT owned and joint ventures, and the remaining 19 firms are foreign owned and joint ventures. As domestic private firms dominate this sub-industry, the firm sizes are generally small.

With regard to the risks inherent in their products, food production and processing enterprises are much more optimistic than the rest of the firms, with over 83% firms believing that their products present no hazards at all. This figure is almost 20% higher than the proportion from the whole sample. While it is very possible that this sub-industry is quite safe, one needs to be reminded that danger is a relative term. Firms may evaluate the risks in their products against products in industries with high levels of risk, like manufacturing, resulting in a high proportion reporting safe products.

7. 2   Measures to Manage Product Quality

Since product quality is vital for the sustainability of enterprises, it is also important to examine what

---

[1] Statistics about safe production in 2006 can be found from http://www.chinasafety.gov.cn/anquanfenxi/2007-01/11/content_214963.htm.

[2] Total accidents and total deaths from non-coal mining, however, cannot be directly found from the above website, but coal mining takes the major proportion. Based on the accidents disclosed on the above website, coal-mining accidents cause about 76% of all deaths in the mining industry.

measures firms have taken to ensure the quality of their products. In this section we mainly consider the establishment of quality control departments among all firms, measures to inspect product quality, and firm efforts in establishing brand names.

Quality Control Department

Overall, firms in the sample realize the importance of quality management, and make the effort to establish quality management departments and set up written product quality standards. There were 1,121, or 88.41% of the firms indicating that they had a quality management (QM) department in 2005, and only 115, or 9.07% of firms do not have quality control departments[3]. 84.63% of the firms also indicate that they have written quality management standards. We focus on discussing the establishment of quality control departments as it is highly correlated with written quality management standards. In particular, we inspect the incentives and the timing of the establishment of the QM department.

Firms may feel it necessary to establish a QM department because they realize that better inspection of product quality is essential for their long-term developments. We investigate whether firms with different ownership structures, and whether firms facing different degrees of competition behave differently with regard to QM establishment. Indeed, domestic firms and joint ventures behave differently; with joint ventures having a higher percentage of firms with quality control departments than domestic firms (Figure 7.9).

Figure 7.9

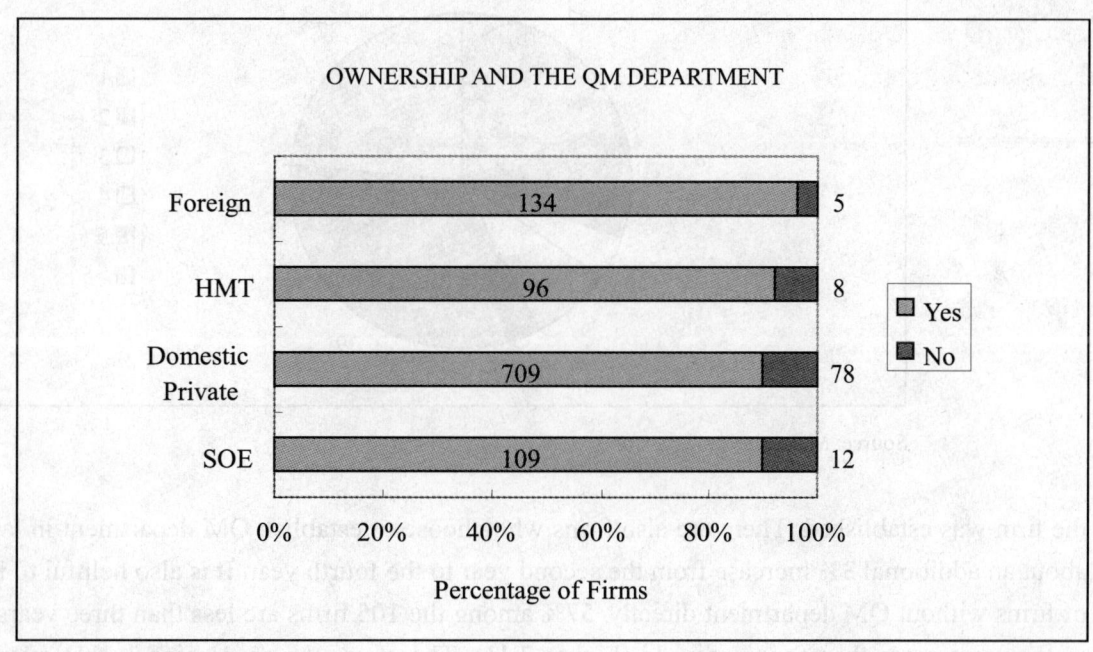

Source: Main Survey

With regard to the timing of QM department establishment, firms can either establish it at the very beginning, or to establish it at a suitable time after the firm has survived the initial years of operation. Figure 7.10 indicates that the majority of firms (82%) choose to establish their QM department in the year

---

[3] The percentages are calculated using the total number of firms as the denominator, instead of using all of those who provide answers to this question. The remaining 2.52% firms missed this question.

Figure 7.10

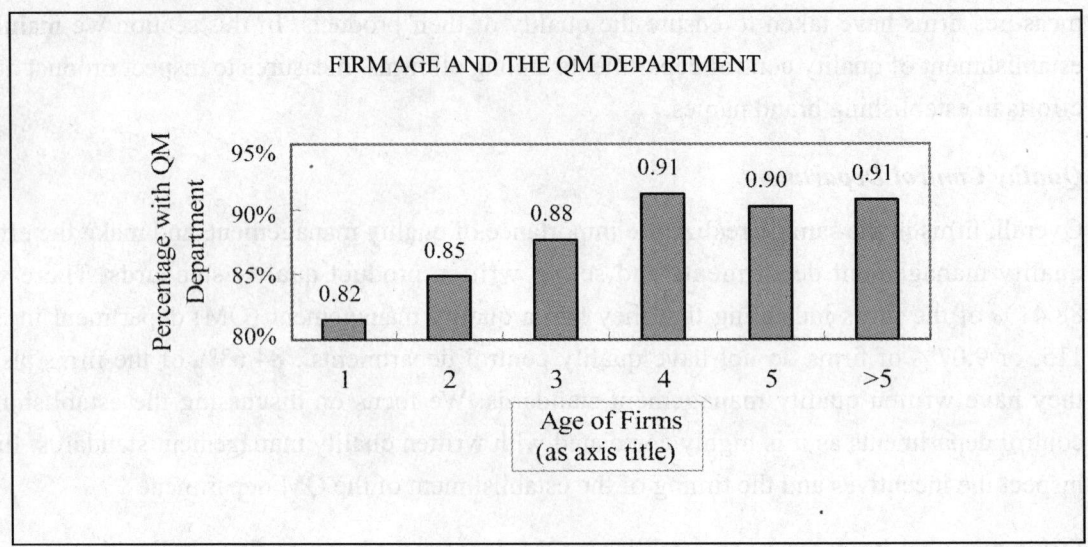

FIRM AGE AND THE QM DEPARTMENT

Source: Main Survey

Figure 7.11

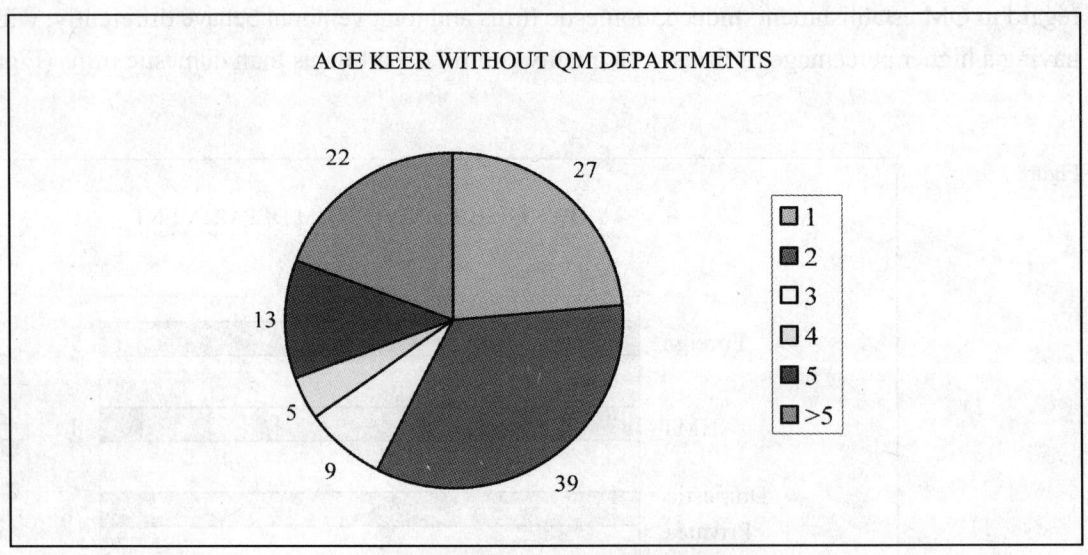

AGE KEER WITHOUT QM DEPARTMENTS

Source: Main Survey

the firm was established. There are also firms who choose to establish QM department in later years, with about an additional 3% increase from the second year to the fourth year. It is also helpful to inspect the age of firms without QM department directly. 57% among the 105 firms are less than three years old, and 31% of them are more than four years old (Figure 7.11). Therefore, the conclusion is that over 90% of firms choose to establish their QM departments in the first 5 years of their businesses, but if a firm does not have a QM department after 5 years of its establishment, it has little incentive to do so. A standard related to age is firm's size, since firm size tends to increase once a firm starts to make stable profit. This implies that the percentage of firms with QM department will be greater for firms of larger size. This is confirmed in Figure 7.12[4].

---

[4] There are 117 firms who missed either employment size information or the quality management department information. The percentage is calculated based on firms that provide both pieces of information.

Figure 7.12

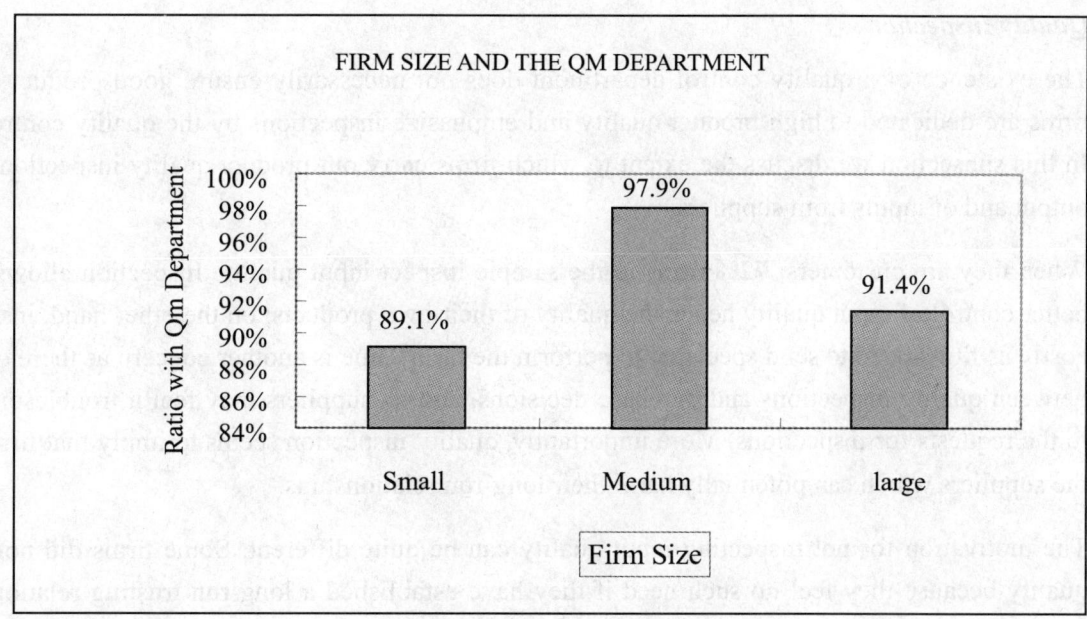

Source: Main Survey

It is also possible that firms establish QM departments simply because they are obliged to do so to satisfy the requirements of their customers. To check the extent to which firms are obliged to establish a QM department by customers we can compare the behavior of exporting firms with that of non-exporting firms. 94% of the exporting firms have QM departments, which is 6% higher than non-exporting firms (Figure 7.13).

Figure 7.13

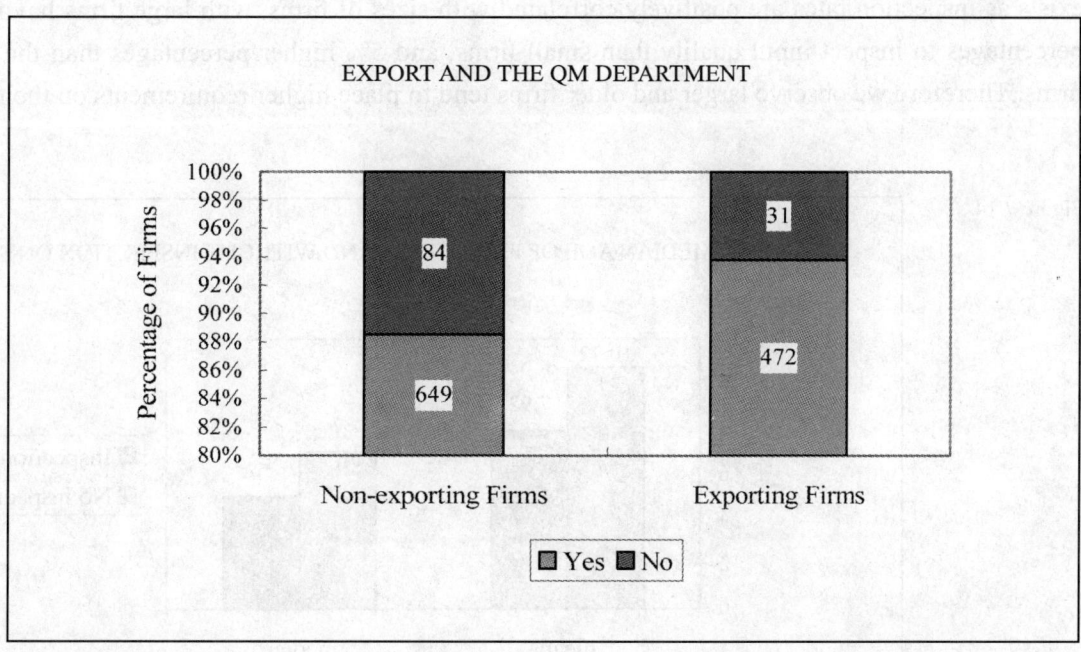

Source: Main Survey

Quality Inspection

The existence of a quality control department does not necessarily ensure good product quality unless firms are dedicated to high product quality and emphasize inspections by the quality control department. In this subsection we discuss the extent to which firms carry out product quality inspections of their own output and of inputs from suppliers.

When they are customers, 72% firms in the sample inspect input quality. Inspection allows firms to gain better control of input quality hence the quality of their own products; on the other hand, inspection is also costly as firms need to send specialist to perform the task. Time is another concern as there often exist lags between quality inspections and purchase decisions, and its suppliers may feel it troublesome to conform to the requests for inspections. More importantly, quality inspection seems to imply that firms do not trust the suppliers which can potentially harm their long-run relationships.

The motivation for not inspecting input quality can be quite different. Some firms did not inspect input quality because they feel no such need if they have established a long-run trusting relationship between each other. If this is the case, then older firms may have a tendency to waive input quality inspection. Other firms waiving input inspection may be because they do not have enough bargaining power to request such checkups. Since young firms and small firms are relatively weak in bargaining with their suppliers, we expect that they have a lower probability of checking input quality if the age and size effect dominates.

To check the age effect, we plot the mean and median age for the inspection and non-inspection groups in Figure 7.14. The median age is provided to avoid the impact of outliers on mean values. To check the size effect, the inspection rates for firms of different sizes are plotted in Figure 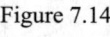 . The age effect indicates that older firms have a higher probability of inspection. The mean age of the inspection group is 2.6 years older than that of the non-inspection group, and the median age difference is 2 years. Size effect also exists as inspection rates are positively correlated with sizes of firms, with large firms having 15% higher percentages to inspect input quality than small firms, and 5% higher percentages than the moderate size firms. Therefore we observe larger and older firms tend to place higher requirements on their suppliers.

Figure 7.14

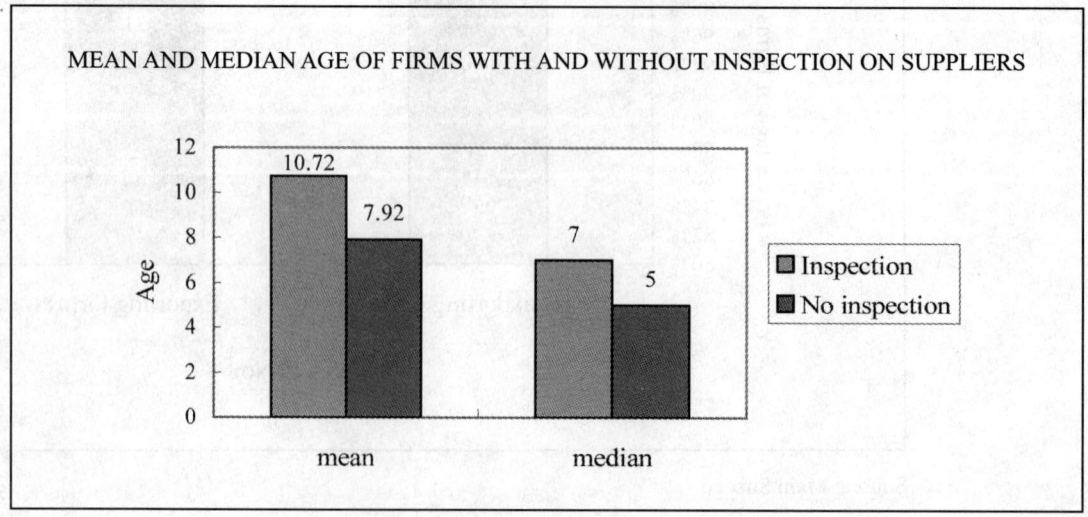

Source: Main Survey

Figure 7.15

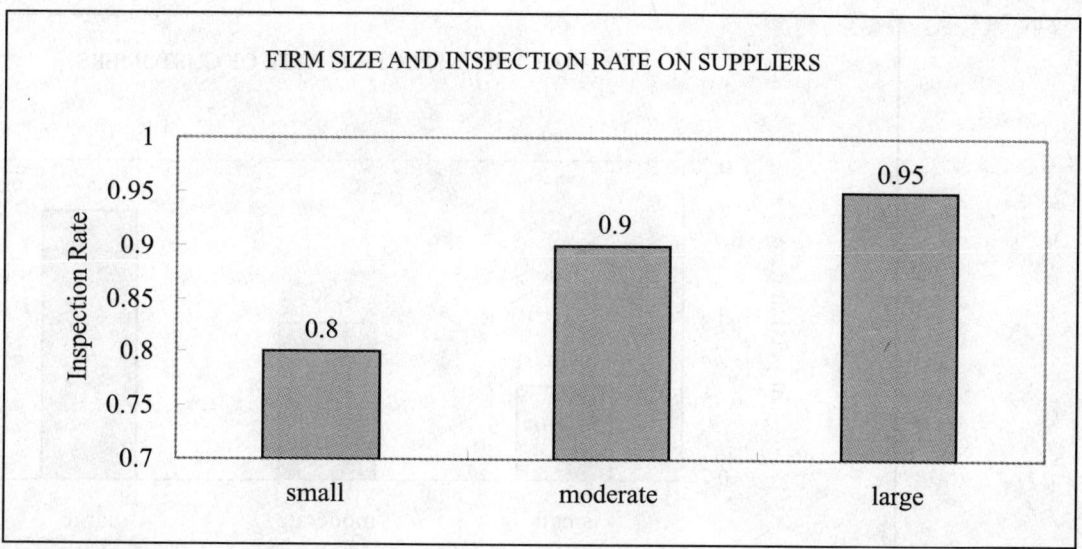

FIRM SIZE AND INSPECTION RATE ON SUPPLIERS

Source: Main Survey

Figure 7.16

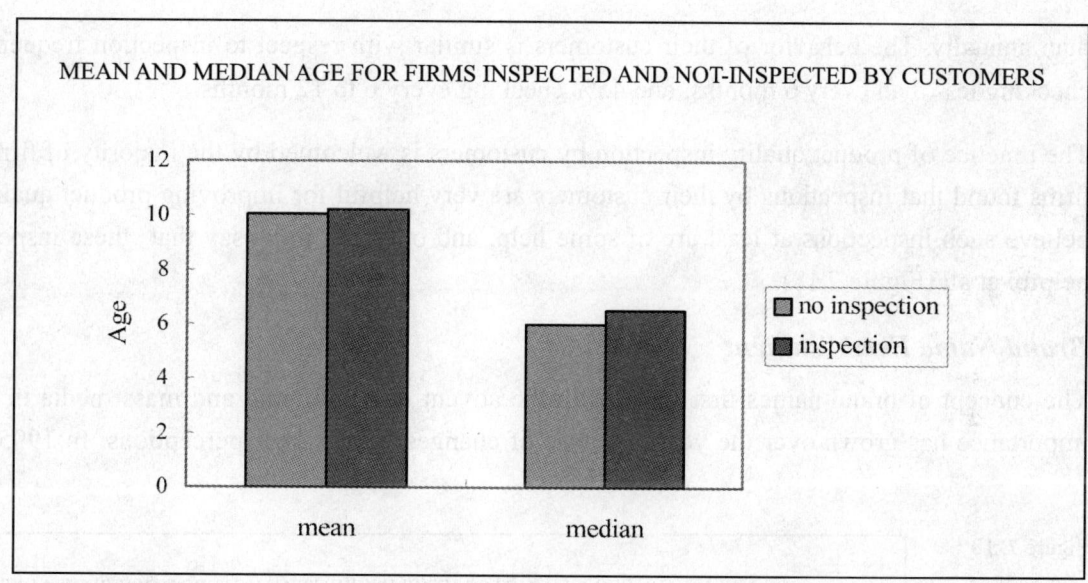

MEAN AND MEDIAN AGE FOR FIRMS INSPECTED AND NOT-INSPECTED BY CUSTOMERS

Source: Main Survey

Does age and size effect exist when firms are acting as suppliers? We compare the mean and median age of firms for the inspection and non-inspection groups in Figure 7.16, and the customers inspection rate for firms with different sizes in Figure 7.17. It is interesting to notice that age is not a factor in determining whether customers request product quality checks, as the inspection and non-inspection groups share similar mean and median ages. On the other hand, size effects still exist and we observe that larger firms are more likely to be subject to quality inspection. Therefore, overall smaller firms are less strict about their input quality, and their customers are also more lenient on their product quality.

As inspections are costly, firms need to decide upon the frequency of inspection of their suppliers. In this regard, 41% of firms report to check input quality every 6 months or less, another 50% do so every 6 months to one year. Only 9% indicate that they check the product of their suppliers less frequently

Figure 7.17

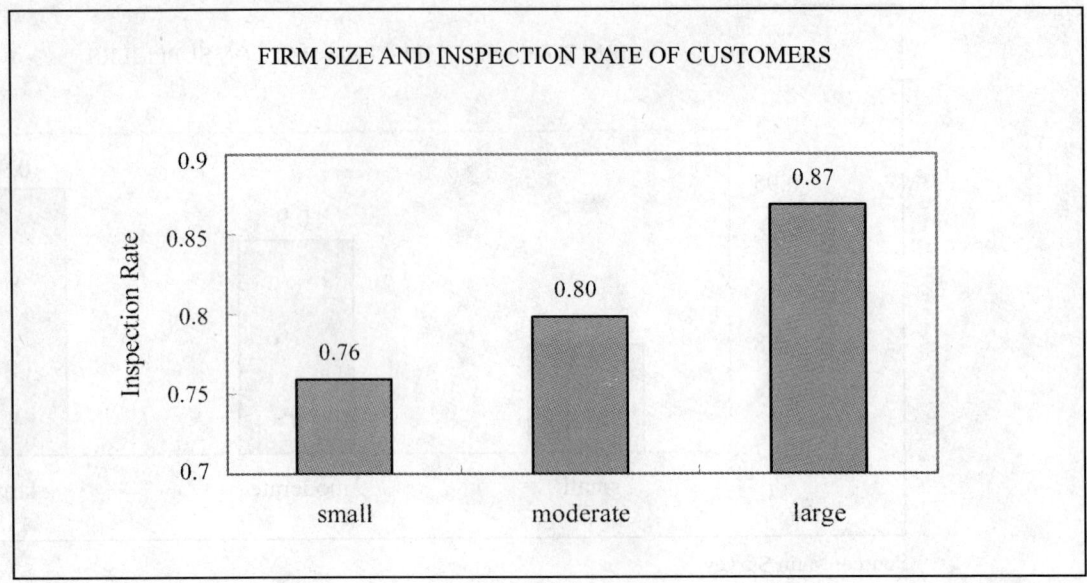

Source: Main Survey

than annually. The behavior of their customers is similar with respect to inspection frequency, with 42% checking less than every 6 months, and 45% checking every 6 to 12 months.

The practice of product quality inspection by customers is welcomed by the majority of firms. 84% of all firms found that inspections by their customers are very helpful for improving product quality, 15% firms believe such inspections at least are of some help, and only 1% firms say that these inspections are not helpful at all (Figure 7.18).

Brand Name Establishment

The concept of brand names first arose with the advent of advertising and mass media in the 1930s. Its importance has grown over the years because of changes in customer perceptions. In 1995, Yankelovich

Figure 7. 18

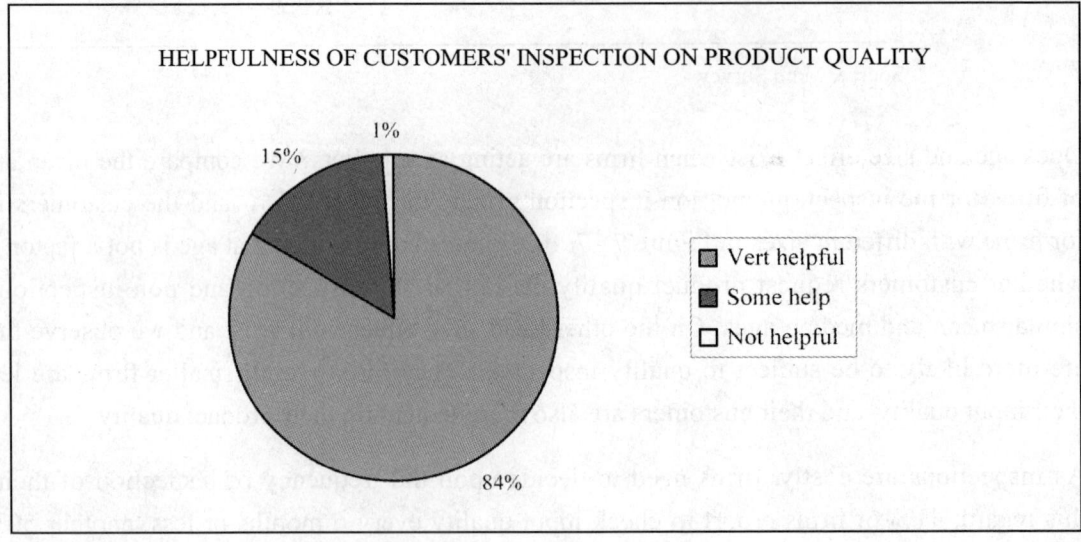

Source: Main Survey

Partners, a market research firm, reported that studies of consumers showed an almost unbelievable increase in reliance on brand names. In two years, the percentage of American consumers who said brand names figured significantly in their product decisions jumped from 52 percent to 67 percent. Therefore, an essential method for ensuring long-term profitability is to establish a brand name and foster brand name loyalty among customers. In this subsection, we investigate how much effort firms put into brand names.

Firms can establish their brand names through careful design of the product, its logo, and advertising, etc. Even though these efforts are difficult to measure, firms' expenditure on brand name establishment is a good proxy for it, as a profit-maximizing firm will choose to control its costs as efficiently as possible. Figure 7.19 provides the average cost in brand name establishment for all firms over the past three years. On average, firms spend 4.3 million Yuan in establishing their brand names. Among firms with different ownership structures, expenditures by domestic firms are below average while joint ventures are above average. With an average of 9.47 million Yuan, Foreign owned & Joint ventures spent five times more than

Figure 7.19

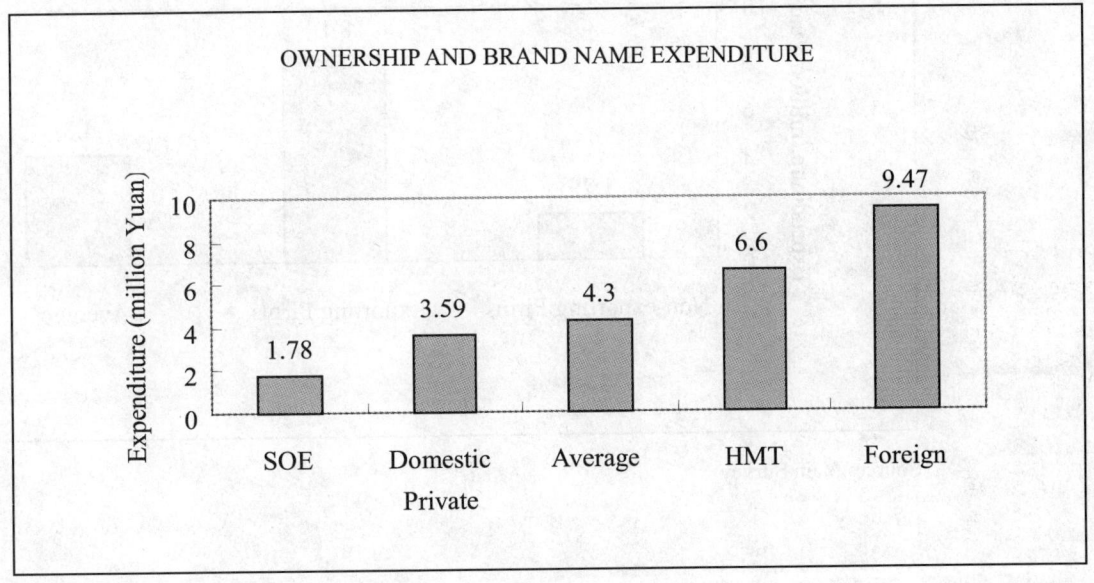

Source: Main Survey

SOEs. Even domestic private firms spent twice as much as SOEs.

The different attitudes of SOEs and joint ventures toward brand name establishment can also be the result of market competition. If a firm wishes to survive through fierce competition, it will make every effort to sell its products through a good brand name. Indeed, firms facing fierce competition spent a mean of 540 million Yuan, while firms facing moderate competition spent a mean of 10 million Yuan, and those facing low competition spent only 2.5 million Yuan. As mean values are easily affected by extreme values, we also inspect the maximum expenditure in each category. The maximum costs are 12,000 million, 2,000 million, and 100 million, respectively for firms facing fierce, moderate and low competition.

While expenditures directly spent on brand name establishment can help enterprises to gain market share in the short run, firms need to be reminded that the fundamental element that ensures brand name is product quality. Firms are doomed to fail if they focus only on short-term profit through massive expenditures on advertisement but neglect product quality. For example, the diary enterprise Sanlu had been the number one seller of infant formula with a valuable brand name for about 20 years. However, after the public discovered that it was also ranked number one in putting melamine into infant formula, this brand name is destroyed and Sanlu cannot avoid the fate of failure in 2008.

If firms wish to enter and gain market share in international markets, they have incentives to establish their brand name through understanding the needs of the local customers and through advertising. Figure 7.20 clearly indicates that exporting firms do spend more than non-exporting firms on average.

Figure 7.20

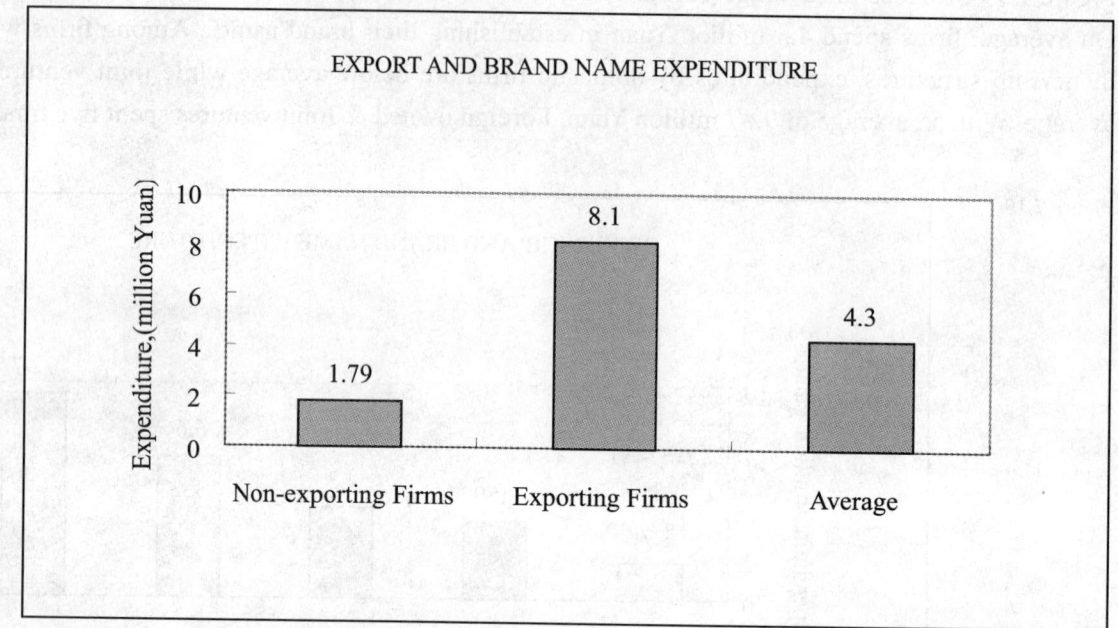

Source: Main Survey

7. 3 Factors Affecting Product Quality and Firm Efforts in Product Quality Management

In this subsection we discuss factors that can affect product quality and also the factors affecting the level of effort which firms devote to product quality management. We have discussed some of the factors that can have an impact on product quality, such as the ownership structure, the age and size of firms, etc. In this subsection we focus on discussing how competition and CSR awareness affects firm behavior in improving product quality.

Competition

Competition can be one of the main driving forces for firms to improve product quality, as better quality can help firms outperform competitors in the long run. The sample does show that competition stimulates improvement in product quality.

First of all, as shown in Figure 7.21, firms surviving in fiercely competed markets are more confident about their product quality, with over 70% of such firms claiming their products are better, which is 35.6% higher than that reported by firms in low-competition markets. One may worry that firms indicate low market competition just because they are at the industries that face entry barriers. This sample, however, shows that there is no significant difference in confidence in product quality for firms with and without entry barriers. Both have 69% of firms reporting that their products are better than those of competitors.

Such confidence does not come without reason. The sample shows that firms in fiercely competed markets have the highest proportion of quality standards (Figure 7.22). In response to high quality standards than

Figure 7.21

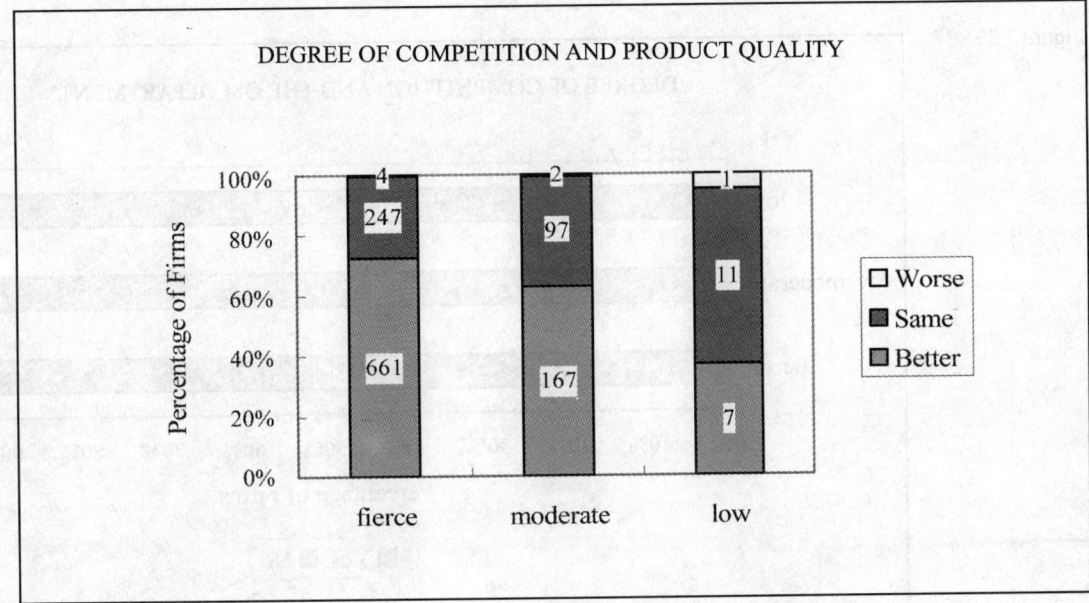

Source: Main Survey

Figure 7.22

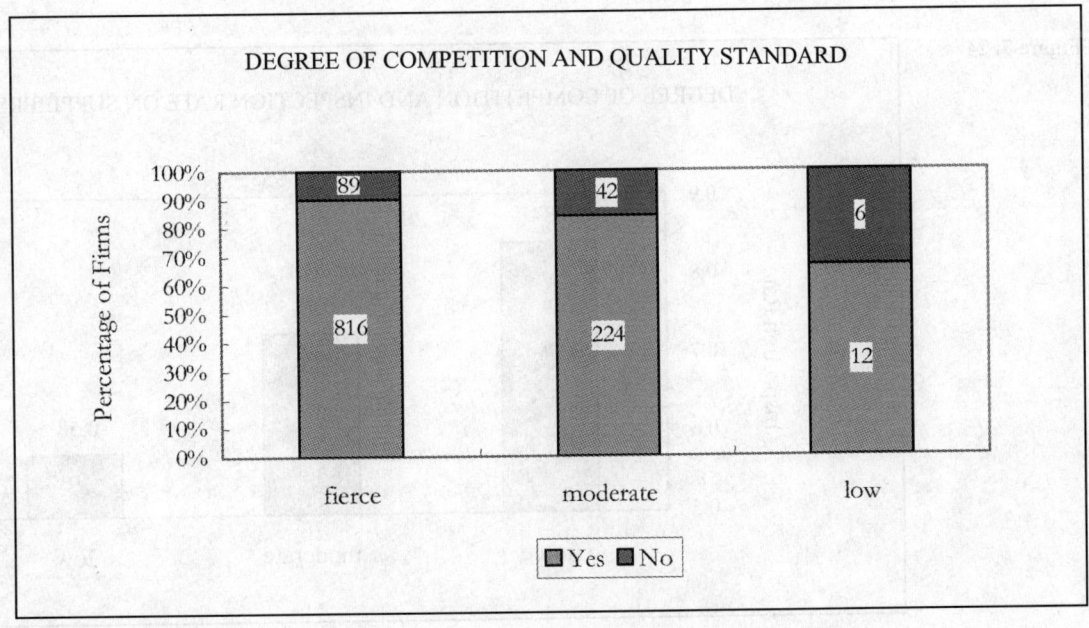

Source: Main Survey

those without such constraints, firms are more likely to establish quality control departments. As shown in Figure 7.23, the sampled firms facing fierce competition outperform those facing low competition by 10 percentage points in establishing QM departments.

In addition to investing in brand names, firms in fiercely-competed markets make greater efforts to control input quality. Figure 7.24 compares the inspection rate of their suppliers for firms facing different degrees of competition. The outcome is clear: firms facing fierce competition are pressured by the market to ensure good product quality, which propels them to inspect their suppliers. 84% of these firms will choose to inspect input quality. In contrast, only 58% of firms facing low competition choose to do so. As a result,

Figure 7.23

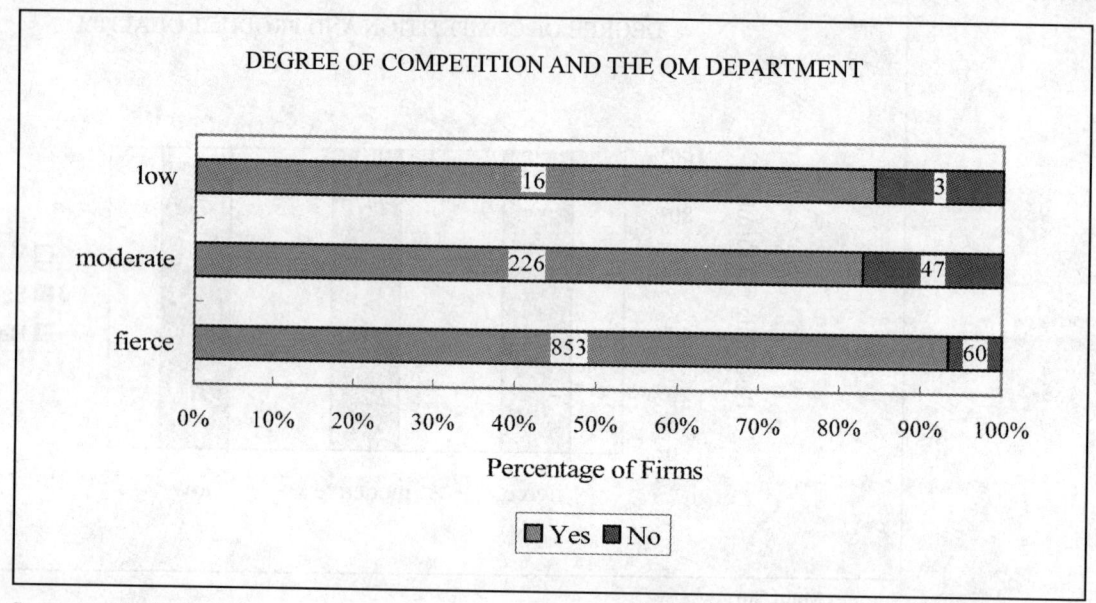

Source: Main Survey

Figure 7. 24

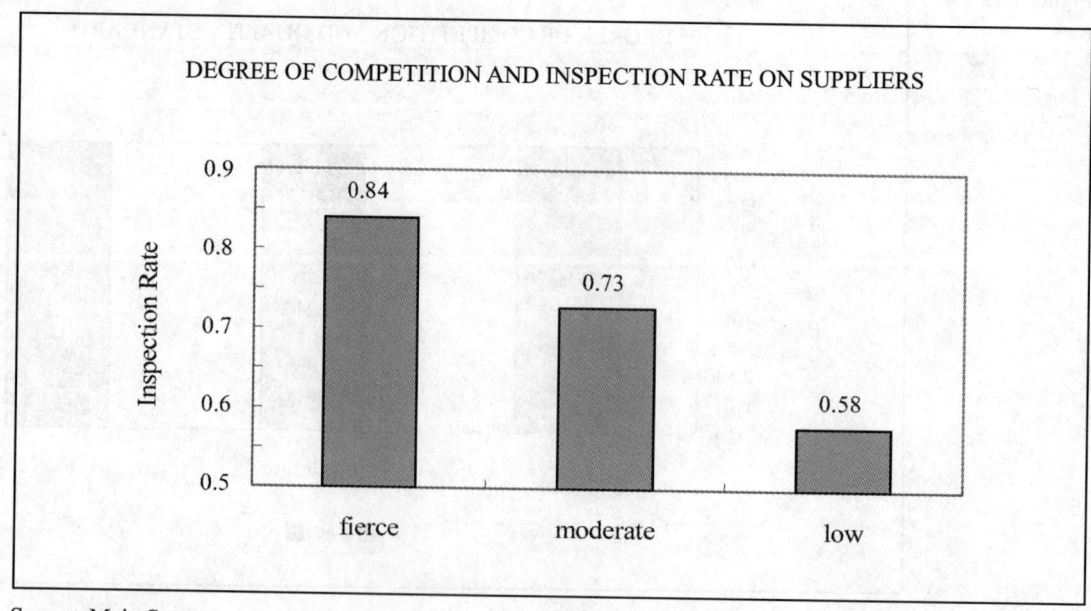

Source: Main Survey

firms in fiercely competed markets have the highest proportion of firms with registered brand names (Figure 7.25). They also have higher proportions of ISO 9001 certificates for their products (Figure 7.26).

Overall, the analysis in this subsection shows that competition is a fundamental factor in improving product quality. Firms facing fierce competition in general have better product quality than others. It follows that fostering a suitable institutional environment for healthy competition among firms can be an important task for a government aiming to improve product quality.

Figure 7. 25

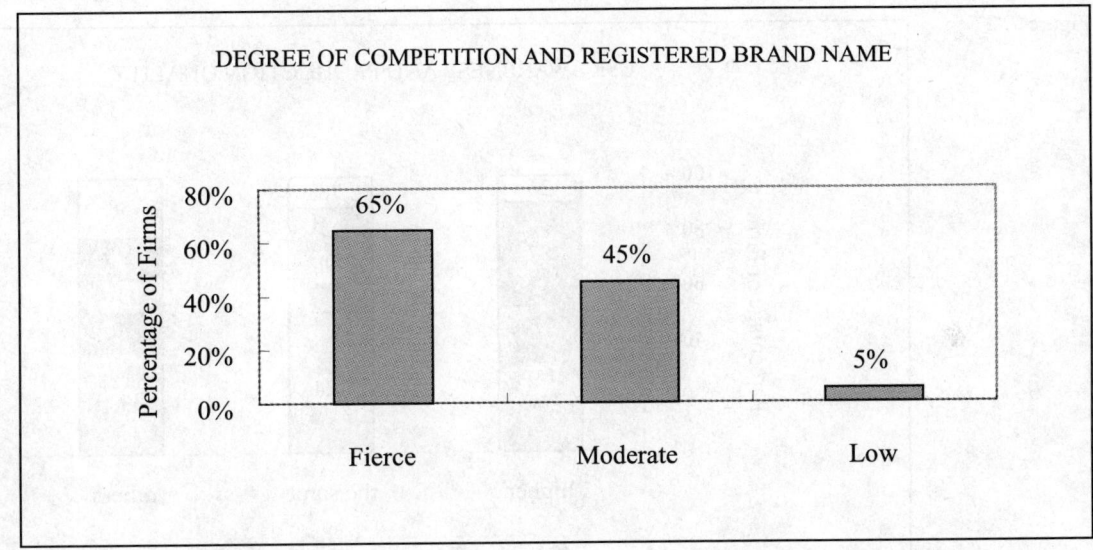

Source: Main Survey

Figure 7. 26

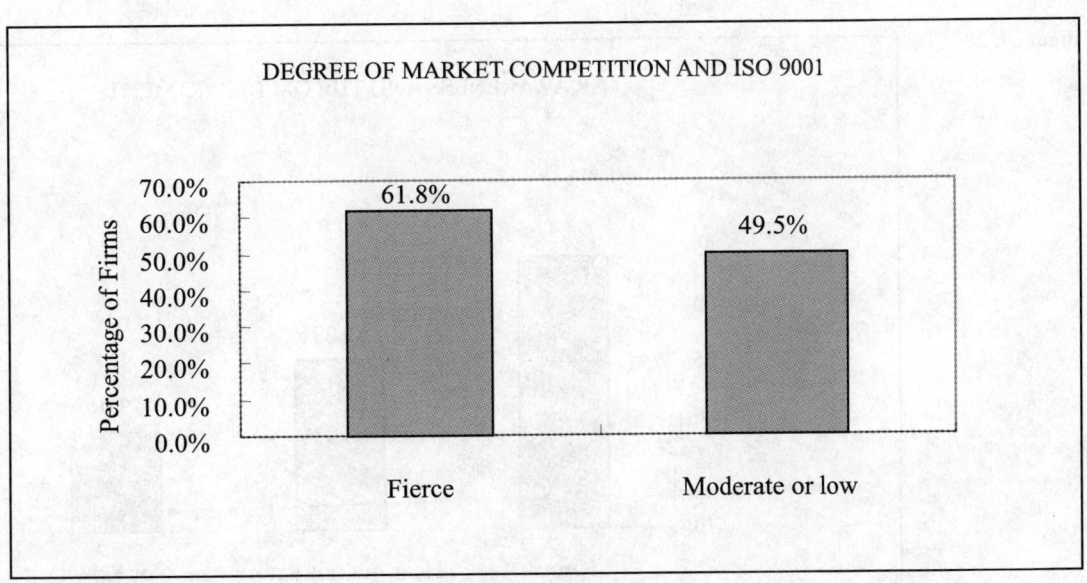

Source: Main Survey

CSR awareness

Similar to the results of studies on the impact of competition, more awareness of CSR is also associated with better product quality and better quality management. Figure 7.27 indicates that higher proportion of firms believe their products are better than others if firms know about CSR. They also spend more effort in establishing quality control departments. As shown in Figure 7.28, 94.47% of firms knowing about CSR report having a quality control department, which is about 10% higher than the knowing a little group and about 15% higher than those admitting not knowing about CSR.

Figure 7. 27

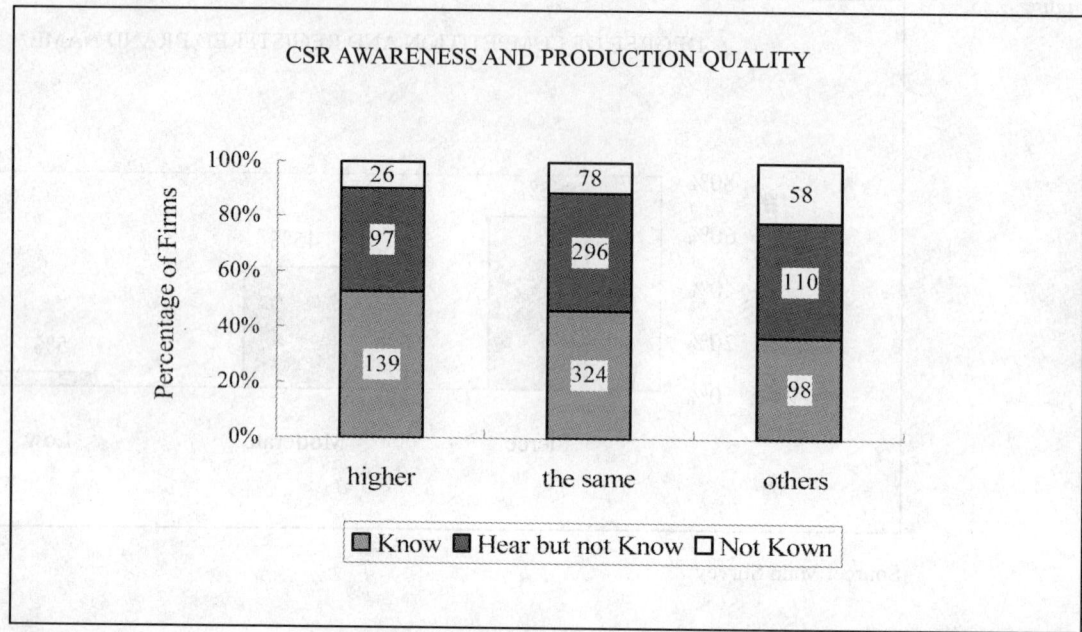

Source: Main Survey

Figure 7. 28

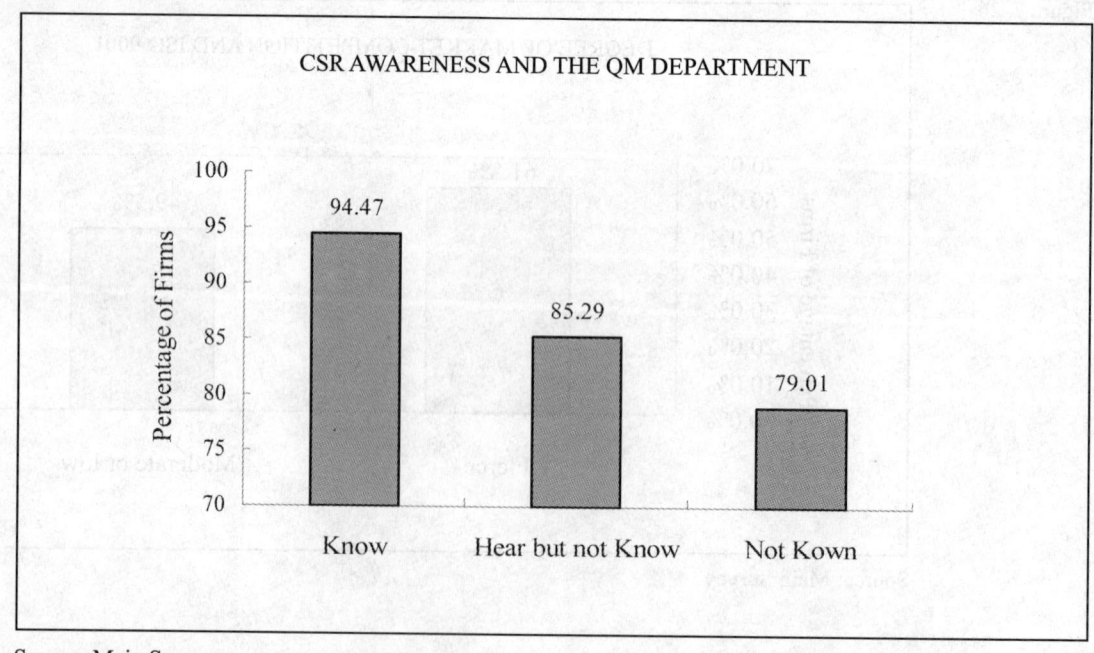

Source: Main Survey

In addition to establishing quality control departments, firms more aware of CSR also tend to be more likely to inspect their suppliers' products. Figure 7.29 shows that 88% percent of firms knowing about CSR inspect their suppliers, while 76% of those hearing of but not knowing about CSR inspect their suppliers and only 69% of those not knowing about CSR inspect their suppliers.

Firms knowing about CSR also spent more on establishing their brand names. Figure 7.30 reports the median expenditure on brand names in the past three years. The median expenditure is 0.2 million for the

Figure 7.29

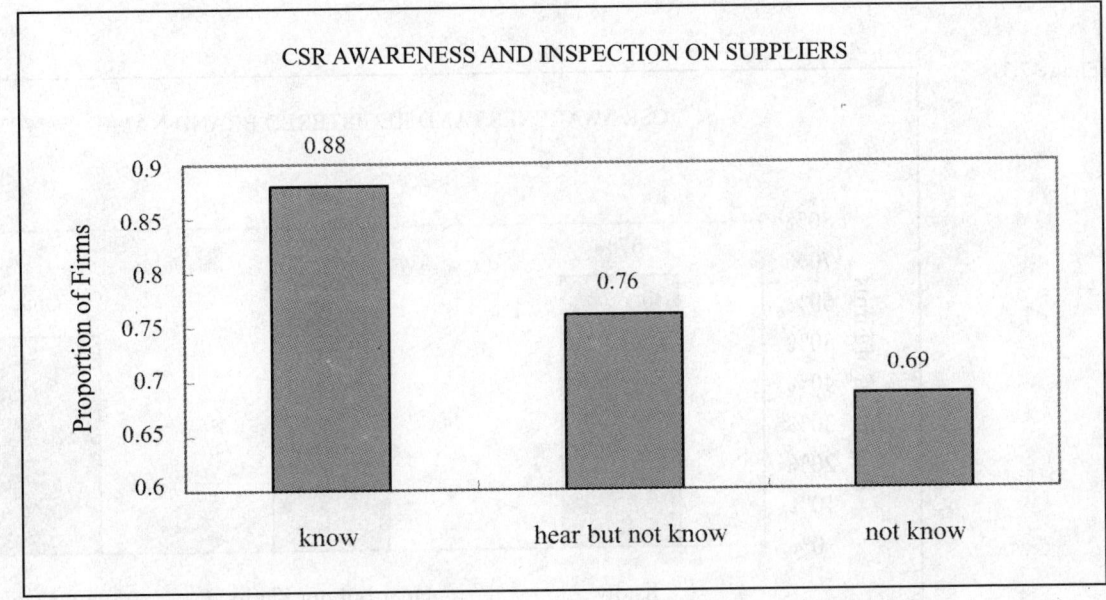

Source: Main Survey

Figure 7.30

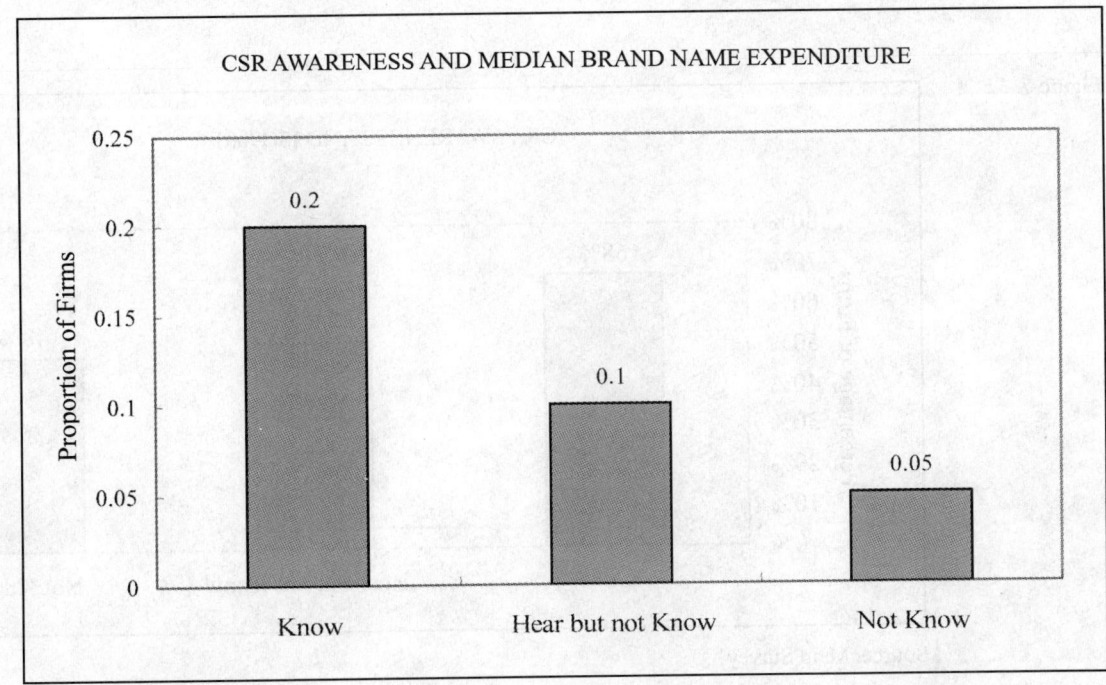

Source: Main Survey

group knowing about CSR; it is 0.1 million for the group reporting knowing a little about CSR, and it is only 0.05 million for those not knowing CSR at all. Accordingly, it is not surprising to see that firms more aware of CSR tend to register their brand names with a higher probability (Figure7.31).

Finally, if we use the proportion of firms with ISO9001 as a more objective measure of product quality, we again observe that the more CSR aware the firm is, the higher the proportion of their products to obtain ISO9001 certificates. The percentage for the knowing CSR group is almost 20% higher than the not-knowing CSR group, as shown in Figure 7.32.

Figure 7.31

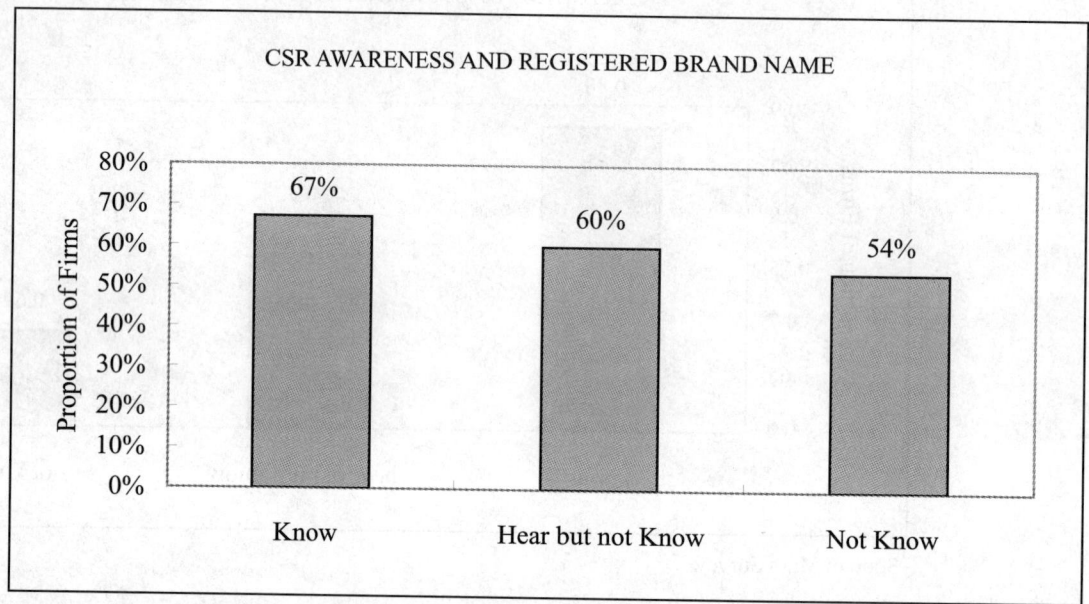

Source: Main Survey

Figure 7. 32

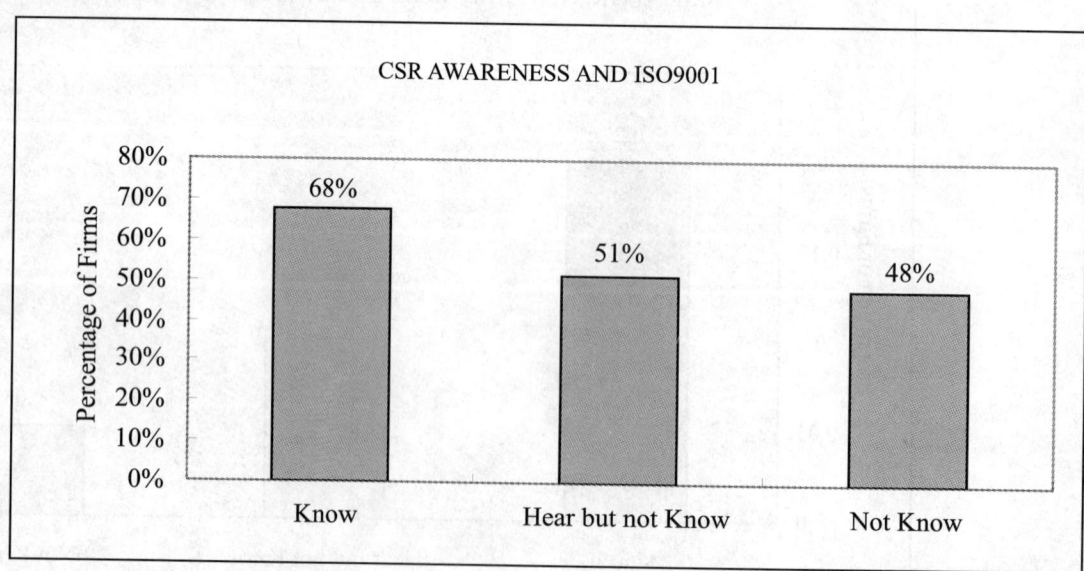

Source: Main Survey

7.4　Summary

This chapter describes the status quo of product quality, the measures firms take to improve it, and the factors that can influences product quality as well as firm effort in managing it. The survey reveals that joint ventures, firms facing fierce competition and those knowing about CSR are more confident about the quality of their products. Firms exert quality control through several measures. One is to establish a quality control department. Over 80% of firms in the sample have QM departments and the majority of them choose to establish QM department at the year of establishment of the enterprise. The second measure is to obtain product quality certificates, like ISO 9001, and meeting national standards. The third measure firms can take is to establish product brand names, and the last one is to closely inspect the product quality of suppliers and to satisfy the inspection needs of their customers.

A common characteristic observed over all the four measures is that firms facing fierce competition often outperform those who face moderate and low degrees of competition. When firms face fierce competition either from domestic or international markets, they spend much more on brand name establishment, they are also much more careful in inspecting the quality of the input for their products. Similar observations hold for firms knowing CSR. Therefore, to improve product quality, policies can focus on ensuring a fair and transparent competition environment, and helping firms to be more aware of their corporate social responsibilities.

Chapter 8
Governance Structure

Fundamental changes in economic structure have accompanied China's rapid economic growth over the past several decades. In particular, China has transformed from complete reliance on state-owned and collective enterprises to a mixed economy where private enterprises play a leading role (Garnaut, Song, Tenev and Yao (2005)). In this chapter we focus on studying the governance structure of the sampled firms, and how various factors affect it and firm performances. In section 8.1 we describe the ownership structure of the sampled firms. As *gaizhi*, the Chinese term meaning "transforming the system", has become a major phenomenon in most parts of the country, in section 8.2 we focus on comparing the *gaizhi* firms with firms born as private enterprises. Section 8.3 discusses other factors that can affect the governance structure of an enterprise.

8. 1 Ownership Structure at a Glance

As discussed in Chapter 2, 68.7% of the sample firms are domestic privately owned. The rest of the firms are about equally distributed among SOEs, HMT, and foreign owned or joint-ventures. Even though SOEs account for only about 10% of the sampled firms, their sizes are relatively large. Figure 8.1 presents the size distribution for the different types of ownership status. More than half of the SOE firms are medium or large in scale. With only 3% of large firms, domestic private firms have the smallest percentage of medium

Figure 8.1

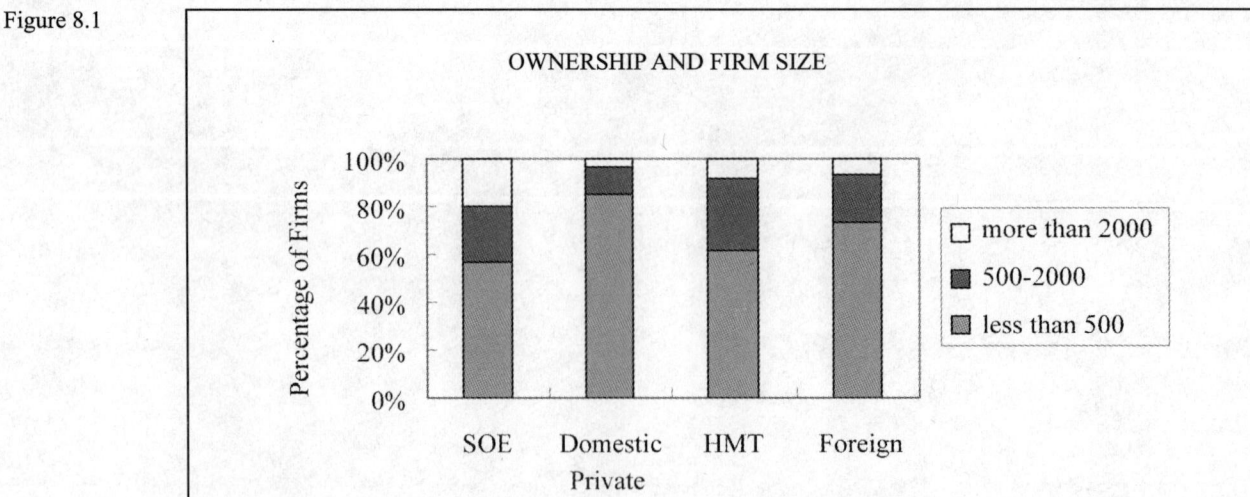

Source: Main Survey

156

Figure 8.2

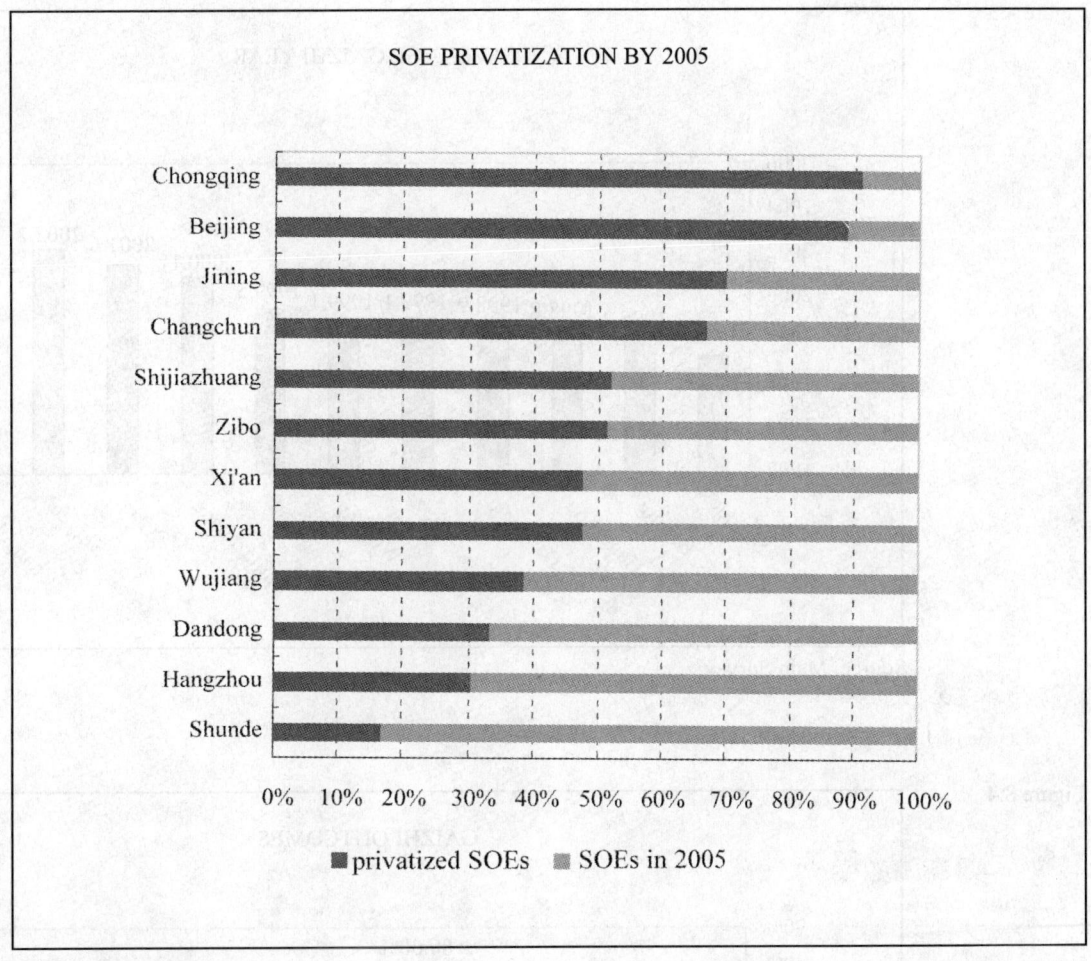

SOE PRIVATIZATION BY 2005

Source: Main Survey

and large firms.

The *gaizhi* of SOEs has been a major theme in the past decade. It has not only led to drastic changes in economic development, but has also deeply influenced the lives of millions of workers and their families. Our sample provides a chance to observe the *gaizhi* process in more detail. If we compare the percentage of privatized SOEs with the proportion which were still state-owned in 2005 across cities (Figure 8.2) and study the average *gaizhi* time (Figure 8.3), we can divide cities into four groups: heavily privatized and *gaizhi* started early; least privatized but *gaizhi* started early; least privatized and *gaizhi* started late; moderately privatized, and *gaizhi* started not too recently. Shunde, Beijing and Hangzhou belong to the first group. Over 70% of the firms in these three cities had been privatized with the average *gaizhi* date no later than 1999. Dandong and Jining belong to the second group. They were among the earliest to start the *gaizhi* process, but up to 2005 no more than 30% of SOEs had been privatized. Chongqing belongs to the third group. On average *gaizhi* in this city happened in 2004, and *gaizhi* was completed in less than 20% of the firms by 2005.

After *gaizhi*, the majority (80%) of firms that were originally SOEs became domestic private firms, another 12.2% became collective enterprises, and the remaining 8% were distributed between HMT & Joint Ventures and Foreign & Joint Ventures (Figure 8.4). This outcome reflects the belief of the Chinese

Figure 8.3

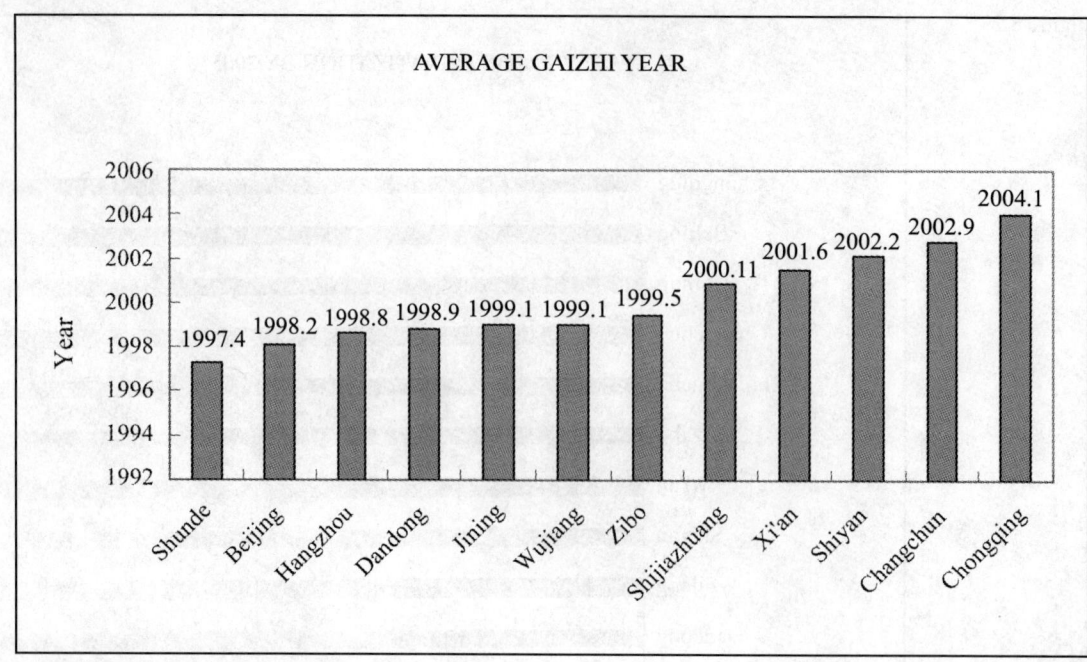

Source: Main Survey

Figure 8.4

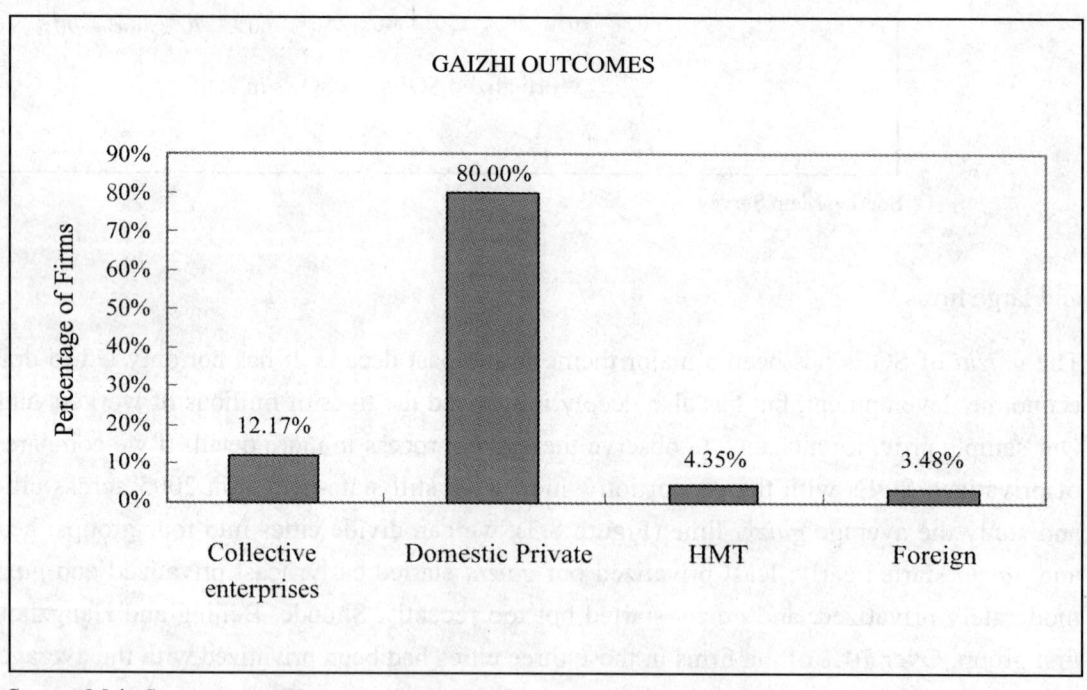

Source: Main Survey

government that privatizing SOEs into domestic private firms should be the main theme of *gaizhi*, and it has been very cautious toward letting foreign firms take full control of the firms which were originally SOEs.

Figure 8.5

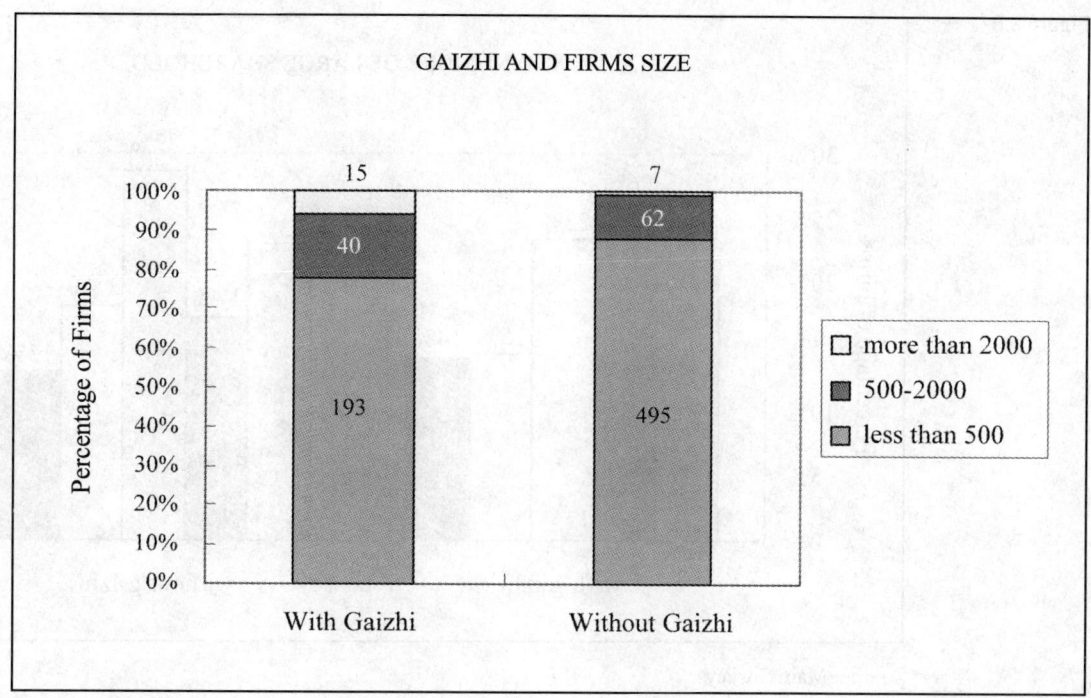

Source: Main Survey

8. 2   The Impacts of *Gaizhi*: Domestic Enterprises with and without *Gaizhi*

In this subsection we focus on comparing the governance structure of domestic enterprises with and without *gaizhi* to further study the impacts of *gaizhi* on governance structure. Garnaut, Song, Tenev and Yao (2005) has systematically studied the magnitude, forms, and consequences of *gaizhi* using data collected from 700 enterprises in 11 Chinese cities for the year 2001. Our study complements theirs with more recent data. Furthermore, as our surveyed cities do not overlap with those in Garnaut, Song, Tenev and Yao (2005)[1], this study will provide geographic diversification for understanding the impact of *Gaizhi*. We divide the 812 private firms into two groups: 248 firms (30.54%) that have been privatized (firms with *gaizhi)*, and 564 firms (69.46%) that are not *gaizhi* firms (without *gaizhi)*. Compared with other private enterprises, firms with *gaizhi* in general are larger. Figure 8.5 compare the firm sizes between these two types of firms. The *gaizhi* group has higher proportions of firms whose sizes are larger than 500 employees. That is, 22.18% firms with *gaizhi* hire more than 500 employees, while 12.23% firms without *gaizhi* hire 500 and over employees.

The *gaizhi* firms and the *non-gaizhi* firms are different in shareholder structure. As shown in Figure 8.6, 26% of the *gaizhi* firms choose to have only one big shareholder, which is 9% higher than the *non-gaizhi* firms. The *non-gaizhi* firms appear to prefer the two-big-shareholders structure more. In addition to the differences in shareholder structure, firms with *gaizhi* are also different from those without *gaizhi* by the proportion of the largest shareholder's former occupation in the industry sector. 71.8% of the largest shareholders of the firms with *gaizhi* had experience of working in the same industries. This percentage is

---

[1] The eleven cities are Harbin, Fushun, tangshan, Lanzhou, Weifang, Cining, Zhenjiang, Huangshi, Chengdu, Hengyang, and Guiyang.

Figure 8.6

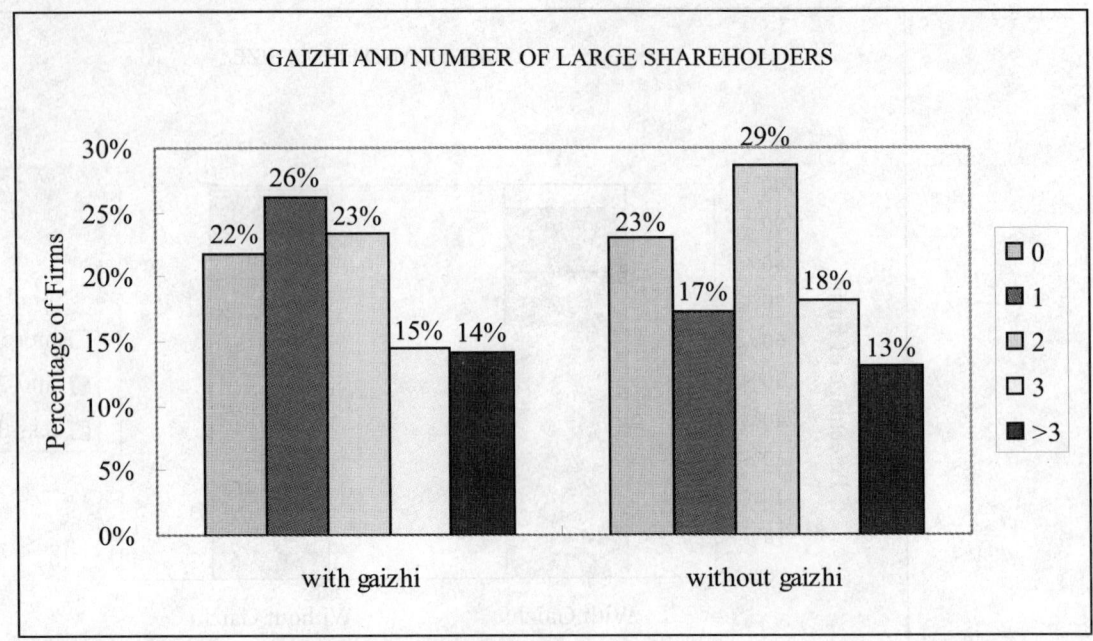

Source: Main Survey

about 7.4% higher than those without *gaizhi* (Figure 8.7).

Whether a firm has a board of directors makes a fundamental difference to the governance the enterprise. In the sample, 64.3% firms reported that they had a board of directors, but the establishment of boards of directors also differed greatly based on ownership structure and on whether a firm is export- oriented. As shown in Figure 8.8, the establishment rate of boards at SOEs is only 27%, which is almost 40% lower than that for domestic private firms. HMT & Joint Ventures had the highest rate of 91%, and it is 8%

Figure 8.7

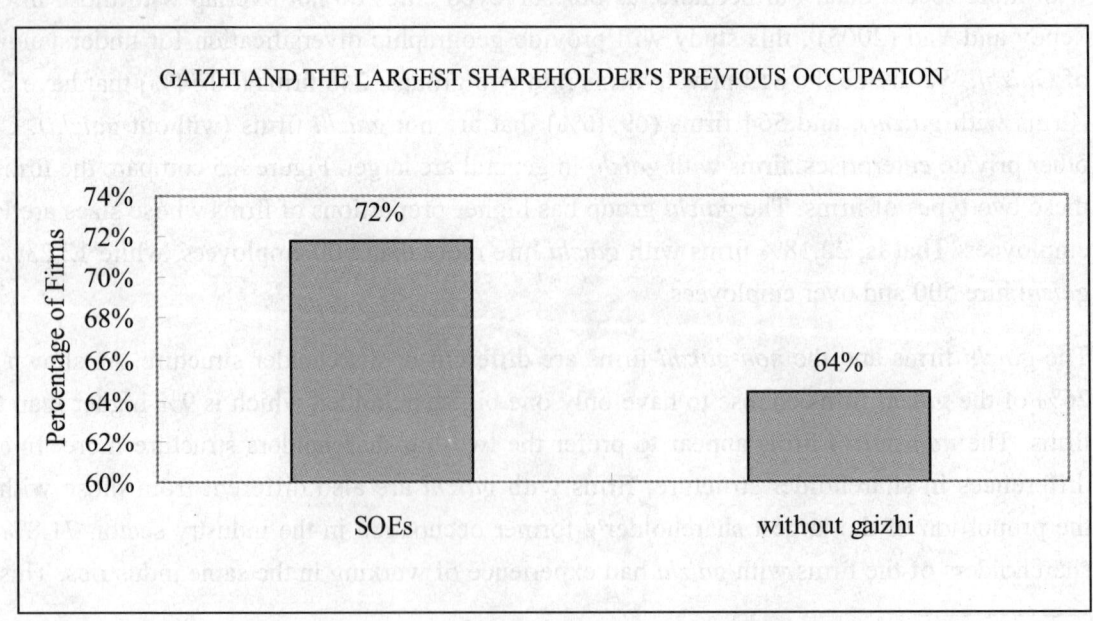

Source: Main Survey

Figure 8.8

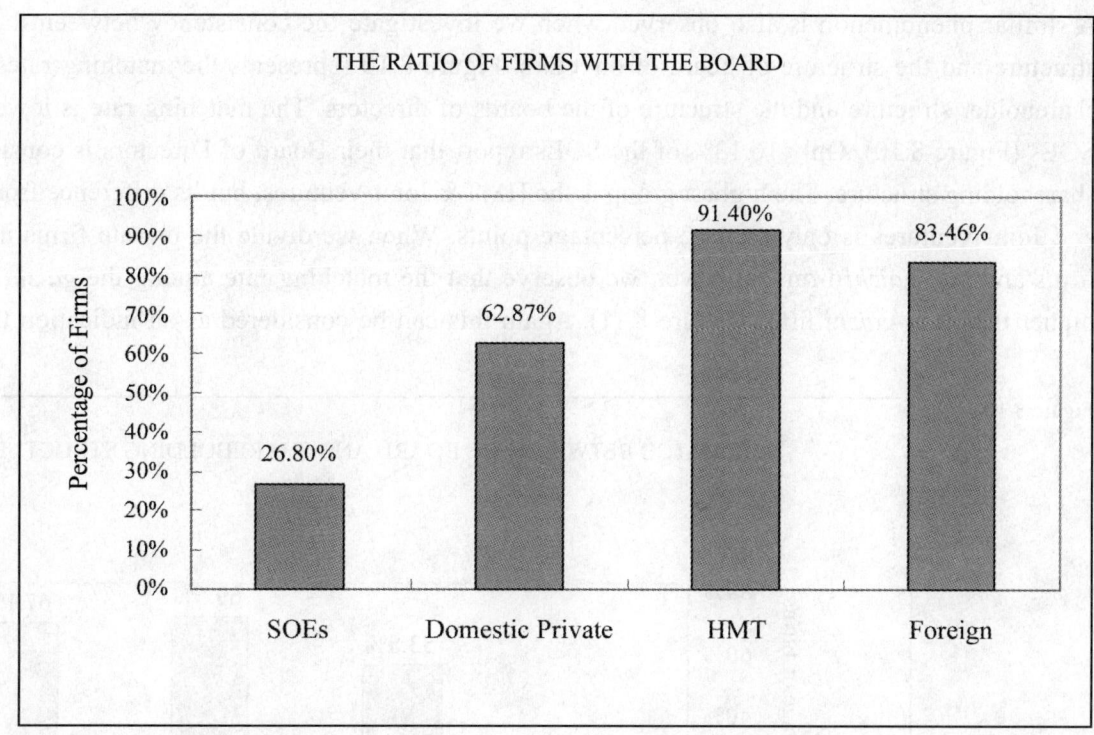

THE RATIO OF FIRMS WITH THE BOARD

Source: Main Survey

higher than Foreign & Joint Ventures. Among the domestic private firms, however, Figure 8.9 shows that nearly 70% of the *gaizhi* firms have established Boards of Directors, while less than 50% of the *non-gaizhi* domestic private firms do so. Comparing the lower setting up rate in the non-privatized SOEs and the high rate in the *gaizhi* firms, one can infer that setting up Boards of Directors is viewed as an important step for the transformation of SOEs.

Figure 8.9

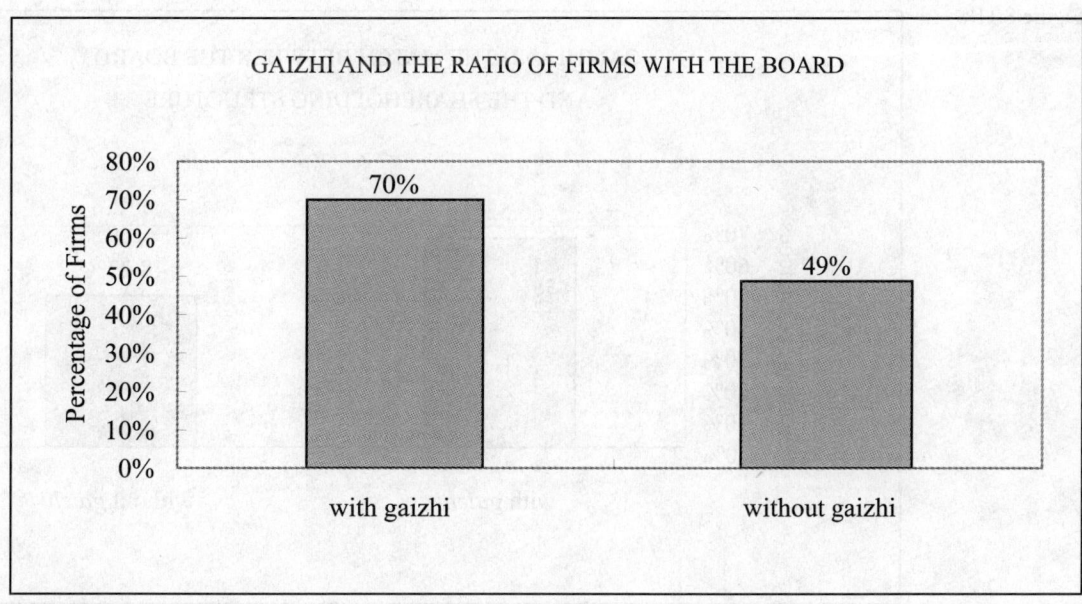

GAIZHI AND THE RATIO OF FIRMS WITH THE BOARD

Source: Main Survey

A similar phenomenon is also observed when we investigate the consistency between the shareholder structure and the structure of board of directors. Figure 8.10 represents the matching rates between the shareholder structure and the structure of the boards of directors. The matching rate is lowest among the SOEs (Figure 8.10). Only 16.13% of the SOEs report that their Board of Directors is consistent with the shareholding structure. The highest group is the HMT& Joint Ventures, but its difference from the Foreign and Joint Ventures is only about 2 percentage points. When we divide the private firms into the *gaizhi* firms and *non-gaizhi* firms, however, we observe that the matching rate among the *gaizhi* firms is 18% higher than *non-gaizhi* firms (Figure 8.11). Again this can be considered as an indication that the *gaizhi*

Figure 8.10

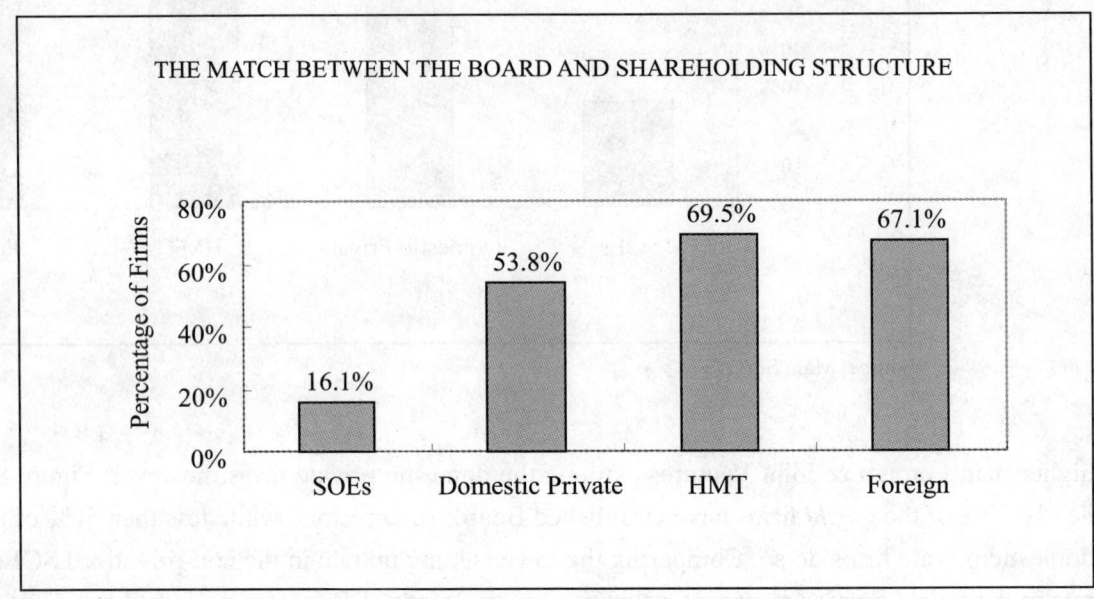

Source: Main Survey

Figure 8.11

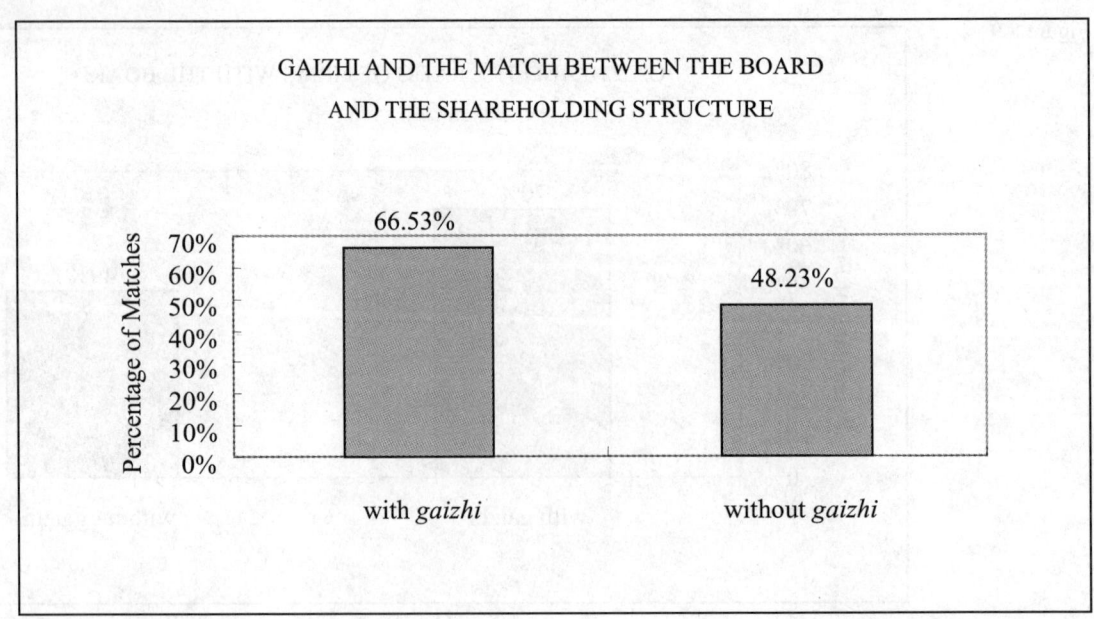

Source: Main Survey

162

firms are more determined to establish a modern governance structure.

Whether the board of directors is independent from the management group can be evaluated by whether the members of the two groups are different. Among the 807 firms responding to this question, 55% of the sample firms indicate that members of the board of directors are different from those of the management group. But as firms may tend to 'window dress', we need to investigate this indicator further from the perspectives of region, ownership structure and size.

Figure 8.12 shows by city the percentage of respondents who indicate that membership of the board and the management group are different or are almost the same. Xi'an ranks the first with over 80% of firms reporting that their board of directors and the management group are two different groups. Beijing and Hangzhou ranked just after Xi'an, with nearly 70% firms believing that the two groups are different. The central cities, Changchun and Shijiazhuang are ranked at the bottom, with over 70% indicating overlapping boards the management groups. To cross-check the honesty of firms in commenting the overlapping degrees, they were also invited to comment the non-overlapping degrees of the boards and the management group for other firms about the same size in the same city. Each firm was given three choices: none of its peers has the same board and management group; only a few do so and most of them do so.

Figure 8. 12

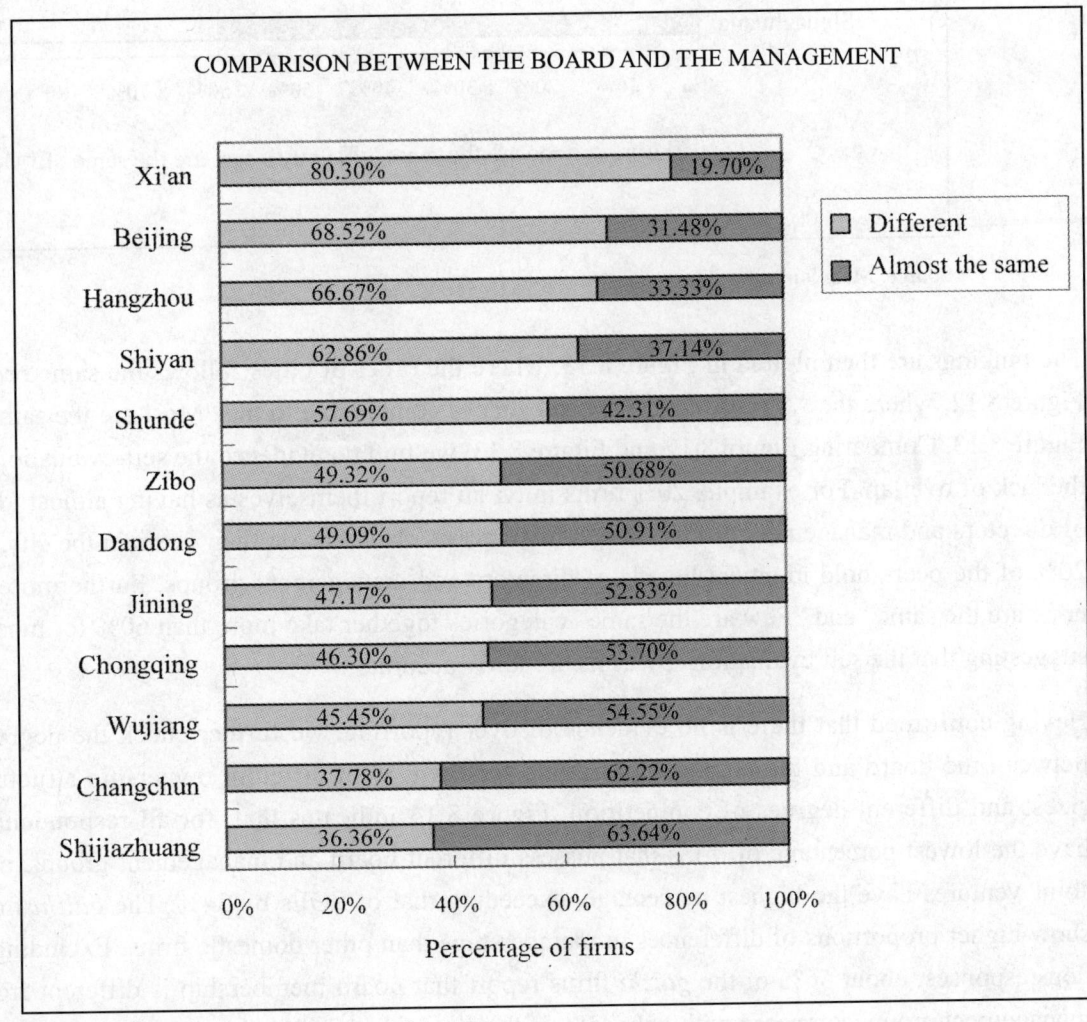

Source: Main Survey

Figure 8. 13

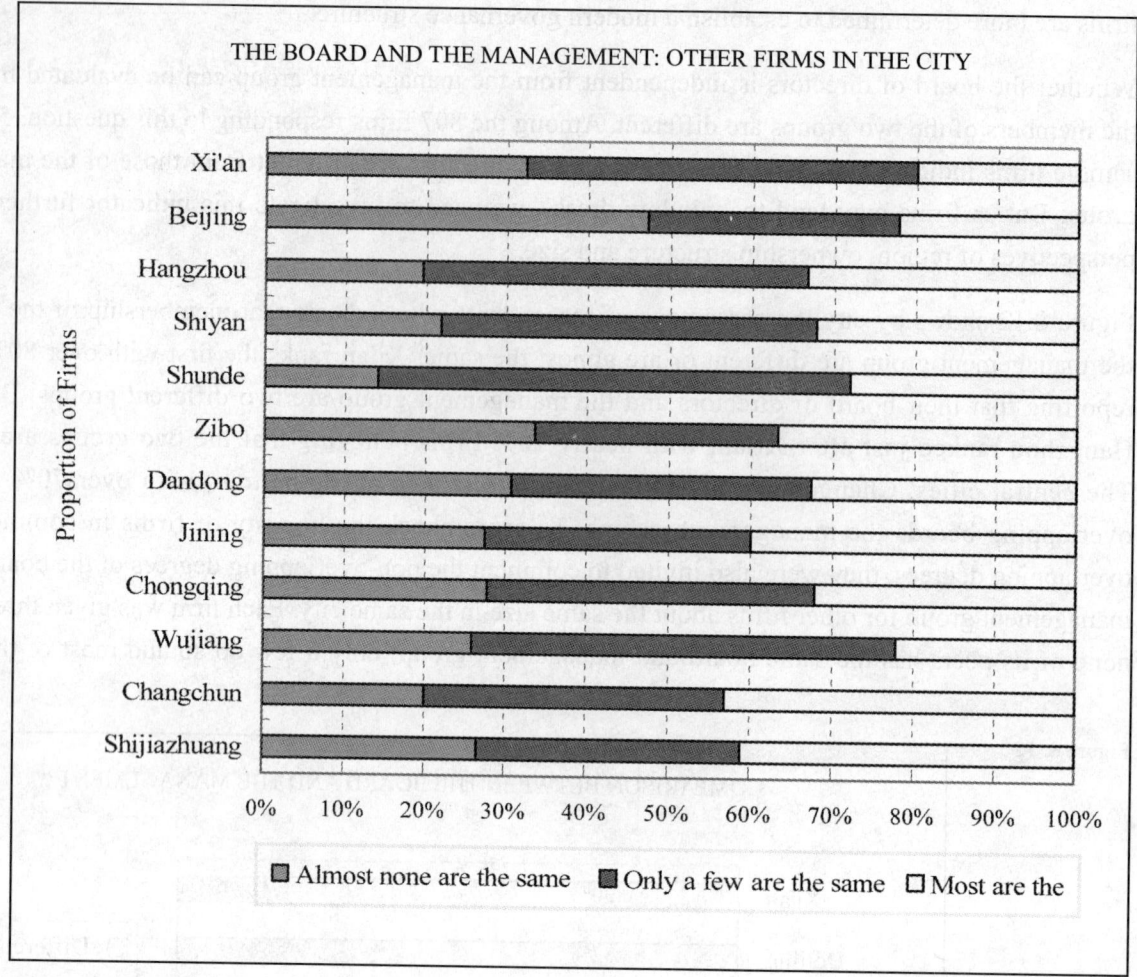

THE BOARD AND THE MANAGEMENT: OTHER FIRMS IN THE CITY

☐ Almost none are the same   ■ Only a few are the same   ☐ Most are the

Source: Main Survey

The rankings are then plotted in Figure 8.13, where the order of cities follows the same order as those in Figure 8.12, where the "Almost the same" category is comparable to the "Most are the same" category in Figure 8.13. Comparing Figure 8.12 and Figure 8.13, we find no evidence the self-evaluations exaggerated the lack of overlap. For example, 20% firms in Xi'an report themselves as having almost identical boards of directors and management groups. When firms act as observers on their peers in the city, they also feel 20% of the peers hold identical boards of directors and management groups. Furthermore, the "Almost none are the same" and "Few are the same" categories together take more than 60% for most of the cities, suggesting that the self evaluations by firms are fairly accurate.

Having confirmed that there is no evidence of over reporting, we further check the degrees of overlap between the board and the management group for firms with different ownership structures, different sizes, and different degrees of competition. Figure 8.14 indicates that, for all respondent firms, SOEs have the lowest percentage of firms that possess different board and management groups, and Foreign & Joint Ventures have the highest percentage, exceeding that of SOEs by 34%. The *gaizhi* firms, however, show higher proportions of differences in memberships than other domestic firms. Excluding non-missing non-responses, about 56% of the *gaizhi* firms report that board membership is different from that of the management group, compared with only 45% of the *non-gaizhi* firms (Figure 8.15).

Figure 8.14

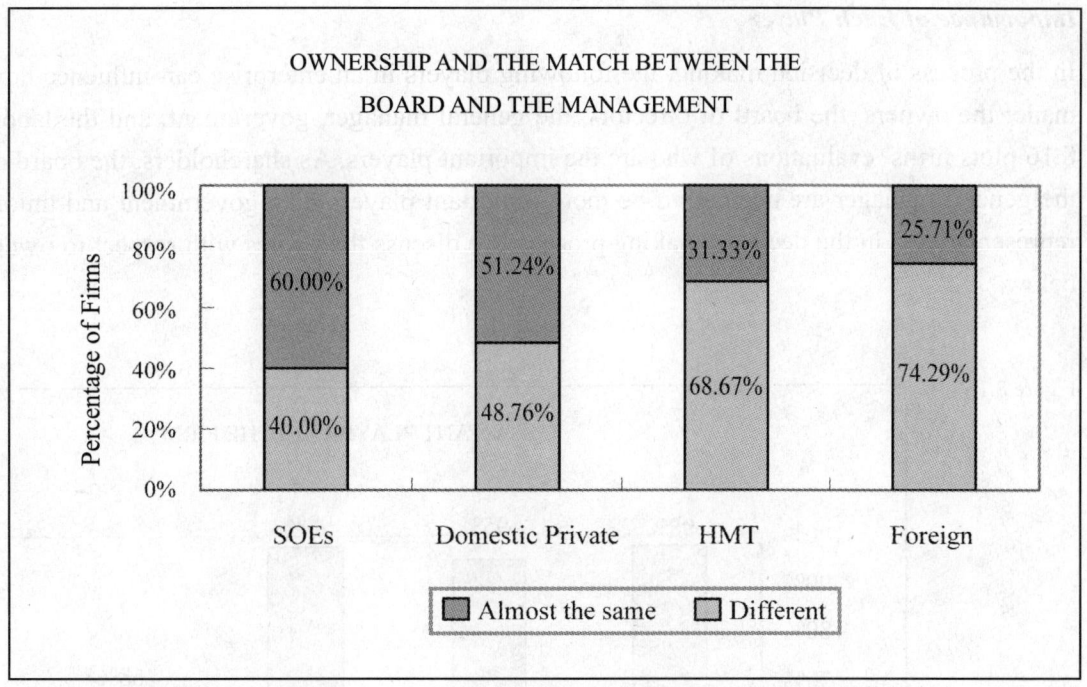

OWNERSHIP AND THE MATCH BETWEEN THE
BOARD AND THE MANAGEMENT

Source: Main Survey

Figure 8.15

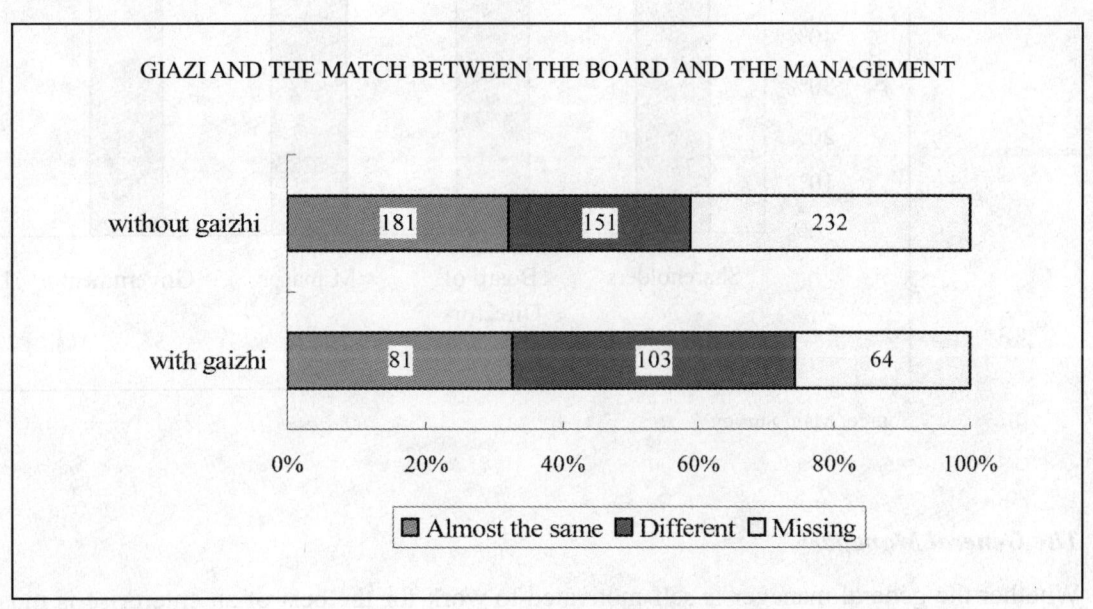

GIAZI AND THE MATCH BETWEEN THE BOARD AND THE MANAGEMENT

Source: Main Survey

8. 3   Management Systems

In this subsection we discuss management systems mainly from two perspectives. The first is how important are the different players in the management of the firm, and second, we discuss the rules and regulations, risk control and information disclosure by the sample firms.

Importance of Each Player

In the process of decision making, the following players in an enterprise can influence how decisions are made: the owners, the board of directors, the general manager, government, and the labor union. Figure 8.16 plots firms' evaluations of who are the important players. As shareholders, the board of directors and the general manager are deemed to be more important players than government and unions (or workers' representatives) in the decision-making process, we discuss their roles with respect to ownership structure below.

Figure 8.16

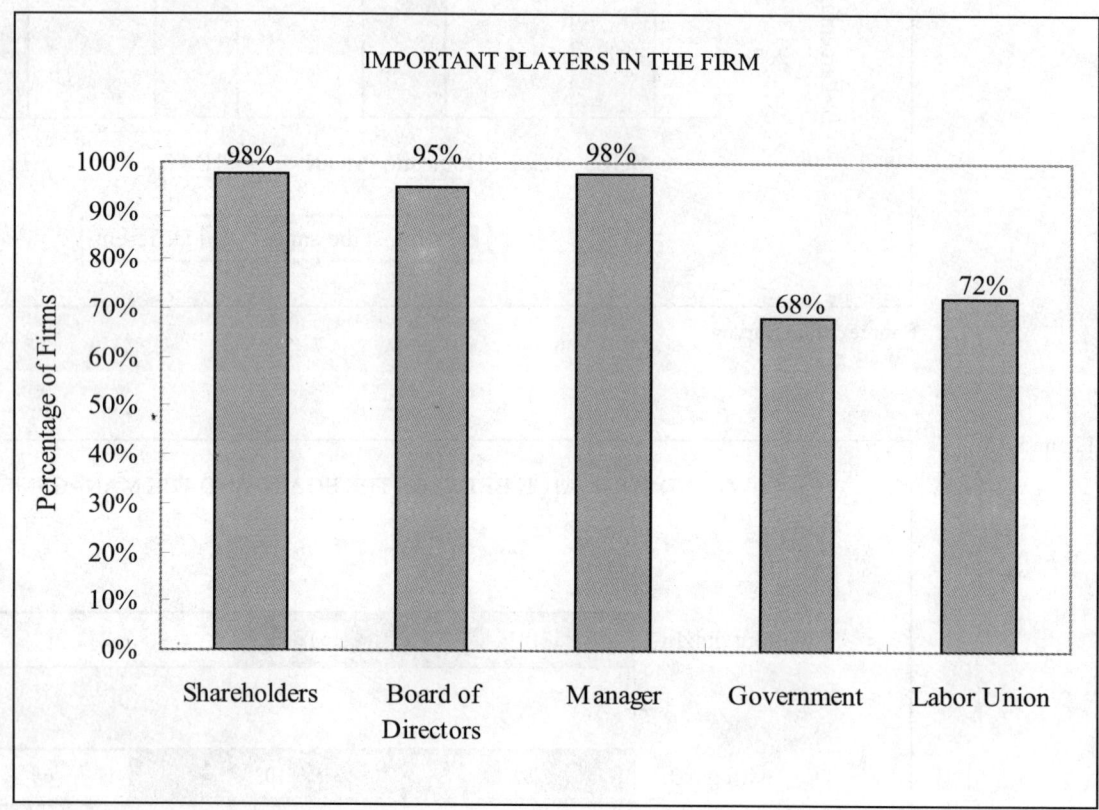

Source: Main Survey

The General Manager

Whether the general manager is self-motivated to work for the best of an enterprise is mostly determined by whether his/her own interests are aligned with those of the enterprise. Therefore, making the manager a shareholder is a commonly used method of providing managers more incentives. As shown in Figure 8.17, over 65% of the firms make such arrangements in 10 out of the 12 cities. Beijing and Xi'an, however, have the lowest shares of general managers who are also shareholders. Further, general managers in 78% of domestic private firms are the shareholders; incontrast, this ratio is about 50% for joint ventures. SOEs have the lowest share of shareholder managers of only 24% (Figure 8.18). This implies that SOEs use different incentive schemes for motivating managers. In addition to rewards measured by money or shares in the company, a high proportion of managers in SOEs originally worked for the government.

Figure 8.17

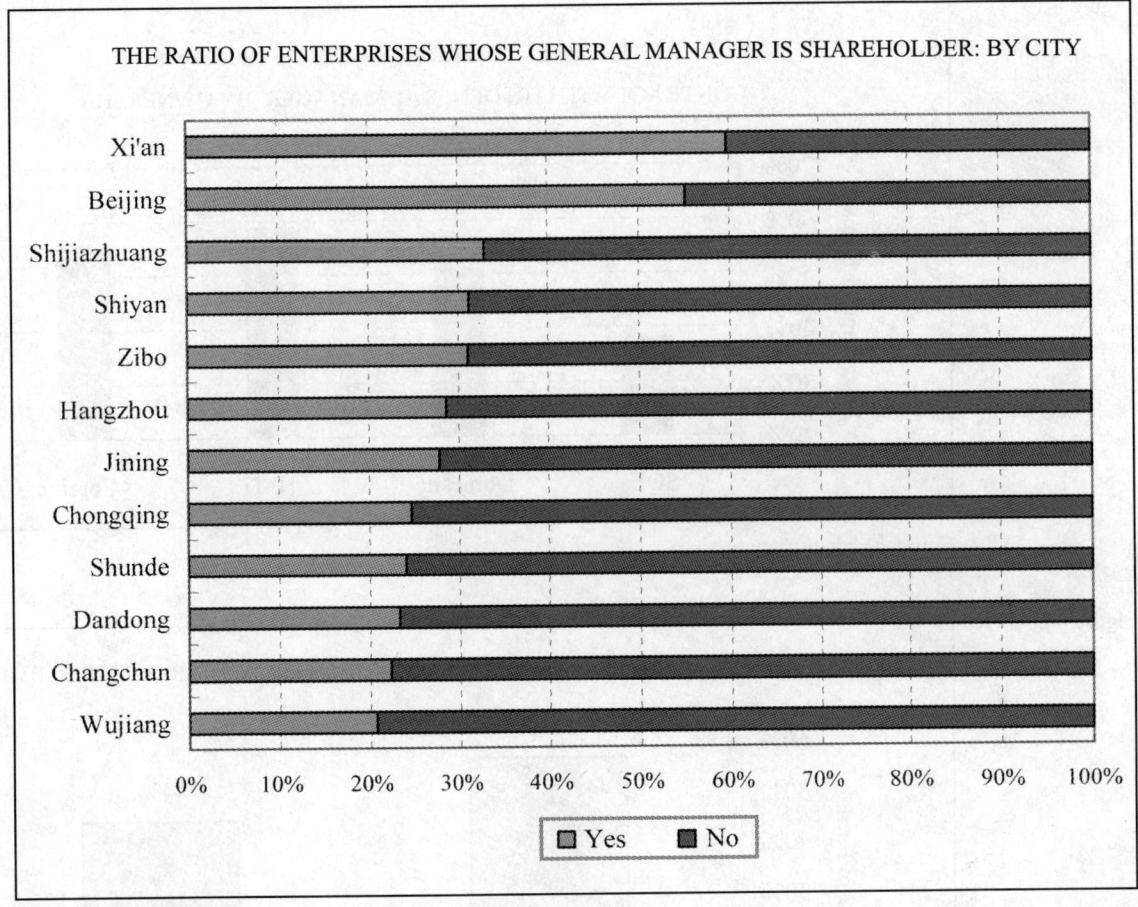

THE RATIO OF ENTERPRISES WHOSE GENERAL MANAGER IS SHAREHOLDER: BY CITY

Source: Main Survey

Figure 8.18

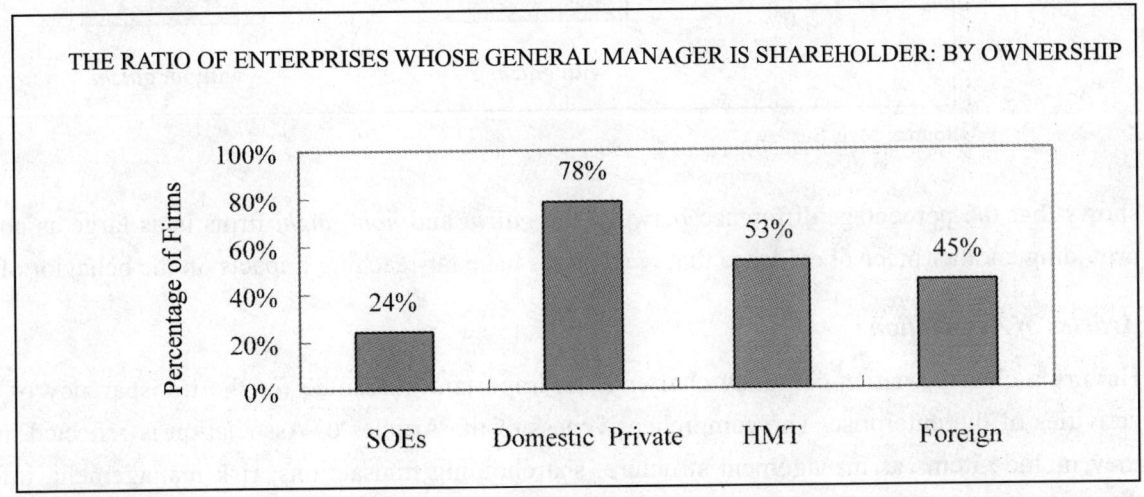

THE RATIO OF ENTERPRISES WHOSE GENERAL MANAGER IS SHAREHOLDER: BY OWNERSHIP

Source: Main Survey

A general manager may, as an additional benefit, sign a contract with the enterprise that he/she serves. Different owners have different policies towards signing contracts to their general managers. Nearly 60% of joint ventures sign contracts with their general managers, while SOEs have the lowest share (Figure 8.19). However, after *gaizhi,* they are more likely to sign contracts with the general manager. Figure 8.20

Figure 8.19

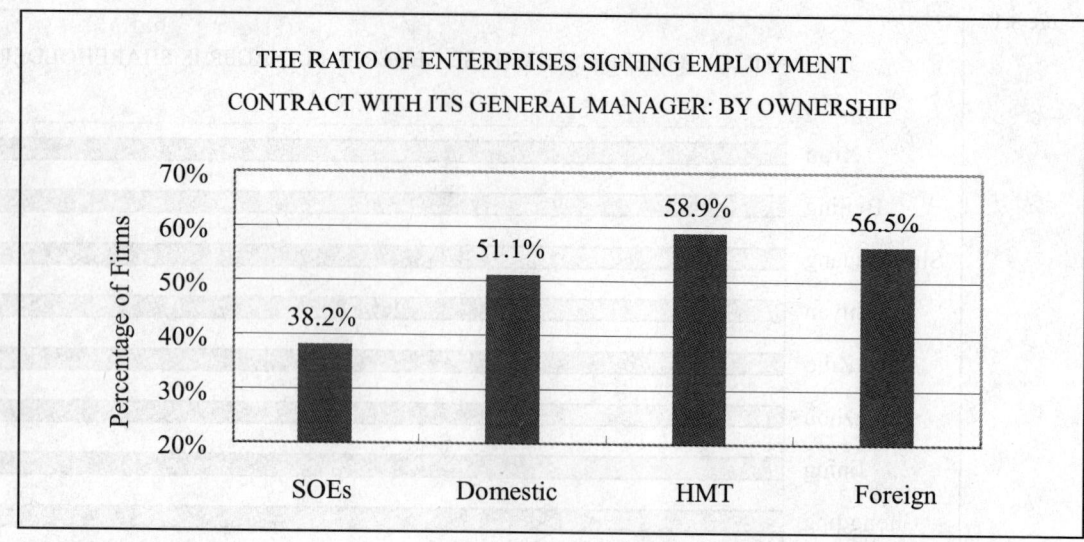

THE RATIO OF ENTERPRISES SIGNING EMPLOYMENT
CONTRACT WITH ITS GENERAL MANAGER: BY OWNERSHIP

Source: Main Survey

Figure 8.20

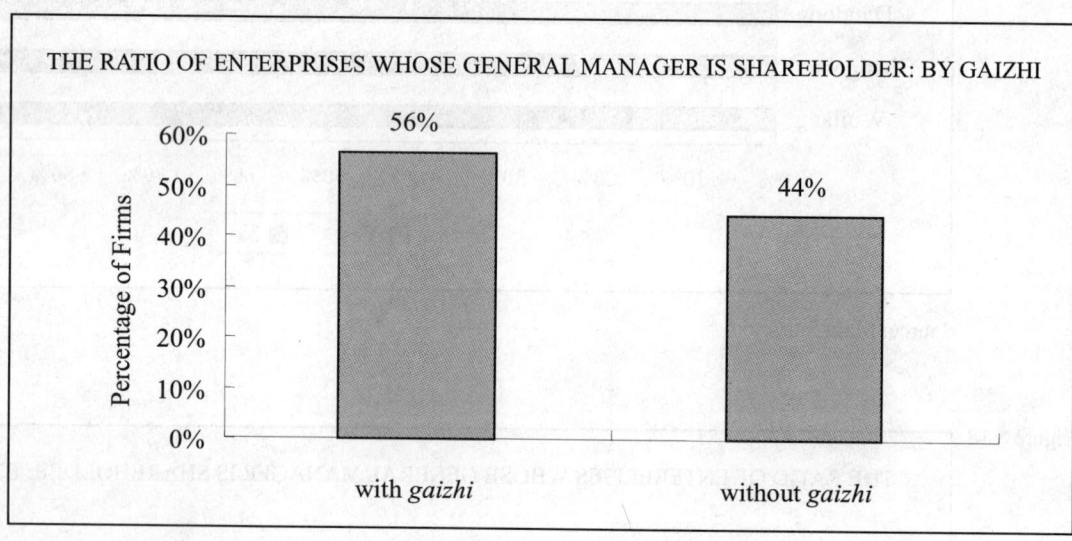

THE RATIO OF ENTERPRISES WHOSE GENERAL MANAGER IS SHAREHOLDER: BY GAIZHI

Source: Main Survey

shows that the percentage difference between the *gaizhi* and *non-gaizhi* firms is as large as about 12%, providing another piece of evidence that *gaizhi* does have far-reaching impacts on the behavior of firms.

Articles of Association

Having a clearly written company charter is an important guarantee for the transparency of the daily activities of the enterprise. The comprehensiveness of the Articles of Association is reflected in whether they include items as management structure, shareholding transactions, risk management, information disclosure, principles for profit distribution, finance management and auditing, etc. If we study whether firms have included the above items in their Articles of Association from the perspective of ownership structure, we observe that the charters of SOEs are relatively incomplete for management structure, shareholding transactions, and principles for profit distribution as compared with other types of firms. SOEs only come close to domestic private firms and Foreign & Joint Ventures in finance management and auditing, which probably is because SOEs need to deal with various kinds of inspections from the

government and other institutions. Figure 8.21 presents the proportion of firms including Corporate Constitution in the management structure. It shows that SOEs has the lowest proportion of firms while HMT
and Foreign & Joint Ventures have the highest proportions of firms to do so. This pattern is similar toward
whether insider transaction, profit distribution rules, financial management rules are included in corporate
constitution in enterprises with different ownership structure.

Figure 8. 21

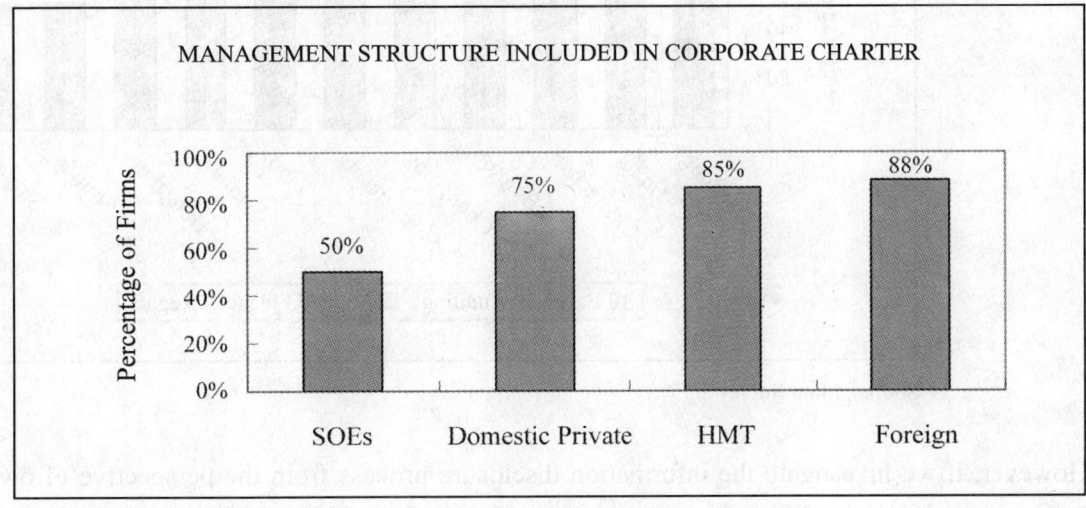

Source: Main Survey

The *gaizhi* firms can serve as an control group for comparing the coverage of SOEs and private enterprises
in terms of Articles of Association. As shown in Table 8.1, the *gaizhi* firms in general have more complete
Articles of Association. For example, 84% of the *gaizhi* firms have management structure in their Articles
of Association, 14% higher than the *non-gaizhi* firms; regulations for insider transactions and finance
management are stricter in the *gaizhi* firms than those in the *non-gaizhi* firms. Finally, a higher proportion of
the *gaizhi* firms have profit distribution rules written into their articles of Association to avoid future conflicts.

Table 8. 1

ARTICLES OF ASSOCIATION in *GAIZHI* AND *NON-GAIZHI* FIRMS

	Management Structure	Insider Transaction	Profit Distribution Rules	Financial Management
Gaizhi firms	84.27%	45.97%	66.13%	75.4%
Non-gaizhi firms	70.92%	36.35%	59.22%	67.2%

Auditing and Information Disclosure

Auditing the financial health of enterprises through a third-party professional institution is the basis for the
provision of audited financial reports to shareholders. Overall, the majority of firms emphasize these two
tasks. Xi'an seems to do best with 93% of the firms having audits and 92% of the firms providing audited
financial reports. Even for the lowest city, over 60% of the sample firms will go through the process of
auditing and providing audited financial reports (Figure 8.22).

Figure 8.22

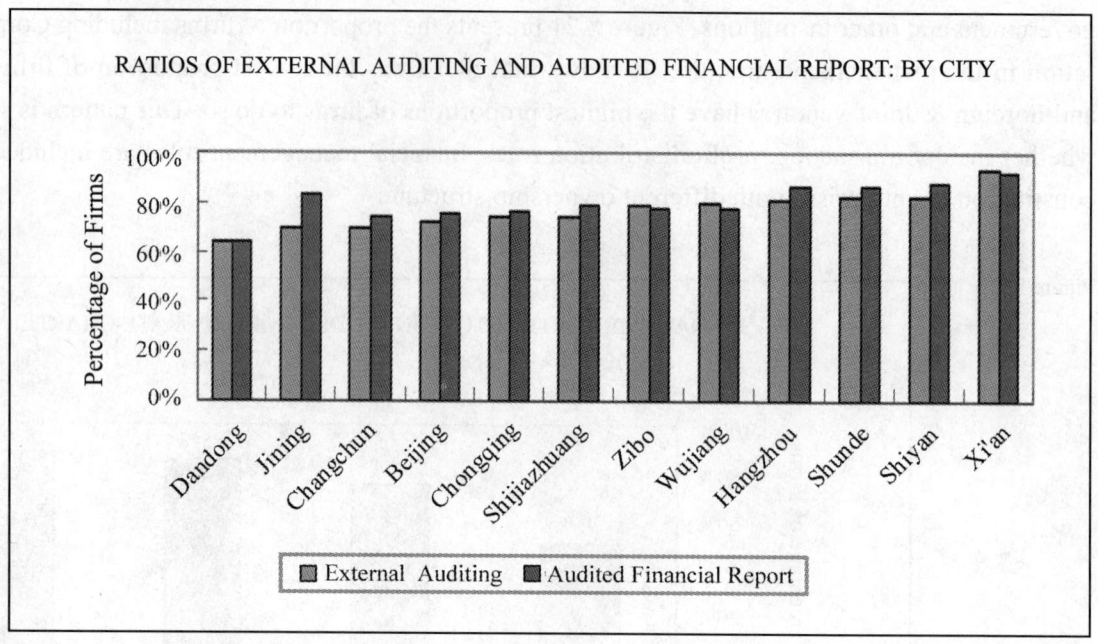

RATIOS OF EXTERNAL AUDITING AND AUDITED FINANCIAL REPORT: BY CITY

Source: Main Survey

However, if we investigate the information disclosure process from the perspective of ownership structures, we find that the differences are quite significant. Only 80% of SOEs perform third-party auditing, and only 62% of them provide audited financial reports to shareholders. Joint ventures, on the other hand, carry out audits and provide regular audited financial reports for over 90% of the firms in this group (Figure 8.23). The behavior of SOEs toward informing shareholders about important decisions is similar to their behavior toward audited financial reports. The *gaizhi* firms, however, appear to do better than *non-gaizhi* firms in disclosing information. For example, about 9 percent more of the *gaizhi* firms will provide external financial reports than the *non-gaizhi* firms.

Risk Control and Education Levels

With the deepening of globalization and the acceleration of economic development in China, risk management is critical to the survival and prosperity of firms. In this subsection we investigate whether firms have risk management systems and whether firms have periodic evaluations of potential risks. In addition, we also examine the differences in educational levels among firms with different governance structures, as the education level can affect the implementation of firms' governance quality and risk control.

Based on the sampled data, the majority of the firms in China do not have risk management systems. Only 20.99% firms reported they have established risk management systems. In particular, 16% of the sample firms report they do not know what risk management systems are. From the ownership point of view, only 19% of SOEs and domestic private firms have established risk management systems (Figure 8.24). There is little difference between *gaizhi* and *non-gaizhi* firms in this respect.

The general picture of educational levels is drawn from four angles: the education level of the general manager; the proportion of members with at least a bachelor degree in the management team, the proportion of employees with at least a bachelor degree, and the proportion of workers with junior high education level.

Figure 8.23

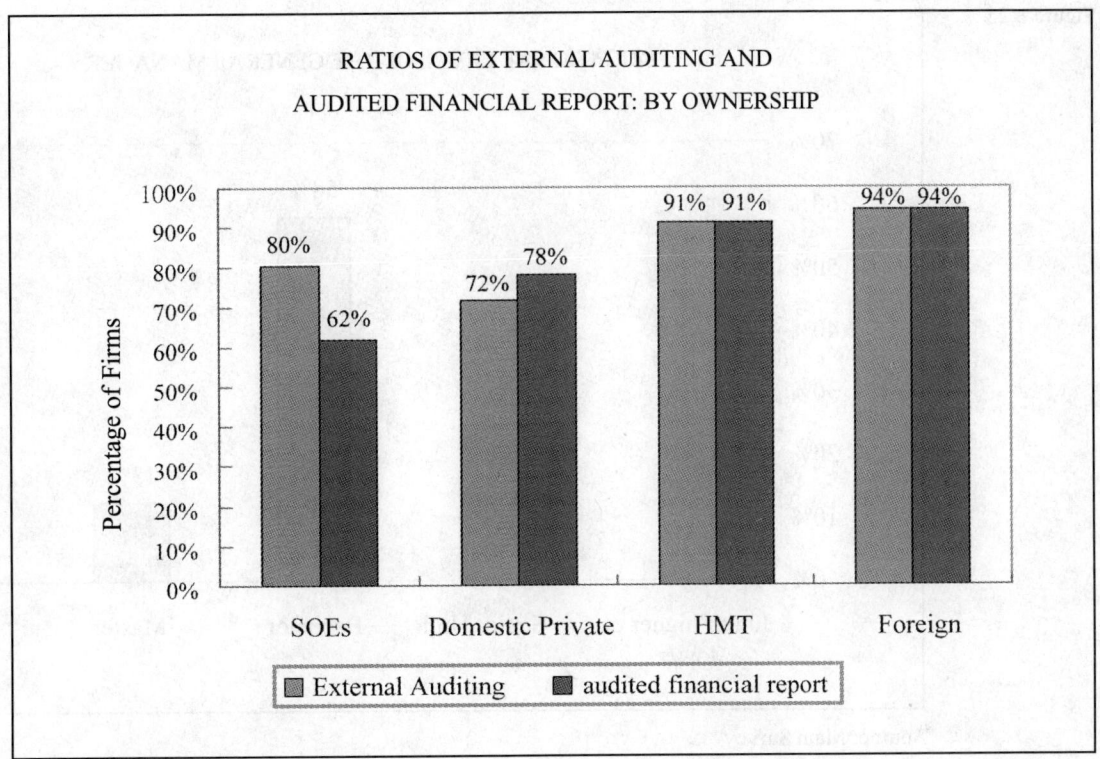

RATIOS OF EXTERNAL AUDITING AND
AUDITED FINANCIAL REPORT: BY OWNERSHIP

Source: Main Survey

Figure 8.24

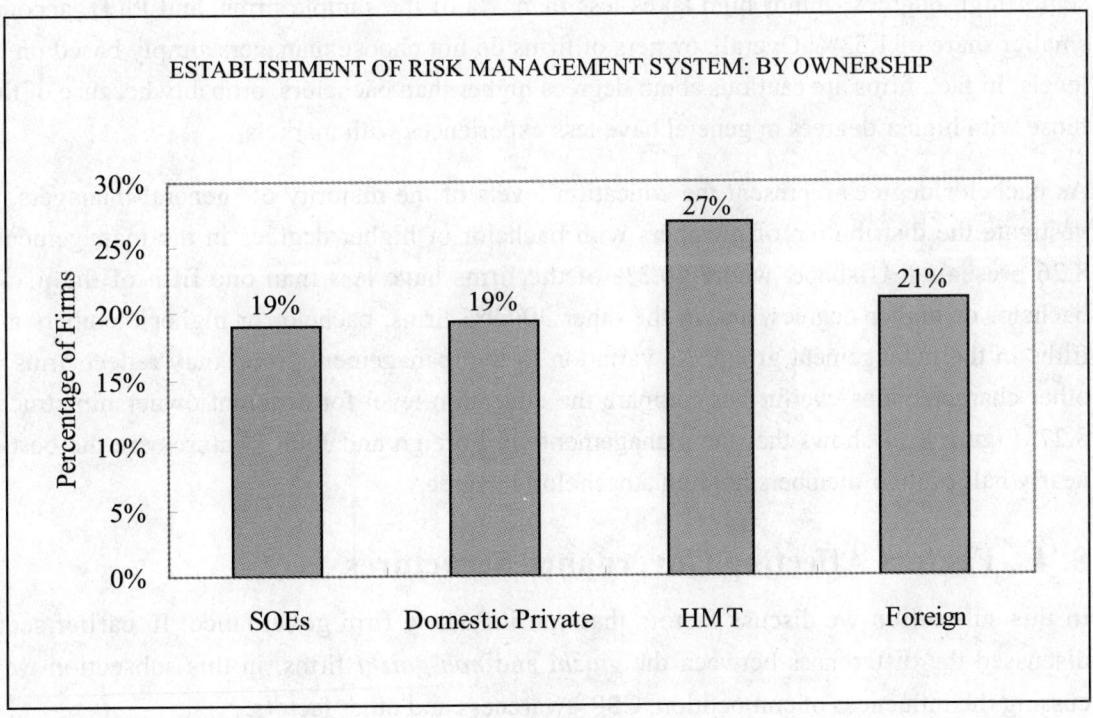

ESTABLISHMENT OF RISK MANAGEMENT SYSTEM: BY OWNERSHIP

Source: Main Survey

The distribution of the education levels for general managers has a bell shape (Figure 8.25), with the peak at the bachelor level: over 58% of general managers hold a Bachelor's degree. Besides the bachelor

Figure 8.25

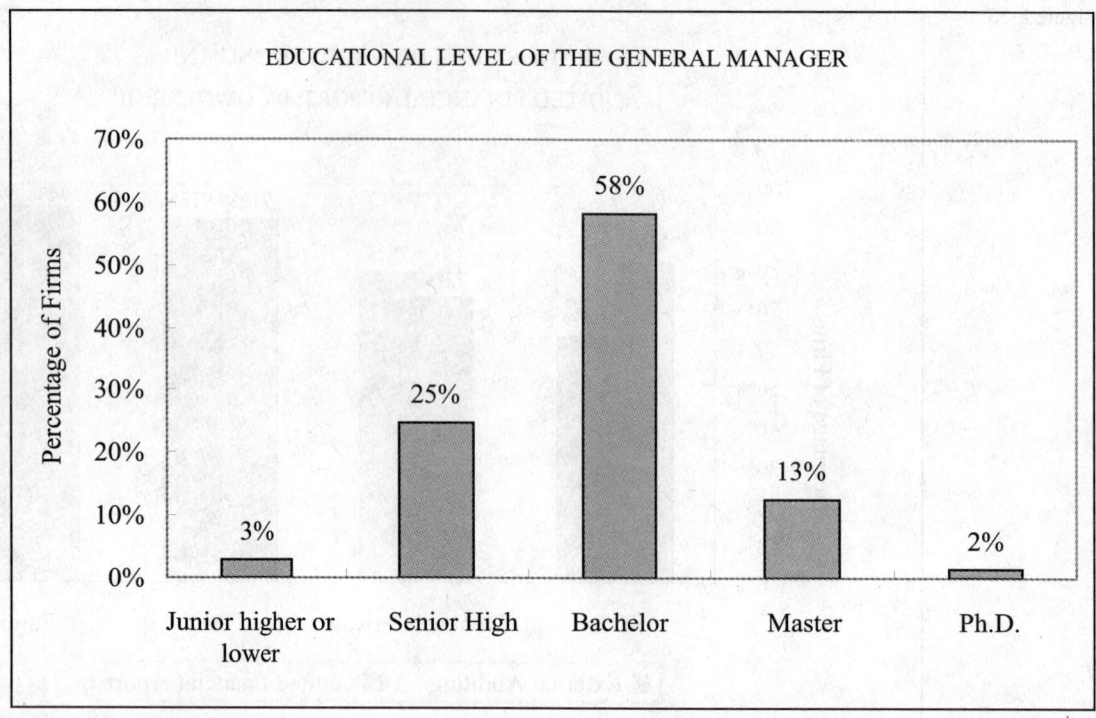

Source: Main Survey

degree, the next highest category is senior high, with over 24% of firms having general managers with senior high degrees. Junior high takes less than 3% of the sample firms, and Ph.D. account for an even smaller share of 1.53%. Overall, owners of firms do not choose managers simply based on their education levels. In fact, firms are cautious about degrees higher than bachelors, probably because of the concern that those with higher degrees in general have less experiences with markets.

As bachelor degrees represent the education levels of the majority of general managers, we further investigate the distribution of members with bachelor or higher degrees in the management team. Figure 8.26 presents a U-shape, where 40.3% of the firms have less than one-fifth of the managers holding bachelor or higher degrees, and in the other 30.69% firms, bachelor or higher members take over three-fifths in the management group. As variation in the management group may reflect firms' differences in other characteristics, we further compare the education level for different ownership structures in Figure 8.27. Figure 8.27 shows that the managements in Foreign and Joint Ventures are the best educated with nearly half of their members holding a bachelor's degree.

8. 4 Factors Affecting Governance Structures

In this subsection we discuss factors that can influence firm governance. In earlier sections we have discussed the differences between the *gaizhi* and *non-gaizhi* firms, in this subsection we focus on discussing the influences of competition, CSR awareness and other factors.

Competition

Market competition is the first factor that we inspect, as pressure from the market may force firms to work at improving their governance structure to increase profit. We do find that the governance structures

Figure 8.26

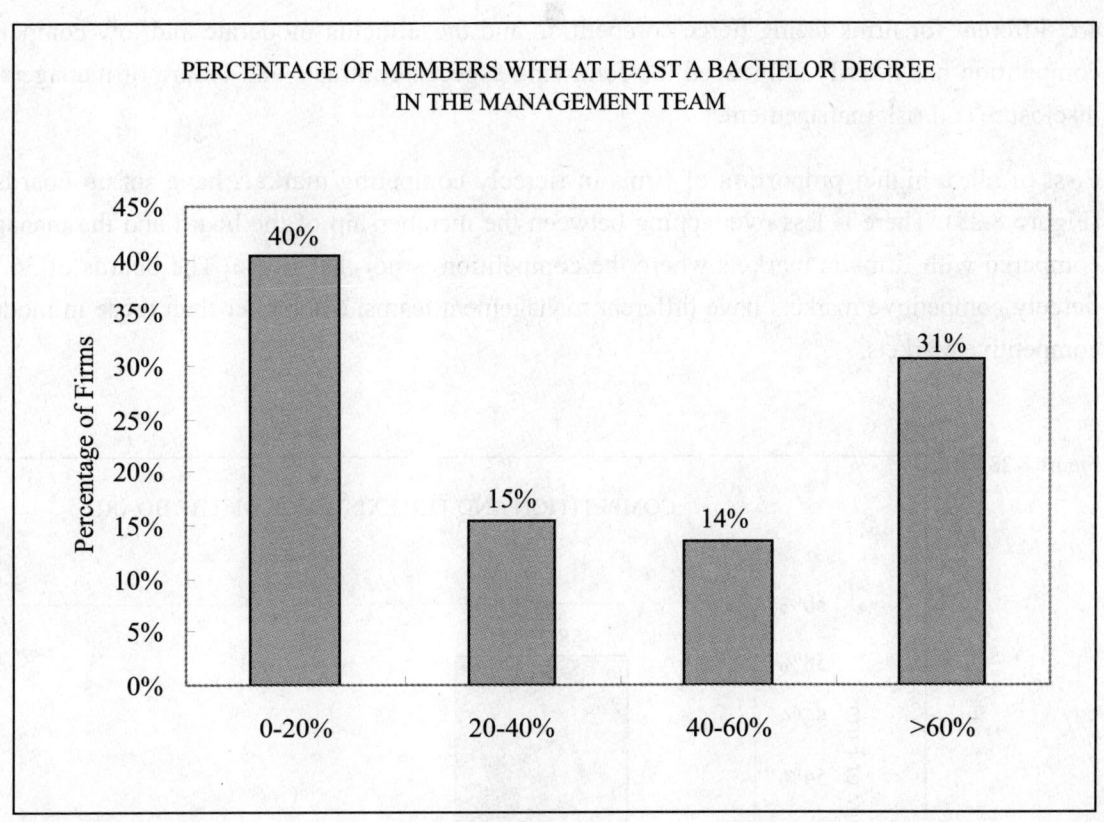

PERCENTAGE OF MEMBERS WITH AT LEAST A BACHELOR DEGREE
IN THE MANAGEMENT TEAM

Source: Main Survey

Figure 8.27

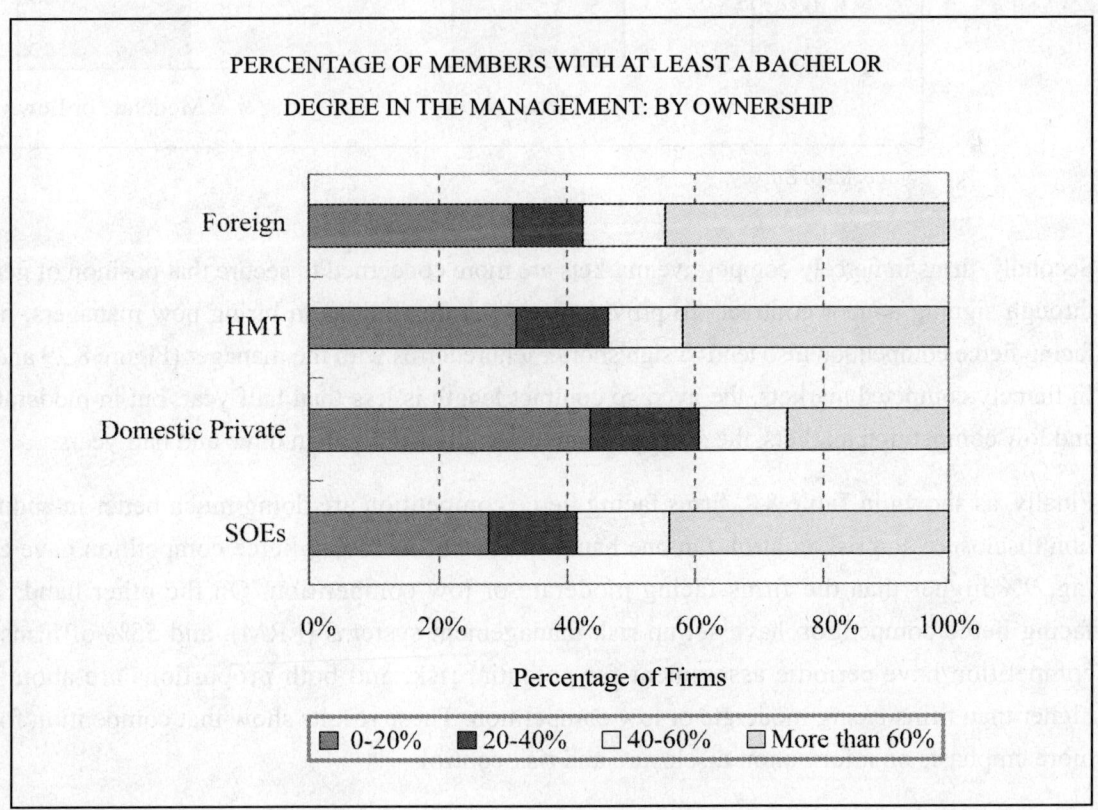

PERCENTAGE OF MEMBERS WITH AT LEAST A BACHELOR
DEGREE IN THE MANAGEMENT: BY OWNERSHIP

Source: Main Survey

are different for firms facing fierce competition and those facing moderate and low competition. Market competition has heavily influenced the following aspects: contracts and tenure of managers, information disclosure and risk management.

First of all, a higher proportion of firms in fiercely competing markets have set up boards of directors (Figure 8.28). There is less overlapping between the membership of the board and the management teams compared with firms in markets where the competition is not that fierce. The boards of 36.76% firms in fiercely competitive markets have different management teams, 6% higher than those in moderate and low competitive markets.

Figure 8.28

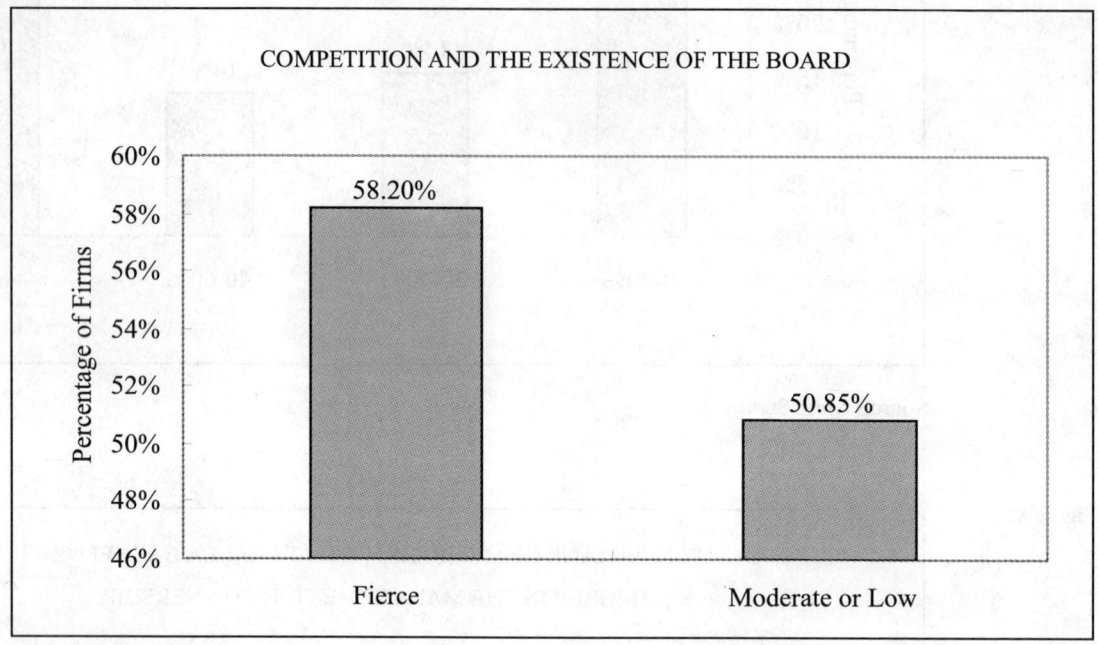

Source: Main Survey

Secondly, firms in fiercely competitive markets are more concerned to secure that position of general manager through signing a labor contract. To provide firms the flexibilities in hiring new managers, however, firms facing fierce competition also tend to sign shorter tenure terms with the manager (Figure 8.29 and Figure 8.30). In fiercely competed markets, the average contract length is less than half year, but in moderately-competed and low competition markets, the average contract length is more than three and half years.

Finally, as shown in Table 8.2, firms facing fierce competition are doing much better in auditing, information disclosure and risk control. On one hand, 77% of firms facing fierce competition have external auditing, 9% higher than the firms facing moderate or low competition. On the other hand, 21% of firms facing fierce competition have set up risk management systems (ERM), and 55% of firms facing fierce competition have periodic assessment for potential risk, and both proportions are about 6 percentage higher than firms facing moderate or low competition. These results show that competition forces firms put more emphasis on information disclosure and risk control.

Figure 8.29

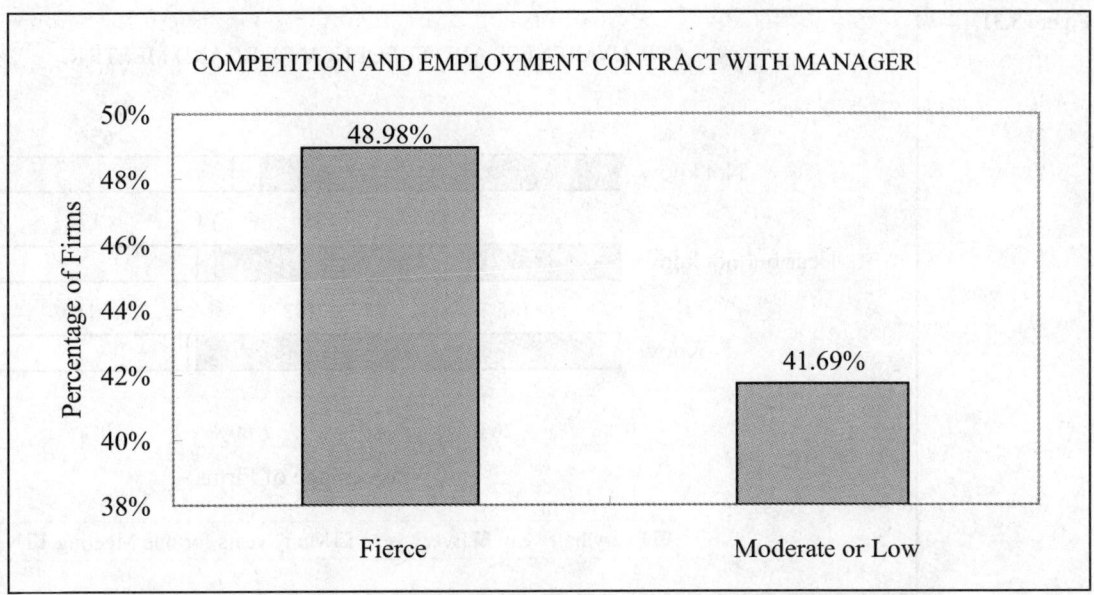

COMPETITION AND EMPLOYMENT CONTRACT WITH MANAGER

Source: Main Survey

Figure 8.30

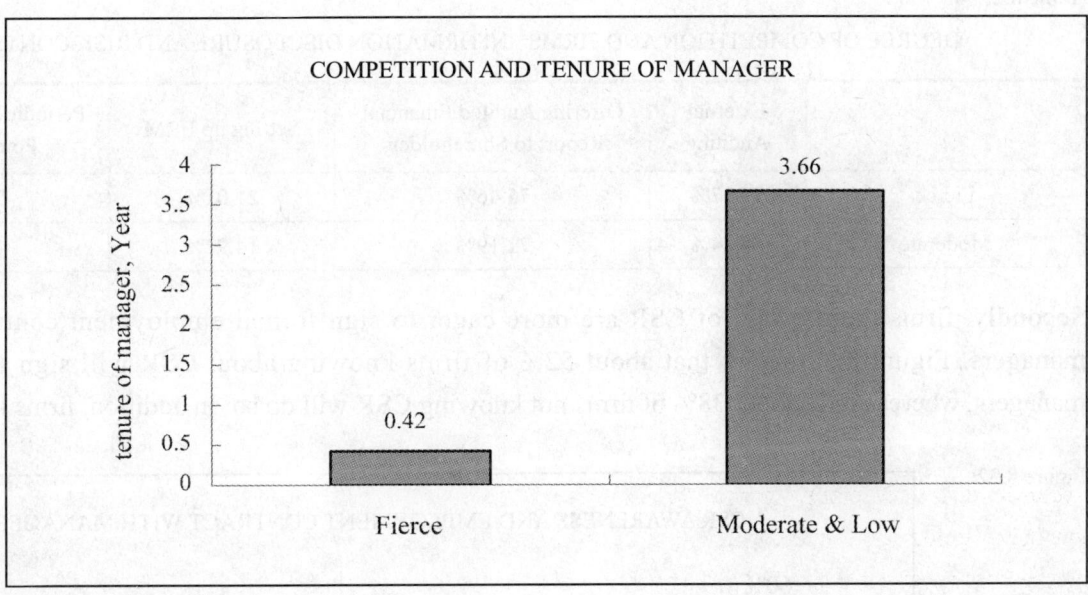

COMPETITION AND TENURE OF MANAGER

Source: Main Survey

CSR awareness

The awareness of CSR is the focus of this study and it remains open whether firms which are more aware of CSR will have different governance structure than those less aware of CSR. Our sample shows that the answer is yes. First of all, firms more aware of CSR appear to respect the Board more than those less aware of CSR. Figure 8.31 provides a piece of evidence. Firms more aware of CSR tend to hold more frequent board meetings. Firms not knowing about CSR, on the other hand, have a higher probability of never holding any Board meetings.

Figure 8.31

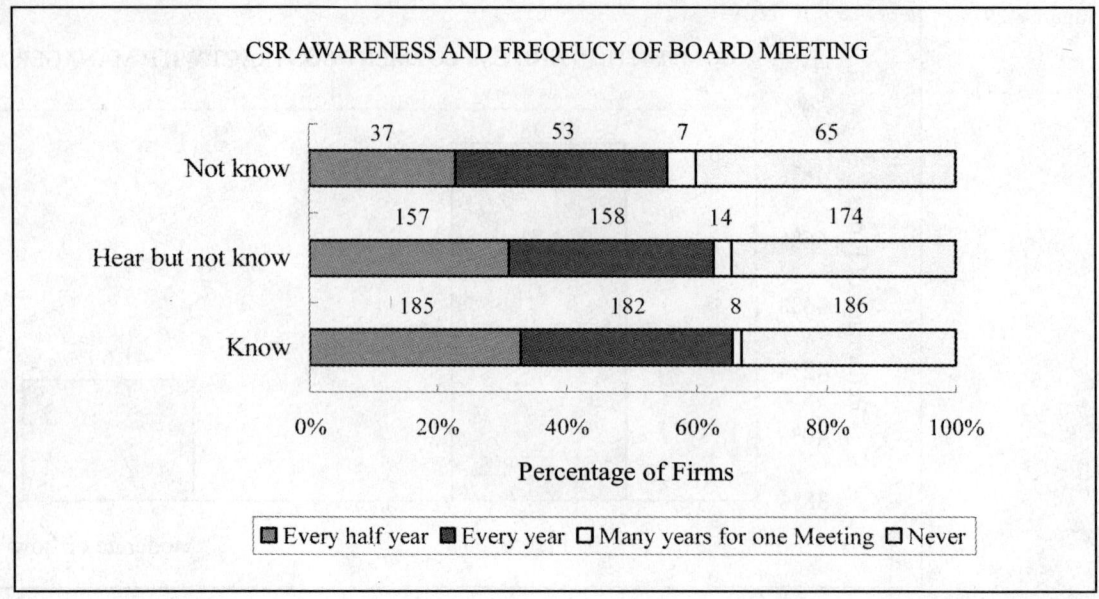

Source: Main Survey

Table 8.2

DEGREE OF COMPETITION AND FIRMS' INFORMATION DISCLOSURE AND RISK CONTROL

	External Auditing	Offering Audited Financial Report to Shareholders	Setting up ERM	Periodic Assessment for Potential Risk
Fierce	77.17%	75.46%	21.01%	54.66%
Moderate	68.14%	71.19%	14.92%	48.14%

Secondly, firms more aware of CSR are more eager to sign formal employment contracts with the managers. Figure 8.32 shows that about 52% of firms knowing about CSR will sign contracts with managers, whereas only about 38% of firms not knowing CSR will do so. In addition, firms knowing about

Figure 8.32

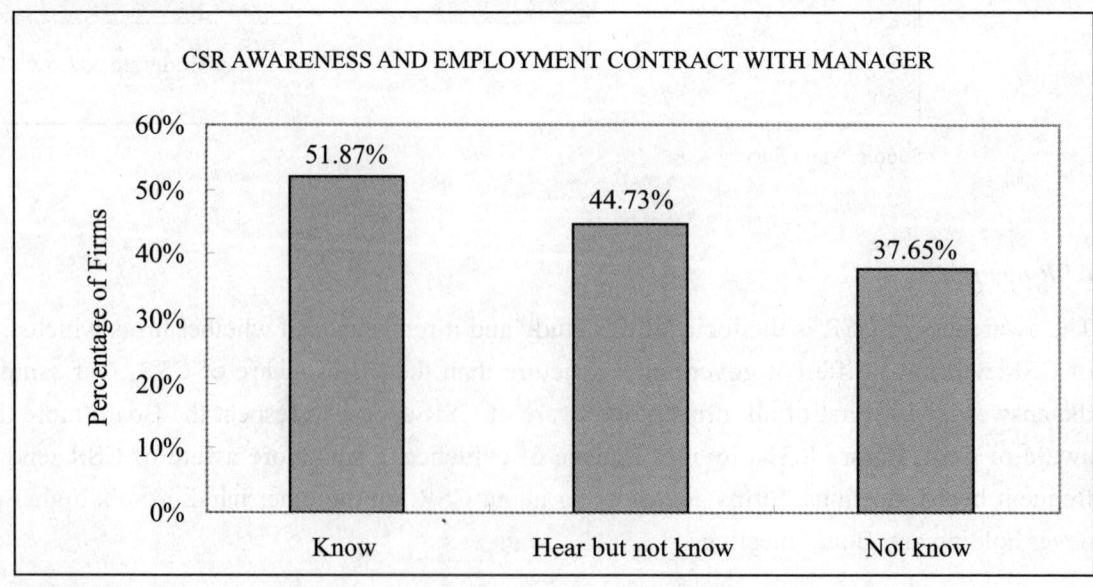

Source: Main Survey

176

CSR also do better in information disclosure and risk control, as shown in Figures 8.33 – 8.34. Figure 8.33 show that 84% of firms knowing CSR have external auditing, but only 54% of firms not knowing CSR do. Firms more aware of CSR are also more cautious about risk control through periodic assessment of potential risk. Over 60% of those familiar with CSR periodically evaluate potential risks, about 25% higher than those not knowing CSR (Figure 8.34).

Finally, firms more aware of CSR also work harder to establish internal values and to convey them to employees through clearly expressed corporate value statements and codes of conduct. As shown in Figure 8.35, 63.5% of firms knowing CSR have established corporate values and codes of conduct, 35% higher than those not knowing about CSR. This shows that while corporate values and codes of conduct

Figure 8.33

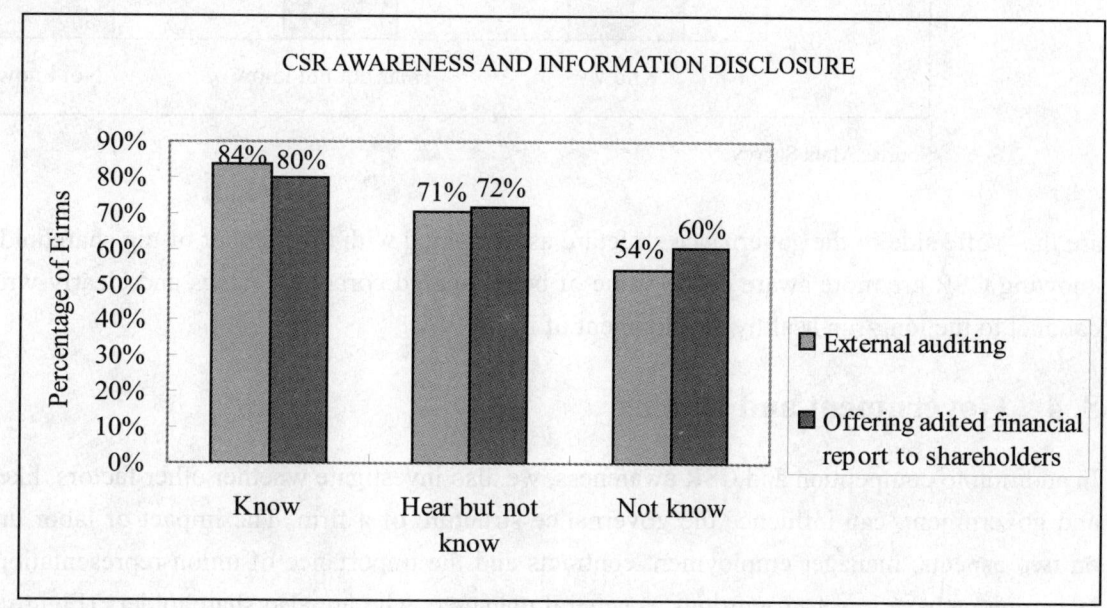

Source: Main Survey

Figure 8.34

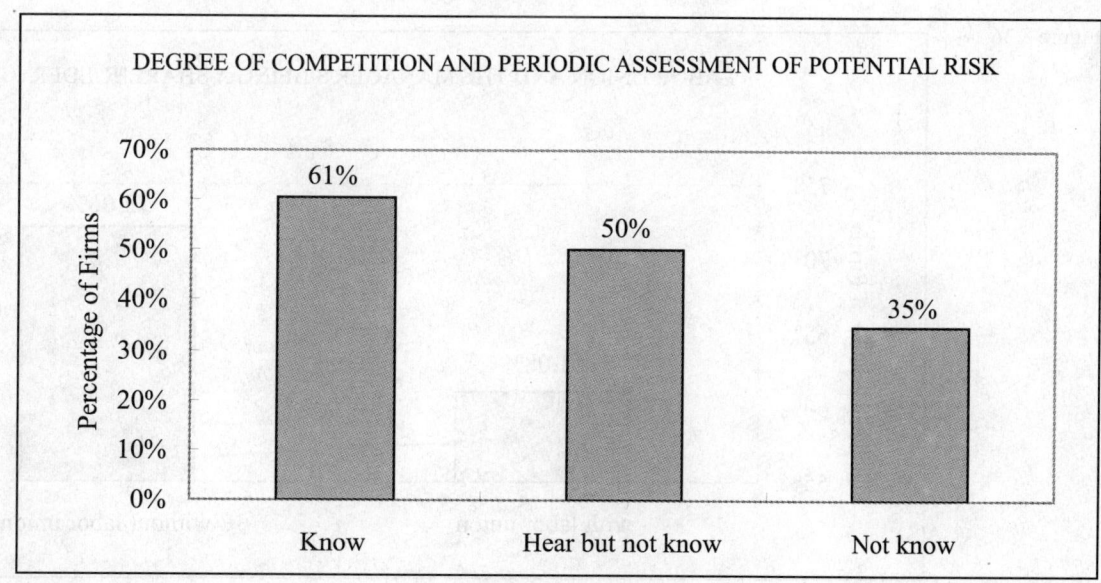

Source: Main Survey

Figure 8.35

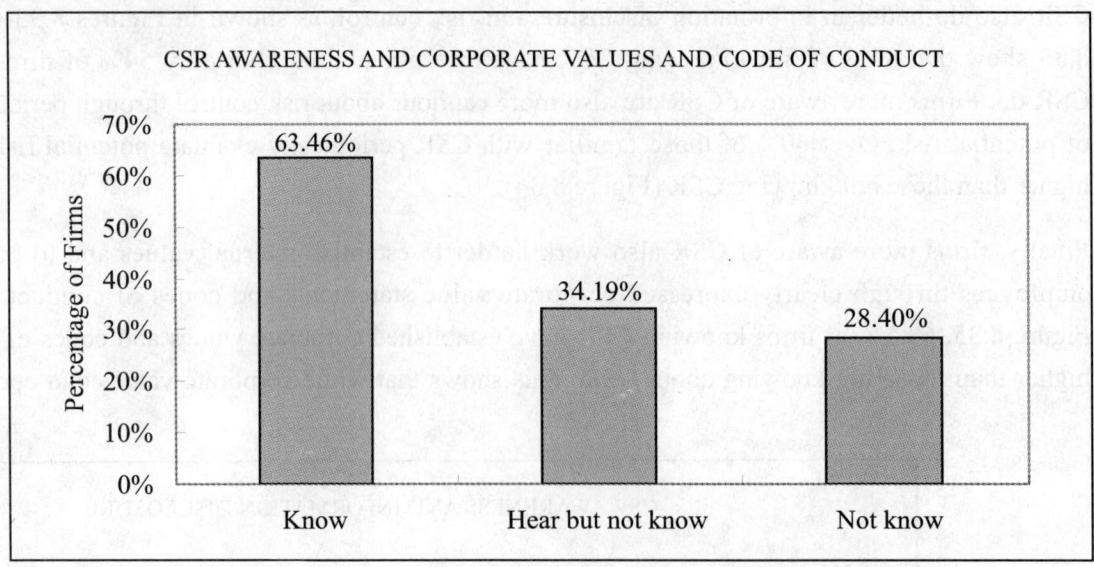

Source: Main Survey

are the "soft" side of the governance structure as compared with the number of big shareholders, the firms knowing CSR are more aware of the value of better shared corporate values and clearly-written codes of conduct to the long-run healthy development of firms.

8. 4   Government and Unions

In addition to competition and CSR awareness, we also investigate whether other factors, like labor unions and government, can influence the governance structure of a firm. The impact of labor unions focuses on two aspects: manager employment contracts and the importance of union representation. Firms with labor unions have lower proportions of general managers who are also shareholders (Figure 8.36), but the proportion of managers with employment contracts is higher (Figure 8.37).

Figure 8.36

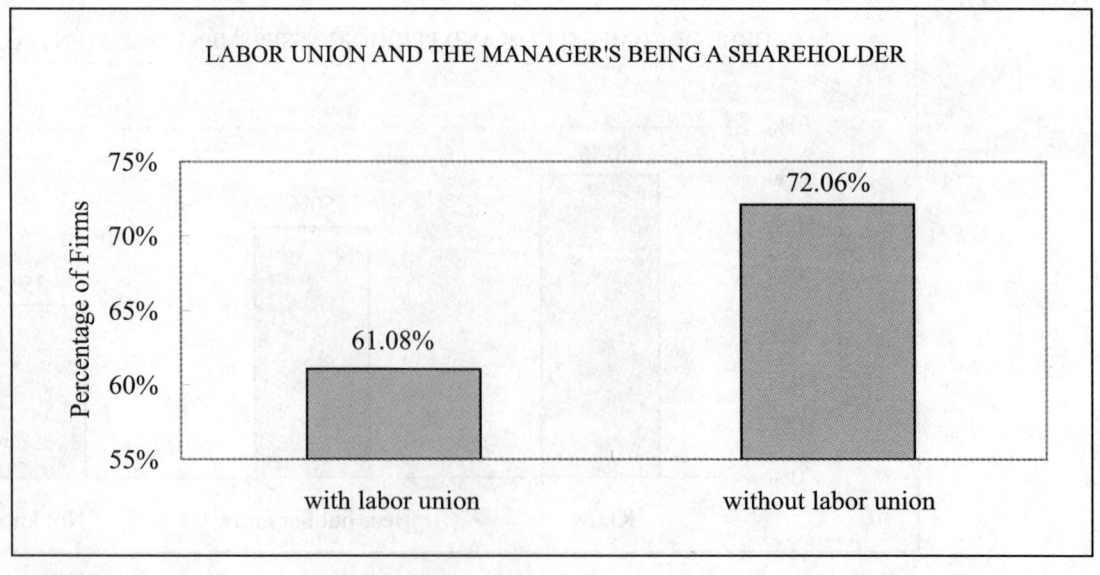

Source: Main Survey

Figure 8.37

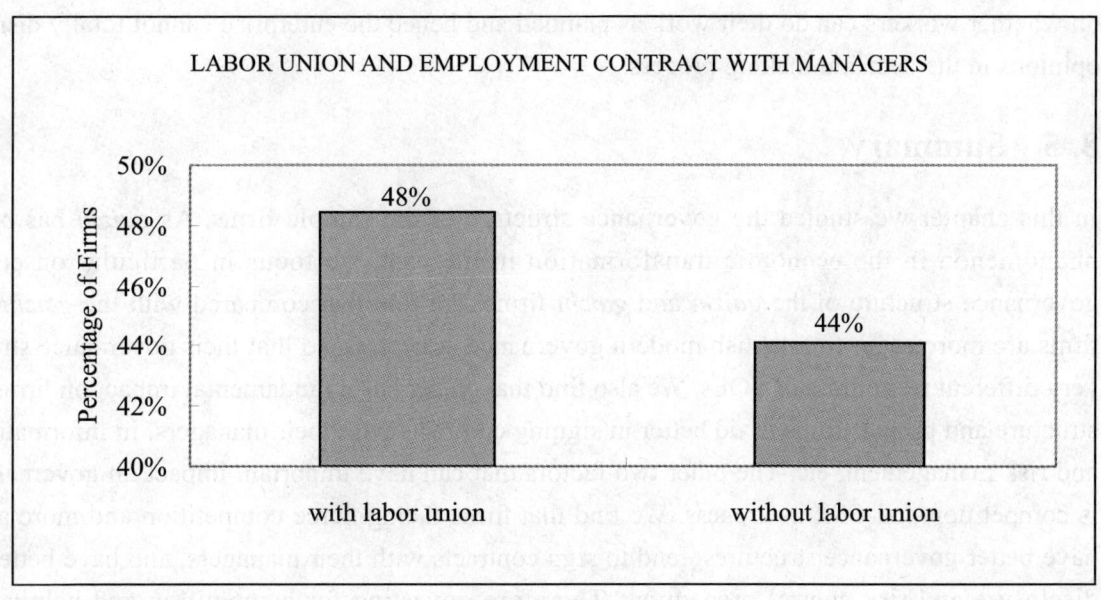

Source: Main Survey

As SOEs tend to have higher proportions of labor unions, we investigate the influences of unions and government in decision making for firms with different ownership structures. It is interesting to observe that government influence on different types of firms seem to be very similar, with the difference between the highest and lowest percentages being only 3%.

Another interesting phenomenon is that labor unions (or worker representatives) are believed to play more important roles than the government in both SOEs and domestic private firms (Figure 8.38). SOEs pay more attention to worker sentiments in the decision making process probably because by nature SOEs are obliged to help relieve employment problems. The operation and survival of domestic private firms rely

Figure 8.38

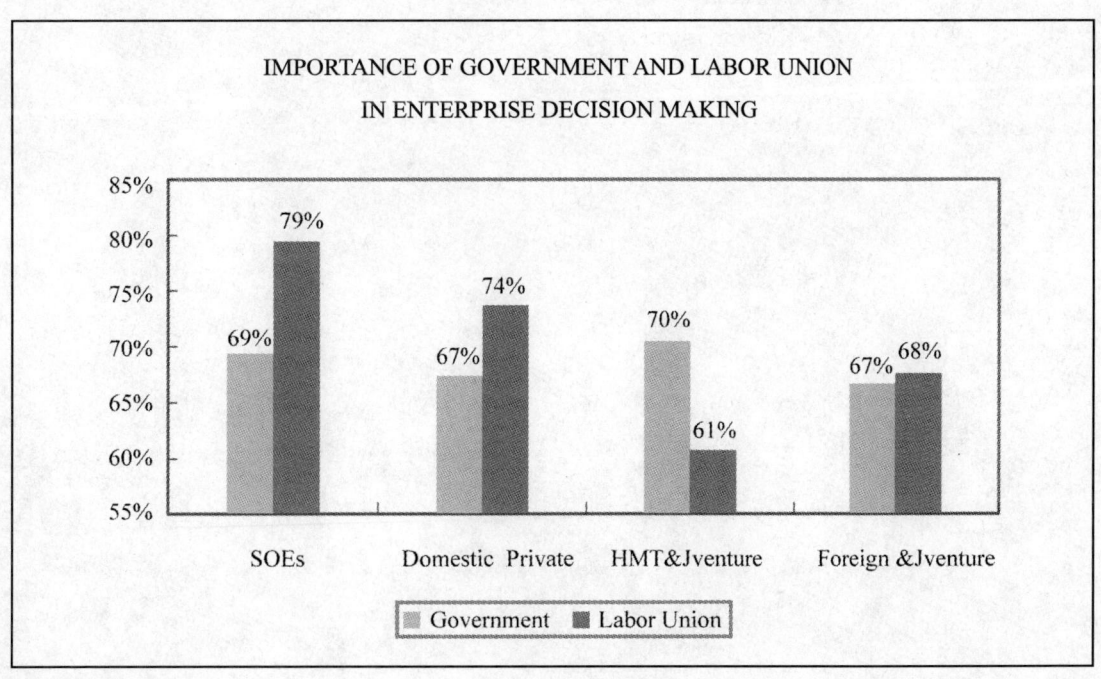

Source: Main Survey

on whether workers can do their work as planned and hence the enterprise cannot totally dismiss workers' opinions in the decision-making process.

8.5 Summary

In this chapter we studied the governance structure of the sample firms. As *gaizhi* has been a central phenomenon in the economic transformation in the past, we focus in particular on comparing the governance structure of the *gaizhi* and *gaizhi* firms. We find that compared with the *gaizhi* firms, *gaizhi* firms are more eager to establish modern governance structures, so that their governance structure can be very different from those of SOEs. We also find that *gaizhi* has a fundamental impact on firms' governance structure and propels firms to do better in signing contracts with their managers, in information disclosure and risk management, etc. The other two factors that can have important impact on governance structures is competition and CSR awareness. We find that firms facing fierce competition and more aware of CSR have better governance structures, tend to sign contracts with their managers, and have better information disclosure and risk control procedures. Therefore, investing for competition and helping firms to be more aware of CSR can be indirect but powerful ways of influencing firms to improve their governance structure.

Chapter 9
Markets, Legal Environment and CSR

Chinese firms are being interwoven into the global market through the division of labor in the global supply chain. Even if a firm only serves the domestic market, it is more or less linked to the global market through its down-stream customers that may be either exporters or FDI firms inside China. CSR is a concept originated in the developed countries. The most effective channel for the diffusion of CSR in developing countries is the global supply chain. Consumers in developed countries care about the environmental and labor standards affecting the products they consume. This is transformed into demands upon companies in developed countries either through direct civil society pressure or through government regulation. Those companies then pass the demand on to the producers in developing countries that provide them with final or intermediate products. A recent study conducted in Shenzhen found that international companies are keen to impose labor and environmental standards on their Chinese suppliers (FIAS and BSR, 2007). Domestically, firms with better CSR records may also pass their own codes of conduct to their suppliers purely because they prefer higher labor and environmental standards.

However, there are also doubts about how effective the supply chain is at diffusing good CSR practice. Within developing countries, there is a concern that supply chain pressures are a way for companies in developed countries to pass their duties onto suppliers in developing countries (Chen, 2006). This concern seems to be echoed, albeit from the negative side, by Phillip Rudolph of the Ethical Leadership Group who, commenting on the case of ILRF vs. Wal-Mart, believes that Wal-Mart's incorporation of its code into its supplier contracts only creates a duty on Wal-Mart's suppliers, but not on itself (Rudolph, 2006). However, the intention of ILRF is exactly to break Wal-Mart's chain of duty shifting. Even in the worst case that the supply chain only provides a channel for companies in developed countries to pass their duties to companies in developing countries, it may not be a bad thing for a developing country as a whole. It definitely benefits the working population, and for the reasons that the next chapter will study, it may also provide strong incentives for firms to find ways to improve their profitability.

The central task of this chapter is to study if and how the supply chain works to enhance the CSR performance of the sample firms. The next chapter will study the linkage between CSR records and the financial performance of firms. Related to this chapter's task is a test of whether outside pressures or the volition of firms are the drivers for the transmission of CSR through the supply chain. This test has policy relevance. If firms impose CSR requirements on their suppliers at their own volition, then government policies and market disciplines are unnecessary, or at least much less necessary, to promote CSR. If firms transmit CSR requirements because of the pressures that they face, then it means that market disciplines, government policies, and civil society pressures are necessary to promote good CSR practice.

Another task of this chapter is to study how the sample firms and the legal environment in each sample city interact with each other to strengthen or weaken the functioning of the legal system. Supporting the legal system is one of the components of good CSR practice. This includes refraining from bribing judges and respecting court rulings, among other things. Before dealing with these two tasks, however, this chapter will start with a section describing the market positions of the sample firms.

9. 1　Market Positions of the Sample Firms

The markets of our sample firms are quite competitive. As reported by respondents entry barriers are limited. There are a total of 34% of the sample firms that reported entry barriers. Among them, 85% mentioned government permits, 17% high requirements for initial capital, 14% regional protectionism, 6% market restrictions (e.g., only SOEs are allowed to operate), and 10% other barriers. Government permits are a conventional means of government regulation, so they are not necessarily real barriers to entry. Apart from this, then, the percentages of firms with other complaints are small. In particular, there are only 4.8% of the sample firms complaining about regional protection, a finding that contradicts the claim that regional protectionism is a serious problem in China (e.g., Young, 2000).

Market competition is intense for the sample firms. Seventy-six percent of them believed that competition in their industry was high and the rest said that it was reasonable or even low. Consistent with the high level of competition, 55% of firms complained that the prices of their products were falling and 89% of them complained that the prices of their inputs were rising, however, there were only 25% of firms reporting increases in the prices of their products and 19% of them reported no change. Supposedly, these firms are more likely to be those producing intermediate goods in short supply.

The markets for the sample firms are mostly local as on average 46% of their sales are within their own province (Figure 9.1). However, there are a large percentage of firms with considerable market presence. Figure 9.2 presents the distribution of the sample firms' market shares in their respective industry within their own province and in the country. There is a bi-modal distribution for both the share in the provincial

Figure 9.1

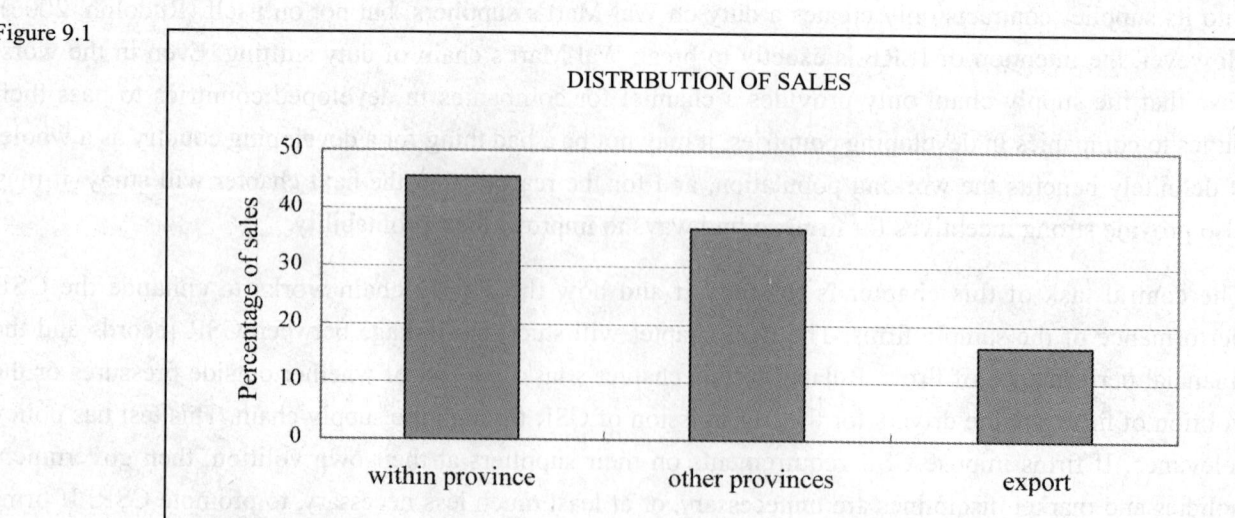

Source: Main Survey

market and in the national market. That is, there are more firms with small shares or large shares than firms with medium-level shares. While 20% of the sample firms have less than 1% market share in their own province, 32% of them have more than 20% market share. As for shares in the national market, 39% of the firms have a market share of less than 1%, but there are also 16% with a share of more than 20%.

Figure 9.2

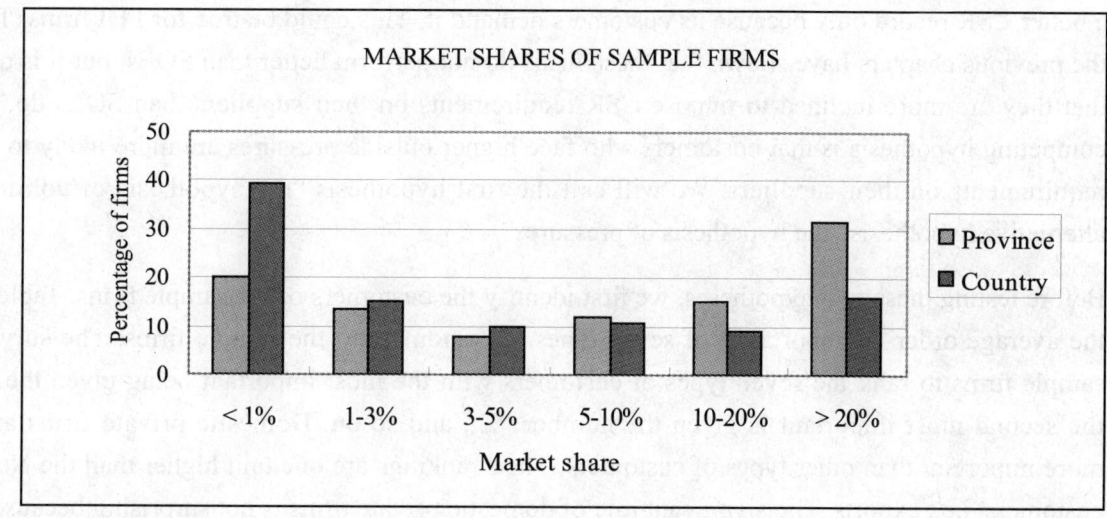

Source: Main Survey

9. 2　The supply Chain and CSR

The supply chain can be one of the significant factors that raise a firm's CSR awareness, especially when the market for the end products is in developed countries. Consumers in developed countries care about the labor and environmental standards as well as the quality of the products they consume. In addition, governments in developed countries implement much more stringent labor and environmental standards and quality control than in developing countries. These consumer and government pressures will then be transmitted through the supply chain to reach the producers in developing countries. This section analyzes how the supply chain affects the CSR performance of the sample and how these sample firms transmit CSR requirements through the supply chain.

Customers and CSR Requirements

Most of the sample firms have stable customers. On average, the largest three customers accounted for 60% of their total sales in 2005. In addition, they have had business with these three largest customers for an average of 7.2 years, and with the largest customer for 9.1 years. Not all customers place labor or environmental standards on their suppliers. Among the sample firms, 24.1% do not face customers' requirements for labor standards and 39.5% do not face customers' requirements for environmental standards. Among those that do have to meet customers' labor or environmental standards, about half of them said that their customers began to place these requirements before 2002.

Different customers may have different requirements for a supplier's CSR standards. A natural hypothesis is that customers that maintain higher CSR standards themselves would be more likely to put higher requirements on their suppliers. However, the underlying presumption of this hypothesis is that CSR is a conscious action of a firm's own volition, which is not always true. It is perfectly possible that a firm maintains higher CSR standards only because the government and consumers force it to do so, or because workers demand it. In this case, maintaining higher CSR standards is mostly seen by the firm as a factor that increases its operating costs, so it is unlikely that the firm would impose it on its suppliers. Likewise, a firm with a not-so-good CSR record may impose higher CSR requirements on its suppliers than a firm with a better CSR record only because its customers demand it. This could be true for FDI firms. The results of the previous chapters have shown that these firms do not perform better than SOEs, but it is quite possible that they are more inclined to impose CSR requirements on their suppliers than SOEs do. Therefore, a competing hypothesis is that customers who face higher outside pressures are more likely to impose CSR requirements on their suppliers. We will call the first hypothesis "the hypothesis of volition", and this alternative hypothesis "the hypothesis of pressures".

Before testing these two hypotheses, we first identify the customers of the sample firms. Table 9.1 presents the average order of importance of seven types of customers to the sample firms. The survey asked the sample firms to rank the seven types of customers with the most important being given the number "1", the second most important is given the number "2", and so on. Domestic private firms and SOEs are more important than other types of customers. Their rankings are one unit higher than the No. 3 source of customers, i.e., exports. The significant role of domestic private firms is not surprising because they are the majority in the market. The reason that SOEs are more significant than FDI firms is that many FDI firms are engaged in processing trades and import more intermediate goods than SOEs.

Table 9.1

ORDER OF DIFFERENT TYPES OF CUSTOMERS BY IMPORTANCE

	Domestic private firms	SOEs	Export	FDI SMEs	Firm's own retail sales	FDI large firms	Other
Average order of importance	1.73	1.91	2.94	3.16	3.5	3.65	4.13

Note: The order of importance is a value between 1 and 7, with a smaller number indicating a higher order of importance.
Source: Main survey.

Our next task is to test the two hypotheses with data collected on the sample firms. The main survey asked the sample firms to evaluate different types of customer-intensity of requirements on labor and environmental standards. They are SOEs, domestic private firms, FDI SMEs, FDI large firms, importers in developed countries, and importers in developing countries. Four answers were given: most firms have requirements, some of them do, none of them do, and do not have such customers. To make the analysis simpler and more transparent, we group the first two answers together to study the percentage of the sample firms believing that at least some of each type of firm have requirements. The results are presented in Figure 9.3.

Figure 9.3

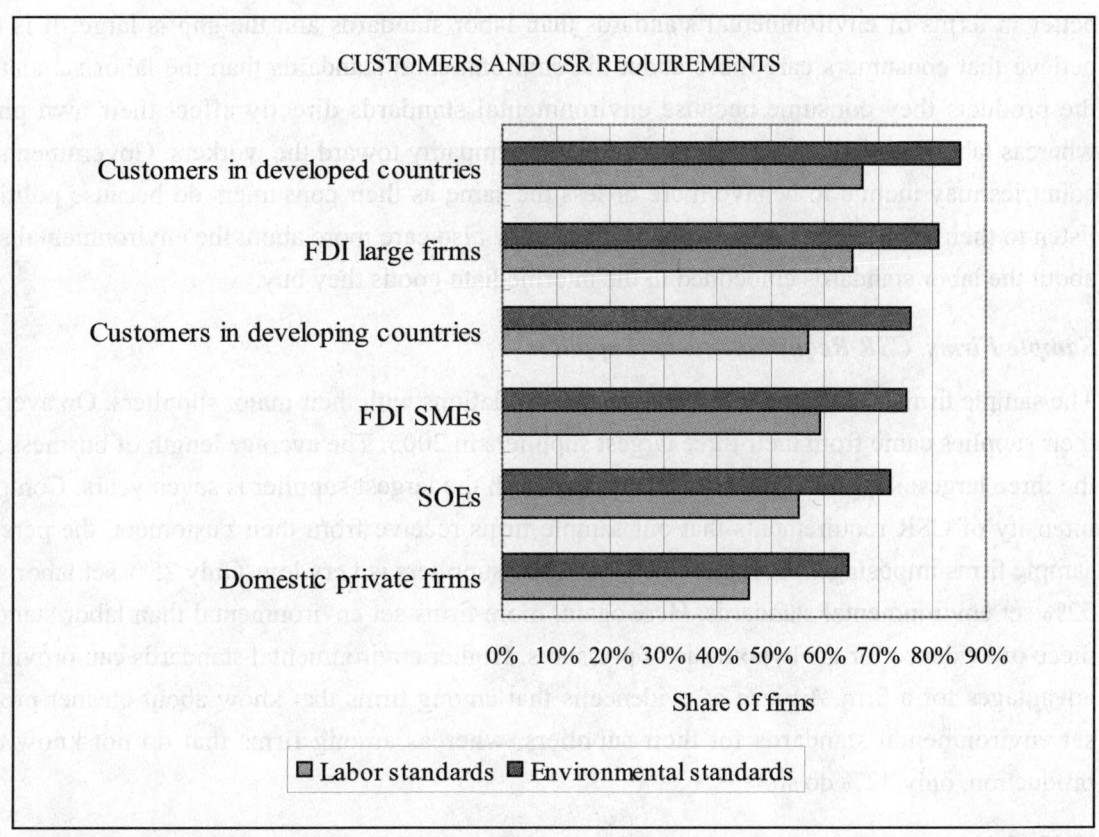

Source: Main Survey

The figure invariably favors the hypothesis of pressures because the order of performance matches the order of pressures faced by the different types of customers, but not the order of their performance. In terms of their own performance, SOEs perform better than other types of firms, especially in labor protection; but their ranking here is much behind that of the FDI firms. On the other hand, it is evident that the ranking in Figure 9.3 matches the order of pressures. Customers in developed countries and large FDI firms are ranked No. 1 and No. 2 in terms of both labor and environmental standards. This is so because they directly face pressures in their home countries and are under global watches. The finding that large FDI firms perform slightly worse may have something to do with the smaller pressures they face in their home countries because they also sell their products inside China where standards may be lower. Customers in developing countries are ranked No. 3 in terms of environmental standards, but No. 4 in terms of labor standards. It is often the case that countries place harsher environmental standards on imports than on domestic products, so the ranking makes sense. FDI SMEs are ranked No. 4 in terms of environmental standards and No. 3 in terms of labor standards. Compared with large FDI firms, these firms are under much smaller pressures from their home countries or global watches. Indeed, they behave more like domestic firms in China. Lastly, SOEs and domestic private firms are ranked No. 5 and No. 6 in terms of both environmental and labor standards. SOEs perform better than FDI firms in many aspects of CSR, but they may behave just as what we discussed earlier, that is, seeing the compliance as a cost, and thus would not impose it on their suppliers. However, they are more visible than domestic private firms, so they are more likely to impose requirements on their suppliers than domestic private firms.

Another piece of evidence supporting the hypothesis of pressures is that all kinds of customers perform better in terms of environmental standards than labor standards and the gap is large. It is reasonable to believe that consumers care more about the environmental standards than the labor standards carried by the products they consume because environmental standards directly affect their own physical health whereas labor standards are only related to their sympathy toward the workers. Governments in importing countries may incline to behave more or less the same as their consumers do because politicians need to listen to their voters. For similar reasons, firms may also care more about the environmental standards than about the labor standards embedded in the intermediate goods they buy.

Sample Firms CSR Requirements on Suppliers

The sample firms also have quite stable business relations with their major suppliers. On average, 66.5% of their supplies came from their three largest suppliers in 2005. The average length of business relations with the three largest suppliers is 6.2 years, and that with the largest supplier is seven years. Compared with the intensity of CSR requirements that our sample firms receive from their customers, the percentage of our sample firms imposing CSR requirements on their suppliers is very low. Only 25% set labor standards, and 52% set environmental standards. Here again, more firms set environmental than labor standards, another piece of evidence for the hypothesis of pressures. Higher environmental standards can provide competitive advantages for a firm. A piece of evidence is that among firms that know about cleaner production, 64% set environmental standards for their suppliers, whereas among firms that do not know about cleaner production, only 42% do so.

Half of the sample firms began to set labor or environmental standards before 2002. Among the firms that do impose labor or environmental standards, about 80% conduct regular audits on their suppliers.

The main survey asks about the kind of labor standards if any that a firm imposes on its suppliers. The majority, 69.3%, of the firms that do impose labor standards adopt the national standards; 26.1% use their own standards; and the rest, 4.8%, use international standards.

It is of interest to look at how the CSR performance of firms affects the requirements they place on suppliers. Figures 9.4 and 9.5 present the relationship between pension coverage and environmental certification and firm requirements on their suppliers. Figure 9.4 shows that among firms with pension

Figure 9.4

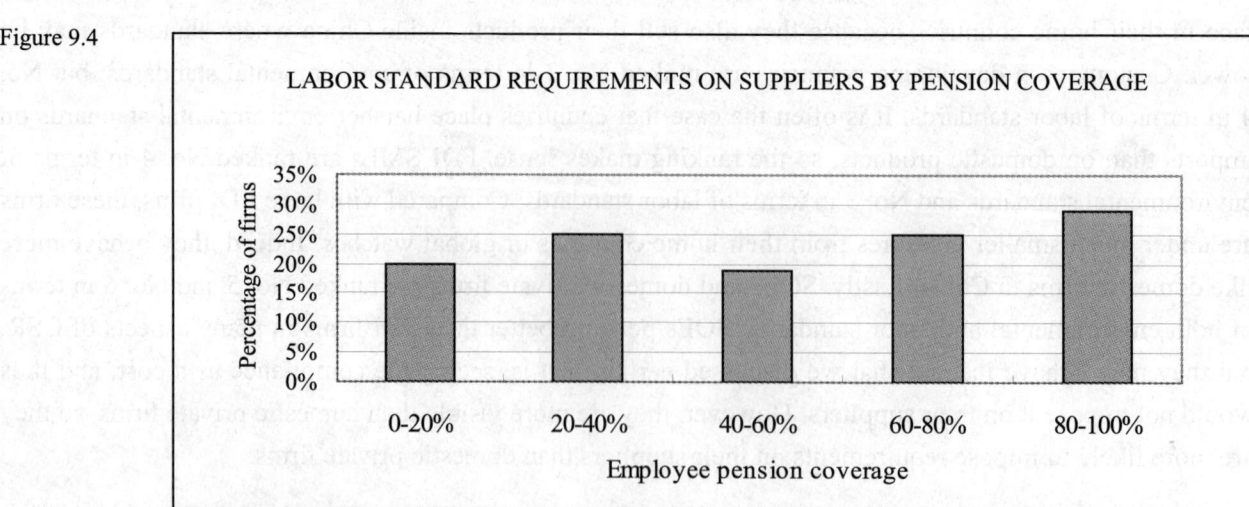

Source: Main Survey

186

Figure 9.5

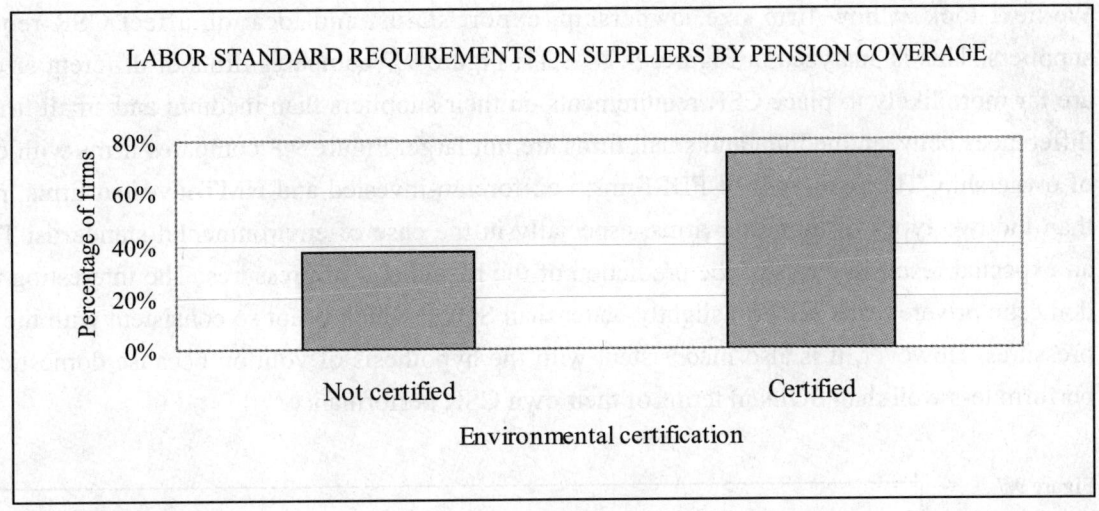

Source: Main Survey

coverage higher than 40%, those with higher rates of pension coverage tend to be more likely to impose labor standards on their suppliers, and Figure 9.5 shows that firms with environmental certification are far more likely to impose environmental standards on their suppliers than those without. Figure 9.6 makes a further comparison among three kinds of firms with different degrees of CSR awareness, know well, know some, and don't know. It is evident that firms with better CSR awareness are more likely to impose labor or environmental standards on their suppliers. These three pieces of evidence seem to suggest that the hypothesis of volition has force in explaining the CSR requirements placed on suppliers. However, better CSR performance and CSR awareness themselves may be a result of outside pressures. In fact, Figure 9.6 itself casts a doubt on the hypothesis. It shows that regardless of their CSR awareness, the percentage of firms imposing environmental standards is twice as high as that of firms imposing labor standards. If the requirements on suppliers arose as a result from the volition of firms, we should not expect to see such large discrepancies. It can only be a result of outside pressures that place more weight on the environment than upon labor protection. The following analysis also supports this claim.

Figure 9. 6

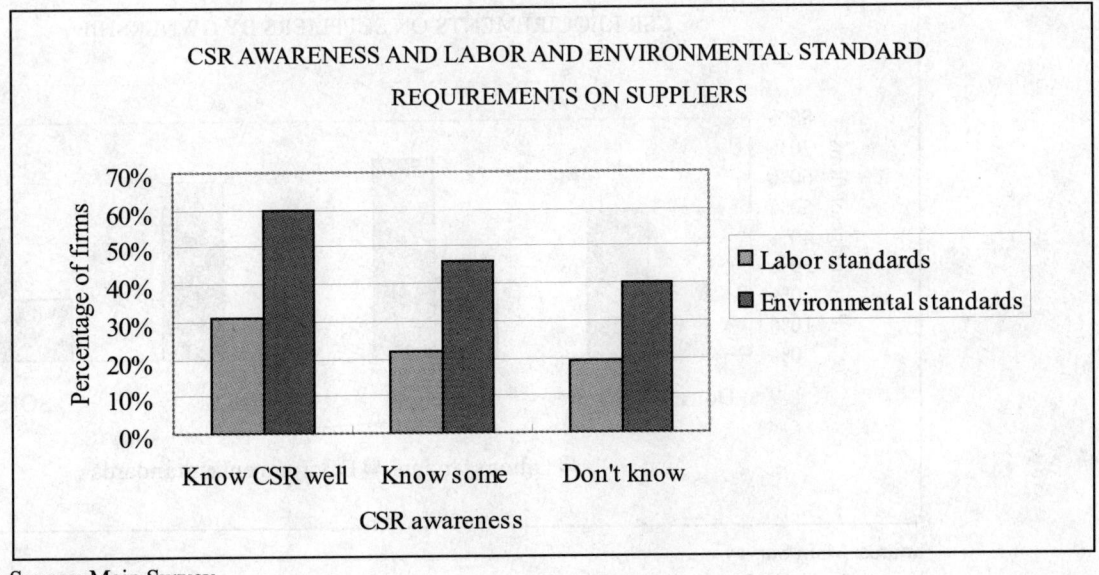

Source: Main Survey

We next look at how firm size, ownership, export status, and location affect CSR requirements on suppliers. This is analyzed in Figures 9.7 – 9.11. Figure 9.7 compares firms of different size. Large firms are far more likely to place CSR requirements on their suppliers than medium and small firms though the differences between medium and small firms are not large. Figure 9.8 compares firms with different types of ownership. The two types of FDI firms, i.e., foreign-invested and HMT-invested firms, perform better than the two types of domestic firms, especially in the case of environmental standards. This should be an expected result in terms of the prediction of the hypothesis of pressures. The interesting finding is that domestic private firms perform slightly better than SOEs, which is not so consistent with the hypothesis of pressures. However, it is also inconsistent with the hypothesis of volition because domestic private firms perform less well than SOEs in terms of their own CSR performance.

Figure 9.7

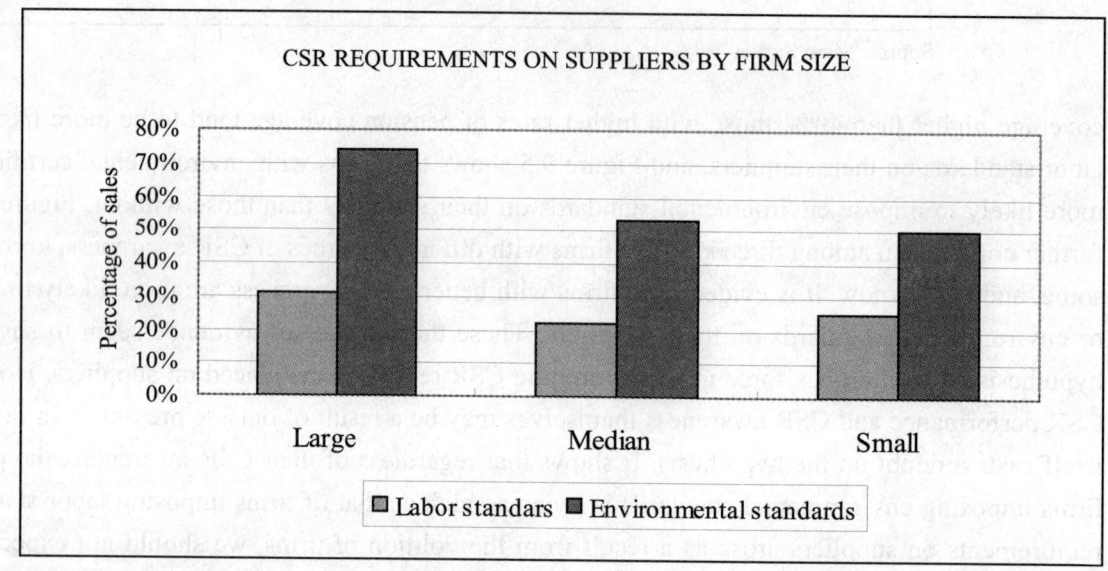

Source: Main Survey

Figure 9.8

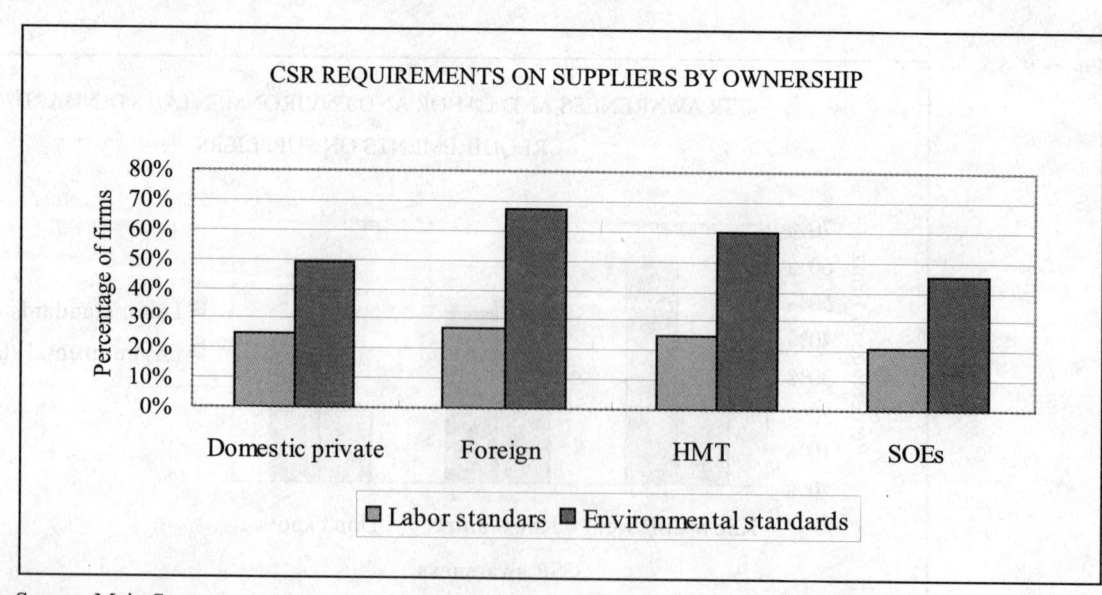

Source: Main Survey

188

Figure 9.9

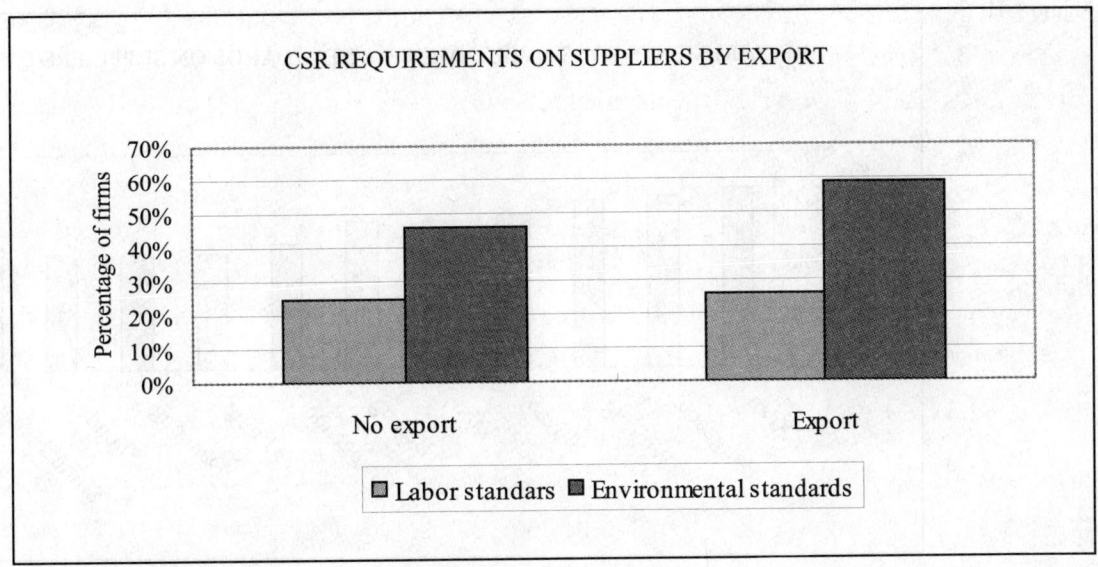

Source: Main Survey

More exporting than non-exporting firms place both labor and environmental standards on their suppliers (Figure 9.9). In the previous chapters, it was usually found that exporting does not affect CSR performance of firms. It is then interesting to find that exporting firms are more likely to require their suppliers to comply with CSR standards. However, this pattern of behavior can still be explained by the hypothesis of pressures. Notice that the difference between exporting and non-exporting firms is small for labor standards, but is large for environmental standards. One explanation based on the hypothesis of pressures is that exporting firms face more pressures from the importing countries, but they can pass the pressures on environmental standards to their suppliers whereas they cannot do that for labor standards because environmental quality can be transmitted through products, but labor standards, which are more difficult to verify, cannot.

Figures 9.10 and 9.11 rank the sample cities by labor standards and environmental standards, respectively.

Figure 9.10

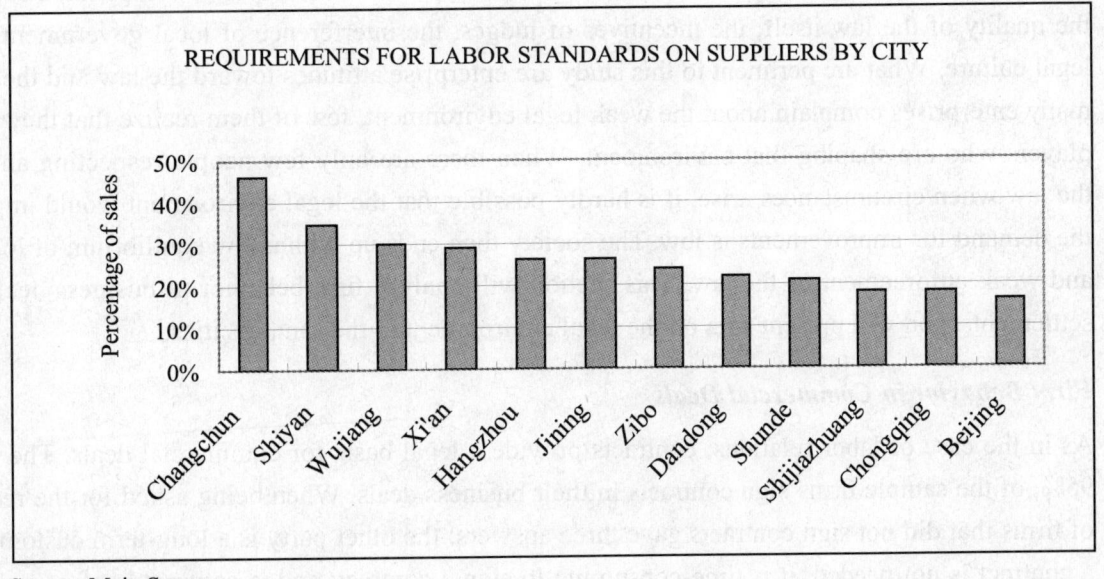

Source: Main Survey

Figure 9.11

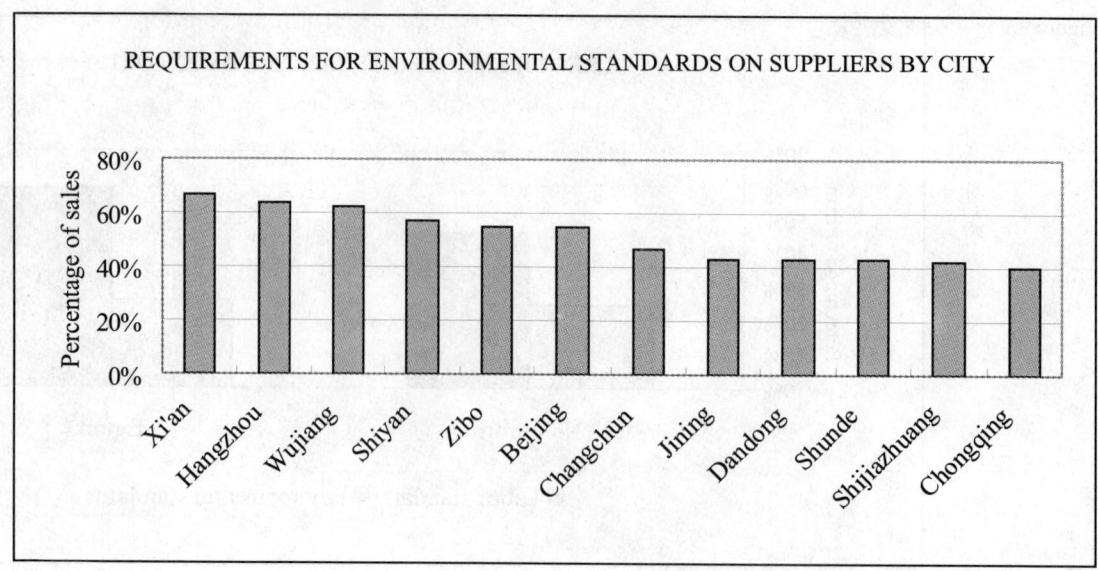

Source: Main Survey

There are no clear regional patterns in the two rankings. The forerunners are from all the three regions. Shiyan, Wujiang, and Xi'an are among the best four cities for both labor and environmental standards. Neither the hypothesis of volition, nor the hypothesis of pressures can provide a full explanation. City-specific government policies or firm characteristics are likely candidates for the explanation.

9. 3   Commercial Deals and Dispute Settlements

The commercial environment in China is far from perfect. The two most important obstacles for smooth commercial deals are triangular debts and weak enforcement of the law. Triangle debts are created by deferred payments for purchases. Once a customer defers payment for its purchases, the chain reaction starts: the supplier begins to defer its payments to its own suppliers, partly because of the shortfall in its cash flow, partly because of its intention to pass the cost to the next firm; and then these suppliers begin to do the same to their up-stream firms. Weak enforcement of the law has more complicated causes including the quality of the law itself, the incentives of judges, the interference of local governments, and a weak legal culture. What are pertinent to this study are enterprise attitudes toward the law and the courts. While many enterprises complain about the weak legal environment, few of them realize that they are one of the players who are shaping that environment. When there are only few people respecting and resorting to the law when circumstances arise, it is hardly possible that the legal environment would improve because the demand for improvements is low. The society then ends up with a low equilibrium of low demand for and weak enforcement of the law. This section will analyze firm behavior in business deals and dispute settlements, and will present data on the legal environment in the sample cities.

Firm Behavior in Commercial Deals

As in the case of labor relations, contracts provide a legal basis for commercial deals. The vast majority, 95%, of the sample firms sign contracts in their business deals. When being asked for the reasons, the 5% of firms that did not sign contracts gave three answers: the other party is a long-term customer/supplier so a contract is not needed; it is time-consuming to sign a contract; and, a contract is of no use because it is

190

not going to be enforced once it is breached. Seventy-six percent of them mentioned the first reason, seven percent the second reason, and twenty-six percent the third reason. The last figure is encouraging because it says that there are only 1.3% of the sample firms that do not have any confidence in the legal system, assuming that the firms signing a contract see it as providing some legally binding constraints. Another encouraging sign is that among the firms signing a contract, 71% use a standard contract provided by the government or a third party. Besides saving costs for all the firms, a standard contract is particularly useful for small firms because they do not have enough knowledge to deal with the legal details in business deals. As a result, the number of cases of is reduced, which in turn contributes to a better legal environment.

About 70% of the sample firms get a credit period for their payments to suppliers, and 65% of them give a credit period to their customers. The length of the credit period is about three months in both cases. Large firms have considerable advantages over SMEs. While 67% of small firms and 78% of medium firms get a credit period from their suppliers, 80% large firms can do so. On the other hand, while only 59% of large firms give a credit period to their customers, 73% of medium firms and 65% of small firms have to do so. Large firms have more leverage than SMEs. For example, they have larger manufacturing capacities than smaller suppliers. They also have better innovation capacities so their products obtain certain monopoly power in the market.

Dispute Settlements

An important factor affecting trust in the legal system is the quality of the courts and the enforcement of court verdicts, which are the weakest parts in China's system. In contemporary China, the rate of rulings of a lower level court rejected by a higher level court can be a good indicator of court quality. Lower level courts need to submit their rulings to a higher level court for review. If the higher level court believes that there are defects in a ruling, it can reject the ruling and ask the lower level court to re-try the case. For enforcement, the best indicator is the percentage of court verdicts that are actually carried out. There are loud complaints from the business community that the verdict cannot be enforced when one wins a case. Weak capacity of the courts, lack of a full-coverage credit reporting system, lack of independence of the court, and a weak legal culture have all been mentioned as the causes. Figures 9.12 and 9.13 then rank the sample cities by their average rejection rates and enforcement rates for 2001-2005, respectively. There were only six cities that provided data for the rejection rate, though. Shijiazhuang had a very high rejection rate. In the period of 2001-2005, more than one fourth of its court rulings were rejected by higher level courts. Zibo and Shiyan also had double-digit rejection rates. There were eight cities that provided data for the enforcement rate. Wujiang, Zibo, and Shunde were the three best performers with their enforcement rates all passing 90%. Dandong was the worst having a rate of only 57%.

Overall, the sample firms have relatively good faith in the courts because they are the first choice for dispute settlement. Figure 9.14 ranks five choices for settling disputes by the percentage of firms making a particular choice in their last commercial dispute. Seventy-two percent of firms chose the courts to settle their last commercial disputes. The second choice was private settlement through the mediations of friends and social leaders, but only 30% of the firms used this choice. Therefore, the courts are overwhelmingly the most popular choice for enterprises to settle their commercial disputes. It is noteworthy, however, there were also 16% of the sample firms that chose not to take any action in their last dispute. While other causes were possible, the distrust of the court could be an important one.

Figure 9.12

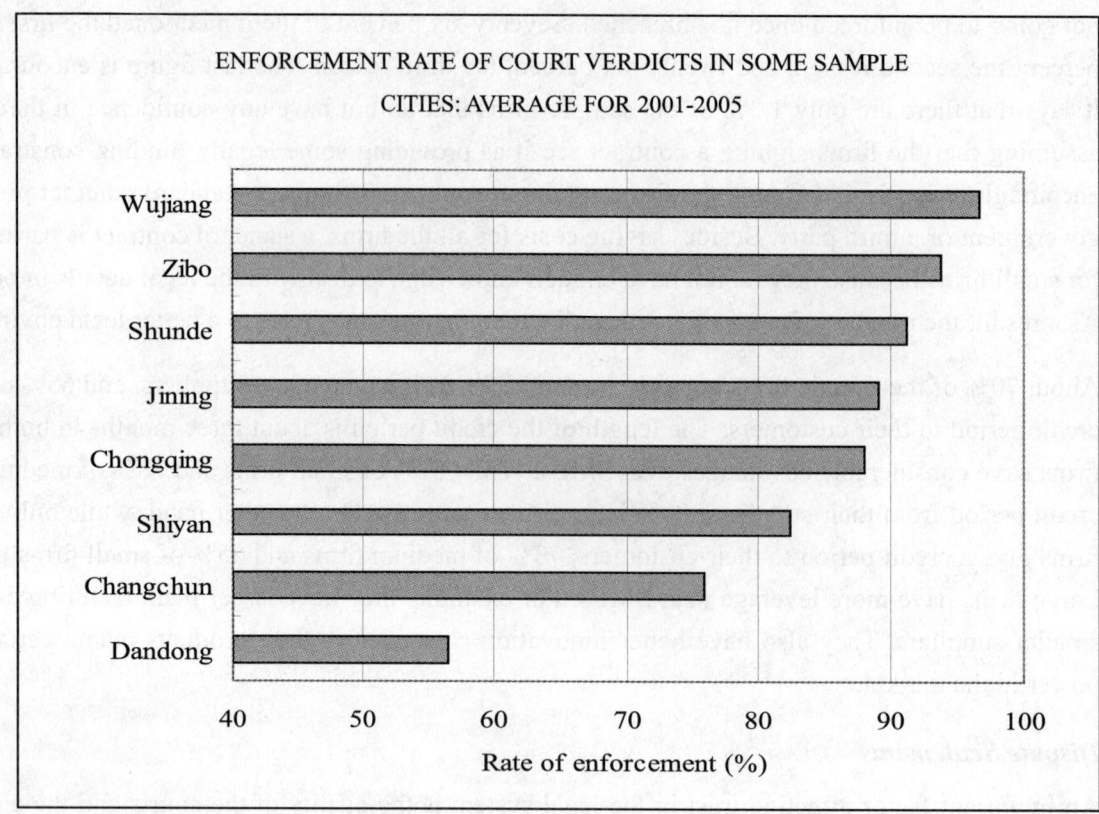

ENFORCEMENT RATE OF COURT VERDICTS IN SOME SAMPLE
CITIES: AVERAGE FOR 2001-2005

Note: Cities not shown did not provide information.
Source: City survey.

Figure 9.13

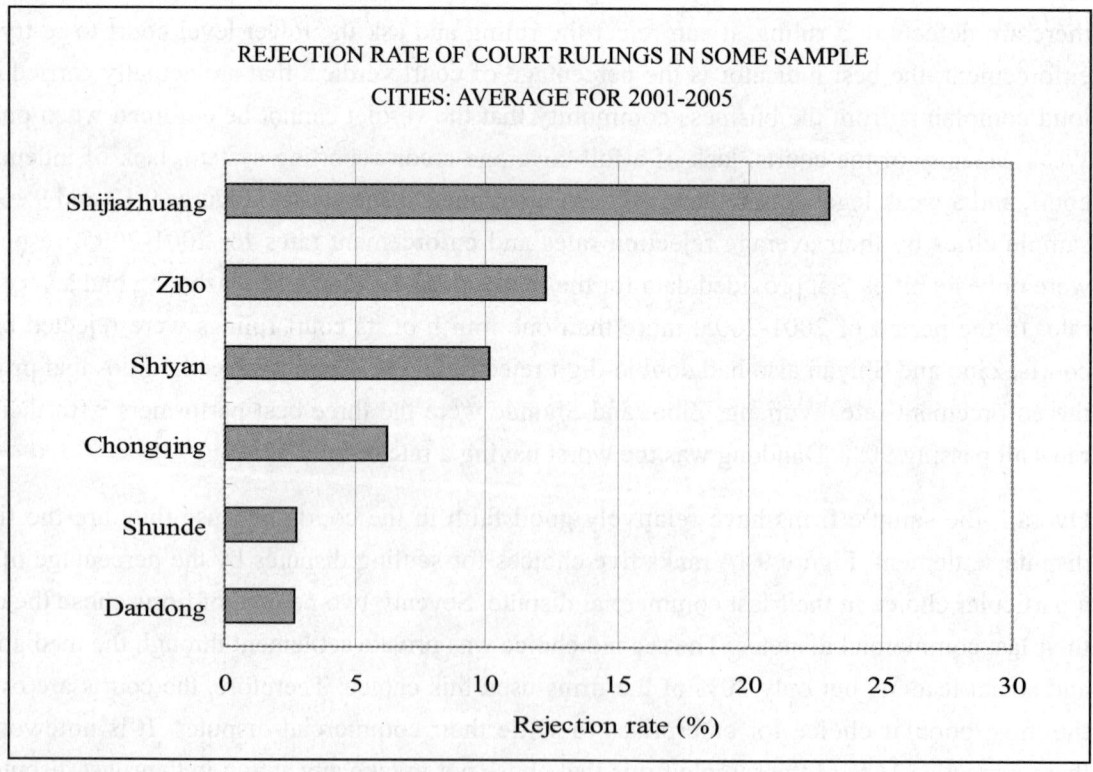

REJECTION RATE OF COURT RULINGS IN SOME SAMPLE
CITIES: AVERAGE FOR 2001-2005

Note: Cities not shown did not provide information.
Source: City survey.

Figure 9.14

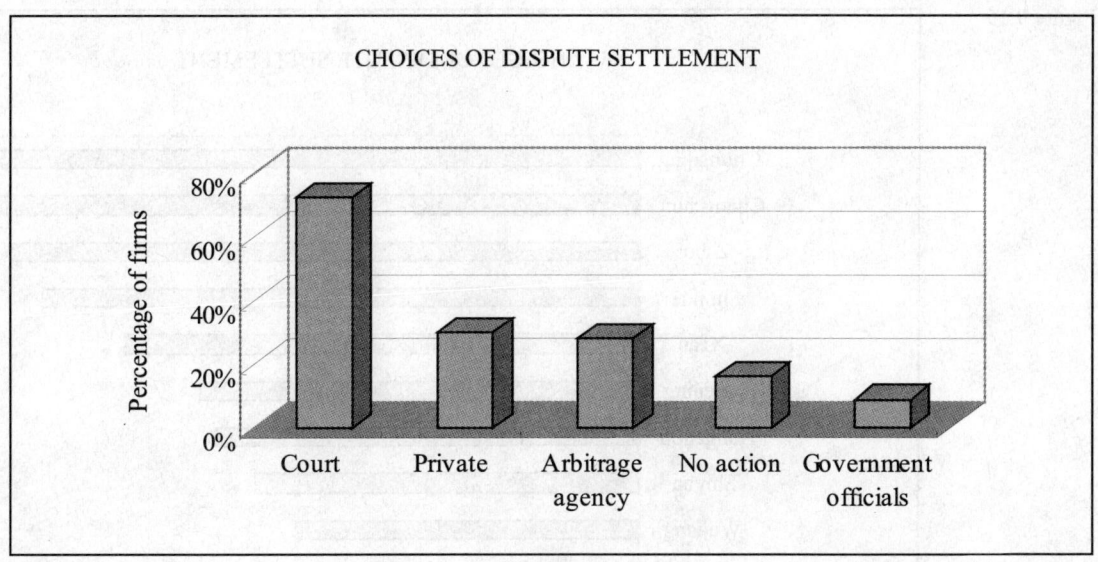

Source: City survey.

The finding that the court is the most preferred means for dispute settlement is somewhat surprising because it is often believed that the court system is very weak in China. While our finding could be interpreted as a piece of evidence for the improvement of the Chinese court system, other explanations are possible. One of them is that out-of-court mechanisms are not well developed in China. It seems that business people are moving away from traditional informal settlement mechanisms, possible because their business dealings have gone beyond family and friend circles. However, formal out-of-court mechanisms such as arbitragy have not been properly developed, or have not been recognized by the business community. The court is an expensive device for dispute settlements; more out-of-court mechanisms should be used.

As for the evaluation of the quality of the court, the sample firms' answers are encouraging. Ninety-six percent of those choosing a court settlement believe that the court verdict is just, and ninety percent of them believe that the judge is trustworthy. However, 92% of the firms that chose the court won their cases, so the high approval rates may be biased upward. It is also noteworthy that the approval rate for court efficiency is only 69%, and the approval rate for efficiency in verdict enforcement is 71%.

Are there any relationships between the choice of using the courts and the general quality of the legal system in specific cities? Our data show that there are some relationships, especially for cities that have the weakest legal quality. Figure 9.15 ranks the sample cities by the share of firms choosing the courts in their last commercial dispute. Figure 9.13 shows that Shijiazhuang, Zibo, and Shiyan had double-digit rejection rates, and Figure 9.12 shows that Shiyan, Changchun, and Dandong had low enforcement rates. Except for Changchun and Zibo, the other three cities have low shares of firms choosing the courts. However, it is worth noting that Wujiang and Jining had relatively high average enforcement rates in 2001-2005, but their share of firms choosing the courts were low. In particular, only 28% of the firms in Jining chose the courts. Since Figures 9.12 and 9.13 do not have data for all the cities, a complete assessment of the ranking in Figure 9.15 is impossible. But the cases of Wujiang and Jining suggest that there are reasons other than the quality of the court and the enforcement of court verdicts that determine firms' use of the court.

Figure 9.15

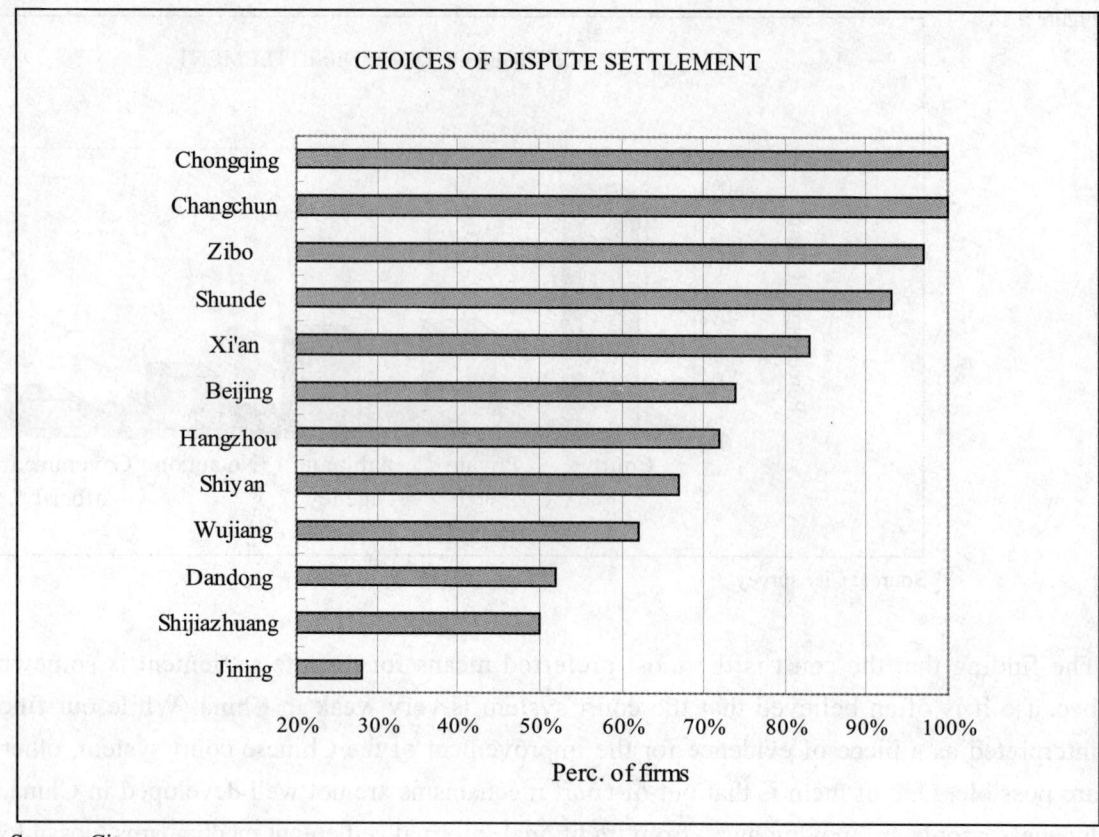

CHOICES OF DISPUTE SETTLEMENT

Perc. of firms

Source: City survey.

9. 4   Summary

This chapter has studied the link between the supply chain and CSR performance and the interactions of the sample firms and the legal system in each sample city. For the first task, the analysis is centered on the test of two competing hypotheses, i.e., the hypothesis of volition and the hypothesis of pressures. The first hypothesis states that firms pass their CSR requirements onto their suppliers out of their own wishes, i.e., their preferences for better labor and environmental standards. The second hypothesis states that firms pass their CSR requirements on only because they face outside pressures from other firms, consumers, or government regulations. The analysis has found strong evidence to support the hypothesis of pressures and tends to reject the hypothesis of volition.

It has been found that our sample firms invariably place more emphasis on environmental standards than on labor standards when they set requirements for their suppliers. This is so because higher environmental standards can be a source of competitiveness in the product market as cleaner production is becoming an industrial standard in both developed and developing countries. The market is good at what it aims at promoting, that is, it induces firms to achieve higher rates of profits. However, the low percentage of firms requiring labor standards for their suppliers is worrisome and needs to be corrected. Our finding that outside pressures are the most significant forces to induce the requirement shows that besides the market, government regulations and civil society organizations should also play stronger roles in promoting labor protection.

Overall, our sample firms place high confidence in the legal system reflecting the continuous improvements made in recent years. However, the low percentages of firms choosing the court as the venue for dispute settlement in cities like Wujiang, Dandong, Shijiazhuang, and Jining are north further studies. The two cases of Wujiang and Jining are particularly puzzling because city-wide statistics show that the legal environment in these two cities is of reasonable quality. If the city-wide statistics are accurate and our sample firms are representative of the firms in the two cities, a conclusion is that there is either a lack of a legal culture or better developed out-of-court mechanisms in these two cities. At any rate, the finding of this chapter is by no means conclusive due to the limited information collected in our surveys. More studies are needed in the future to get a fuller picture of the dynamics of the interactions between firm behavior and the development of the legal system.

Chapter 10
CSR and Firm Performance

The previous chapters have presented data on CSR performance and studied its determinants. This chapter tries to link CSR with firm performance by studying the contribution of CSR to firm profitability and labor productivity. CSR is too often seen as a burden that increases the operating costs of firms. Therefore, it is important to develop a business case for CSR in order to persuade firms to adopt it. Chapter 1 cites from the UNIDO 2002 report six areas where a business case for CSR can be established. In this report, however, we concentrate on studying three sets of factors that contribute to the business case for CSR. We do this not only because of the limitation of data availability, but also because of the significance of these three sets of factors.

The first set of factors is related to human capital retention. Better treatment of employees attracts and retains better workers. This can be true for any firm in a labor market where workers are in ample supply and thus their benefits are often neglected, but is especially true for firms that rely most on the quality of human capital in their labor force.

The second set of factors is related to the Porter hypothesis. This hypothesis proposes that higher environmental standards imposed by the government will stimulate innovations that will not only cover the costs of meeting the standards, but also bring new profits to firms. In a developing country context, meeting higher environmental standards, and cleaner production in particular, may have the advantage of increasing the competitiveness of firms in the international market. To the extent that environmental standards are much higher and consumers are much more environmentally conscious in developed countries than in developing countries, meeting higher environmental standards makes it easier for firms in developing countries to sell their products in developed countries. The results of the previous chapter show that our sample firms are more likely to receive labor and environmental requirements from international customers and FDI firms. So meeting higher labor and environmental standards has the potential to enlarge the market shares of firms.

The third set of factors has to do with public relations and firm reputation. Better CSR performance has the potential to improve the public relations of a firm and makes it easier for it to attract quality business partners, bank loans, and government support. Better CSR performance can help a firm to get access to external formal finance because it increases the transparency of firm activities and enhances its credibility. To an outsider, a firm that has a clearly defined board structure and employee remuneration system is more transparent than a firm that does not have those things, and a firm that commits to social responsibility is more trustworthy in terms of loan repayments than a firm that only looks after its own narrowly defined interests. This is verified by a recent study that finds that outside investors do care about CSR performance when they make their investment decisions (Beloe, Harrison, Greenfield, 2006). On another front, Chinese governments at various levels provide financial and policy support for selected firms as a tool to pursue particular goals, noticeably technological advancements and ecological conservation. For the same reason that better CSR performance attracts external finance, it is easier for a better CSR performing firm to obtain government support.

Existing studies, however, have not provided strong evidence to show that CSR brings significant and systematic tangible benefits to firms although the IFC Developing Value report identifies 240 real-life cases in over 60 countries that support the business case for development with sustainability (Developing Value, 2005). The FIAS-BSR report on a group of Chinese ICT suppliers in Shenzhen finds that "suppliers overwhelmingly believe that there is not a clear, demonstrable business case for driving social and environmental improvements and that the costs of those improvements tend to outweigh the benefits" although certain aspects of benefits do exist (FIAS and BSR, 2007; pp. 24). A study by the Canadian Business for Social Responsibility (CBSR) finds that it is not common for small and medium enterprises to take any measures to improve their CSR practices and the tangible and intangible benefits are tenuous when some firms do (CBSR, 2003). However, the existing studies heavily rely on case studies to draw conclusions. One of the advantages of this study is that it is based on survey data with a relatively large sample and sophisticated statistical methods can be applied to draw more reliable conclusions.

The previous chapters have shown and discussed many aspects of CSR. It is impossible for this chapter to link all of them to firm performance and access to finance. Instead, we will concentrate on several key elements of CSR performance. Specifically, we will only study two aspects of labor standards, quality control, and environmental standards, respectively, and their relationship to productivity and profitability. The two aspects for labor standards are whether a firm provides written contracts to its employees and whether it allows collective wage bargaining. Chapter 4 found that written contracts are the most significant factor determining whether a firm provides various types of benefits to its employees. On the other hand, allowing collective wage bargaining is an indication of the strength of the labor union in a firm. The two aspects for quality control are whether a firm obtains ISO9001 or other quality certifications and whether it maintains higher quality standards than the national standards. The first aspect is essential for quality control and the second aspect shows the achievements of quality control in a firm. Finally, the two aspects for environmental standards are firm achievements in meeting national standards for environmental protection and whether it makes use of environmental or biological labeling. The first aspect shows a firm's overall quality in environmental protection and the second aspect shows its commitment to clean production and informing the public of the possible environmental or biological consequences of using its products.

The above CSR performance indicators may be simultaneously determined with firm financial performance and other factors, or in the worst case, the causality is reversed, that is, CSR performance is determined by financial performance. To deal with this issue, customer-imposed requirements for labor and environmental standards will be used as the "instruments" for firms' own CSR performance. Chapter 9 has shown that CSR requirements are passed through the supply chain not because of firm volition, but because of external pressures from governments and the general public. So they are likely to be exogenous to firms receiving them.

10. 1   CSR Records and Firm Performance

We choose to study the three indicators of firm performance introduced in Chapter 2, that is, pre-tax profit/sales (profit rate), pre-tax profit/fixed capital (return on capital), and sales/worker (labor productivity). The first is a good indicator for the overall efficiency of firms; the second is a measure of efficiency in capital utilization; and the third is a measure of efficiency in the use of labor. Since we do not know the date on which our sample firms adopted each CSR measure, we will concentrate on analyzing the financial performance of 2005. Whenever needed and possible, however, we will supplement our analysis by studying the averages or trends in the period of 2000-2005.

We first study how the two labor standards affect the above three financial indicators. For labor contracts, the comparison is made between firms that offer contracts to all their employees and those that do not offer them to any or only some employees. For collective wage bargaining, the comparison is made between firms that allow for it and those that do not. Tables 10.1 and 10.2 present two sets of results. The results for labor contracts are mixed. Firms offering contracts have much higher labor productivity than firms that do not offer them, but their average rate of return to capital is barely higher and their average profit rate is actually lower. The results for collective bargaining are much more favorable, though. Firms that allow collective bargaining perform significantly better than firms that do not on all the three indicators of financial performance.

Table 10.1

LABOR CONTRACTS AND FIRM PERFORMANCE

	# of cases	Profit rate (%)	Return on capital (%)	Labor productivity (1,000 yuan)
With contracts	960	1.7	25.7	48.3
Without contracts	308	2.8	25.1	39.6

Source: Main survey.

Table 10.2

COLLECTIVE WAGE BARGAINING AND FIRM PERFORMANCE

	# of cases	Profit rate (%)	Return on capital (%)	Labor productivity (1,000 yuan)
Allowed	626	3.5	28.8	49.6
Not allowed	548	0.3	23.1	44.0

Source: Main survey.

The above results generally favor the proposition that better firm performance is correlated with better labor protection although the negative correlation between labor contracts and profit rate needs further exploration. One possible explanation is that profits are volatile so one year data are not reliable. To check on this possibility, we perform the comparison again with the average financial performance over the period 2001-2005. The results are presented in Table 10.3. Now, although the gap in labor productivity is narrowed down, the gap in rate of return on capital increases, and the profit rate becomes the same for both groups of firms. So it is possible that the lower profitability of firms with contracts in Table 10.1 is only caused by data volatility.

Table 10.3

LABOR CONTRACTS AND AVERAGE FIRM PERFORMANCE IN 2000-2005

	# of cases	Profit rate (%)	Return on capital (%)	Labor productivity (1,000 yuan)
With contracts	960	2.8	28.3	39.6
Without contracts	308	2.8	26.0	33.3

Source: Main survey.

The situation is not so favorable when we come to the results for product quality. Tables 10.4 and 10.5 show that firms without any quality certification and firms maintaining lower quality standards invariably perform better than their respective counterparts except in the case of return on capital where firms maintaining higher quality standards perform better. Averaging over the period of 2001-2005 does not help although some of the gaps are narrowed down (e.g., the profit rates for certified and non-certified firms become 2.7% and 2.9%, respectively).

Table 10.4

QUALITY CERTIFICATION AND FIRM PERFORMANCE

	# of cases	Profit rate (%)	Return on capital (%)	Labor productivity (1,000 yuan)
Certified	810	1.4	22.0	45.0
Not certified	458	3.0	32.0	48.4

Source: Main survey.

Table 10.5

PRODUCT QUALITY AND FIRM PERFORMANCE

	# of cases	Profit rate (%)	Return on capital (%)	Labor productivity (1,000 yuan)
Higher than national standards	718	0.9	27.1	41.3
Same as or lower than national standards	550	3.5	23.3	52.9

Source: Main survey.

The results for environmental protection are much better. The survey asks the sample firms whether they have met the environmental protection standards for gas emissions, waste water, solid wastes, noise, and biodiversity, if they are relevant to their production. We divide the firms into two groups based on their answers to this question: one that meets all the applicable standards, and one that do not fulfill at least one of the applicable standards. Table 10.6 then compares the financial performance of these two groups of firms. Except for the profit rate, the first group performs better than the second group and the gaps are reasonably large. The second group only performs slightly better than the first group in terms of the profit rate.

Table 10.6

ENVIRONMENTAL PROTECTION AND FIRM PERFORMANCE

	# of cases	Profit rate (%)	Return on capital (%)	Labor productivity (1,000 yuan)
All environmental standards fulfilled	1078	2.0	26.4	47.1
One or more environmental standards not fulfilled	190	2.2	20.3	41.1

Source: Main survey.

Table 10.7 then shows how environmental/biological labeling affects financial performance. In this case, firms with environmental/biological labeling perform better than those without in profitability and labor productivity and the gaps are very significant. However, they have a lower rate of return on capital than the other group. This pattern of performance gaps does not change when we look at the averages for the period of 2000-2005.

Table 10.7

ENVIRONMENTAL/BIOLOGICAL LABELING AND FIRM PERFORMANCE

	# of cases	Profit rate (%)	Return on capital (%)	Labor productivity (1,000 yuan)
With labels	146	3.4	20.3	55.8
Without labels	1018	1.7	26.6	45.2

Source: Main survey.

We have data for the year when a firm started environmental/biological labeling, so we can conduct a difference-in-difference (DID) analysis for the effects of the labels. The DID estimator has the advantage of eliminating the time trend that may bias the estimator based on simple averages. The treatment group consists of the firms that had adopted the labels by 2005, and the control group consists of the firms that had not adopted the labels by 2005. Since firms began the labeling in different years, the calculation is a bit complicated. For the treatment group, we first obtain the difference between a year after the labeling and the year immediately before labeling. Since we have data for 2000-2005, we can calculate the difference for five years (i.e., first year after labeling, second year after labeling... and fifth year after labeling). The average of these differences is then the difference for the treatment group. For the control group, we first get the differences between any year in 2001-2005 and its one-year lag, two-year lag... and five-year lag, and then average them out to get the difference for this group. Finally, the difference between the difference for the treatment group and the difference for the control group becomes the DID estimator for the effect of labeling. Table 10.8 reports the two sets of first-step differences for both groups of firms and the DID estimator for each indicator of performance. The results invariably favor the firms with labeling. The first-step differences of the control group are negative for profitability and the rate of return on capital but those of the treatment group are positive. As a result, the DID estimators for these two cases are very large, being 6.5% and 11.6%, respectively. The DID estimator for labor productivity is relatively small, being only 1,700 yuan. These results are quite different from those reported in Table 10.7. Since the DID estimator eliminates the time trend that the simple averages in Table 10.7 may contain, more confidence should be placed on the results reported in Table 10.8.

Table 10. 8

DID ESTIMATION FOR THE EFFECTS OF ENVIRONMENTAL/BIOLOGICAL LABELING

	# of cases	Profit rate (%)	Return on capital (%)	Labor productivity (1,000 yuan)
First-stage difference				
Treatment group	146	4.2	6.5	15.6
Control group	1018	-2.3	-5.1	13.9
DID estimator		6.5	11.6	1.7

Source: Main survey.

10. 2 Supply Chain Requirements and Firm Performance

One potential drawback of the analysis in Section 10.1 is that CSR and financial performance may be simultaneously determined by other factors, or even worse, CSR records may be determined by financial performance. That is, there may be a problem of endogeneity. A remedy for this potential drawback is to find features of CSR performance that are exogenous to firm behavior and study how they are related to firm performance. The CSR requirements exerted through the supply chain can be good candidates. As we found in Chapter 9, these requirements are transmitted through the supply chain by external pressures coming from government regulation and consumer demand rather than by firm volition. As long as it faces these external pressures, a firm will be likely to require CSR standards of all of its suppliers, regardless of their performance records. Therefore, CSR requirements through the supply chain are exogenous to a supplier.[1]

Studying these requirements is interesting on two fronts. On the first front, we want to use them as "instruments" for the CSR performance of our sample firms. This is parallel to the instrumental variable method in econometrics. On the second front, the impact of these requirements on firm performance are interesting in their own right because they tell us whether they are burdens or stimuli for better firm performance. Here we analyze two of them: the timing for a sample firm to receive demands for labor standards and the timing for it to receive demands for environmental standards, both from its customers. We can perform the DID analysis again. But before we do that, we want to make sure that these two variables of timing are good representations of a firm's CSR records so that using them as "instruments" makes sense.

We check the correlations between these two "instruments" and the sample firms' four indicators for labor and environmental standards that we studied in the last section. Table 10.9 compares the percentage of firms fulfilling a particular item of labor or environmental standards when it faces supply-chain requirements and that for when it does not. It is clear that firms facing either supply-chain requirement invariably have better CSR records than firms that do not. The gaps are reasonably large. In addition, it is worth noting that both supply-chain requirements have correlated effects: the requirement on labor standards raises firms' performance in environmental standards to the same extent as it does on firms' performance in labor standards; vice versa. Therefore, the two supply-chain requirements are indeed good "instruments" for the sample firms' own CSR performance records.

---

[1] There is a possibility that a customer finds out its suppliers based on criteria that affect their performance. For example, a customer would like to buy from a supplier that has a new product and then put CSR requirements on it. This new product will of course bring a higher profit rate for the supplier. So in this sense, CSR requirements become endogenous, that is, suppliers subject to these requirements have better performance potentials from the very beginning. However, this argument has a flaw. Every customer is trying to find the best suppliers and every surviving supplier has customers, which means that every firm in our sample has some sort of performance potential. However, not all of our sample firms receive CSR requirements from their customers. Therefore, performance potentials cannot be a cause for CSR requirements.

Table 10.9

SUPPLY-CHAIN REQUIREMENTS AND SAMPLE FIRM CSR PERFORMANCE

CSR performance / Supply-chain Requirements	Labor contracts	Collective bargaining	Environmental standards	Environmental/ Biological labeling
Labor standards				
No	74.7%	52.6%	82.7%	11.7%
Yes	78.1%	54.9%	90.2%	14.4%
Environmental standards				
No	73.7%	52.6%	80.5%	11.1%
Yes	78.1%	54.0%	90.2%	14.1%

Source: Main survey.

We then next study how these two requirements affect firm profitability rates, return on capital, and labor productivity.[2] Table 10.10 compares the average performance of four groups of firms: those not subject to any supply-chain requirements, those subject to requirements for labor standards, those subject to requirements for environmental standards, and those subject to both requirements. Except for the rate of return on capital, firms subject to one or two supply-chain requirements perform better than firms not subject to any requirements. The differences between one requirement and two requirements are small except in the case of return on capital. Therefore, we will only study the effect of both requirements when we next conduct the DID analysis.

Table 10.10

SUPPLY-CHAIN REQUIREMENTS AND FIRM PERFORMANCE

	# of cases	Profit rate (%)	Return on capital (%)	Labor productivity (1,000 yuan)
No requirements	668	1.1	29.5	45.6
Labor standards	389	3.4	25.1	47.2
Environmental standards	593	2.9	21.1	47.3
Both standards	381	3.3	25.0	47.8

Source: Main survey.

---

[2] In econometric jargon, this study is equivalent to a reduced-form regression.

The treatment group then is defined as those firms receiving requirements for both labor and environmental standards, and the control group is defined as firms that do not receive any requirements. The results are presented in Table 10.11 using the same format as in Table 10.8. The DID estimator shows that the supply-chain requirements have a positive effect on all the three financial indicators. The effect on the profit rate is 3%, which is very large because the sample average over the period 2000-2005 was only 2.5%. The effect on the rate of return on capital is 6.2%, which is one fourth of the sample average over the period of 2000-2005. The effect on labor productivity, however, is small, being only 800 yuan.

Table 10.11

DID ESTIMATION FOR THE EFFECTS OF SUPPLY-CHAIN REQUIREMENTS

	# of cases	Profit rate (%)	Return on capital (%)	Labor productivity (1,000 yuan)
First-stage difference				
Treatment group	381	0.1	-0.6	14.5
Control group	668	-2.9	-6.8	13.7
DID estimator		3.0	6.2	0.8

Source: Main survey.

In summary, we have found that requirements of labor and environmental standards through the supply chain help to improve firms' financial performance, especially their profitability. This result has two implications. First, it shows that external CSR pressures are not burdens, but stimuli for better firm performance. Second, to the extent that external CSR pressures are good "instruments" for firms' CSR performance, this result confirms the results found in the last section that better CSR performance by firms improves their financial performance.

10. 3   Explaining CSR s Positive Impacts

At the outset of this chapter, we mentioned four major reasons why better CSR performance works to increase the financial performance of firms, i.e., through the retention of more talented employees, by inducing innovations, enlarging market shares, and increasing the probability of getting external finance. This section studies which reasons are responsible for the positive impacts that better CSR records have on firms' financial performance.

Labor Standards and Human Capital

It is usually very hard to measure employee quality because it is often determined by unobserved personal characteristics. To study how labor standards affect a firm's ability to retain better employees, an alternative is to look at employee turnover rates. A low turnover rate has the advantages of allowing firms to invest in employee training and for employees to accumulate specific knowledge and develop loyalty to their firm. It is natural to expect that better treatment of employees induces them to stay longer in a firm and thus result in a lower turnover rate.

The main survey provides information for the average years that blue-collar and white-collar workers work in a firm, respectively. Job tenure in SOEs is exceptionally long being around 16 and 17 years for blue-collar and white-collar workers, respectively. This has to do with two things, one being SOEs' long history and the other their high job security. Therefore, we exclude SOEs from our analysis.

We use pension coverage to approximate conformity with labor standards. Figure 10.1 compares firms with different rates of pension coverage in terms of the average job tenure of their blue-collar and white collar workers, respectively. While the increase of job tenure is not clear for firms with rates of coverage less than 80%, firms with more than 80% of pension coverage have significantly longer job tenure than firms with smaller rates of coverage for both blue-collar and white-collar workers. The insignificant trends for smaller rates of coverage are likely to be a result of our choice of using the average job tenure as the studied indicator. It is possible that firms with lower rates of coverage give pensions to employees on a more selective basis than firms with higher rates of coverage, and those with pensions tend to stay with one firm for a long time. It is only when the coverage gets close to 100% that firms get a decisive advantage over firms with lower rates.

Of course, the above analysis does not establish a clear causality running from higher rates of pension coverage to longer job tenure. It is possible that a firm provides pension to workers only because they intend to stay longer with it. What really happens in the field is likely to be a reinforcing process between firms offering better treatments and employees wanting to stay longer. What is important here is that it is an indispensable part of this process that better treatment leads to better volition because otherwise it does not make sense for firms to offer better treatments.

The Porter Hypothesis

The central argument of the Porter hypothesis is that higher environmental standards lead to more innovation. We use qualification for ISO 14000 as the indicator of fulfillment of environmental standards

Figure 10. 1

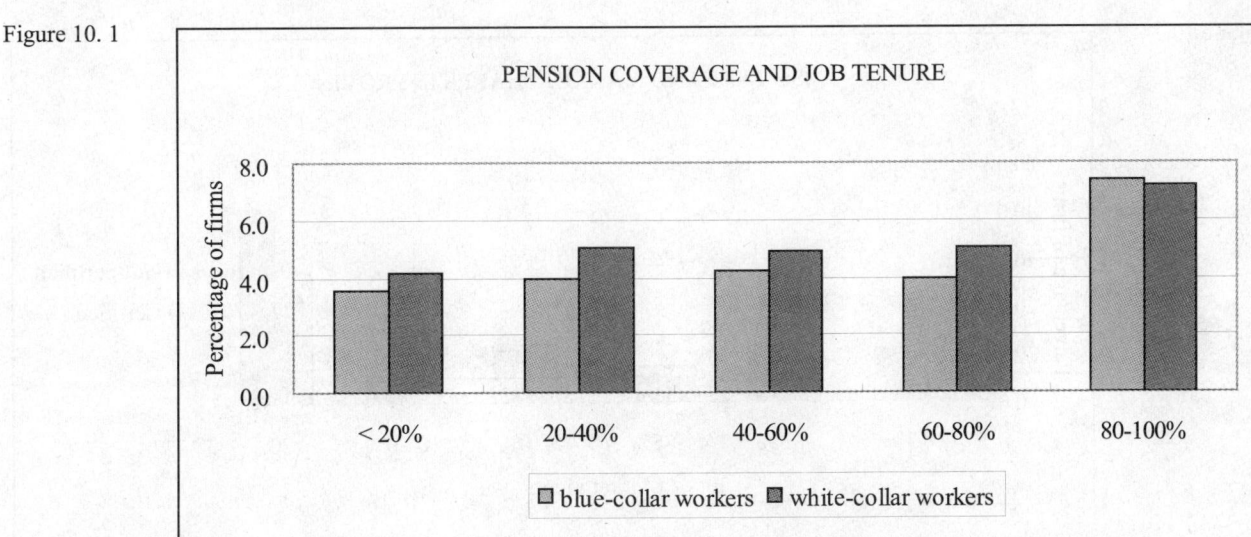

Source: City survey.

by firms. The main survey also provides information on fixed investment, number of new products, and number of patents between 2001 and 2005. However, there are many missing entries for the last two items, so we will only study fixed investment.

The main survey provides information for the year of a firm getting the ISO 14000 certificate so we can apply the DID method again to get results with clear causality. The treatment group contains firms that had obtained the certification by 2005, and the control group contains firms that had not done so by the same year. We study both the total investment and investment rate, i.e., total investment divided by the stock of fixed capital. For the treatment group, we calculate the difference between the means of years before and after obtaining the certification. For the control group, we first obtain the difference between the means before and after each year between 2002 and 2004 and then calculate their means, which is subtracted from the difference we obtain for the treatment group to get the DID estimator. However, the DID estimators for both indicators show that obtaining the ISO 14000 does not increase investment. In the case of total investment, the first difference obtained for the treatment group is 50.42 million yuan, but the first difference of the control group is 90.42 million yuan, so the DID estimator for obtaining the certification is -40.0 million yuan. In the case of the investment rate, the first difference of the treatment group is -0.98%, but the first difference of the control group is 14.84%, so the DID estimator for obtaining certification is -15.82%. That is, meeting environmental standards actually reduces investment by firms. So the Porter hypothesis has to be revised. As we discussed at the beginning of this chapter, the Porter hypothesis can also hold if meeting higher environmental standards helps a firm to obtain a larger market share. Therefore, our next task is to study whether qualification for ISO 14000 leads to a larger market share.

The main survey only provides information for firms' market shares in 2006, so we cannot perform the DID estimation, but instead have to rely on just comparing cross-sectional means. Figures 10.2 and 10.3 compare the distribution of firms with ISO 14000 and the distribution of those without in terms of their market shares in their own province and in China, respectively. The patterns of the distributions resemble what we got in the whole sample (Figure 10.2), that is, there are more firms at the two ends than in the middle of the distribution. Both figures show that the distribution of certified firms dominates that of non-

Figure 10.2

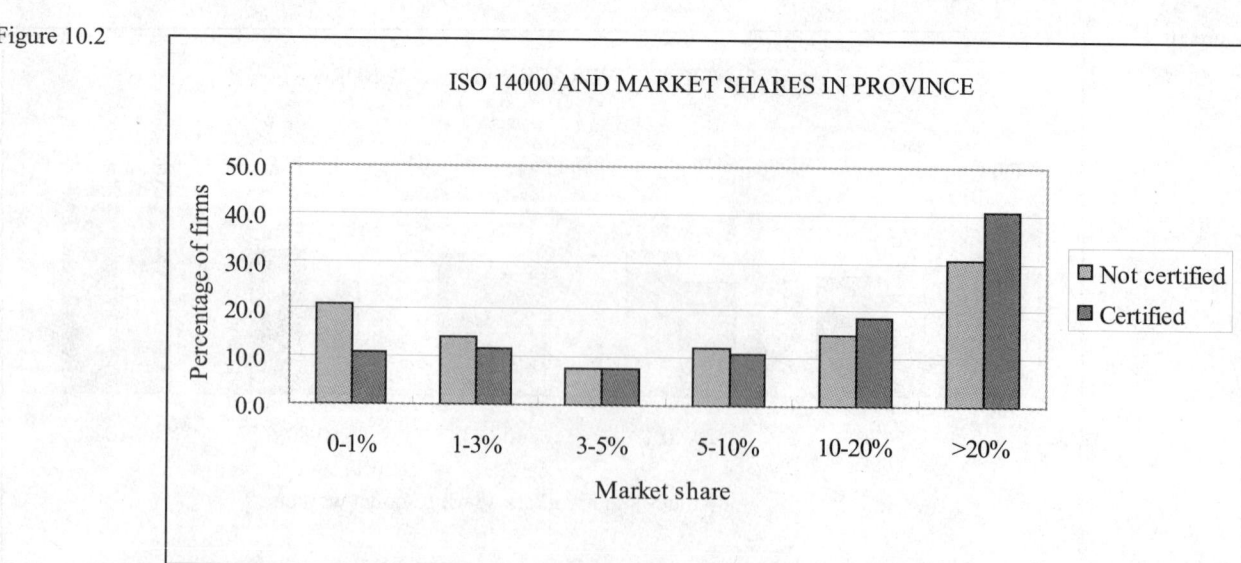

Source: City survey.

Figure 10.3

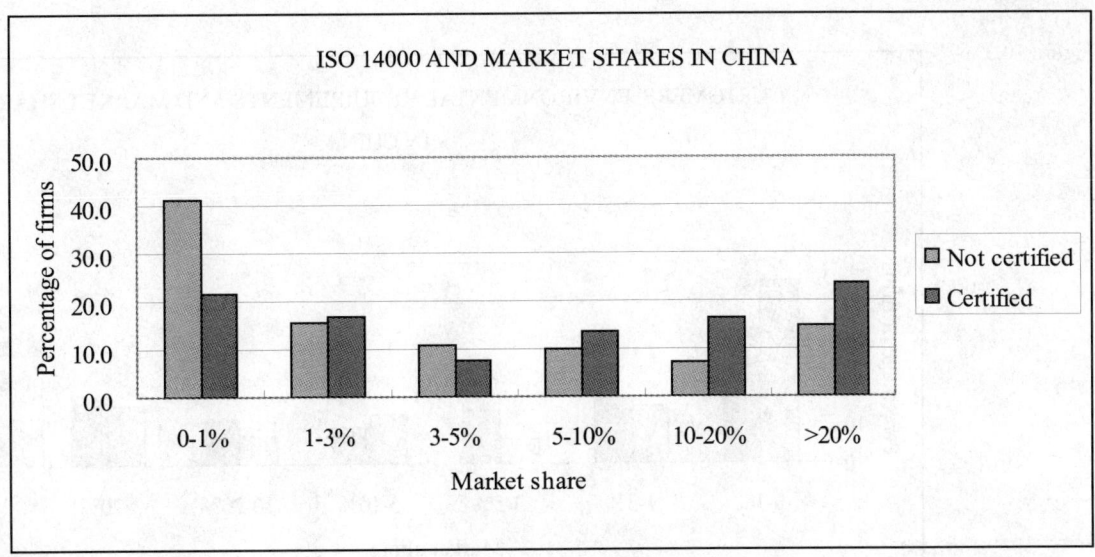

Source: City survey.

certified firms. That is, meeting environmental certification shifts the distribution toward the higher end of market shares. In other words, it increases a firm's chances of having a larger market share.

This analysis, of course, suffers from the potential problem of endogeneity. It is possible that it is the firms with larger market shares that are more likely to obtain the ISO 14000 because they have more financial resources to afford it. In addition, obtaining the certificate and having a larger market share may be determined simultaneously by other factors. To take care of the endogeneity problem, we follow our earlier approach of using environmental requirements imposed by customers as an "instrument" for a firm's own environmental record. Figures 10.4 and 10.5 then replicate Figures 10.2 and 10.3 by replacing ISO 14000 with customer' environmental requirements. In the case of market shares in a firm's own province, having environmental requirements from customers ubiquitously shifts the distribution toward the higher end of market shares (Figure 10.4). The shift is weaker in the case of market shares in China. Compared with

Figure 10.4

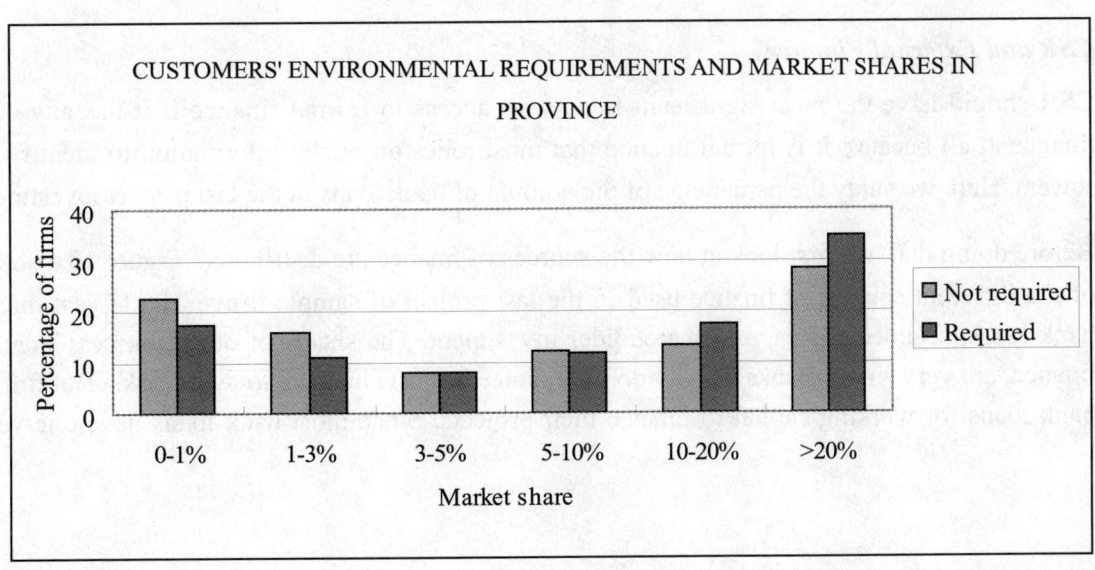

Source: City survey.

Figure 10.5

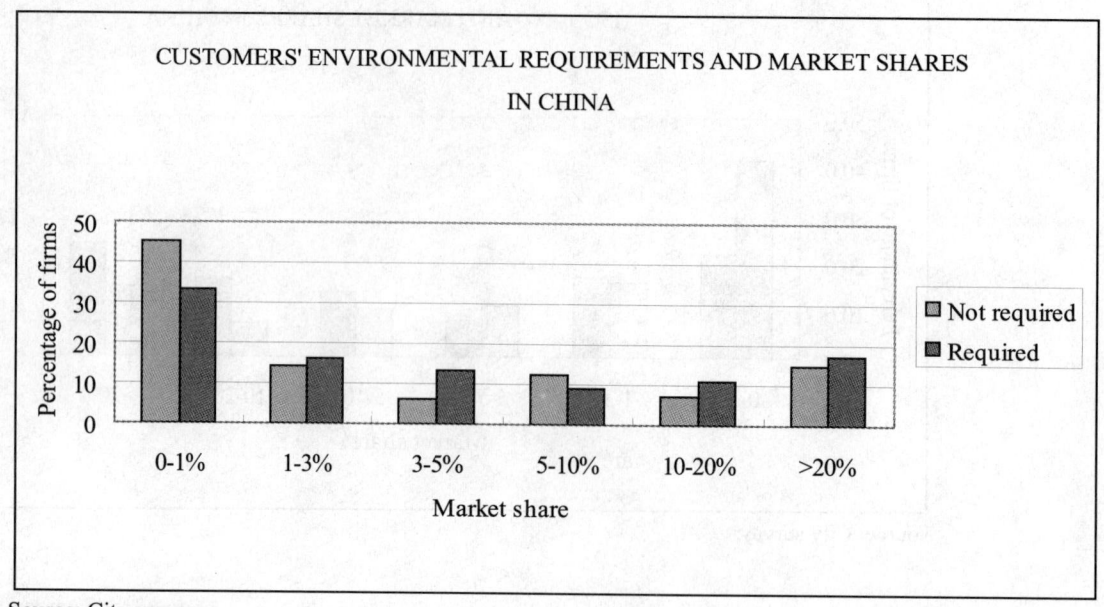

Source: City survey.

firms without customer requirements, firms with customer requirements are found considerably less often in the category of less than 1% of market shares than in the two categories of more than 10% of market shares. However, the two kinds of firms alternate their positions in the medium range of market shares.

In summary, the Porter hypothesis holds in our sample firms not through the channel of inducing more innovations, but through larger market shares. Firms in China, domestic and FDI alike, are lagging behind international technological frontiers. In fact, they can simply adopt the existing technologies to meet higher environmental standards without spending much on new investment. On the other hand, meeting higher environmental standards makes it easier for a firm to find new customers who care about the environment either because they are committed to cleaner production or because they face pressures from the customers in the final product market.

CSR and External Finance

CSR should have the most significant impact on access to formal finance if it has any effects on firm finance at all because it is formal finance that most relies on public information to identify the right borrowers. Here we study the percentage of the amount of bank loans in the last project investment by firms.

Before doing that, we first look at how the sources of finance are distributed. Figure 10.6 shows the shares of the different sources of finance used in the last project of sample firms. The largest three sources are bank loans, retained profits, and shareholder investment. The shares of other sources, including informal finance, are very small. Banks usually do not finance projects in order to avoid risks. But firms often divert bank loans for working capital to finance their projects. Since most bank loans have one-year terms, this

Figure 10. 6

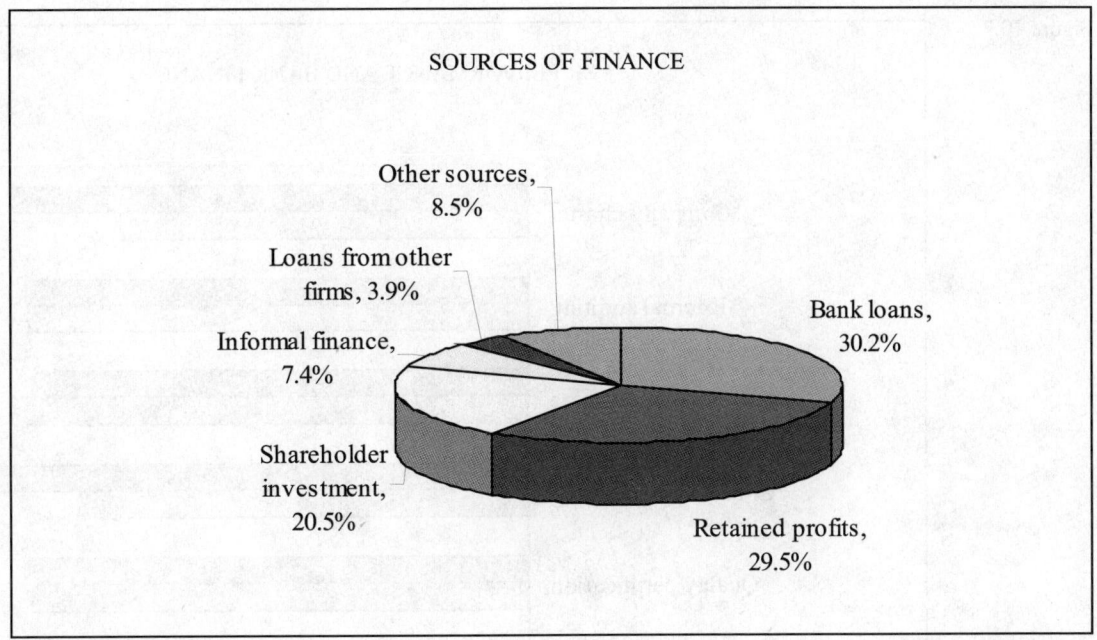

SOURCES OF FINANCE

Other sources, 8.5%

Loans from other firms, 3.9%

Informal finance, 7.4%

Bank loans, 30.2%

Shareholder investment, 20.5%

Retained profits, 29.5%

Source: City survey.

source of project finance is very costly because projects can seldom begin to generate revenues in one year. Under current bank practice, however, the scope of choice for firms is very limited. The high reliance of our sample firms on bank loans, retained profits, and shareholder investment is consistent with the findings of Li and Liu (2006) in recent research for CPDF. In addition, a low percentage of informal finance is also found in his study.

In addition to the CSR indicators studied in Sections 10.1 and 10.2, we add two more for corporate governance because the transparency of governance affects bank assessments of firm credibility. The two additional indicators are whether a firm has articles of association and whether it conducts external auditing. Having articles of association is the basic requirement for good corporate governance and external auditing is essential for transparency.

Figure 10.7 provides a comparison between firms performing a particular CSR item and those without. Except in the two cases of labor contracts and environmental/biological labeling, better CSR performance records lead to a higher percentage of formal loans in the last investment. Having articles of association, allowing collective wage bargaining, and fulfilling environmental standards are particularly significant in raising the percentage of bank loans. In contrast to the case of financial performance, quality control here is shown to slightly benefit a firm.

Figure 10.7

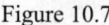

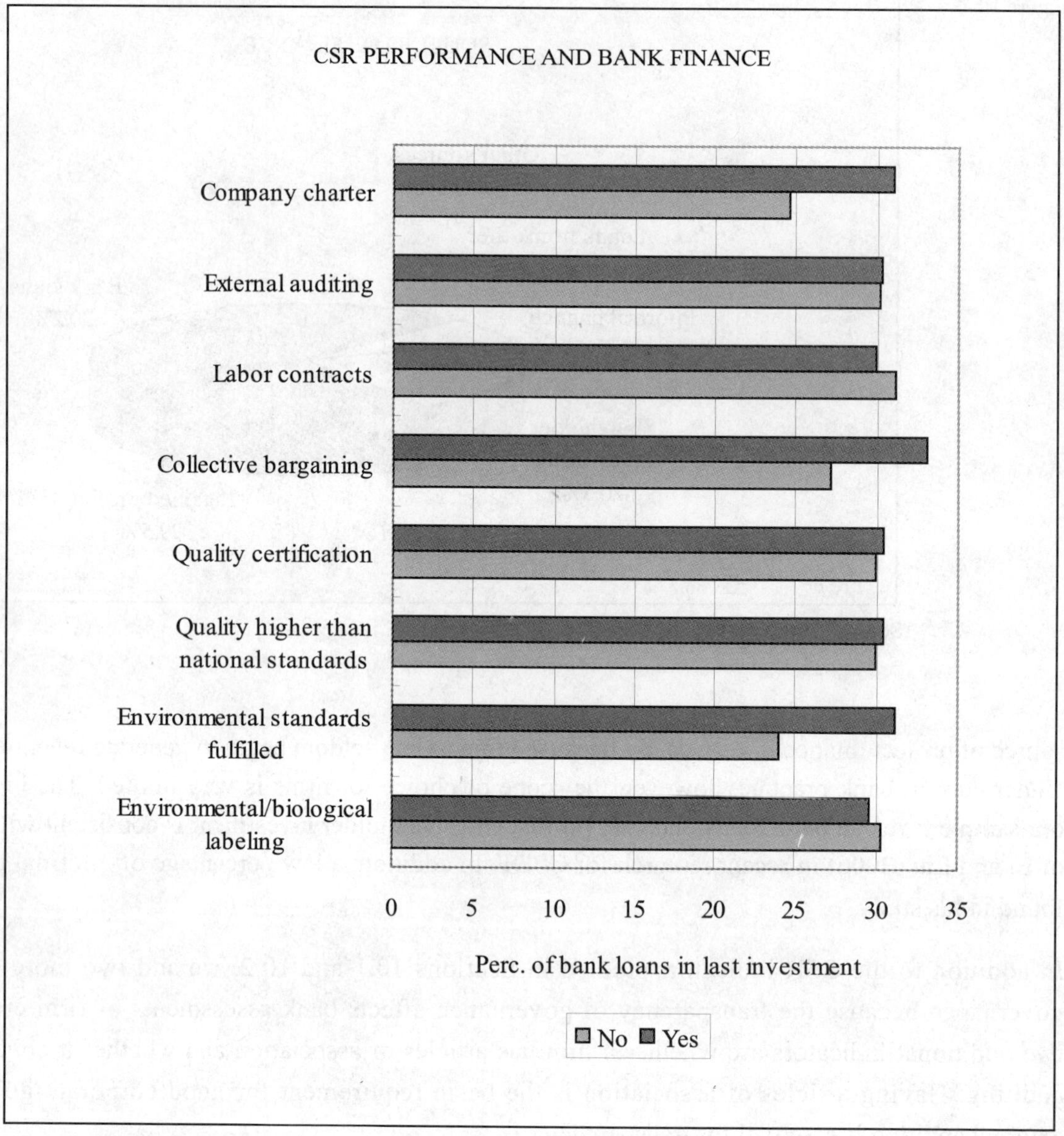

CSR PERFORMANCE AND BANK FINANCE

Company charter

External auditing

Labor contracts

Collective bargaining

Quality certification

Quality higher than
national standards

Environmental standards
fulfilled

Environmental/biological
labeling

0   5   10   15   20   25   30   35

Perc. of bank loans in last investment

☐ No ■ Yes

Source: City survey.

Again, the CSR records of firms may be simultaneously determined together with their access to formal finance. We then study how customer requirements for labor and environmental standards affect formal finance. Figure 10.8 presents the results. Firms subjected to requirements for labor standards perform significantly better than firms subjected to no requirements, but firms subjected to requirements for environmental standards perform slightly worse than those subjected to no requirements. However, firms subjected to both labor and environmental standards perform better again than those subjected to no requirements.

Figure 10.8

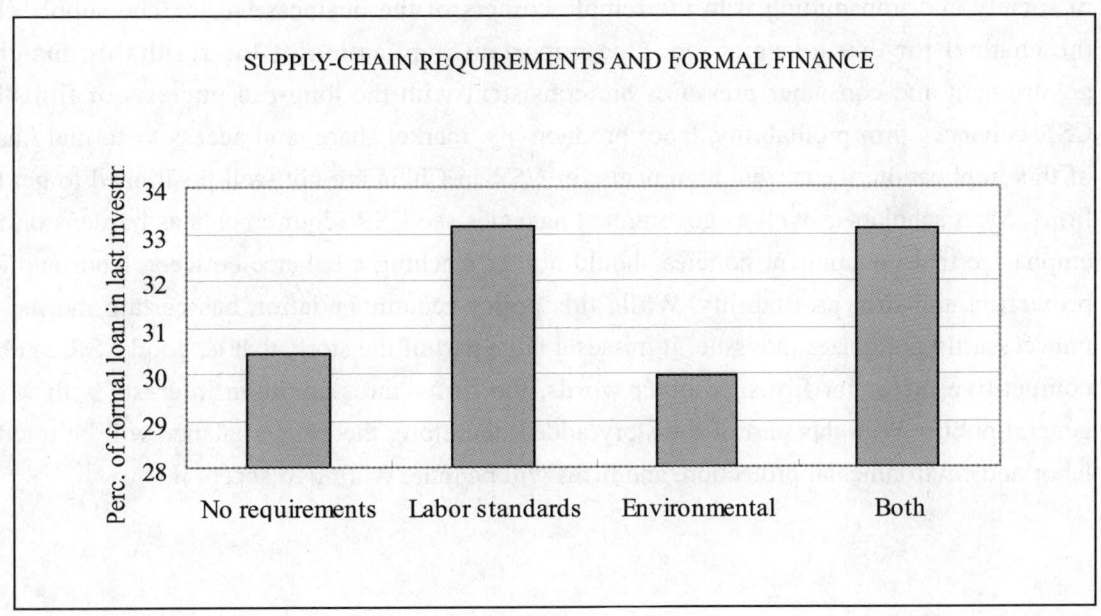

Source: City survey.

10. 4   Summary

This chapter has provided solid evidence of the correlation between the CSR records of firms and their financial performance. Using supply-chain CSR requirements as "instruments", we have also established a causal relationship running from CSR performance to financial performance. The results of the DID analysis are especially strong in supporting this one-way causality for profitability and labor productivity. Our further analysis shows that the causal effects of CSR on firm financial performance have been most likely created by the following three factors: better workforce, larger market shares, and better access to external finance. These results are important for promoting CSR among Chinese firms.

The most important message from these results is that CSR is a factor in competitiveness rather than a burden on a firm. The short-term costs of establishing CSR seem to be high, but the longer-term payoffs are even higher. Although we do not have sufficient data for a cost-benefit analysis, the wide spread of CSR practices among the sample firms and the evidence provided in this chapter make it clear that good CSR brings firms tangible financial gains.

The second message from the results in this chapter is that supply-chain pressures are effective ways of enhancing the CSR performance of firms, and ultimately, their financial performance. This is particularly important when firm awareness of CSR is low. The effectiveness of supply-chain pressures comes from their attachment to business transactions, that is, if a firm wants a deal, it has to take the CSR requirements. As long as it begins to enhance its CSR performance, a firm will gradually find the benefits and begin to internalize them as a part of its competitive strategy.

The third message is that government and consumer pressures can act as a catalyst in triggering CSR in society and transmitting it to the remote corners of the business world. The supply chain provides the channel for that transmission. One important implication of the results in this chapter is that government and consumer pressures are consistent with the long-run interests of firms because good CSR enhances firm profitability, labor productivity, market share, and access to formal finance. In terms of this implication, the current arguments for CSR in China are not well positioned to get the support of firms. Most scholars as well as government agencies see CSR requirements as burdens on firms and thus emphasize that government policies should aim at reaching a balance between labor and environmental protection and firm profitability. While this policy recommendation has certain merits, the argument unnecessarily politicizes the issue. It misses a large part of the story, that is, good CSR can be an effective competitive factor for firms. In other words, the firm shares common interests with workers and the general public. With this part of the story added, therefore, the policy balance will be tilted toward more labor and environmental protection, and firms will be more willing to accept it.

Chapter 11
Policy Recommendations

The results of this study have strong implications for government policies and business operations. This chapter will first summarize the main findings and then put forward a set of recommendations for government and enterprises, respectively. We would like to emphasize that our findings are based on the analysis of a relatively large sample of 1,268 firms from twelve cities with different geographic, social, political, and economic characteristics. Although this does not mean that our sample is representative of the whole country, the size of the sample allows us to test our results by sophisticated statistical methods and thus gives us confidence in our findings. At the very minimum, this study provides the first set of systematic empirical results for CSR and its relationship with firm performance in China. In particular, it builds up a clear business case for CSR in China.

11. 1   Summary of findings

Chapters 3 – 10 provide rich sets of results. Two sets of findings are especially consistent through all these chapters and bear important policy implications. One is that market competition and supply chain pressures have an unambiguous effect in promoting CSR among firms, and the other is that there is a real business case for CSR because it improves firm profitability by helping firms to retain a more stable workforce, gain a larger market share, and obtain more external finance. More specifically, the main findings of the chapters are:

CSR Awareness

- A firm is more aware of CSR than other firms if it is an SOE, an exporting firm, a large firm, a firm operating in a competitive market, or a firm with better educated management.

- CSR activities are mainly confined to the first generation type, i.e., providing donations and meeting the expectations of the law.

- Joining business associations helps firms to increase their CSR awareness.

Labor Standards

- Only half of the respondents in the individual survey had a written contract with their employers in their last job. The majority of the contracts were short term. Worker age (middle-age workers are favored) and education, firm ownership, size, and sector are factors affecting whether a worker can get a written contract. Firms offering written contracts tend to have shorter working hours, pay their workers higher wages and provide larger coverage for pension and medical insurance.

- Labor unions play a positive role in worker protection. Firms with a labor union tend to have shorter working hours and offer a larger coverage for pension and medical insurance. However, they do not offer significantly different wage rates from those offered by firms without unions.

- Collective bargaining does not provide tangible benefits to employees. It still takes time for collective bargaining to have an impact.

- SOEs and foreign-invested firms and Hong Kong, Macao, and Taiwan-invested firms are much better than domestic private firms at treating their employees.

- Local employees enjoy much better treatment than migrant employees.

Environmental Standards

- Firms facing more intense competition put more effort into complying with national environmental standards and spend more on environment-related investment.

- Firms that are more aware of CSR perform better in protecting the environment in all aspects than firms with low awareness.

- Domestic private firms have the smallest proportion of firms with ISO14000, and are the least aware of cleaner production.

- There are large regional and industry variations in environmental protection, suggesting that government efforts and industrial policies are an important driver for better environmental protection.

Quality Control

- Over 80% of the sample firms have a quality management department and the majority of them chose to establish the department when they established the enterprise.

- In addition to establishing the quality management department, firms enhance their product quality by obtaining product quality certificates, such as ISO9001, establishing product brand names, and inspecting the product quality of their suppliers.

- Joint ventures are more confident about the quality of their products.

- Firms that are more aware of CSR are likely to spend on establishing brand names and inspecting their suppliers.

- Firms in more competitive markets often outperform those operating in markets with moderate or low degrees of competition. These firms spend much more on establishing brand names. They are also much more careful in inspecting the quality of their suppliers.

Corporate Governance

● Firms operating in more competitive markets are more likely to have a better governance structure, hire professional managers, and have better information disclosure and risk control.

● Firms that are more aware of CSR perform equally well in these respects.

● Privatized (gaizhi) firms are more eager to establish modern governance structures and provide contracts for their managers than traditional SOEs. They also do better in information disclosure and risk control.

The supply Chain and CSR

● The majority of the sample firms are subject to labor and environmental requirements imposed by their customers. By the frequency of requirements, the order is: customers in developed countries, large FDI firms in China, customers in developing countries, small and medium FDI firms in China, SOEs, and domestic private firms.

● However, only one fourth of the sample firms place labor standards and half of them place environmental standards on their suppliers. Firms' own records of labor standard compliance are not a significant factor affecting their decision to impose labor standards on their suppliers, but their better environmental compliance does increase their tendency to impose environmental standards on their suppliers.

● Large firms are far more likely than SMEs to impose CSR requirements, especially environmental standards, on their suppliers. Foreign and HMT-invested firms are doing better than domestic firms, and exporting firms are doing better than non-exporting firms. In both cases, environmental standards are more emphasized than labor standards.

● In general, firms impose CSR requirements on their suppliers not because they value CSR themselves, but because they face outside pressures to do so.

● Firms favor court settlements over private settlements in commercial disputes. There is weak evidence showing that firms in cities with a better legal environment tend to trust the court more than firms in cities with a slacker legal environment.

CSR and Financial Performance

● Better compliance with labor and environmental standards is associated with higher rates of profitability and labor productivity, but better quality control does not have a significant impact on either profitability or labor productivity.

● In the case of environmental standards, a causal relationship between better compliance and better financial performance can be established.

● There is also a causal relationship between supply chain requirements of labor and environmental standards and better financial performance.

- The positive effects of CSR on financial performance come through the following channels: lower turnover rates, larger market shares, and better access to external finance.

11. 2　Recommendations for the government

The results of this report have important policy implications. They provide clarification for several important areas in the current CSR debate in China.

- The "race to the bottom" story does not hold; instead, there is a story of "race to the top". That is, market competition has not forced firms to lower their CSR standards, but instead has encouraged them to enhance their CSR performance. This has a lot to do with the business environment in China. One critical factor is the transmission of international standards and practices through the international supply chain. Another factor is the demonstration effect of better performing firms, including SOEs and FDI firms. In such a business environment, trying to save on cutting CSR expenditures will not fulfill the goal of long-term profitability; instead, better CSR performance can help firms get ahead of others in retaining a better workforce, getting a larger market share, and obtaining more external finance.

- Multinational companies have played a positive role in promoting CSR in China while not having hurt the profitability of Chinese firms in serious ways. This positive role is played through supply chain transmission of international standards and the local demonstration effects of FDI firms.

- SOEs are doing better than other types of firms in most areas of CSR. However, they do not play an active role in transmitting their code of conduct to a larger part of the business world.

- Firms adopt CSR more because of the external pressures they face than because of their own willingness.

Based on these clarifications and the relevant results summarized in the last section, we propose the following recommendations for the Chinese government. They may also be useful for governments in other developing countries.

- Leveling the playing field and providing equal opportunity to all firms are not only pivotal for fair competition, but also helpful in promoting CSR. Competition is good for CSR.

- Setting up their own CSR standards is needed by national soverments and a country's civil society so as to take a proactive role in promoting CSR and gain ground in multinational endeavors. However, those standards should not be used to discourage international companies from pressing their suppliers to implement higher standards. International companies can serve as catalysts for better CSR.

- Better implementation of existing laws and government regulations provide incentives for firms to build CSR into their business strategies.

- Policy and media coverage should direct attention away from the first generation type of CSR activities in which philanthropy is the most significant part; instead, they should induce more efforts on the part of the enterprises to build CSR into their business strategies.

11. 3   Recommendations for enterprises

The most important result that this study offers to enterprises is that CSR can be an important source of competitiveness in China. In particular, we have the following recommendations for companies.

● Enterprises should seriously consider making CSR an integral part of their business strategies. CSR can be a means of value creation for enterprises. Seeing CSR only as a cost burden is short sighted.

● The kind of CSR activities that may bring immediate payoffs are improving the treatment of workers, increasing compliance with environmental standards, and strengthening corporate governance.

● SOEs should think hard about how to cash-in on their superior CSR performance in the market. They can play this card in getting more orders and better deals in the international market. They should also transmit their own code of conduct through their own supply chains, for doing so not only brings significant social gains, but also helps leveling the playing field in which they operate.

● Multinational companies should continue to use CSR as leverage in the marketplace. Companies producing in China should continue to be the role models for better CSR performance. Companies having suppliers in China should continue to impose certain code of conduct on these suppliers, but in the meantime realize that standards applied in the developed world may not be applicable in the developing world. It is thus important for them to manage a delicate public relations campaign in their home countries.

● Small domestic firms may be under smaller pressures to strengthen their CSR. However, they would better be prepared if they wanted to expand to medium and even large scale. They should realize that CSR can be one of the bottlenecks in this transformation. Getting acquainted with CSR is the first step towards putting them on the right track.

● Overall, firms need to scale up their efforts to comply with the national laws and regulations regarding labor, environment, and product quality. Opportunism will bring short-term benefits, but honesty will deliver payoffs that last longer.

REFERENCES

Bai, Chong'en, Changtai Xie, and Yingyi Qian (2007). "China's Rate of Return to Capital." *Comparative Studies*, Vol. 28, pp. 1-22.

Bromley, Daniel (2006). *Sufficient Reason*. Princeton, Princeton University Press.

Beloe, Seb, Julia Harrison, and Oliver Greenfield (2006). *Coming in from the Cold Public Affairs and Corporate Responsibility*. Report prepared for Blueprint Partners, SustainAbility, and World Wildlife Foundation (WWF).

BSR (2006). "Introduction to CSR." www.bsr.org.

CBSR (2003). *Engaging Small Business in Corporate Social Responsibility: A Canadian Small Business Perspective on CSR*. CBSR report.

CCER (2007). *A Research Report on China's Rate of Return to Capital*. CCER China Economic Observer.

Chen, Ying (2006). "Business as Usual in the 21st Century." *Leading Perspectives*, Summer 2006, pp. 8.

CPDF (2005). *Sichuan SME Mapping*, CPDF.

Collingsworth, Terry (2006). "The Wal-Mart Litigation: Challenging Code of Conduct Regimes." *Leading Perspectives*, Winter 2006, pp. 14.

Developing Value (2005). *The Business Case for Sustainability in Emerging Markets*. Joint report published by SustainAbility, IFC, and Ethos Institute.

European Union (2001), *Promoting a European Framework for Corporate Social Responsibility*. Brussels: Commission of the European Communities.

FIAS and BSR (2007). *Corporate Social Responsibilities in China's Information and Communications Technology (ICT) Sector*, report prepared for United Nations Environmental Programme.

Friedman, Milton (1962) *Capitalism and Freedom*. Chicago, University of Chicago Press.

Garnaut, Ross, Ligang Song, Stoyan Tenev, and Yang Yao (2005). *Ownership Transformation in China*, The World Bank.

Garnaut, Song, Tenev, and Yao (2005), "China's Ownership Transformation", International Finance Corporation.

GRI (2000). *Sustainability Reporting Guidelines on Economic, Environmental and Social Performance*, June 2000. New York, Global Reporting Initiative.

Guo, Jihui (2006). "Corporate Social Responsibility Breaks the Ice in China: Moving onto the Balance Beam of Multi-stakeholders." www.chinagate.com.cn, September 25, 2006.

Guo, Jun (2005). "A Healthy Attitude toward CSR." www.finance.sina.com.edu, November 28, 2005.

Guo, Jun (2006). "CSR: Challenges and Opportunities for Labor Unions in China." Background paper.

Huang, Shuhe (2007). *Speech in the National Conference for Central Government Owned SOEs to Save Energy and Reduce Emission*, Beijing, August 28, 2007.

IFC (1999). *The Emerging Private Sector in China*, Washington D.C.: World Bank.

IFC (2002) "The Environmental and Social Challenges of Private Sector Projects: The IFC Experience", International Finance Cooperation.

Jingji Guancha Wang (2007). "1,400 Foreign Companies Signed a Joint Statement to Take Social Responsibility." http://www.eeo.com.cn/eobserve/Politics/beijing_news/2007/08/28/81698.html.

Li, Lulu and Duo Liu (2006). *A Study of SMEs' External Finance in Fivue Cities*. CPDF report.

Li, Ziyang (2006). "The Only Responsibility of Enterprises Is to Make Profit." www.China-Review.com, May 31, 2006.

Lin, Justin Yifu, Fang Cai, and Zhou Li (1996).*The China Miracle*, Hong Kong, Chinese University of Hong Kong Press.

Lomborg, Bjørn (2001). *The Skeptical Environmentalist*, Cambridge, Cambridge University Press.

Lu, Feng and Liu Liu (2007). "Measurements of China's Relative Labor Productivity Growth (1978-2005) — Rethinking the Relationship between the Balassa-Samuelson Effect and Renminbi Real Exchange Rate." *China Economic Quarterly*, Vol. 6, No. 2: 357-380.

NBS (2006). *Statistical Report of National Economy and Social Development: 2005*, February 28, 2006 http://www.stats.gov.cn/ndtigh/qgndtigb/t20060227/402307796.htm

NLU (2006). *NLU Bluebook 2005: Promoting the Legal Rights of Employees*, NLU, 2006.

Peng, L., Long, B., and Pamlin, D. (2005), "Chinese Companies in the 21st Century: Helping or Destroying the Planet? , Trade and Investment Program, WWWF.

Porter, Michael, and Claas van der linde (1995). "Toward a New Conception of the Environment-Competitiveness Relationship. *Journal of Economic Perspectives* , Vol. 9, No. 4, pp. 97-118.

Reinhardt, F.L., (2000), "Down to earth: applying business principles to environmental management", Harvard Business School Press.

Rudolph, Phillip (2006). "Why the Case against Wal-Mart Should Not Have been Brought and Why It Should Fail? *Leading Perspectives* , Winter 2006, pp. 15.

SETC (2003). *Tentative Standards for Small and Medium Enterprises*, SME Department, SETC, document [2003] No. 143.

Shan, Weijian (2006a). "The World Bank s China Delusions. *Far Eastern Economic Review*, September 2006, pp. 29-32.

Shan, Weijian (2006b). "China s Low-profit Growth Model. *Far Eastern Economic Review*, November 2006, pp. 23-28.

Song, Linfei (2007). "The Environmental Wars in Shanxi. Paper presented in the Symposium on Social Justice, The Hongfan Institute for Legal and Economic Studies, Beijing, August 3-4, 2007.

Soros, George (2005). *Soros on Globalization*, New York, Public Affairs.

SEPA (2006), "Environmental Protection in China: 1996 – 2005(White Book) , the State Environmental Protection Administration of China, 2006

UN (1987) "Our Common Future", the 1987 UN Commission on Environment and Development report.

UNIDO (2002). *Corporate Social Responsibility: Implications for Small and Medium Enterprise in Developing Countries*, United Nations Industrial Development Organization.

WBCSD (2001), *Corporate Social Responsibility: Making Good Business Sense*. WBCSD. Washington, www.wbcsd.org.

Yao, Yang, and Ye Zhang (2007). "A Study on the Domestic Technological Contents of Chinese Products: Evidence from the Country and Jiangsu and Guangdong Provinces", CCER Working Paper No. C2007013, July 2007.

Yao, Yang, and Linfeng Zhang (2007). "An Analysis of the Competitiveness of Domestic Chinese Exporting Firms and Their Technological Upgrading", CCER Working Paper No. C2007012, July 2007.

Young, Alwyn (2000). "The Razor's Edge: Distortions and Incremental Reform in the People's Rupublic of China. *Quarterly Journal of Economics*, vol. 115, no. 4, pp. 1091-1135.

Zhang, Junfeng (2006). *Speech in the First International Forum of CSR in China*, Beijing, February 22, 2006.

Zhou, Weidong (2006). "Will CSR Work in China?" *Leading Perspectives*, June 2006, pp. 5.